THE YOUNG ADULT

THE YOUNG ADULT

Identity and Awareness

Edited by

Gerald D. Winter

St. John's University

Eugene M. Nuss

University of Bridgeport

Scott, Foresman and Company

Library of Congress Catalog Card No. 70-75378

Regional Offices of Scott, Foresman and Company are located
in Atlanta, Dallas, Glenview, Palo Alto, Oakland, N.J.,
and London, England.

Preface

A review of any segment of periodical literature provides conclusive evidence that there is widespread concern for today's adolescent in America. Not only does everyone have an opinion about today's adolescent, but adolescent development has become a legitimate field of scholarly study. No longer is adolescence relegated to an "in-between" status—following childhood and preceeding adulthood. Rather, a strong case has been made that "adolescenthood" is equal in importance to all other stages of development.

The typical view of "adolescenthood" is rather grim. Some writers describe it as a time of over-reaction to environment. More than a few suggest that there exists a sort of intra-tribal warfare between teen-agers and adults. There is general agreement that the adolescent has neither the privileges and immunities of an adult nor the privileges and immunities of a child. It is only rarely that one discovers a writer who sees adolescence as a period in which self-fulfillment is promoted, creative expression nurtured, and social development achieved.

Can adolescence be all that bad? And, if it is, has it always been such? Must it continue to be the ogre phase of human development? These questions intrigue the researcher, challenge the teacher and social worker, and haunt parents.

The primary purpose of this book of selected readings is to explore the nature of adolescence in a psychosocial perspective—that is, to describe and interpret the forces within the individual as they interact with the dynamics of his social environment. The readings vary in point of view and in approach to the problems and steps to correct them. Several articles emphasize the sometimes vicious, frequently ambivalent pressures that adult society imposes upon its young. Conversely, promising ideas are advanced which, if implemented, would go far toward creating a "new look" in adolescence.

This book is intended to be used as a supplement to a main text. It does not inquire with equal attention into all aspects of adolescence. For example, physiology is not treated in detail. We believe that this basic area can better be handled in a textbook.

The readings are centered around fundamental questions that our society asks about adolescents:

1. What are today's adolescents really like? Are they different from youth of other generations?
2. How serious is the sex conflict for the "typical adolescent"? Does the conflict tend to distort developing personalities?

3. How do adolescents work out their problems? Are major difficulties that are encountered during this period resolved, or do they simply accumulate to produce an "ailing" subsociety now—a "sick" society later?
4. How can adolescents best be served in their development? Can the institutions of society insure a healthy environment for the optimal psychosocial development of its youth?
5. Are other societies as concerned with the adolescent years as we are in America, or is adolescence more particularly an American phenomenon?

This collection of readings has been put together with the student in mind. Nearly all the articles included have been read by our classes, and their favorable responses suggested that a book of this sort would serve a useful purpose among students of human behavior.

We express our appreciation to the authors and publishers for permission to reprint the materials selected for this volume. We also thank Dr. Lorin McMackin, chairman of the Department of Educational Foundations, University of Bridgeport, for the advice and patience he generously extended to us during the organization and writing of this book.

G. D. W.
E. M. N.

Table of Contents

Chapter 1 Characteristics of Adolescence and the Adolescent

Chapter 2 Sex: The Adolescent's Personal Dilemma

Chapter 3 Problems of Special Significance to the Adolescent

Chapter 4 Adolescence in Cross-Cultural Perspective

Chapter 5 Promoting Healthy Adolescence in American Society

Chapter 1
Characteristics of Adolescence and the Adolescent

Americans have a penchant for stereotyping. Labels are applied to groups with reckless abandon. Are the terms used in the description of adolescence representative of facts or, as in the case of most stereotyping, are they simply defensive attempts to come to grips with a phase of life that is poorly understood in our society?

This section examines some of the characteristics of the person we call the adolescent, within the context of his subculture. The approach used is interdisciplinary and embraces physical, social, and psychological adolescence. In order to comprehend the characteristics of adolescence it is essential to understand each of these areas and their interaction.

The student of adolescence must decide which ideas will withstand the rigors of scientific inquiry. The articles in this chapter provide divergent points of view and contribute to the expanding awareness of "young adulthood."

Other than physical change, what are the *distinctive* characteristics of the phase of life called adolescence? To what extent do those characteristics that are newly explored contribute to our knowledge of human development?

The Mystique of Adolescence

Joseph Adelson

University of Michigan

What is the adolescent image? The author feels that the adolescent has changed his role from victim to victimizer. Is this true, or is it the adult role that is changing? Perhaps the answer lies in the fact that today there is more awareness of the problems of being an adolescent in an adult world. Or is it possible that the "mystery" of adolescence prevents any valid study of its nature?

In recent years the adolescent has come to weigh oppressively on the American consciousness. Just a few years ago he was of little substance in our collective imaginings, in fiction, and in the mass media. He was represented as a figure of fun: callow, flighty, silly, given to infatuations, wild enthusiasms, and transient moodiness. His prototype was Andy Hardy, Henry Aldrich. Or he was sometimes seen as a latter-day and rather harmless Werther: sensitive, emotionally afflicted, overly sentimental. In either case the figure was seen as lovable, though sometimes exasperating, and not to be taken too seriously. He would get over it—whatever *it* might be—in time. I shall call this type the adolescent as Fool.[1] The Fool exists outside the world of adult happenings; he is blessedly innocent of complication, guilt, or responsibility. He is a fool not in being duped, but because he is unrelated to the intrigues and corruptions, or the moral seriousness, of adulthood. He inhabits an Eden of preresponsibility.

These days two new images, weightier and more ominous, have superseded the Fool figure, and between them they divide the contemporary sense of the adolescent. One of these I shall call the adolescent as Visionary. He is distinguished by a purity of moral vision which allows him to perceive or state the moral simplicity hidden by adult complication. In the way of prophets, he is also a Victim. He is betrayed, exploited, or neglected by the adult world. His needs go unrecognized by adults too busy in their own affairs; or as an innocent bystander he may be victimized by adult corruption. The prototypes here are J. D. Salinger's adolescents, Holden Caulfield or Franny Glass. Whereas the Fool is essentially unrelated to the adult world, the Visionary-Victim is connected to it in being passive and powerless. Perceptive, articulate, morally precocious, his only resources are in-

Reprinted by special permission of The William Alanson White Psychiatric Foundation, Inc., from *Psychiatry*, Vol. 27 (1964), pp. 1–5.

[1]Compare Orrin E. Klapp, *Heroes, Villains, and Fools: The Changing American Character* (Englewood Cliffs, N.J.: Prentice-Hall, Inc., 1962).

sight and knowledge, and the strength which may eventually accrue from them.

The antitype to the Visionary is the newest and most disturbing representation of the adolescent, as Victimizer. Leather-jacketed, cruel, sinister, and amoral, he is the nemesis-hero of a new genre of fiction and film. Here, as one example, is the plot of a typical fiction of the genre. A man accidentally incurs the hatred of some hoodlum youths who threaten to kill him. He appeals to the police for protection, but they are impotent to help him. The story ends as the night closes in, and the man, alone and helpless, awaits his death at the hands of the youths. The story's mood is paranoid; the adolescent is the persecutor, the killer. This adolescent stands in utter contrast to the Visionary; one is innocent, the other evil; one is powerless, the other omnipotent.

The emergence of these images makes it clear that the adolescent occupies a peculiarly intense place in American thought and feeling.[2] As prophet and victim, he joins and replaces the child-innocent who once played these roles exclusively. As victimizer, he is the carrier of the society's projections; sadistic and sexual motives are imputed to him, and he joins or replaces the gangster, the Negro, and other projective enemies. Nor is it only in our dark imaginings that these adolescent types hold so central a place. A good deal of recent social thought sees in the adolescent's character and situation the key to our moral and social pathology. Curiously, it is in their response to the adolescent that the social criticism of the Left is joined by the social criticism of the Right. Both see our youth as reflecting what is most ignoble and most portentous in our time.

I have stressed this mystique of adolescence because it has influenced both work and thought in the social sciences. The attention of social scientists has been captured by two conspicuous but atypical enclaves of adolescence, drawn from extreme and opposing ends of the social-class continuum, and representing exceptional solutions to the adolescent crisis. The victimizer corresponds, of course, to the delinquent. The visionary-victim corresponds—though this may not be apparent at first—to the sensitive, articulate, intense, intelligent type of upper-middle-class adolescent on whom the psychoanalytic theory of adolescence is almost exclusively based.

Now in most ways these two adolescent types could not be more dissimilar. The estranged lower-class youngster relies largely on alloplastic solutions to the adolescent crisis, living out mutely, in urgent yet aimless acts of violence or bravado, a sullen resentment against the middle-class world and its values. The estranged upper-middle-class youngster is largely autoplastic in response, subject to acute intrapsychic upheavals which are expressed in neurotic symptoms, affect storms, character eccentricities, and a general value ferment. Paradoxically, these two extremes are alike, and their alikeness is in being

[2]Yet this is not to say that these motifs have been restricted either to American thought, or to the representation of adolescence. The themes of saintliness and violence have been endemic in recent European writing as well, and have also figured in the depiction of postadolescent prototypes—for example, the Beats as "holy barbarians." An interesting variation is seen in the effort to fuse saintliness and violence, as in the writings of Jean Genet, Norman Mailer, and William Burroughs.

different from the normative adolescent—that is, the socially modal adolescent. The extremes are alike in showing an unusual degree of independence from the family; they are alike in disaffection, in acting out or thinking out a discontent with the social order; they are alike, above all, in their adoption of radical solutions to that key problem of adolescence, the task of ego-synthesis. I want to suggest that one cannot generalize these processes to the adolescent population at large. The adolescent at the extremes responds to the instinctual and psychosocial upheaval of puberty by disorder, by failures of ego-synthesis, by a tendency to abandon earlier values and object-attachments. In the normative response to adolescence, however, there is more commonly an avoidance of inner and outer conflict, premature identity consolidation, ego and ideological constriction, and a general unwillingness to take psychic risks.[3]

Now having stated my thesis, let me pause here to say something about its origins. These conclusions derive from a national survey of adolescent boys and girls.[4] A colleague and I studied, by means of a rather extensive semistructured interview, 3,000 youngsters, including about 1,000 boys between 14 and 16, and about 2,000 girls between 12 and 18. Let me say at once that we were very much aware of the limitations of this sort of interview; one must write questions suitable for the lowest common denominator, and the interview setting is one which maximizes cautious, shallow, and platitudinous responses. But we were, if anything, hypersensitive to these problems, and mined the questionnaire with a great number and variety of projective items. Thanks to IBM technology we were buried in data; but I want to bypass a discussion of specific findings and approach these interviews as personal documents, to consider them impressionistically, discursively, clinically. The great advantage of this kind of project is that it permits study of those adolescents who make up the middle majority, who evoke neither grief nor wonder, and who all too often escape notice. When one looks at the normative forms of the adolescent experience, one is led to think twice about the received version of adolescence.

Let me begin with the question of autonomy and conflict. Many writers take the position that at puberty the child is under great pressure to detach himself from the family emotionally, to find a pattern of disengagement. The instinctual revival brings with it a return of Oedipal dangers and temptations. The home is a hothouse and the youngster must discover a way out, a means of escaping his dependent status in the family, and even more urgently, the dimly recognized drives and feelings toward his parents. The psychosexual irritation pushes the child from home, leading him to negotiate or battle with the parents for greater freedom. The conflict of generations is joined. Theorists add to this the psychosocial pull of the child's need to be his own man, to forge an individual identity—those needs which draw him toward the future. These forces give the adolescent peer group its critical

---

[3]It should be clear that I am speaking here of institutionalized patterns, rather than voluntaristic "choices."

[4]A full report on this research, in co-authorship with Elizabeth Douvan, will be published shortly by John Wiley. A report on one aspect can be found in Douvan and Adelson, "The Psychodynamics of Social Mobility in Adolescent Boys," *J. Abnormal and Social Psychol.* (1958), 56:31–44.

importance. Peer group and culture supplant the family as the locus of authority and the giver of norms. Through his immersion in the peer group, through the incorporation of peer ideals and values, the youngster gains the support he needs to win autonomy from the family. And the peer group provides a haven in which the delicate task of self-exploration and self-definition can be accomplished.[5]

This view of adolescence has a good deal to recommend it, but my reading of the interviews suggests that it needs revision in some important particulars. It exaggerates the degree of conflict between parent and child; it wrongly estimates the autonomy issue; and it misinterprets the role of the peer group. The normative adolescent tends to avoid overt conflict with his family. This is not to say that conflict is not present, but it is largely unconscious conflict—undersurface resentments which do not necessarily liberate or enlarge the personality, but which, paradoxically, increase the child's docility toward his parents. Even when one does find overt conflict one senses that it has an *as if* quality to it, that it is a kind of war game, with all the sights and sounds of battle but without any bloodshed. More often than not the conflicts center on trivia, on issues of taste—clothing, grooming, and the like. It can be argued that these issues are trivial only to the adult, that they are of great symbolic importance in the adolescent's quest for autonomy. True; but one can reply that parent and child play out an empty ritual of disaffection, that they agree to disagree only on token issues, on teen issues, and in doing so are able to sidestep any genuine encounter of differences.

Much the same is true of autonomy. There are autonomies and autonomies. The American adolescent asks for and is freely given an unusual degree of behavioral freedom—the right to come and go, to share in setting rules, and so on. But it is far more problematic whether he asks for or achieves a high degree of emotional autonomy, and it is even more doubtful whether he manages much in the way of value autonomy. Indeed, the ease with which the adolescent acquires behavioral freedom may tend to interfere with the achievement of emotional and ideological freedom, for reasons I will mention in a moment. As to the peer group, its supposed functions—as an arena for the confrontation of the self, for the testing and trying out of identities—are present for many adolescents, but for many more the peer group is used for the learning and display of sociability and social skills. The peer culture is all too often a kind of playpen, designed to keep children out of harm's way and out of parents' hair. It may not work out this way; the children may begin throwing toys at each other, or—what is worse—may begin throwing them at the grown-ups in the living room. But generally it does work out just this way. The peer group, with its artificial amusements and excitements, more often than not acts to hinder differentiation and growth.

This is especially evident in the area of values and ideology. The traditional idea of the adolescent experience holds that the youngster

[5]A full yet succinct review of this general position can be found in Leo Spiegel, "A Review of Contributions to a Psychoanalytic Theory of Adolescence: Individual Aspects," in *Psychoanalytic Study of the Child*, 6:375–393 (New York: Internat. Univ. Press, 1951).

becomes involved in an intense concern with ethics, political ideology, religious belief, and so on. The moral parochialism of early childhood was thought to be smashed by the moral fervor and incipient cosmopolitanism of adolescence. The youngster's need to detach himself from the family and its view of the moral and social order, his need to redo the ego-superego constellation, his need to find new and more appropriate ego ideals, his need to use ideology as a solution for instinctual problems—all these needs came together, so it was thought, to produce a value crisis somewhere in the course of the adolescent career. This pattern can be found in adolescence, but it is found in a bold, sometimes stubborn, often unhappy minority. Our interviews confirm a mounting impression from other studies that American adolescents are on the whole not deeply involved in ideology, nor are they prepared to do much individual thinking on value issues of any generality. Why is this so? I would guess because to think anew and differently endangers the adolescent's connection to the community—his object attachments—and complicates the task of ego synthesis.

Let me sum up in the language of personality theory. The inherent tensions of adolescence are displaced to and discharged within the matrix of peer-group sociability. Intrapsychically the defenses and character positions adopted are those which curtail experience and limit the growth and differentiation of the self—repression, reaction-formation, and certain forms of ego restriction. These modes of dealing with inner and outer experience join to produce a pseudo-adaptive solution of the adolescent crisis, marked by cognitive stereotypy, value stasis, and interpersonal conformity. It is a solution which is accomplished by resisting conflict, resisting change, resisting the transformation of the self. It settles for a modest, sluggish resynthesis of the ego that closely follows the lines of the older organization of drives, defenses, values, and object-attachments. It is characterized by an avoidance of identity-diffusion through identity-coarctation.

One is left to wonder whether this form of adolescence is a new thing in this country, or whether Americans have always been falsely bemused by one or another mystique of adolescence. Of course we cannot know; if, as this paper has suggested, today's adults have egregiously misunderstood the adolescents they see before their very eyes, then it would be prudent, to say the least, to avoid generalizations about historically earlier patterns of adolescence. In all likelihood, the degree of tension and disorder has always been more apparent than real. It is always more likely that passion, defiance, and suffering will capture the fancy, and that the amiable, colorless forms of adaptation will be ignored.

And yet—and yet—one feels, nevertheless, that the contemporary modes of adolescence do involve something new, that Friedenberg,[6] among others, is correct in saying that adolescence is disappearing as the period during which the individual can achieve a decisive articulation of the self. If this is so—and granting how large an *if* this is—then perhaps one important reason that can be singled out is the extraordi-

---

[6]Edgar Z. Friedenberg, *The Vanishing Adolescent* (Boston: Beacon, 1959).

nary attenuation of today's adolescence. Given the long preparation required for advanced technical training, given the uselessness of the adolescent in the labor market, parent and child settle down for a long, long period of time during which the child will, in one way or another, remain a dependent being. Traditionally, adolescence has been the age in which the child readied himself to leave home; accounts of adolescence in the earlier part of this century often describe a decisive encounter between father and son, a decisive testing of wills, in which the son makes a determined bid for autonomy, either by leaving home, or threatening to do so, and meaning it. The adolescent then had little of the freedom he has today; he was kept under the parental thumb, but he used his captivity well, to strengthen himself for a real departure and a real autonomy. Nowadays the adolescent and his parents are both made captive by their mutual knowledge of the adolescent's dependency. They are locked in a room with no exit, and they make the best of it by an unconscious *quid pro quo*, in which the adolescent forfeits his adolescence, and instead becomes a teen-ager. He keeps the peace by muting his natural rebelliousness, through transforming it into structured and defined techniques for getting on people's nerves. The passions, the restlessness, the vivacity of adolescence are partly strangled, and partly drained off in the mixed childishness and false adulthood of the adolescent teen culture.

The Problem of Generations

Bruno Bettelheim

University of Chicago

The author interrelates the psychological differences between girls and boys in our culture with the contrasts of differing generations. What implications has this interrelationship upon the study of young adults? What are Bettelheim's views regarding the degree of complexity of male adolescence as compared to female? Are boys more often considered because their problems in adjustment in this period are more critical than those of girls, or is it because writers are principally men and focus on the male? How valid is the "confusion of sex roles" and how does it affect the study of adolescence? The psychological differences between the sexes and a historical perspective of the older generation may be important aspects

From *Youth: Change and Challenge*, ed. Erik H. Erikson, © 1961 by the American Academy of Arts and Sciences, © 1963 by Basic Books, Inc., Publishers, New York.

of the understanding of adolescence. In the following article a number of interesting observations are offered for consideration.

What strikes the psychologist forcefully when he surveys the available literature on adolescence and youth is that, if the amount of discussion were indicative, then all or nearly all problems of youth would appear to be those of the adolescent male. True, the more serious authors nod in the direction of female adolescence and recognize that it creates problems, too. But having done so, they turn so exclusively to the problems of the male adolescent that the net impression remains: female adolescence, if it exists at all, does not create problems equally worthy of the sociologist's or the psychologist's interest.

But whether we view adolescent development from a sociological or a psychological viewpoint, the problems confronting boys and girls should be parallel. The reassertion of sexual desires on reaching physical maturity is typical of both sexes, as are the psychological problems of repressing or satisfying these drives; of postponing the consummation of some and of sublimating the rest. So also, in modern times, are the social and psychological problems of achieving self-identity on a more mature basis, and of finding one's place in society.

Is it really so much easier for the adolescent girl to find her self-identity as a woman and her place in society, than for the boy to gain his as a man? True, Erikson describes cases of negative identity in women, but most of his writings on adolescence concern males, and other recent students of the problem such as Friedenberg and Goodman deal almost wholly with male youth.[1] Though Freud's original work was based on the study of hysteria in females, and though he devoted much thought to their difficulties in achieving sexual maturity, a problem typical of middle-class youth, his later writings centered mainly on the development of the male. In another context I have discussed how, in regard to puberty rites, nearly all psychoanalytic interest centers on boys, neglecting the far-reaching meaning the rites have for both boys and girls in achieving sexual maturity and adult status.[2]

Since I, too, have had to rely on available sources, and since they are so much richer in content and more abundant than any one man's observations can be, my discussion too will be weighted toward male youth; but at least I wish to acknowledge this deficiency in my remarks, and try to rectify it in part. I venture to say that those who conceived of this issue of *Dædalus* were caught in much the same predicament, since a careful reading of the suggestions they kindly offered me permits a consideration of the feminine only by stretching the points they detailed. Yet there must be a reason why the male adolescent and his problems dominate public attention and that of the scholarly expert.

---

[1]Erik H. Erikson, *Identity and the Life Cycle* (New York: International Universities Press, 1959). Edgar Z. Friedenberg, *The Vanishing Adolescent* (Boston: Beacon Press, 1959). Paul Goodman, *Growing Up Absurd* (New York: Random House, 1960).

[2]Bruno Bettelheim, *Symbolic Wounds* (Glencoe, Illinois: The Free Press, 1954).

Perhaps my particular topic allows for a first approximation as to why this is so: I was asked to discuss the problem of the generations from the psychologist's point of view. Unfortunately I shall have to transgress heavily into the field of sociology, since in my opinion the problem of generations is at best a psychosocial one, and can never be dealt with on a purely psychological basis.

It may be that the problem of generations is what gives us adults so much trouble, and not the problems of adolescence or youth; and this is why, when we concern ourselves with the problem of youth in our society, it is that of male youth. If delinquency worries us, it is chiefly male delinquency, though to their families and themselves, female delinquents are at least as great a problem.

For the same reason we are concerned with Johnny's not learning to read, or not getting enough science and math, as if reading problems were foreign to Jane, or as if she were automatically good at math and science. And if not, it is thought to matter little, since the number of female contributors to the sciences is relatively negligible. But such an evaluation of women's potential is both shortsighted and wasteful. Despite all the obstacles to women's higher education in the physical sciences, it was a young woman who did pioneering work in radioactivity, a development in physics which eventually led to the present clamor for more science education in our schools.

Since it is adults who conduct the studies and write the articles, and since these adults are predominantly male, they write most of where the shoe pinches them—that is, in regard to the problem of generations. They are neglectful of where the shoe hurts the young—that is, with the problem of sexual maturity and with finding one's place in society. True, each of these is well recognized as problematic, but especially so where they coincide with what is bothersome to adults, the relation of the generations to each other. They are neglected where they trouble adults less, as in the female.

I hasten to add that this respite in regard to the girls' part in the problem of generations is fast disappearing. I submit that already it creates more emotional hardship than that of the males, which at least is officially recognized. Why, then, is the problem of generations so much more acute in the male than in the female?

To put it crassly: the self-identity, and even more the self-realization of the young man, implies to a large degree his replacing the preceding generation. In order to come into his own, the old man (or whoever stands in his place) must move over; or, in the folklore of my native Austria, he must move into the old people's quarters (*Ausgedinge*). This happens as soon as the son is ready to take over the farm, and with it, all other prerogatives including the main building: the farmhouse.

Such ascendancy of youth over old age proceeds smoothly, at the right age and in the correct form, if it tallies with the survival needs of the entire family and with the facts of biology, in short, if it takes place in concordance with nature and nurture. The well-being of the farm family depended on a vigorous male being in charge at least of the farming, if not also of the family. For centuries most men lived on farms tilled by small landholders or serf-tenants, or else made a living as small artisans or shopkeepers. In those times economic success and often mere survival depended on the physical strength and skill of the head of the family. So it seemed "natural" that as the father's vigor declined, a son just reaching the prime of his strength and mental abilities should take over.

When this was so, and since the father's life was meaningful, that of the son who at first helped him and then followed in his footsteps was automatically meaningful, too. An old Chinese proverb summed things up: "He who has sons cannot long remain poor; he who has none cannot remain rich." This was something both fathers and sons understood. The son growing up was secure in everyone's knowledge that he added substantially to the economic well-being of the family. Seeing also that his contributions increased in importance as he approached maturity and the peak of his physical strength, just as his father was declining in vigor, he had no need to worry about his work achievement (as would now come through more indirect employment on the labor market) and whether it supported his claim to have reached manhood.

Such an easy succession of the generations, even in times past, was mainly an "ideal" solution to the changing of the guards. But actuality often approached this ideal; and if not, the biological realities made it seem like the given order of things, since production depended so largely on the male's prowess.

True, even when the level of technology was so low that physical strength counted most, one's experience and skill, the know-how of work and of life, had to be added to strength to succeed; but all one's experience and knowledge were of little avail without physical strength, because it alone powered the economic process. There was no point, therefore, in a selfish holding on to knowledge or even to property rights, because they were only theoretical if they could bring no return, once physical power had failed.

While there were always some old men who held on beyond reason, along with other conflicts of interest and generations, these were clearly men smitten with blindness or carried away by unreasonable emotions. An intelligent self-interest in both old and young still required a transition of power and privilege at the point when physical decline set in among the aging and manhood was gained by the young. An old man might stand in the way of his sons, but his fate was then ordained. Thus O'Neill's Ephraim Cabot is unwilling to recognize his son's contribution; but when the son walks off, not with the farm but with his father's young wife, the father ends up in possession of a farm that he alone cannot tend to.

It is when physical strength is no longer essential for survival or economic success that the biological process of aging as well as of maturing no longer, of necessity, conditions the taking over of the dominant position by youth. What once formed the "ideal" solution, because conditioned by the nature of man, suddenly turns into an arbitrary "ideal" without any necessary or natural basis. Such an ideal soon becomes hard to put into practice, and eventually even ceases to be an ideal.[3]

Even before modern times, wherever physical strength was not essential to survival because the life-assuring labor was performed by others, the problem of generations was acute. This was true, for example, of former ruling classes, and later on of the upper middle classes. It was also true in the Greece of Alcibiades and in Catiline's Rome. Whenever there was no natural order to the ascendancy of the generations, problems arose between them similar to those that are now typical for all in a machine age, when almost nobody's survival depends on physical strength.

If the young man's coming into his place as head of the living unit is not thus assured by the natural order of things, if he cannot be sure that the dominant position will be his at a foreseeable and not too distant moment, then he cannot wait for it in good grace. Then he must fight for it, for both his rights and his obligations, and the sooner the better, because only both in their combination make for the realm of the mature man.

If such a transition does not occur smoothly, is not accepted as natural and inevitable by both partners, then the older generation is likely to view the younger with suspicion, and justifiably so, because youth taking over is no longer necessary and natural. Why should the older generation voluntarily abdicate if it has nothing to gain by it and loses nothing by holding on?

Many if not most adults have an emotional need for children and enjoy bringing them up. It is such a truism that children for their part need their parents for physical and emotional survival that I mention it only to round out the picture. Once childhood is past, however, the picture changes. At certain times in history the older generation had an emotional need to see its way of life continued by the coming generations. This was particularly true when the parent generation had begun a work it could not complete and which it felt would remain pointless if uncompleted, be it the clearing of the land or the raising of a cathedral. Yet the more we came to doubt that things would continue in the old ways, that we were toiling for eternity, the less emotional need was felt by the older generation for the next one to continue what it so auspiciously had begun.

With the advent of modern technology and mass society, only very few have so intimate a feeling for their life's work, such a personal investment in it, that they need to see it continued by others. Short of such a desire, the older generation has little psychological need for youth. If youth tends to move away and build a life very different from that of the old folk, whom they only sporadically remember or visit on special occasions, then even the hope for emotional comfort from youth becomes unrealistic. While youth may still have some emotional

---

[3]Still, we are not yet too far removed from it in our deeper feelings about what makes for the secure order of things. Witness the feeling of relief, in the last election [1960], when both parties offered young and vigorous candidates for a position being vacated by an old and tired man. Though there is no doubt that millions loved and venerated the old man more than either young candidate, the feeling was prevalent that age had to step aside in favor of youth for the good of the commonweal.

and economic need for parents, most parents have little emotional need, and very few an economic one, for a youth striving to be free of its elders. It is because parents still have an emotional need for children, but not for an independent youth, that they often show strenuous resistance when youth fights for its independence. It is also what makes them so critical of certain exaggerations or passing effects of youth's battle for self-realization.

Such resentment and ambivalence about youth's striking out on its own matters little if youth can readily remove itself from the impact. The development of youngsters who went West or ran away to sea was not hampered by adult criticism of their ventures, though their development to full emotional maturity may have known other vagaries. But if youth stays at home or close to home and still fights for its independence from those it depends on, both sides show an emotional deficit.

The resultant scarring of personality in a delinquent youth, for example, is recognized by society as serious. The misanthropic nagging and dissatisfaction of his elders are less well recognized as the price they pay for the conflict. Hamlet thus has his counterpart in King Lear, who, unwilling to make room for youth, tries instead to put reins on the younger generation and to saddle it with a burden of gratitude. It is poetic justice that Cordelia, willing to serve age by foregoing the right of youth to a life of its own, suffers destruction, too.

In the psychoanalytic literature certain aspects of the problem of youth are traced back to a revival and a more violent acting out of the oedipal situation in adolescence. And it is true; something akin to the oedipal situation may be found among the children of most known societies. Specific variations will depend on who is head of the family and to what degree; the character of the persons who minister to the child; how large or small the family is; and how intense or weak is the emotional attachment of specific family members to one another and to the child. But the same cannot be said for the repetition of oedipal conflicts in adolescence.

The girl who marries at fifteen or sixteen and soon thereafter has children of her own is not likely to be beset by a repetition of her oedipal longings for her father or by any fierce competition with her mother for his emotions. As suggested earlier, the repetition of the oedipal conflict is not an issue of nature but depends very much on the structure of family and society.

Only a youth who is kept (or keeps himself) economically and emotionally dependent on the older generation will experience the repetition of the conflict that psychoanalysts observe so frequently nowadays among middle-class adolescents. To cite Hamlet again as the most familiar instance of a revived oedipal conflict in youth—if Hamlet, like Fortinbras, had fought for a kingdom across the sea instead of wishing to inherit his father's place, no tragedy would have taken place; but because he wished to take over from a generation unwilling to yield, rather than to find and win a world of his own, the old oedipal feelings were reactivated and led to the tragedy that destroyed them all. If Hamlet had known for sure what he wished to achieve on his own in life, he could not have been pressed into becoming the avenger of his father. For Hamlet's father, like Lear, put a private burden on his child's too weak shoulders.

Here, then, is another aspect of the conflict of generations: the parent who sees his child's main task in life as the duty to execute his will or to justify his existence (which is different from a parent's devotion to an unfinished labor which the child, on his own, later wishes to bring to fruition). The son who does not revolt when he is expected to devote his life only or mainly to achieving what the parent could not, usually perishes as Hamlet did.

In the present-day world with its tamer middle-class society, we find that the conflicts between a youth either afraid of or prevented from coming into its own and an older generation unwilling or unable to give way, are no less tragic though played out in more muted tones. It follows that whenever society is so organized that youth remains dependent on the older generation, because of the duration of the educational process or for other reasons, and this older generation is not ready to step aside economically, politically or emotionally, a psychological impasse is created which may then be aggravated by unresolved oedipal conflicts.

Here it might be well to remind ourselves that no oedipal situation would exist if the parents were not deeply involved with their child. The revival of the oedipal conflict in adolescence is often due to a parents' wish or need to remain as important to his child in adolescence as he was during infancy.

I venture to guess that many more (particularly middle-class) youths come to grief nowadays because of their parents' insistence that the former justify them as parents than because of any revived oedipal desire for their mothers or fathers. (This again is different from youth's independent wish to prove its own worth and not the worth of a parent.) One form of such an insistence is the overt and covert pressure on youth to provide the parents with what was lacking in their own lives. The mother's pressure on her daughter to live out vicariously her unfulfilled daydreams of popularity or to make a notable marriage can effectively block the girl's efforts to find self-realization in ways that are genuine to her. Often it is both parents who expect their sons to excell in athletics and who take for granted their right to assume that their child will do better than they did.

Nowadays it is usually both middle-class parents who put pressure on youth of both sexes to enter the prestige colleges; this pressure is reinforced by a parallel one from the schools and the general public. I have found those parents most insistent and most unreasonable in such demands who never went to college themselves or never graduated.[4] Many a college youngster needs to ward off this undue attempt to run his life as his parents or teachers want, and longs to carve his own way. He decides that the only way to manage this is to drink, do poorly in college, or flunk out. That is not his original desire; he acts out of a

[4]Similarly, I know of no Latin scholar who has bought a copy of *Winnie Ille Pooh* for his children; but tens of thousands who never studied Latin have bought the book for their children and have expected them to enjoy it and to acquire an understanding of Latin culture from it. Actually, such a translation is at best a sophomoric prank; taken seriously, it should be obvious on whom the joke is played.

necessity to prove himself master of his own fate.

All this is only part of an attitude that expects American children to do better than their parents, and often, seen objectively, the task is even quite feasible; but to children and adolescents the demand seems emotionally impossible, because it comes at a time when their opinion of their parents' achievements is unrealistically high. Contrary to all psychoanalytic writings that teach clearly how the child and adolescent is overawed by his parents' power and wisdom, both society and his parents continue to expect the emotionally impossible of youth. Offhand, I can recall no single statement in which consideration of what is expected of high school and college youth is directly linked to the achievement of the youth's parents. While we are more than ready to praise the self-made man, we are reluctant to apply the correlate of such praise: to recognize how difficult it is to outdo one's parents.

True, many youngsters end up doing better than their parents, either socially, economically, or intellectually; but I wonder how the score would show up on a balance sheet that also took account of emotional well-being. A vast number have risen in this way, but then they have hardly been able to manage life, even with the help of a psychoanalyst. If we consider, in evaluating those who do better in life than their parents, not only the externals but also the inner life, perhaps the picture of success that emerges would give us food for second thoughts.

To put the burden of surpassing one's parents on the relations between parent and child leads of necessity to unresolvable conflicts. If youth succeeds, it emasculates the parent. As a result, youth cannot feel successful—partly out of guilt, and partly because he cannot be sure if it was he or his parent who wanted him to succeed. That is, he cannot be sure who it is that truly structures his life.

As for the older generation, the conflict shows many faces. It may take the form of contempt if youth does not fight back (they are weak) or of hostile anxiety if it does (they are delinquent). And if youth has serious doubts about whether it will ever succeed, it must still either rebel or submit in cowardly fashion, or else find some devious (neurotic) way to sidetrack the issue. (To be neither son nor man avoids the fight altogether and hurts the father most, as when the son is a "beat.") Hence the eternal historic and dramatic predicament of the crown prince: If he submits to his father's superannuated clinging to office, he will be a weakling when he finally inherits the throne. If he rejects a role of empty waiting, he must head the revolt against his father.

But what about the girl? Must her mother abdicate for her to come into her own? Not as long as her psychosocial identity resides in childbearing and homemaking. The older generation may stand in her husband's way of realizing his independence, but as long as she accepts that her independence as a social being rests on his, the older generation may stand in her husband's way but it does not stand in hers. Her mother does not need to move over for her to be herself. On the contrary, the mother's having reached an age when childbearing is no longer possible or becoming makes it obvious to one and all who is now in ascendance, and no fight between the generations is needed to settle the issue. (Some modern mothers who cannot accept their gray hair and fading looks, and with it their sexual decline, create a problem for their daughters similar to that of the boy's.)

But what if the girl's psychosocial identity ceases to reside in child-bearing and homemaking, or exclusively so? Until the industrial era, as Veblen saw, woman's social identity was "essentially and normally a vicarious one," an expression of the man's life at second remove. And so long as she remained (of necessity) a drudge, she accepted this ancillary role and was largely at peace with her lot. But the less this became true, the more her problems of identity and self-realization were compounded. By now, the female adolescent struggles not only with having to decide whether her place is in the home or in society at large, or in both, but to what degree and with what justification. Thus the problems of youth have become nearly the same for both sexes; the sexual difference counts for less, because the conflicts of growing up are so much more psychosocial than sexual.

This, I believe, is one of the reasons why psychoanalysis is so often ineffective in adolescence—not because the sexual pressures are so great, and they are great, but because psychoanalysis, which is so well able to help with problems of sex and repression and personal self-realization, does not help with the problem of social self-realization. Or, to put it differently, pitting a helpful authority (the analyst) against repressive authority figures still leaves the adolescent under the sway of some adult authority which he needs to replace with his own. Or, to put it yet differently: psychoanalysis is devised for and effective in helping persons with their intrapersonal difficulties; hence it tends to approach all problems as such. But the problem of the generations is an interpersonal difficulty. Therefore, to deal with it as if it were intrapersonal only complicates matters instead of simplifying them, and makes resolving them less likely.

Of course, this also is true only for Western middle-class society. How the problem of generations can differ in different cultures may be illustrated by a controversy between American and Japanese psychoanalysts: in Japan the psychoanalyst's task was seen to consist in helping the young individual to give up his search for self-identity; his self-realization was to be sought not in individuation but in accepting his place within the family in the traditional subservient position of the son toward his father. Thus a Japanese patient "as he approached the successful conclusion of his treatment said, 'During my vacation my mother told me on one occasion that I was now pleasing my father better again.' The psychoanalyst, in reviewing the changes in the patient's personality, says, 'His psychic stage is now as harmonious a one as can ever be reached by human beings' i.e., in accordance with the national mores and aspirations of Japan."[5]

[5] J. C. Moloney, "Understanding the Paradox of Japanese Psychoanalysis," *International Journal of Psychoanalysis* (1953), *34*:291–303. He also quotes a statement from the *Tokyo Journal of Psychoanalysis* asserting that the task of psychoanalysis is so to strengthen the ego that it can and will respond to the demands of the superego. Those demands in turn are viewed as basically the demands of the emperor, since he represents the all-embracing ethos of his nation.

Most serious writers on the problem of youth have recognized that youth's present difficulties in Western society are closely related to changed social and economic conditions and to the ensuing difficulty for youth in finding self-realization in work. As Goodman observes: "It's hard to grow up when there isn't enough man's work," and he continues, "To produce necessary food and shelter is man's work. During most of economic history most men have done this drudging work, secure that it was justified and worthy of a man to do it, though often feeling that the social conditions under which they did it were not worthy of a man, thinking, 'It's better to die than to live so hard'—but they worked on. . . . Security is always first; but in normal conditions a large part of security comes from knowing your contribution is useful, and the rest from knowing it's uniquely yours: they need you."[6]

Just as in this country an earlier generation needed youth because the economic security of the family depended on its contribution, so in Russia today youth is needed because only it can carry on the task of creating the new and better society; and in Africa because only it can move society from tribal confusion toward modern democracy. If the generations thus need each other, they can live together successfully, and the problem of their succession, though not negligible, can be mastered successfully. Under such conditions youth and age need each other not only for their economic but even more for their moral survival. This makes youth secure—if not in its position, at least in its self-respect. But how does the parent in modern society need the next generation? Certainly not for economic reasons any more, and what little expectation a parent may have had that his children would support him in old age becomes superfluous with greater social security. More crucially, the status-quo mood of the older generation suggests no need for youth to create a much different or radically better world.

In many respects youth has suddenly turned from being the older generation's greatest economic asset into its greatest economic liability. Witness the expense of rearing and educating youth for some twenty or more years, with no economic return to be expected. Youth still poses emotional problems to the preceding generation, as of old. But in past generations these emotional problems were, so to speak, incidental or subservient to economic necessity. What at best was once the frosting on the cake must now serve as both solid food and trimmings—and this will never work.

Thus the economic roles, obligations, and rewards are no longer clearly defined between the generations, if not turned upside down. Therefore, another aspect of the relation between the generations looms ever larger, in a balance sheet of interaction that is no longer economic but largely emotional. Modern man, insecure because he no longer feels needed for his work contribution or for self-preservation (the automatic machines do things so much better and faster), is also insecure as a parent. He wonders how well he has discharged that other great function of man, the continuation of his species.

At this point modern youth becomes the dreaded avenging angel of

---

[6]P. Goodman, *op. cit.*

his parents, since he holds the power to prove his parents' success or failure as parents; and this counts so much more now, since his parents' economic success is no longer so important in a society of abundance. Youth itself, feeling insecure because of its marginal position in a society that no longer depends on it for economic survival, is tempted to use the one power this reversal between the generations has conferred on it: to be accuser and judge of the parents' success or failure as parents.

How new is all this? It is very hard to compare one age with another. But the Alcibiades or Catiline of antiquity would not have had their followings if the problem of youth having to test itself against an older generation had not existed in those times; nor do Plato's indictments of what he saw as obstreperous youth sound very different from those leveled at our young people today. I may be the victim of those distortions of perspective that make things distant seem far smaller than those looming in the foreground.

Whether this is error in judgment or not, the fact remains that the present problems of Western youth in finding self-definition, and with it security, seem more complex than those of other generations. I say Western youth because, while Russia appears to have its equivalent of the Teddy boys and while Isael does not seem altogether happy with all aspects of Kibbutz-reared youth, the problems there seem different not only in quantity but also in quality. The main difference lies not so much in the particular tasks society sets for its younger generation but in how clearly the latter realize that only they, the generation of the future, can achieve these tasks.

This difference is critical, for, contrary to some people's opinion, youth does not create its own cause for which it is ready to fight. All it can do is to embrace causes developed by mature men. But youth can only do this successfully if the older men are satisfied with providing the ideals and do not also wish to lead the active battle for reaching them. Or, to put it differently, a youth expected to fight for his personal place in a society of well-defined direction is not lost but on his way. A youth expected to create a new but not yet delineated society finds himself a rebel without a cause. Only when each group has its own important tasks, when one without the other cannot succeed, when age provides the direction but youth the leadership and the fighting manpower, is it clearly understood that whether the battle is won or lost depends on youth's fulfilling its all-important share of the total struggle.

As to who is to provide meaningful work for youth, I believe the answer is that nobody can do that for another. This is why I believe that the well-meant discussions and advice as to what industry should do to make factory work more meaningful has the problem all wrong. Nobody can make life or work more meaningful for others. Nor do most tasks have an absolute significance, not even the growing of food.

On our own plains, for example, stand acres of corn cribs filled to overflowing, while youth continues to leave rural America in droves. Yet its first response to the contemplated Peace Corps for underdeveloped areas was electric. This was the more striking since American farms are now largely mechanized (it is clean work), while the very goals of the Peace Corps include the mechanization of agriculture wherever it is still largely manual (which is "dirty" work). So it is not the work task (growing food) which attracts or repels youth, but the clear evidence that "they need you."[7]

Yet when it became apparent that to join the Peace Corps candidates had to be screened, take examinations, and then be assigned tasks, enthusiasm faltered. It was not initially aroused by the chance to enter one more rat race of competitive examinations nor by the prospect of being sent where the managers of the Corps wanted them to go. They did not want to be emissaries, even of their country. They had jumped at the chance to go where they were needed and to prove how well they could do. They hoped to develop themselves while helping others to develop their country. When it became clear that they were expected to represent something else (in this case American goodwill abroad), they lost interest and, of the many who initially applied, few presented themselves for the scheduled examinations. A chance to act on their own fervor caused a stir; but faced with one more competition, they might as well continue the college rat race for suburbia.

True, a society of plenty can tempt people to waste their time by filling it with empty entertainment or meaningless comfort, or to strive for the wherewithal to do so. But no one need fall for this temptation nor can even the best TV programs make life more meaningful for viewers. At best they can provide the raw material which the individual can then forge into a meaningful life.

Just as freedom and democracy cannot be handed down but have to be fought for, just as knowledge cannot be poured into the heads of our students but only situations created that induce them to seek it, so too industry cannot make work more meaningful for the worker. Only he can first find out what kind of work may be meaningful to him, and then go out and seek it, or at least a reasonable compromise between what is personally meaningful work and what jobs are available to him. I think those who complain that work is not more meaningful are in the wrong, too. What is wrong is that more people do not strive to find meaning in their lives; if they did, they would radically alter our economy and with it our working conditions.

Thus the older generation never has provided meaningful work or life for youth. All they have striven for was a deeper meaning in their own lives, and when they did that, segments of youth could at least follow their lead. It was the mature Marx, not the adolescent, who created Marxism, which then provided the basis for meaningful effort by a whole generation of youth. It was not the youthful but the mature Roosevelt who stimulated another generation of youth to find meaning in life through improvement and through efforts to reorganize society.

Surely, we too give lip-service to the conviction that man's best hope is the next generation, but this hope does not seem very strong or at-

---

[7]A crude index of how far we are from understanding the goals of youth lies in the fact that some United States agricultural extension agents working with 4-H clubs were recently sponsoring a new scheme for keeping youth on the farm: rousing their interest in the care and breeding of race horses!

tractive if we of the older generation do not pursue it with equal vigor. Neither our conviction that the West is declining nor our fear that atomic destruction will wipe man from the earth, realistic as each may well be, offers much hope for assertive self-realization, now or ever. If I cannot feel myself full of vitality because of my hopes for a life in the future, if the world I am about to create will not be better than that of my fathers, better not to live in this world, better to retire from it or feel alive in the moment, no matter what price I must pay in the future. So reasons the criminal delinquent who seeks a moment of heightened self-assertion in the anxious excitement of the criminal act, or through the kick he finds in his drugs.

As one delinquent youngster complained, "You can't live, if there's nothing to push against." What he meant is that you cannot test your own worth, your own strength and vitality, the very things you feel most dubious about as an adolescent, when all you can push against is a vacuum, or an adult society more than ready to give way, to act more youthful than even befits youth. Without something definite to push against, youth feels lost. Many causes are embraced by youth, not for the cause itself, but because in fighting for it, its strength can be tested against something. Hence youth favors causes that run against the established order, even an ultraconservative cause, because nothing is quite so safe a testing ground as the well-established order.

In Germany today, delinquent youth is often spoken of as the half strong (*die Halbstarken*). They are half strong because for them the older generation and its values mean the Hitler generation. But the ideas and values of those elders proved deficient in all important respects, while the generation of the fathers was cut down by heavy German losses during the war. Hence youth could not test itself against them and remained only half strong.

In the United States a very dissimilar but parallel process took place. The depression led to serious doubts about the values and ideas of the older generations as to the merits of a free enterprise society. The response of the older generation was frequently an inner abdication of the truly parental role. Since that generation felt it had embraced the false goddess of material success, they relinquished being mentors of the next generation and tried instead to be their pals, if not also their peers. They did not, however, give up wanting their children to give meaning to their own now emptier lives. While German fathers were either absent, or died in the war, or were morally destroyed by becoming Hitler's servants, many middle-class American parents simply abdicated their parental function but still wanted their parenthood proved successful by their children's achievements in life.

In terms of generations, then, the question that haunts every young person is: Am I as good, as much a man as my father? as much a woman as my mother? This is something to measure up against, to find out if one has it in him to push things a bit further than the parents were able to do. But if the question has to be: Am I as much a man as my father should have been, as my mother wants me to be? Or in reverse, and hence even more void of direction, the anxious question: Am I the girl my father does not want me to be? Then the person is lost, without guideposts in his struggle to find out what kind of person he is and what kind of a person he wishes to be, as compared with the generation of his parents.

Where is youth to go? How is it to shape itself and its relation to the older generation, the image it must either want to emulate or to supersede with a better one? If I am not mistaken, it is in Jack Kerouac's *On the Road* that two beat characters have the following conversation: "We got to go and never stop till we get there," says the first. The other wonders, "Where are we going, man?" and the answer is, "I don't know, but we gotta go."

These two young men are not in flight from society. They seek a goal—that much is clear. Otherwise, the first would not say they must go until they get there, nor would the second ask where they are going. If they were merely in flight, the first might have said they must go and never stop, and the question of destination would not have come up. More than that, they are in a great hurry to get started toward their goal; but this goal is elusive, and so they are people lost in their search, so lost that they no longer know which direction to take. Worse, they doubt that there is any direction. Therefore, their search for only an unknown goal becomes empty roaming. As long as they are on their way, they feel alive. If they stop, they fear to die. Therefore, any and all kinds of spurious activities will do, to keep from recognizing how lost they are.

Why is this goal eluding modern young man in search of himself? If manhood, if the good life in the good community, is the goal of adolescence, then the goal is clear, and with it the direction and the path. But what if existing manhood is viewed as empty, static, obsolescent? Then becoming a man is death, and manhood marks the death of adolescence, not its fulfillment. The bouyancy of youth is fed by the conviction of a full life to come, one in which all great things are theoretically attainable. But one cannot believe in the good life to come when the goal is suburbia. One cannot realize one's values by climbing the ladder of the business community, nor prove one's manhood on the greens of the country club; neither can one settle into security in an insecure world.

If there is no certainty of fulfillment, then it is better not to give up the promise of youth with its uncertainty, its lack of definite commitment. Youth at least offers a chance to escape the premature death of rigidity or the anxious confusion of a life that is disgraceful when it is without direction. Neither rigidity nor a confused running in many directions at once (and running after status or money are only the worst among nondirections) is an attractive goal for the young man trying to emerge from his state of uncommittedness into one of inner stability. Better to be committed to such uncommittedness than to commit oneself to spending the rest of one's life as a hollow man.

One's fathers (at least, the best of them) did a good job of showing the young how hollow a life they had built. Let this be a warning not to join them in the waste lands. Better not to enter this land of walking shadows, of immaturity posing as maturity. Better to assert defensively one's uncommitted immaturity, one's remaining poised at the threshold of a life one does not wish to enter. It is the romantic position, but alas, the position of a generation which has little belief in the romance of a better world, a generation whose dreams are not to be striven for but subjected to analysis.

I have said that the present difficulties of youth are related to changed economic and social conditions, and to how much harder it has grown for youth to find its fulfillment in work. In this respect the fate of the girl can be even harder than the boy's. It is impressed on her from an early age that her main fulfillment will come with marriage and children, but her education has nevertheless been the same as that of boys, who are expected to realize themselves mainly through work and achievement in society. To make matters worse, the years in college or even graduate school have further prepared the female elite to seek self-realization in work, while society at large continues to stress that they must find it in motherhood.

Only very occasionally, for boys, is fatherhood added like an afterthought as part of their self-image as mature men. And nowhere, to the best of my knowledge, or only most incidentally, is the complementary image of being a husband even dimly outlined. Yet it should be obvious that women will not find fulfillment in being wives if their partners do not see being a husband as essential to their own self-realization.

True, not long ago there was a time when work around the house was hard, and it could and did proceed in conjunction with raising children and creating a home. But if modern labor-saving devices are relieving women of the most backbreaking work, they have also done away with the satisfactions it yielded. For girls, too, if machines do it better and faster, it is hard to grow up if there's not enough woman's work to be done. Buying ready-to-wear clothes for her family is a vicarious act. It reflects only her husband's ability to provide the money to buy them, but no unique or essential labors of her own. Since the same is nearly as true for cooking and the home arts, what remain, apart from child-rearing, are the most stultifying tasks—dusting, making beds, washing dishes. And beyond that lie mainly the refinements of homemaking, or what Veblen termed an occupation of ceremonial futility.

Many of the young woman's free-time activities are equally futile. I do not refer only to gardening, which replaces the conspicuous embroidery of an earlier age, or to the bridge circle or country-club life designed to help her husband toward his own type of ceremonial futility. I refer also to much that passes, unexamined, as more valuable pastimes, such as the PTA or the League of Women Voters. When used to cover up a vacuum of truly significant activities, of serious involvement, even these lose the genuine satisfactions they could otherwise confer. For, as Veblen also observed, "Woman is endowed with her share—which there is reason to believe is more than an even share—of the instinct of workmanship, to which futility of life or of expenditure is obnoxious," and such an impulse, when denied expression, leaves them "touched with a sense of grievance too vivid to leave them at rest."

But if a girl tries to fulfill her instinct for workmanship, she is subject to pressures not directed at boys. Many young men show little interest in marriage, even through their early thirties, and are allowed to go their way. At worst, a man may come in for gentle nagging at home, and his friends may tease him about it; but in the final analysis they accept his wish to postpone getting married and founding a family; they tacitly acknowledge that he is not ready yet, that he needs more time to find himself in his work life before he can settle down to family life. Such men are often popular, both in married and unmarried circles, and feel no adverse effect on their sense of accomplishment. In brief, a man is considered a failure if he does not support himself, does not achieve in work, but his marital status little affects people's estimate of him.

All this is very different for the girl. A woman, no matter how gifted or successful in her work life, is judged a failure if she does not marry fairly soon. From adolescence on, therefore, the pressure to marry interferes with her ability to find self-realization in her own personal way. Discrimination usually begins in youth, when there is some indulgence for the boy's nonconformity or revolt because he must "sow his wild oats"; much less tolerance is accorded the girl who seeks to find herself through such a period of nonconformity.

Many a college boy goes through a crisis of identity during his first years away from home, after exposure to many new ideas. Later, in his last years at college, he may suddenly throw himself into his studies, trying to find new identity in his work achievement. Many a girl finds herself in a parallel position; but then she suddenly realizes that with her new dedication to hard work and study, she is failing to compete in the marriage market. Knowing that she wants to have a family one day, and fearing that with her present single-minded absorption it may slip through her fingers, she stops herself dead in her tracks; or worse, she cannot make up her mind which she really wants, and may lose out on both means of self-realization if marriage has become the only possibility.

Nor is it only the college girl who suddenly kills her excitement about biochemistry because she realizes she is passing up desirable dates. The noncollege girl goes through a similar experience. She too is caught in the realization that society insists she can only find self-realization through an early marriage. So she gives up her tentative new interests as impractical and buckles down to a course in beauty culture or secretarial work. Later, as the young wife of a skilled or unskilled worker, she is exactly as restless and bewildered as the college girl who gave up biochemistry to achieve married life in the suburbs. Neither girl can understand why, though now a success in the eyes of others, all the meaning of life is evading her. This meaning she now looks for in the task of bringing her children up right, which means finding vicarious satisfaction in their lives, with all the consequences discussed earlier.

Here the worker's wife is perhaps the worst off, because she lacks even the secondary gains of her suburban counterpart. Many such women, uprooted too often, no longer try to fill their emptiness with family gossip or church activities, but try to find, if not meaning, at least some escape from emptiness through a job. Unfortunately, it is rarely the kind of work that gives meaning to their lives; but at least it provides association with equals and is preferred to the drudgery of homemaking.

Yet it is not only the instinct for workmanship which is too often frustrated in the modern young woman; frequently it is also her sexual instinct. While sexual difficulties are neither a recent curse of youth, nor restricted to one sex alone, the American attitude toward sex and the educational system have here, too, burdened female youth more than male youth.

Early in this article I referred to the puberty rites of preliterate societies. These elaborate rituals mark the reaching of sexual maturity and assure the initiates of their new adult status. In most of these societies sex was never at all secret nor was pregenital sex experience forbidden. The child learned what sex was all about as he grew up, watching older persons and animals in intercourse. In farming societies, the fecundity of animals is always a central economic issue, so if adult sex is no longer open, at least animal procreation in all its ramifications is still freely observed and discussed in most parts of the world.

Not so in American middle-class society; and what observations are available to the growing child are shrouded in secrecy, if not in embarrassment or outright shame. We all know that shame and embarrassment about the normal bodily functions make sex experiences difficult for much of modern youth. But compensatory efforts to make of sex relations more than they can ever be are equally confounding. I am speaking of the many literary descriptions of intercourse as an earth-shaking event (for example, Hemingway's description in *For Whom the Bell Tolls*). Obviously, one's own sexual experiences, however rewarding, have no such cosmic effect and hence do not seem to come up to par.[8]

Laurance Wylie . . . describes how, in a large segment of the French middle classes, the adolescent boy receives his training in love-making from an older woman and then in turn initiates a girl younger than himself in the art he has learned. There is much more than simple experience involved in this way of teaching sex to an inexperienced young man. His very inexperience makes him attractive to the mature woman. In the typical American pattern, ignorance is supposed to be the best teacher of the ignorant in sexual matters. But here the young man's inexperience makes him feel clumsy and insecure in seducing his girl, who, as likely as not, had to seduce him into becoming the seducer in the first place.

---

[8]One may also wonder about the success of *Hiroshima, mon Amour* among the intelligentsia. This is a film in which a love affair is significant not because of what it means to the two partners, or of what they find in each other, but because it is played out against a perspective of world history: the German occupation of France and the bombing of Hiroshima. If the earth has to shake or world history to look on before a love affair can be meaningful for the partners, youth must find itself in awkward straits in its love relations. (I have discussed other difficulties many Americans encounter in finding meaning in their intimate relations in *The Informed Heart*, The Free Press, 1960.)

American middle-class youth learns about sex in the back seat of a car, or during a slightly drunken party, or because there was nothing better to do to kill boredom (read: sexual frustration and anxiety). The first sexual experience often leaves ineffaceable impressions, marred by a total lack of experience on either side. Both partners feeling anxious and insecure, neither one can offer encouragement to the other, nor can they take comfort from the accomplished sex act, since they cannot be sure that they did it well, all comparisons lacking.

To use Wylie's example again, the young Frenchman not only knows that his inexperience makes him sexually attractive, he also receives the accolade of the person from whom it counts most: an experienced woman has found him not only sexually attractive but from her rich experience (based on comparisons) she has also assured him that he is a manly lover indeed. Thus, secure in his masculinity, he in due course will be sexually attracted by a young girl's inexperience, rather than frightened by it, as his American counterpart usually is. She, feeling that her innocence, or at least her inexperience, makes her attractive, will not feel clumsy because of it, and he, encouraged by previous experience, will feel himself well able to satisfy his girl sexually.[9] Feeling sure that he can satisfy her, she will feel she has satisfied him.

This, of course, is comparing a French "ideal" type of introduction to sex with an American "ideal" type. In actuality, there are as many variations in France as in the United States in the ways youth is introduced to sex. Still, the French way is as typical there as the other is of middle class youth in America. What goes far beyond a mere paradigm of sex behavior in the two countries is the way youth is prepared for the expected sexual role. In France, as in many other lands, both boy and girl from early childhood on are prepared, the first to take the more dominant, the other the more yielding role, not only in sex but also in the family.

In earlier times there have been societies, or at least subsocieties, in which the woman was dominant in the home and even in intimate relations. This situation may still be found in certain segments of the French middle classes, and it used to be characteristic of some orthodox Jewish groups. It seems that successful family life can be organized on such a basis as long as the man's dominance in his sphere is clearly recognized and never challenged by women. The man's sphere is usually the work life, be it in the professions, in business, or politics.

In the orthodox Jewish groups referred to, the man's unquestioned superiority in the all-important religious sphere permitted both to accept gladly the wife's dominance in running the home and often also the shop. With the areas of dominance thus clearly marked out, the wife could be dominant in her sphere without extending it to running her husband's life or her children's. Though such a woman was dominant in the home, no "mom-ism" resulted. Secure in her sphere, it did not occur to her to challenge the man's. More importantly, she did not expect her husband to be dominant at home or in business. Therefore, she was not disappointed in what she expected of him, and hence she

---

[9]This has been described in Strauss's *Rosenkavalier.*

did not need to make up for it by nagging him or dominating her children.[10] The woman who engages in "mom-ism" and wishes to "wear the pants" does not act out of an original desire to go her husband one better, but in defense and retaliation.

Certainly, our educational system does not prepare the girl to play the more dominant role in the home sphere, nor the more surrendering role, either in sex or other areas of experience. Instead, she is raised in contradiction. On the one hand, she is told that to be feminine means to be yielding, to be courted, and that this is the desirable norm for a woman. She certainly cannot, for example, ask a boy for a date, nor pay the expenses of a date, though in some circles she may sometimes "go dutch."[11]

Contrary to such passivity (waiting to be asked out), where it counts most emotionally, she is taught in school not only to think but also to act for herself. What she is not taught, either at home or in our educational system, is the emotional counterpart of the facts of life: that men and women are neither wholly equal nor by any means opposite sexes, but are complementary; that neither things that are equal nor those that are opposite can be complementary. More importantly, she is not taught wherein men and women are alike—in their talents, aspirations, and emotional needs—and where they are not. From her educationally reinforced but unexamined notion of an equality of the sexes, arise many of the girl's difficulties in her sex relations. For, without clearly understanding her own nature, she does not know where and when to be "feminine" and where and when to be "equal."[12]

For example, in societies in which technology has not yet affected the social conditions of women or their expectations, her sexual life is in far less conflict than in ours. It is still sufficient for her if her lover or husband enjoys sex with her. Since she feels that his enjoyment proves her a good woman, nothing stands in her way of enjoying her-

---

[10]Things changed when such families left the ghettoes and entered modern technological societies. Once the religious sphere lost in importance, while the work sphere grew tremendously important, there were commensurate upheavals in the balance within the family.

[11]I can only mention in passing what would call for lenghy discussion: How a society of relative abundance has changed the dating and mating patterns. In other societies it was well known that the greatest attention one could show the courted person was to devote time and attention to him or her. In our society, in which the phrase "time is money" is more than a slogan, money must often make up for time; a boy's car or the money he can spend on his date now replaces the time and attention spent in being with her.

It is not simply that money is made to make up for emotional dedication, which it can never do; it is also made to prove virility, if not even orgastic potency, for which it is equally unsuitable. Many men who doubt their masculinity and virility try to quiet their fears through their social or economic success. Falsely equating virility with beating the other guy in competition, they must come out on top at all costs. But when success is sought not for itself but to make up for something that is missing, it cannot even be enjoyed for what it is, since it cannot make up for what it is not.

The counterpart of such a situation is found in a wife who feels thwarted in her hope for a virile man who can truly make her feel and be a woman. Heedlessly, she spends his money and eggs him on to achieve further status, since these have to make up to her for what they never can, her empty feeling of being a failure as a woman.

But all this comes later in life. It is not yet a problem of youth unless they have been exposed to it in their parents. Similarly, they cannot take their teachers as images to copy, if teachers in their sphere strive for academic success much as members of the business community use money and the status it confers.

[12]There is a corresponding confusion in the way we look upon initiative in women, for not all "active" women are unfeminine. Women who strive to "wear the pants" do so for defensive and neurotic reasons, just as the very need to be dominant, whether in man or in woman, is due to thwarted desires, if not also to a thwarted personality. Quite different is the striving to achieve for a purpose, for, like men, some women strive to realize their inner potentials—quite outside any context of competing with other men, other women, or any standard of measurement except their own wish to work toward a purpose. Until we distinguish clearly between the two, we shall continue to hold back, by labeling "unfeminine," those girls who seek to further their own natural growth and development.

self; and, not worrying about whether she is frigid or has an orgastic experience, as likely as not she experiences orgasm. He, not obliged by older tradition or by any newer understanding to provide her with an orgastic experience, can enjoy himself, experience orgasm, and thus help her to experience it herself.

In our own society, the male youth needs as much as ever to have his virility attested by his sexual partner, and the female youth has a parallel need. But by now, the boy also needs to have his girl prove him a man by her so-called "orgastic experience," and the girl is even worse off. She not only has to prove him a man by making him experience orgasm; she must also prove her femininity by the same experience, because otherwise she must fear she is frigid. Sexual intercourse cannot often stand up to such complex emotional demands of proving so many things in addition to being enjoyable.

To compound it all, the girl has grown conditioned by all her previous experience in school and college to performing with males on equal grounds, but not on how to complement them.[13] She cannot suddenly learn this in bed. She, trying to make sure that the man has an orgastic experience, and also wondering if she will be able to have one herself, gets so worried that she can truly experience neither, and ends up pretending. In order to prove their manhood or womanhood, the act is now burdened by their having to prove their potency to themselves and to each other, if not also to make the earth shake. Sex becomes another competition of who can make whom have an orgastic experience, and they cannot give up their self-centered needs in the act. The result is that they are unable to enjoy either their mutual desire or the forgetting of self in the experience.

If sexual relations are often less than satisfactory, and if female youth has put work achievement behind her, what is left for the girl by way of self-realization? With home-making now less challenging or satisfying, the children become a concentrated target of the young woman's energies. Here at least, if she starts out feeling less experienced than her mother, she feels considerably more sophisticated. Her world is no longer, as in an older generation, confined to her children, her kitchen, and the church. For years, through the period of her schooling, and perhaps later in a professional occupation, she has worked hard to enlarge her horizon, intellectually and emotionally. Motherhood was depicted to her, and she looked forward to it, as another tremendous, enlarging experience. Yet in reality it forces her to give up most of her old interests, and, unless she is fascinated by the minute developments of the infant, no new and different enrichment is on the horizon. Thus the new world of experience fails to materialize just at the moment

---

[13]Things would not be so bad if the competition were only with persons. To compete with somebody one knows well keeps competition in the human dimension and leads to personal jealousies, hopes and disappointments. But much of the competition where it counts most (merit scholarships, college board) involves not just a person but rather competing with one's whole age group. It is a competitiveness in the abstract, not against another person, but for a score on a test. As if this were not bad enough, competitions other than for grades and scholastic achievement have entered our educational system. All too often, at the same "educational" place where youngsters compete for grades, they are also competing for dates and a marriage partner.

when the old enriching experiences are closed, because the infant demands her concentrated attention.

All this is particularly acute with the first child, because the second and third child provide additional content in the mother's life while she cares for the newcomer. I am convinced she will have to find a solution to this problem. It might mean creating something akin to the extended family, through which some societies solved the problem; this meant entrusting part of infant care to the older children or sharing it with relatives. Another solution would be the care of young children by professional people while the mother pursues her individual interests, at least, for part of her time.

In any case, the young mother is now doubly disadvantaged. She cannot find fulfillment in her wifely and motherly role, because she lacks a partner who can complement her in tasks that cannot be mastered alone, or at least not in an emotionally satisfying way. In addition, she is in conflict between her old traditional role and the image of self-fulfillment through work to which all her schooling has directed her. Or, to put it differently, she is torn between the image of her vicarious role in society as mother and housewife and the self-directed image of herself that developed before marriage. Together, these conflicts are often enough to sour her on motherhood, which she could otherwise fully enjoy.

Resentful in many cases that her husband enjoys what to her seems a fuller life, she tries either to force him to share motherhood with her (which he cannot do without damage to his emotional well-being) or she expects marriage itself to compensate for the frustrated work aspects of her self-realization (which marriage cannot do). Hence she may also sour on her marriage.

The fact that female youth does not react in open conflict with a society that forces her into such an impossible predicament has to do with the actual and socially fostered difference between the sexes. The male delinquent will engage mainly in aggressive acts such as the destruction of property or other forms of aggressive violence; in the "beat," this may be turned inwards, as in the destructive neglect of his own body. In adolescence the female counterpart of violence is sex delinquency, which is less apt to bring the girl into conflict with society.

Yet again this behavior is more often socially imposed than biologically inherent. Many girls who feel "unfeminine" in terms of Hollywood fostered attitudes become sex delinquents to prove they are feminine, or at least to deny that they are not. The nondelinquent, more adult female youth may take things out on her husband and children in less obvious but equally destructive nagging, in a general dissatisfaction that drives her husband to try to achieve for her what only she can achieve for herself.

Others have come to recognize that the problem is largely theirs and are groping for reasonable solutions. Like Negro youth in America, they find themselves a minority with certain psychological advantages. If the majority of young American males can choose their occupations freely but long for more purpose to their labors, the minorities among youth are still fighting with a purpose. Once they do achieve the freedom to pursue self-chosen goals, then the current problems of youth will be no different for boys than for girls, white or Negro.

The elections of 1960 brought an upsurge of purpose, at least in a segment of our population who felt that the new administration had a place for their aspirations, might give them scope to create a better world. This was true for both youth and adult, but youth would not have believed it, if their elders had not shown that their hopes seemed to be justified. As one colleague of mine put it while observing changes on the campus of his university: These students who for years have been rebels without a cause were for the most part too sensible even to rebel. But when they first started to work for Stevenson, and then for Kennedy, and ever since the latter's election, they became dedicated workers for a better future. Yet these, as I say, were only a small segment. The vast majority of the young, like the vast majority of the old, still lacking a direction, seek harder than ever for an empty comfort. This, they hope, may enable them to forget that they have no purpose beyond it, and, as it fails, their search for more of the same becomes increasingly frantic and empty.

Many visitors to Russia, and not only educators, have been struck by how well-behaved Russian children are to their parents, and their parents to them. This mutual respect is entirely different in texture from either fear or the uneasy camaraderie sought by so many parents in our society, where the parent sees his task as that of play companion rather than mentor to the young. Perhaps the explanation lies in what Russian educators have to say about this remarkable difference. They claim that "the good behavior of the children is the result of the clarity and agreement on the part of all teachers [and all adults, we might add] as to their expectations from the children," espectations based on a strong sense of common purpose to create a better social system than has ever existed.[14] Now these for the most part are the children of the people who are still trying to create a new and better society for all, and not of the ruling elite, who already enjoy most of the new advantages. That is why "delinquent" tendencies are found more readily among children of the elite.

Yet even the common purpose of creating a better world, while assuring youth its importance in creating it, is not enough in itself to permit all who seek it to realize themselves. There must be added the clear conception of the usefulness of one's labor; and even then there will always be some who must travel an individual pathway not provided by society, for testing their manhood and worth.

Modern American society has virtually cut off such avenues inside the framework of that society. (Some young people seek them in foreign countries; witness the past attraction of the Spanish Civil War and the current appeal of the Cuban unheaval and of the new African countries.) No longer is there an open frontier for escape from the oppressive feeling that one cannot prove oneself within a rigidly stratified society. Where is a modern Ishmael to roam? Though he may feel

---

[14]B. Spock, "Russian children," *Ladies' Home Journal* (October 1960).

like "methodically knocking off people's hats," he cannot run away to sea because life there is now as regulated and devoid of chances for self-realization as on land. Prevented from knocking people's hats off, or hauled into court or to the psychiatrist for trying to, he feels he has no "substitute for pistol and ball," and may end up using them.

I have said before that for youth to come into his own means to a large degree his replacing the older generation, and that, whether the transition is smooth or hard-won, youth is still on its way. Thus the problem of the generations, when it goes wrong, may be characterized by saying that, whenever the older generation has lost its bearings, the younger generation is lost with it. The positive alternatives of emulation or revolt are then replaced by the lost quality of neither.

And this, I am afraid, is the situation in which large segments of American youth find themselves. They are unhappy when they settle down to continue in a pattern of life that their parents have arranged for them, because they know it to be an empty one. But they find it pointless to rebel, as do those others who, sensing emptiness in the lives prepared for them, fight against it but do not know what to fight for.

Old age is happiest when it can take youth up to the threshold of the good and the new and, like the mythical father of the West, point out the Promised Land to its children, saying: You and only you in a hard fight will have to make this your own; because what is handed down to you, what you have not won for yourselves, is never truly your own.

Youth, on the other hand, is happiest when it feels it is fighting to reach goals that were conceived of but not realized by the generation before them. What the older generation then urgently wished for itself, but had to acknowledge as the hope of the future—this is the legacy of youth. That the preceding generation wished to create such a better world makes it a worthy standard for youth. To come closer to achieving it through its own efforts proves to youth that it is gaining its own rich maturity.

The Myths of Youth

Marie Jahoda and Neil Warren

The authors review much of the literature on adolescence and inject their own critical comments on its merits and relevence. In doing this, what attitude have they toward the myths that surround youth? In an attempt to clarify the concepts of adolescence, people often tend to cloud some issues and oversimplify others. Have the authors fallen into this trap or have they successfully scrutinized the findings and added to our understanding? Time, study, and perspective should be helpful in making a decision.

Increasingly we indulge in searching examination of the societies in which we live. In this the United States excels: Whatever the maladies of American society, the saving grace lies perhaps with the Riesmans, the Whytes and the Harringtons, even the Packards and the Baldwins—men who, with varying degrees of passion and involvement, but always with concern, expose what they see as undesirable, dangerous, or simply ludicrous aspects of the American scene. The Americans, one says, are their own best critics.

A facet of such tendencies toward self-study is a growing concern with youth. The amount of published literature on the young has been steadily rising of recent years; the number of publications on adolescent behavior recorded in the *Psychological Abstracts* has almost trebled since 1930 in absolute terms and, relative to the overall number of publications, more or less doubled. In a way, this journal, and this article, are themselves a continuing part of the same sociocultural phenomenon, an attentive focus on the young which is beginning to be shared throughout the industrialized world.

In almost innumerable journalistic contributions to the understanding of youth this growing segment of the population is often loosely equated with the troublemakers among the young, be they involved in delinquency or in riotous reception meetings for the Beatles, in any case, with the most visible group among them. In a more systematic approach it pays to be pedantic about a definition of this age group and to link it to the usual concepts in the human sciences. Many years ago Charlotte Bühler[1] in her analysis of the five phases in the course of human life suggested a useful functional definition of this stage in life based on a biosocial approach: Youth is an in-between period begin-

From *Sociology of Education*, Vol. 38, No. 2 (Winter 1965). Reprinted by permission of The American Sociological Association.

[1]C. Bühler (1933), *Der menschliche Lebenslauf als psychologisches Problem*, second compl. rev. ed. 1959, Verlag f. Psych., Göttingen.

ning with the achievement of physiological maturity and ending with the acquisition of social maturity, that is with the assumption of the social, sexual, economic and legal rights and duties of the adult. In this period, youth anticipates on a trial pattern various ways in which to be adult. Societies in which physiological and social maturity occur simultaneously have no problems of youth, neither in a practical nor a theoretical sense; agricultural societies such as Eire in which inheritance is by *primogeniture* have a protracted youth which can easily go up to 40 years of age and which seems to impose a great strain on the young. But, short of such extremes, the level of civilization seems related to the number of years which a society accords to youth.

There is evidence to show that the biological onset of youth occurs earlier and earlier as the 20th century progresses. In the U. S. A., physiological maturity has been achieved 1/3 to 1/2 year earlier in every decade, and the situation in Britain and the Scandinavian countries is similar.[2] At the other end the period is shortened, however, at least with regard to age at marriage. In any case, the status of youth spans a period of about 10 or 12 years in those countries from which systematic studies are available.

While from a sociological, particularly a demographic, point of view there would be much to be said for investigating the entire stretch of this period, very few empirical studies have actually done so. Once in a while one comes across an interesting statistic relevant to youth defined as a position in society lasting for years; for example, Mark Abrams[3] has recently drawn attention to the fact that in England there are in the age group 16–24 three single men for every two single girls. But by and large the empirical studies concentrate on a smaller age span. To take the four books here under review, Rosenmayr,[4] in his study of Austrian apprentices deals with 15- and 17-year olds; Remmers[5] in his opinion surveys of American High School students takes age groups from 15 to 17, and does not emerge with results that describe the total position; and the Sherifs[6] deal separately with groups of young people, aged from 13 to 18. A volume edited by Erikson,[7] largely theoretical and descriptive in content, comes nearest to covering the full span of youth even if the definition remains implicit rather than explicit.

Wherever they draw the age line, these various social scientists obviously feel that youth is a topic worth studying, and most of them make the assumption that there are particular psychological and social problems in this period which segregate it from childhood on the one hand, and young adulthood on the other. Others disagree. A provocative book, decidedly a tract, recently published by Musgrove,[8] a British

[2]Ministry of Education, *The Youth Service in England and Wales* (1960), Comnd. 929, H.M.S.O., London.
[3]M. Abrams (1964), *The Newspaper Reading Public of Tomorrow*, Odhams Press, London.
[4]L. Rosenmayr (1963), *Familienbeziehungen und Freizeitgewohnheiten jugendlicher Arbeiter*, Verlag f. Geschichte and Politik: Vienna.
[5]H. H. Remmers (Ed.) (1963), *Anti-Democratic Attitudes in American Schools*, Northwestern University Press.
[6]M. Sherif and C. W. Sherif (1964), *Reference Groups*, Harper, New York.
[7]Erik H. Erikson. (1963), *Youth: Change and Challenge*, Basic Books, New York.
[8]F. Musgrove (1964), *Youth and the Social Order*, Routledge, London.

educational psychologist, takes the position that the psychology of adolescence is an invention of the psychologists; he claims that theories concerning the nature of youth have in fact been used to justify the segregation of the young from adult society—"The position of youth in contemporary society is only intelligible in terms of the rise since the later 18th century of a psychology of adolescence which has helped to create what it describes" (p. 2). Musgrove can even date with precision the beginning of all this: The adolescent, he claims, was invented by Rousseau in 1762. Whatever the force of Musgrove's argument, his extreme position draws attention to a valid point: The topic of youth is shot through with myths of all kinds which, on occasion, may contribute to their own validation. We shall return to this point later, but here it must be pointed out that it is relevant too to a curious controversy—curious on conceptual grounds—which pervades implicitly or explicitly much of the research literature: the controversy over a "youth culture."

Take the volume edited by Erikson, *Youth: Change and Challenge.* The various social scientists who contributed to this symposium presuppose that there is a "youth culture" or "adolescent subculture"; the concept is quite explicit in all the sociological analyses provided (in particular by Parsons and Keniston). The bulk of this symposium appeared as an issue of *Daedalus*, the Journal of the American Academy of Arts and Sciences, in the winter of 1961–1962. And perhaps because of this origin it differs from the other books here under review in several ways. For one thing, its contributions are directed to the educated layman rather than to the professional social scientist. For another, it is the only one not written around detailed research findings: Of course a vast amount of impressionistic experience, both first- and secondhand, has gone into the composition of the papers, but in general they are discursive and theoretical, with many assumptions on empirical matters, often in the form of bald statements of apparent fact. Some are best described as essays.

Eisenstadt and Parsons provide compact summaries of their well-known sociological positions with respect to youth in the framework of society. Erikson reworks his psychological views on identity and fidelity, and other scholars (Naegele, Bettelheim, Denney, Keniston) approach the topic from sociological and psychological vantage-points. There are descriptive and informative chapters on the Peace Corps, on civil rights activists in the U. S., on Japanese, French and Soviet youth. And Erikson claims as a minor scoop Justice Goldberg's contribution (which had not been in the *Daedalus* issue) on the employment problems and consequent educational needs of youth in the context of swift technological development. One of the most searching articles in the collection is that by Reuel Denney on present-day American youth.

Just because this book will probably be read more widely than the more technical reports it may contribute more than others to creating a public image of youth which, in turn, may become a directive to young and old alike about what youth ought to be. This is the justification for a particularly critical examination of some of its assumptions. A great deal of the generalizing and the reporting of impressions is based on college students and, it seems, on students of "elite" colleges at that. This is made quite explicit by several of the contributors. But what of the large proportion of young people who do not go to college? Even in the United States this is a majority of the young, and in some of the modern societies of Europe the percentage receiving higher education of any kind is so small, and the social and psychological differences between college students and others so well established, that to use them as a basis for generalization is clearly inadequate.

Erikson, in his preface, points out the neglect of female youth and of "technological youth." We would also stress the neglect of the lower ranks which comprise the majority of youth. If one takes seriously the implication of the definition of youth as an in-between period during which the young are in some respects like adults and in others like children, sociological and psychological role theories equally predict a period of conflict, uncertainty, insecurity and stress. But surely the function of a theoretical formulation is to provide signposts for empirical research and not to take the prediction for granted? The assumptions by the psychologists contributing to the Erikson volume that youth experiences conflict, by the sociologists that there is a youth culture, remain in that volume unsubstantiated.

What one expects from the empirical literature, then, is an analysis of the conflicts and experiences of the young in response to the particular position assigned to them in modern society and an analysis of what youth culture consists of.

Let us begin with the second point and note that there is more argument and less conceptual clarity than one would wish for. In an article published in 1955 Elkin and Westley[9] maintain that the idea of an adolescent culture is a myth. Elkin and Westley question the validity of the usual picture of the youth culture presented by sociologists and the mass media alike, and point out that it can be maintained only by a biased selection of illustrations. They themselves present some counter-evidence from a study of adolescents in a suburban community of Montreal: They find that these youngsters maintain close and open relationships with their parents, and have values similar to those of their parents—in general, a picture of continuity rather than discontinuity in socialization. Elkin and Westley also suggest that whatever psychological conflicts and tensions are present among the young should not be taken as distinctive characteristics of their age—from childhood to old age there are problems of adjustment. In a further article[10] they say: "Specifically we would suggest that in any particular study, the adolescent pattern be seen as part of its community context, that data on discontinuities be balanced by data on continuities, and that any generalizations specify the extent of social insulation and control provided by the community."

Elkin and Westley's data in support of their argument were not particularly convincing. They interviewed but 20 teen-agers, all about the

---

[9]F. Elkin and W. Westley (1955), "The Myth of Adolescent Culture," *American Sociological Review,* Vol. 20, 680–684.

[10]F. Elkin and W. Westley (1957), "The Protection Environment and Adolescent Socialisation," *Social Forces,* Vol. 35, 243–249.

same age, from a single upper middle-class Canadian community, and obtained life-history material on a further 20. They were, however, able to point to some other empirical studies which tended to bear out their own impressions, in particular Hollingshead's middle-class subjects in *Elmtown's Youth.*

In 1961 James Coleman[11] published *The Adolescent Society*, which had the air of a definitive study and appeared at first sight to dispose of the issue raised on such slender grounds by Elkin and Westley. Coleman reported a large-scale questionnaire and interview survey of ten American high schools, selected for their diversity so as to be to some degree representative of all types of schools and communities throughout the U. S. Valuable information of all kinds was presented by Coleman, which led him to the conclusion that the existence of a separate adolescent subculture is more or less beyond dispute. Coleman stressed an item which shows the nearly half (43%) of the teen-agers studied would incur their parents' disapproval rather than break with their closest friend, and took as an index of "apartness" the relatively small extent to which boys expressed the desire to follow their father's occupation.

If, however, one reads Coleman closely, it is clear that much of his argument for the existence of a separate youth culture consists either of bald statements of assumption or appeals for agreement. He points out that most students of adolescent behavior have agreed on the existence of a subculture, and points to institutional changes in the social structure as historical rationale. There are also certain findings which Coleman reports but does not take into account in the subculture issue. For instance, he finds that the teachers and students prefer "white-collar" students to be leaders, and that "the higher the proportion of white-collar, high-educational background students in the school, the more likely that the leading clique will be a white-collar one—which in these schools means one more oriented to adult goals, a college education, and to school activities and interests" (p. 215).

Moreover, in a recent article Epperson[12] has pointed out that Coleman, in presenting evidence for the existence of an adolescent subculture, has equated "*breaking* with a friend" with "*disapproval* from parents." Besides the difference in emotional importance, there is a major difference in frequency and likelihood of occurrence. Epperson himself asked high school students whose *disapproval* would make them feel most unhappy, and 80% said their parents' rather than their friends' disapproval. Epperson also surveyed pre-adolescent children, with the contention that if adolescents are a distinct social system there should be sharp differences between pre-adolescents and adolescents: He found that, if anything, secondary school students were *more* rather than less concerned about parental reactions than the elementary grade pupils, and that there is no basis for saying that adolescents are more estranged from adult culture than younger children.

All this makes Coleman's empirical rationale for accepting the pres-

[11]J. S. Coleman (1961), *The Adolescent Society*, The Free Press, New York.

[12]D. C. Epperson (1964), "A Reassessment of Indices of Parental Influence in 'The Adolescent Society'," *American Sociological Review*, Vol. 29, 93–96.

ence of an adolescent subculture shaky indeed. Epperson also convincingly dismisses Coleman's evidence concerning the degree to which boys disdained to follow their father's occupation: It is equally possible, he points out, to interpret the results as due to aspirations for upward social mobility (no doubt shared by the parents), to realistic self-appraisals, or to changes in the occupational role-system. All of which seems to leave us back where we started when Elkin and Westley raised the issue.

The entire controversy seems to us to be about a pseudo-problem rather than about a real issue. Coleman and some other authors certainly recognize that it all depends on what you mean by a sub-culture; but they nevertheless take sides on the issue. Now what does one mean by a subculture? Whichever of the many definitions of culture serves as a model, the fact that youth is assigned a special status in society is not a good enough reason to speak of a separate culture. All known societies include some status differentiations among their constituent groups, not only according to age but also sex, occupation and other factors. Unless subculture means more than status, it only leads to a duplication of terms. The additional aspect has to do with the notion that shared experiences lead to shared ways of life and shared values and beliefs. The emphasis is on "shared." It would make little sense to talk of a subculture of Prime Ministers, for example. This interesting status in society does not involve sharing of experience with other occupants of the same status; at least in democratic societies the values and beliefs of Prime Ministers or Presidents tend to differ from each other. Youth, in contrast, has more opportunity for sharing with each other the strains and stresses, rewards and achievements, beliefs and values which go with their status. But as the prefix "sub" indicates, the opportunity is inevitably limited. The major culture of which they are part is transmitted by family, school and community in which they mix with other age groups to varying extents. It follows that such a group in society can usefully be studied from the point of view of what they have in common as well as from the point of view of what they share with the major culture. Both are legitimate approaches whose ultimate value stems from what they reveal. Sub-culture is not a "thing" whose absence or presence can be verified; it is a concept that may lead to fruitful research, and does not exclude other conceptual guides.

What then have empirical studies which are not centered on taking sides on this pseudo-issue contributed to our knowledge of youth? Remmers and Rosenmayr report on extensive and methodologically sophisticated investigations based primarily on questionnaire data.

Anti-Democratic Attitudes in American Schools, edited by Remmers, consists of six studies of a nationally representative sample of American high school youth, and four investigations of attitudes of both students and staff in institutions of higher education in the Midwest. The title of the book roughly defines the particular content of the attitudes selected for emphasis—authoritarianism, social discrimination, prejudice, attitudes toward freedom, and so on. Most of the studies collected here were originally carried out for higher degree theses under the supervision of Dr. Remmers, Founder and Director of the Purdue Opinion

Panel, which provides a continuous inventory of the attitudes of a nationally representative sample of American high school pupils.

The contributions of Remmers' ex-students are careful and workmanlike, but the stamp of the uninspiring format of the Ph. D. thesis is still upon them and they make awkward reading. The strength of these studies, as Remmers points out, lies in their respect for sampling principles: ". . . college sophomores are too often the basis of generalizations for mankind." We agree: To generalize about the young we require national samples. Remmers cites evidence for the validity of the poll; but only one validity check is of any precision. Looked at differently, this validity check is very interesting and, in its way, extremely curious.

It seems that the Purdue Panel polls of high school youth compared very favorably with the established adult opinion polls in predicting the proportion of votes cast for the candidates in three successive presidential elections (1952–60). On at least one occasion, we are told, the Purdue poll was somewhat *more* accurate than the adult polls. Clearly Remmers takes pride in this achievement—it is mentioned at several points in the book. And yet it is very odd. In the first place, to use the voting behavior of one body of people to validate the statements of voting preference of another body of people is scarcely justifiable from a strictly methodological point of view. On the other hand, in spite of this, the predictions were surprisingly accurate. One might almost say that teen-agers are, in this respect, more like adults than adults themselves are! The validity issue apart, as a finding it is surely astonishing. Astonishing from one view—that the youngsters, several months before the actual election date, should be so precisely able to reflect their elders' voting behavior; and astonishing from another—that teen-agers do not differ at all from adults on the issue. For they were asked for whom they would vote if they had a vote, not how they thought their parents would vote; and in any case, a sizeable proportion of the U. S. electorate at any one time would not have a son or daughter in high school.

There are of course many other areas of opinion and behavior; but here is extraordinary and perhaps disappointing evidence of a precise conformity between adolescents and adults in an area of major importance. Remmers himself finds it not at all surprising, but most convincing as evidence for the validity of the poll: "These youngsters, therefore, apparently faithfully reflect their parents' political orientation" (p. 62). He refers us to another article of his presenting further evidence of close correspondence between parents' and children's attitudes. Given more correspondences of this kind, we need hardly bother polling the young. Adult polls will tell us what teen-agers are thinking! Or vice versa—as Remmers sometimes seems to suggest. It should be noted, if only in passing, that not all studies find youth a mirror-image of the adult world. Hathaway and Monachesi[13] have administered the MMPI to a state-wide sample of the young; they find that on

[13]S. R. Hathaway and E. D. Monachesi (1963), *Adolescent Personality and Behaviour*, University of Minnesota Press, Minneapolis.

this instrument youth has more resemblance with the adult schizophrenic and sociopathic than with the "normal" adult population. But to return to Remmers: The content of the reported findings on the "public opinion of tomorrow" is rather gloomy: for example, about one in five of 12th-grade youngsters do not agree with the Bill of Rights and accept tenets of fascism, declaring themselves to be superpatriots (Horton). Of the college studies, one interesting finding (Struening) was that the distribution of authoritarianism and prejudice among the staff of a large midwestern university followed a low-high continuum from social science to physical education and administration. Very gratifying, this—or is it that social scientists know how to fool the F-scale?

There is a suggestion here and there that some of Remmers' students do not entirely trust their own data and their own approach. In the *Daedalus* symposium, Denney, in commenting on an earlier publication by Remmers, questions whether the teen-agers always understood what they were saying in their answers (p. 140); and the book under review lends weight to his doubt. It may well be that questions about property rights, or trial by jury, or relations with foreign countries, to take a few examples without undue malice, are simply lacking in meaning, relevance and immediate significance for a great many teen-agers. But if one asks the questions nevertheless in multiple-choice form and in the school situation, one will get answers for the most part, even though the respondents never think about such things.

What, in contrast, of youth in a European society? Leopold Rosenmayr's survey of young workers in Austria, *Family Relations and Leisure Habits of Young Workers*, is especially interesting for our purposes because it deals with the lower strata of society and because it affords relevant comparisons with Coleman's work. The study was prompted by Rosenmayr's concern that too many emotional and unverified generalizations were being made in discussions of Austrian youth. The focus was on self-report mainly of behavioral information concerning family and social relationships and leisure habits, scarcely at all on personality variables and general values and attitudes, and the approach adopted is one of direct fact-finding. Rosenmayr provides data on which policy, argument, generalization and theory can be built rather than being guided by any major hypothesis or theoretical orientation. The investigation was competently carried out and is well, if rather dully, presented in German with a brief summary in English.

Rosenmayr finds a close relationship between the boys and their parents, particularly their mothers; but then it should be remembered that about a third of the sample lived in fatherless households, mostly due to war casualties. The parents, however, were not often chosen as leisure partners by the boys, and there was evidence of a rapidly decreasing attachment to the parents as the boys grew older. Nevertheless, Rosenmayr finds no indication of an "interim-society" or "youth culture" in Austria, and draws the explicit contrast with Coleman's findings. He suspects that in Austria the main alternatives are "not unstructured peer-contacts versus socio-organizational structures caused and carried by the school, but rather socially unstructured adolescence versus continual parental influence and leisure partnership with them." A comparison with Austrian high school students will be of interest.

One of Rosenmayr's findings is that a third of the apprentices would join a peer group even if their parents forbade it. This is very similar to one of Coleman's findings in answer to a similar question. But Coleman finds the existence of an adolescent society beyond dispute, while Rosenmayr can see no indication of it. Once again, the pseudo-issue raises its head. In fact, in Rosenmayr's work there is little indication of differences in values and major attitudes between the generations for the very good reason that he was interested in family influences and did not ask questions of that kind.

Yet another research problem using completely different techniques is presented by the Sherifs in their book *Reference Groups.* Although the Sherifs employed survey methods, these were definitely secondary to, and consequent on, an investigation of various groups of American teen-agers from different regions and socio-economic levels by means of participant observation. The observers "planted" themselves, and studied the groups with which they became associated with painstaking care over long periods of time, always ensuring that they had a credible reason for their presence. Successive phases of observation focused on different aspects of group behaviour, and independent observers were introduced on certain occasions for a reliability check. Thus the Sherifs' data are notable for their richness of detail and closeness to the real-life situation of adolescents rather than for quantified elegance. The book is very well written, even though it is occasionally repetitive.

The Sherifs argue for looking at youth without value-laden concepts. They assert that they had set out to study the operation of reference groups in determining choices, affiliations and behavior in the natural setting, and chose adolescent behavior as the object of study more or less as a secondary concern "mainly on theoretical and methodological grounds" (p. 40). Nevertheless, by the end of the book they are clearly passionately involved in the "grim picture" of delinquency and in drawing implications (some of which perhaps go further than their basic research findings would in fact suggest) for the amelioration of the problem.

Some of the observations to which the Sherifs gave special emphasis deserve mention here. They found that adolescent groups exist in *all* kinds of neighborhoods at *all* social levels, though only in certain neighborhoods are they designated "gangs" and labelled as pathological formations by the authorities and the public. These groups have their own rules and values, and members of *all* groups indulged in illegal and anti-social activities—though these occupied only a fraction of their time. There were large differences among the kinds of activities that groups of different social levels engaged in, but in all areas the teen-agers were strikingly imbued with the American ideology of success and the desire for material goods. The groups were highly structured, but *informally* so; and the Sherifs continually emphasize the inadequacy of attaching labels denoting individual pathology to delinquent and offensive youth by pointing out that any individual in need of psychiatric help could have lasted scarcely a week in the complex and subtle organization of the groups studied. Anti-social youth is very sociable; the authors refer to statistical analyses which show that a very large percentage (70–90%, probably an under-estimate) of adolescent crimes are committed with companions. The book provides a great amount of insight into how adolescents feel, behave and relate to one another. All the boys they studied displayed a knowledge of "right" and "wrong" as defined by the law and the school, but it was their commitment to the norms of their own group which channelled their behavior. Similarly, in response to direct questions, only about 10% indicated that their parents did not understand them (which is similar to Rosenmayr's finding); but in this case the participant observers were able to report on specific matters like the overall discrepancy between the time the youths wanted to be home and the time the parents wanted them home, and, in general, on how little part the parents played in the adolescents' lives.

The Sherifs, then, have come nearest to dealing with the psychological problem of youth, that is with the way in which young people experience their particular position in society. They have gone further than others in demonstrating what one finds if one looks at youth as a subculture. But, at the same time, they have amply demonstrated the futility of pursuing the question of the existence of a "youth culture" as a research problem, just as they expose the folly of making a sharp break between the "delinquent" and the "non-delinquent." The Sherifs have concentrated on telling us what youths get up to, in greater richness of detail than can be suggested here, and have attempted explanation in terms of the immediate social framework of the behavior, instead of selecting data to bear out their predilections. If one so wished, one could take the Sherifs' report and sift out discontinuities of socialization to prove the existence of a youth culture, or continuities to bear out the opposite contention.

It is the discontinuities which tend to be stressed, and which give rise to the notion of the youth culture. One reason for this may well be that it is all too easy to think only of anti-social, defiant or creative youth, because, mainly through the mass media, these will be the youngsters *of high visibility.* Social scientists are not by their nature exempt from the effects of visibility—particularly as their learned journals have been showing so much concern with deviant and anti-social youth in recent years. In 1930, about 12% of publications on adolescence recorded in *Psychological Abstracts* dealt with delinquency and juvenile misvehavior; in 1950, 59%; and by 1960, 68%—"Crime and Delinquency" having by 1950 acquired a subheading of its own. But it must be remembered that 95% or more of adolescents do *not* come to be officially categorized as "delinquent"; and the majority of those who do, settle down, nevertheless, to adult life without criminality.

On the general public, the influence of visibility in channelling the formation of images of youth is likely to operate unchecked. But this general public includes, paradoxically, *the adolescents themselves.* Not only the average adult's impression of today's youth will be heavily biassed towards teen-age violence, teen-age sexual license, teen-age fashion, newsworthy adolescent feats of all kinds, but also *the self-image of the teen-agers themselves.* Thus in some instances the effects of visibility may well be to make the mythical stereotype based on it come true, owing to acceptance of a version of this stereotype by the very objects of the stereotyped perception. Whether or not there are elements of a self-fulfilling prophecy in the way in which the adult world concentrates on the most visible section of youth, so that today's myth may play its part in producing tomorrow's reality, we can readily agree with Veness[14] (p. 169) that the danger of focussing attention on minorities is that the problems will be exacerbated by the very publicity given to them.

One inference that can be drawn from this argument is that, for research purposes, an essential part of studying the young should be the uncovering of youth's own images and stereotypes, "myths" and projections of youth and life, for these stand the best chance of shaping the reality of youth and, in due course, of adulthood. With the exception of parts of the Sherifs' book, the research literature reviewed is strangely silent on what being young means to the young and on youth's fantasies of being adult. Perhaps this is because the study of personal experiences is unfashionable in much modern psychology. But when the requisite methods are employed, a wealth of information can be obtained: A good example is Veness' use (in conjunction with more conventional techniques) of a short essay entitled "The Best Moments of my Life," and a retrospective autobiographical essay, for which youngsters were asked to imagine themselves at the end of their lives and tell their life stories from the time they left school.

Where authors feel the lack of documentation of youth's inner life, they tend to use world literature to compensate for it. Judging from the sample of books under review, the most available prototype of youth is Hamlet. The Sherifs, Erikson, Bettelheim and Denney refer to Hamlet in their discussions. Three of these writers impose their own theoretical frameworks on events in the play. The Sherifs (p. 5) view Polonius as advocating recognition of the inner promptings of external social norms. Erikson (p. 4) pays tribute to the earlier psychoanalytic interpretation of Hamlet as regression to the Oedipus complex, but brings in his own notions of identity conflict to achieve further understanding. Bettelheim . . . also endorses the Oedipal interpretation, with the corollary of Hamlet's dependence on his father.

For these three writers Hamlet is manifestly a vehicle for interpreting the young in accordance with their own theoretical orientations. They can and will be criticized in this respect by those who prefer other theories. Such arguments may be of value for the clarification of theories, but they will not shed much light on the situation of the young. This is not said, of course, in support of the fallacy that empirical data can be collected and presented without at least implicit theoretical assumptions. But which approach should one adopt if one wants to know about the young rather than about a psychological theory?

[14]T. Veness (1962), *School Leavers*, Methuen, London.

Among the bewildering range of theoretical orientations in the social sciences, there are some (for example, Kelly[15]) which stress the importance of taking account of the actor's definition of his situation, of the "theories" which all men employ in transacting the business of living. An approach of this kind would direct the student of youth to pay attention to the "theories" the young have about themselves. Denney, who also refers to Hamlet does so in a way which is strikingly different from the other three authors, and, it seems to us, is implicitly in agreement with this latter kind of approach.

Denney bids us look at the interpretations of Hamlet by the young in the theatre of today, and cites a recent New York production of the play which "treated what used to be interpreted in the character of Hamlet as a lack of action and an incapacity for action, as a kind of action in itself. . . . Perhaps young people need only look at the heroes of Samuel Beckett to redefine Hamlet as furiously activist, even extrovert! . . . Perhaps this is a world in which any second thought, capable of paralyzing any action, is still preferable to principled decisions that carry overtones of fanaticism." Denney is telling us to take note of the "theories," the projected images and "myths" which are essential to the young in their experience of themselves. Such data are so far not readily available in the research literature on the young. If they were, one might be in a better position to make inferences from the myths which have validity among the young and to dispel some of the myths propagated *about* them.

---

[15]G. A. Kelly (1955), *The Psychology of Personal Constructs*, Norton, New York.

The Teen-Agers

Newsweek

What are teen-agers like today? Are they healthy or unhealthy? Naive or sophisticated? Are the pressures on them greater than ever before or are we exaggerating and overreacting to sensitive times? *Newsweek* attempts to answer these questions in the following articles. Are its findings consistent with yours? Has *Newsweek* described reality or just another fantasy about adolescents conjured up by adults?

They are everywhere—almost 18 million young Americans crowding into classrooms, spilling into the streets, filling cars and stores and beaches. They have been probed and prodded and psychoanalyzed. And yet, as behavioral scientists Bernard Berelson and Gary Steiner point out, the years between childhood and adulthood still remain an "ill-defined no man's land . . . ."

To explore this territory, *Newsweek* has used every available journalistic technique. The staff of Louis Harris and Associates, Inc., interviewed some 775 boys and girls—a carefully selected and representative U. S. cross section of youngsters between 13 and 17. Many of the *Newsweek* survey questions were open-ended—giving the teen-agers a chance to tell their own stories in their own words—and most interviews lasted more than an hour. At the same time, *Newsweek* bureaus and correspondents talked to hundreds of other adolescents at home, at school and at play. These reports were supplemented by interviews with parents, principals, psychologists and others with a claim to special insight into the young. The result of this effort follows—a comprehensive, eighteen-page report on what the *Newsweek* survey and correspondents found; a report on the present physical and mental state of the nation's young; on their spending habits, and on their fads. . . .

Everyone knows all about them. To Eastern Europeans, the teen-agers of California, cavorting on their surfboards or burning on their beaches, seem a shimmering vision of the true capitalist paradise. In Japan, a generation of adolescent kids imitate the typical American teen-ager by drinking *remon*—lemon pop—singing protest songs and strumming *ereki*—electric—guitars.

Reporting to Italian readers, the magazine *L'Europeo* recently concluded: "America's teen-agers make up, as we shall see, the most pitiless, irreducible, indestructible dictatorship in the world." And Manuel Maloof, an Atlanta tavern keeper, says he can "pick 'em up around the eyes, the wrinkles around the eyes, and the way they wear their hair and the way they talk. It's hard to define, but it's the challenge they give you." Of course, Maloof admits, the older he gets the harder it is to tell: "Sometimes it looks like everybody's under 21."

It does indeed. The American population has found the fountain of youth and, swimming in it, grows younger. The nation's official median age is 27.9 and declining. There are some 17.9 million Americans between 13 and 17, the high-school years. At times the world they inhabit seems strange and remote, more exotic than the mythic glades of Ponce de León's Florida. Even those adults who share living space with them are baffled by their tribal ways, secret passwords and ritualistic songs and dances.

Yet the young Americans themselves can supply some guideposts. They think, the *Newsweek* survey discovered, that the world is "fast-moving, modern, competitive and warlike" with "lots to do" and not much time to do it in. They come through as purposeful, pragmatic—and prosperous. As they see it, only a few snakes slither through their paradise. One in every five interviewed thinks the world is "happy," which is a prerogative of age: Teen-age happiness is a private affair that cannot be dismissed by a conspiracy of glum old folks.

The Group. Until the term became synonymous with juvenile delinquency, the Germans called their teen-agers *Halbstarke*, or "half-strong ones." Nobody ever called them teen-agers in America until the 1930s, when the word sneaked into the language from sources still unknown. Not until roughly the same time did systematic American sociology, itself coming of age, recognize the teen-ager as a major phenomenon to be studied and tabulated.

Teen-agers despise being called a group, for fear of criticism. Yet a group is what they are, whether they admit it or not, whether they realize it or not—and few do realize the extent to which they are forced to be a group.

At the root of most binds that tie these youngsters to each other is adolescence. Intellectuals talk about a crisis of identity in today's adult world, but that has been old hat for ages to the adolescent, a person in search of himself with all the advantages of an explorer using a compass and a sextant in an iron mine on a cloudy night. An adolescent is not only half-strong but half-made. Truman Capote's *In Cold Blood* has young Nancy Clutter explaining why she writes in three styles of script: "Because I'm not grown-up enough to be one person with one kind of signature."

Teen-age years are social years, with a bewildering gradation of clubs, cliques, castes and accompanying forms of untouchability. "There are few periods of life," according to sociologist James S. Coleman, "in which associations are so strong, intimate and all-encompassing as those that develop during adolescence." No wonder, then, that today's teen-agers value the social arts above all others.

Asked by the *Newsweek* survey what they like best about themselves, almost one in every three said they were friendly ("I have a nice smile") and well-adjusted ("I get along fine with people"). Almost all (90 per cent) feel that they have a lot of friends, more than half wish they had more. What do they like least? Their own appearance, for 26 per cent—and in the same self-critical vein, their tempers, which 16 per cent tend to lose. Their sense of groupness, if not necessarily togetherness, is confirmed by 77 per cent who say they are the same as others their age (the figure rises to 79 per cent for suburban children and 82 per cent for those in the crowded industrial East).

Contented Kids. If teen-agers take refuge in their supposed sameness, they also differ markedly from stereotyped adult notions of what they are like.

A solid majority are builders, not breakers—not hop-headed hoodlums and hoodlettes churning up the drag strips with their hot rods, rolling in the hay, thumbing their noses at organized society and getting blind drunk on today in the belief that their tomorrows will run dry. They like it here. They want what the adults want them to want. They are essentially content with their lot. They feel at one with the world today and have little doubt their tomorrows will be even better.

They rarely admit to feeling lonely. Fifty-six per cent work to earn money. They disagree heartily with their parents about new dances, rock 'n' roll, television, movies, hair styles and makeup (all of which the youngsters stoutly defend), but they and their parents agree thoroughly on basic goals and values in life. And they believe in God (96 per cent). "You just couldn't go from nothing to so much without something helping," a 15-year-old says.

Likeable and garrulous in a light, laugh-tumbled way that can be charming or infuriatingly ambiguous, American teen-agers are also determined to make life work for them. They respect anyone's competence, including their own. They respect excellence too, but more the excellence of a mixer or an athlete than a scholar. "Excellence is the best in the trade," says a Chicago high-school junior. "I'd even respect an excellent thief."

Though the greatest problem in an adolescent's life is himself, the teen-age generation sees clearly enough that the principal problems confronting the nation are avoiding war (58 per cent) and eliminating racial discrimination (16 per cent). Even more clearly—and candidly—they see how they differ from previous generations. They value their freedom, mobility and improved education. Most voluntarily acknowledge the benefits of "a better standard of living." This generation lives the good life, likes it and wants more. A graduating senior declares his ambition "To be rich, happy, healthy and famous rather than poor, sad, sick and insignificant."

They're Spoiled. When the Gershwins wrote their song, it was only in summertime that the livin' was easy. Now it is a year-round thing for all but the outermost outsiders. A majority find life is easier for them than for their parents, "who had to cut wood and carry water from wells." Are they spoiled? Of course, and spoiling for more. "It's really a blast!" says a 17-year-old girl from Knoxville, Tenn. "We get almost everything we want," confesses a 15-year-old.

With a flourishing economy, their nation can afford to keep a large part of its potentially productive population inside classrooms through high school, basking in the warmth of a social incubator. And in the citadel of conspicuous consumption there is no consumer group quite so conspicuous as the teen-agers, whom Harvard's David Riesman has called "consumer trainees." What wonderful games they play! Big business . . . urges them to get out and do what they love to do anyway—buy.

Only 21 per cent say they don't much care for shopping. Three per cent aren't sure. Seventy-six per cent regard it as one of the experiences they most enjoy: not so much for what they buy—they are fickle and their attachments shallow—but for a sense of independence and possession. Knowledge is power, but so is buying power.

At home, where the heart is, the nation's adolescents have every good reason to be heartened by their parents' spirit of fair play. Neither age group calls the tune but both carry it. A heavy majority of teen-agers get along just fine with their parents. Only 12 per cent think their parents try to run their lives. Eighty-six per cent in the survey say the folks at home mind their own business.

Inevitably there are conflicts. Of 17 per cent who admit they smoke (as much as a pack a day among 17-year-old boys), 82 per cent say their parents know it, 85 per cent say their parents disapprove of it. Fourteen per cent believe their parents should be more understanding. Girls also feel slightly less understood than boys. "My parents don't like me to run around with boys, and I think I should be able to," says a Tulsa, Okla., teen-ager. She is 13.

Since privilege and mobility are two of the teen-age generation's hallmarks, it follows that the most prevalent form of parental punishment should be the withholding of privilege: more specifically, "grounding"—keeping the junior birdman in his hangar or taking away the car keys. Grounding is especially popular (or unpopular) in the lone, flat expanses of the Midwest (40 per cent) and the West (45 per cent) where wheels are not only an essential for getting around but also the center of social life and a major source of status.

A 16-year-old Boston girl, Edna Diggs, says, "A lot of kids don't get enough love at home and go out and get mussed up outside," but the dominant domestic theme remains harmonious. Teen-agers agree with their parents on the value of money, companions, places they go, what they wear, how late they stay up and what they really consider important in life.

Undoubtedly there are still confident disciplinarians such as J. L. O'Shields, an Atlanta service-station owner who raises his children firmly and lovingly and who says: "You've just got to have confidence in them and treat them so they'll have confidence in you." But parental acquiescence, not resolve, impresses teen-age America. A plurality of 45 per cent say their parents, at one time or another, have sometimes been unsure of how to tell them what they should do.

Living in School. To their dismay, parents increasingly find themselves low bidder for their children's confidence and attention. Home life is being preempted by the high school, where the kids spend most of their day (8 A.M. to 4 or 5 P.M. by the time the after-class activities and the bus ride home are added). At school, they make most of their friends, learn most of their lessons and are advised, encouraged, analyzed, consoled and profoundly influenced by specialists in surrogate parenthood, the guidance counselors.

What is school? It is an edifice, occasionally majestic, a single, brooding Victorian pile or a cluster of sunny bungalows connected by breezeways, in which classes are taught, clubs convened, records kept, tests graded, teachers tested, rules ruled, cheats cheated, newspapers published, tales told, hands held, smokes smoked, dances danced, drills drilled, sports played, games played, plays played, bells rung and yells yelled. For the student, the best part of school is friends (38 per cent), followed by social life (16 per cent) and learning (16 per cent) in a dead heat.

High school also separates the teen-ager's world as cleanly as if the United States were riven by the Grand Canyon instead of the Continental Divide. On one side are the blessed, who have earned the right to go on to college and probable prosperity. On the other are the damned, who drop out, stop short or, at best, go on to vocational training schools and sharply circumscribed earning potential. "High school," says a boy in Poughkeepsie, N.Y., "is either the beginning or the end."

Separation between the groups is almost complete. Neither has a bed of roses. The college-bound may have hopes of beating the draft temporarily, but they work under crushing pressure for grades if they want to get into a competitive college.

In the second of the two cultures, teen-agers may feign indifference to higher education or feign faint-hearted ambitions to give it a whirl, but "we know, and deep down they know," says Albany (Calif.) High School principal Harry J. Price, "that they won't be successful." Mrs. Anne Blackstone, counselor at Atlanta's O'Keefe High, says students "have been told and told that today high school isn't enough education to get a good job, that they will have to go on into vocational or technical training," but those who cannot do either "are at the seething point." In Greenville, Texas, a 17-year-old says: "I flunked the college-entrance exams and I don't have any money so I've had it."

Who Doesn't Cheat? Performance in school can change the course of a life. Demands are stringent. The book strap of yesteryear could never go round today's bulky curriculum. "There is more pressure on us to accept adult responsibilities than ever before," says Suzanne Slayden, 17, of Knoxville, Tenn. "The school program is much harder and more advanced." Each year brings more new things to learn in the same number of weeks. Exams, therefore, become hurdles that must be negotiated: over the bar, by knowing, or under it, by cheating.

Columbia University's Dr. Allen Barton, who supervised a study of 99 colleges that concluded half the students in the sample had cheated, believes high-school cheating is even more prevalent "because college is usually more dedicated to ideas and learning." By teachers' and administrators' reports and their own admissions, high-school students copy one another's homework, plagiarize from critical essays, carry crib notes into class and swipe exam questions from teachers' offices.

Moreover, the guilt associated with cheating is diminishing. "Which is more important, the morality of cheating or getting into college?" asks a 17-year-old New York girl. Exactly half feel certain they will go to college, probably a realistic estimate, since 53 per cent actually got

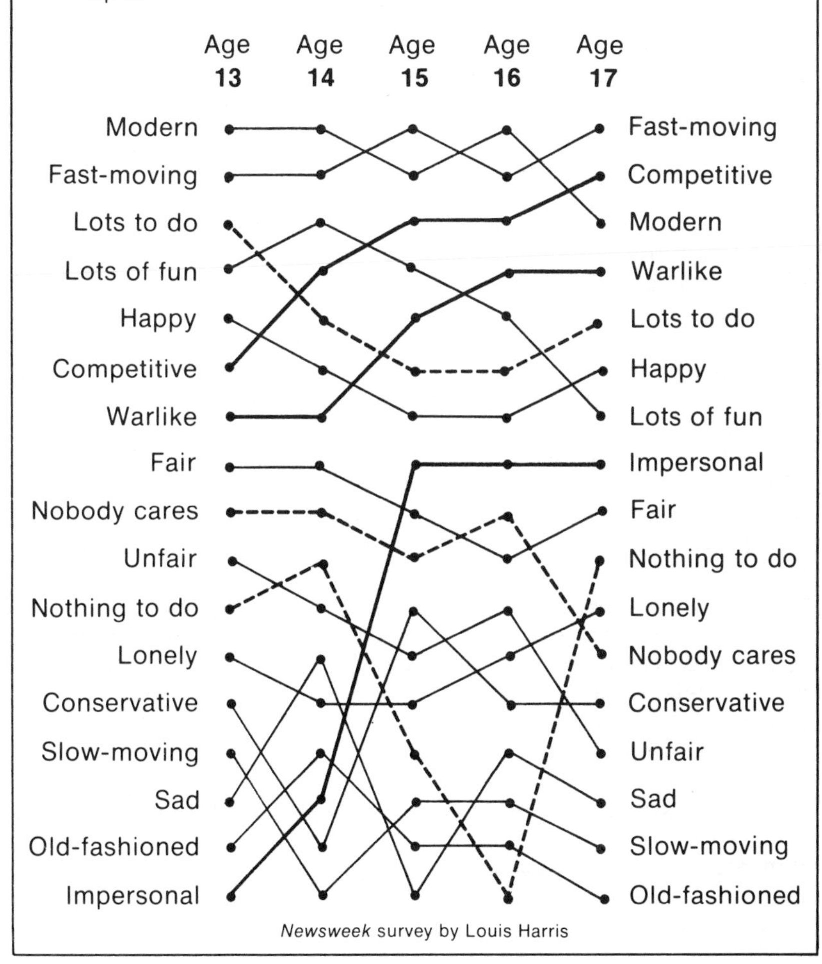

there last year. More than half think high school does a "pretty good job" of preparing them for college. Fifty-one per cent say the same of their preparation for vocations. Most girls want to teach or be secretaries; most boys want to be engineers, technicians, teachers and pilots.

A striking 64 per cent say they own their own encyclopedias or reference books. Boys picked their encyclopedia as the possession they would be most reluctant to give up. Whether this was an eloquent tribute to the joys of the intellect or a kindly attempt to encourage the interviewers, adolescence is not a particularly intellectual time of life.

The teen-ager is preoccupied with things that touch him directly. One student asks for a way to relate Newtonian physics to "the physics of automobile accidents." And there are extracurricular activities to contend with. "I never let my studies interfere with my education," cracks a Missouri senior.

Many students are devoted and even brilliant scholars, of course, but they are a minority. Librarians find adolescent reading tastes heavily influenced by the movies. The *Newsweek* survey shows Sean Connery is the most popular star, and Beverly Goerke, who orders all young-adult books for the Chicago Public Library, reports the Bond books are "the big craze now." "This is not a reading age for teen-agers, you know," observes Virginia Baygulow, a Los Angeles high-school librarian. "There is so much pressure of grades and from the curriculum that even the good student doesn't get a chance to read much on his own."

When a subsidiary of the Charles F. Kettering Foundation took 102 high-school students to Washington, D.C., last month and asked them what was wrong with their high schools, the educators got fascinating answers but no demands for revolutionary changes. During one seminar, however, the youngsters grew impassioned and had to be cajoled, then forced, to break for lunch: Their subject was sex education.

The Place of Sex. "Sex is the biggest topic in any high school and you can't tell me it isn't," said one of the young seminarists. In considering adolescence, says University of California sociologist Edgar Z. Frienberg in his influential book "The Vanishing Adolescent," sexuality "must be regarded in somewhat the same light as photosynthesis in the study of ecology—as the penultimate source of all energy."

As the sea can be seen in a drop of water, the change in teen-age social patterns can be seen in a single word-ending: "going steadily" as opposed to "going steady." It used to be steady, in word if not in deed, and the relationship was given all the solemn trappings of a demi-marriage. At the United Nations, a former guide recalls, teen-agers going steady would insist on squeezing into the same quadrant of a revolving door because "we're a unit."

Now the going is "steadily" because socially mobile teen-agers are wary of entangling alliances and increasingly convinced that a relationship depends on what emotions its partners invest in it, not on what term they agree to call it by. Sociologist Friedenberg finds and applauds a growing sense of "erotic authenticity" among America's adolescents, an ability to rejoice in their whole physical self, to love openly and respond warmly without a neurotic preoccupation with sexual love. "Girls," he says "don't look so much like flaming hors d'oeuvres and more like girls."

"Can you imagine making sex education a compulsory thing?" asks a Nevada girl. "The parents and the church groups would scream and jump up and down." But a good deal of screaming is being done without the facts. Not even those who are studying the question have much information on the actual content of high-school "sex education" courses; many of the courses tender only cautious, academic information on the biological aspects of reproduction. One thing seems certain. America's high schools have not yet acknowledged a revolutionary change in sexual relations. In the words of William Denham, associate professor at Howard University's School of Social Work, "We continue to perpetuate beliefs of a pre-contraceptive era in a contraceptive age."

Today's teen-agers, to put it bluntly but accurately, want to know the how, and their parents want to know the how-much; they want to know if premarital sex is really on the increase among the younger generation.

The *Newsweek* survey questionnaire did not deal with sex habits, partly because the legality of such inquiries among minors is in doubt, and also because such questions evoke an often meaningless jumble of wishes, facts and boasts. Some sources, however, indicate that increasing numbers of teen-agers engage in premarital sex, at least in certain areas and among certain social strata. A New York City boy is convinced that "the majority of teen-age girls sleep with the boy they're going with, from 14 up. It's part of the times." And two obstetric residents at the Emanuel Hospital in Portland, Ore., assert that pregnancy is the leading cause of the city's high-school dropouts.

Across the U.S., illegitimate live births among mothers aged 15 to 19 were 40,000 in 1940, and climbed to more than 101,000 out of 4 million births in 1963. In a recent report, the Connecticut Health Department estimates that one of six teen-age girls in the state was illegitimately pregnant last year.

WHOM THEY ADMIRE

Newsweek asked, which famous people do you admire most?

	% Boys	% Girls
John F. Kennedy	**47**	**50**
Abraham Lincoln	**22**	**16**
George Washington	**10**	**5**
Lyndon B. Johnson	**5**	**5**
Helen Keller	**2**	**8**
Winston Churchill	**4**	**4**
The Beatles	**2**	**5**
Jacqueline Kennedy	**1**	**8**
Benjamin Franklin	**4**	**2**
Franklin D. Roosevelt	**4**	**2**
Elvis Presley	**1**	**5**
Dwight Eisenhower	**4**	**2**
Albert Einstein	**3**	**2**

Newsweek survey by Louis Harris

Yet those who have been involved in the precious few systematic studies of the subject counsel calm. Ira Reiss, a University of Iowa sociologist, believes "there is no indication" that younger teen-agers "are indulging in indisciminate sex practices." He is joined by Paul Gebhard, an associate on the pioneer Kinsey report and now head of the Institute for Sex Research at Indiana University. Among younger teen-agers, Gebhard says, "there hasn't been any real increase in premarital coitus in recent years. The great liberalization has been in the ability to talk freely about sex." Many authorities say the public has confused a demonstrable increase in premarital sex among college students with increased sex in high schools.

Freedom on Wheels. Though boy-girl relations dominate the teen-ager's thinking, they do not occupy all his free time, most of which is spent watching television (favorite programs: "The Man from U.N.C.L.E.," "Hullabaloo"). Just a generation ago, the Saturday movie at the neighborhood house was a regular affair. But the *Newsweek* survey shows that nowadays the majority of teen-agers go to the movies only once or twice a month, where, after Connery, they dote on John Wayne, Paul Newman and Julie Andrews. *Seventeen* is the favorite magazine among the girls, *Hot Rod* among the boys. That sweet old team of a boy and his dog has given way to a boy and his car, or his hopes of owning one.

It is a car, not the truth, that sets them free, gives them a sense of romance. The automobile is this century's riverboat. Eighteen per cent of all boys interviewed said they had one, 8 per cent of all girls. The figure climbs to 41 per cent of all 17-year-old boys, and at affluent Lamar High School in Houston an estimated 75 per cent of the student body own cars. Hot rods are passé, sports cares are in.

Not all teen-agers, however, ride the same curling wave toward tomorrow. Some stand apart from the club: the poor, the unemployed, the juvenile criminals, the joyless boys and gleeless girls in the parts of America's cities that any kid who could would flee like the plague. There are also the Negroes.

Hopeful Outsiders. Negro teen-agers in the *Newsweek* survey set themselves apart with consistent, usually cautious but occasionally astonishing expressions of faith in the future. They have no illusions about life today. Twenty-two per cent say they are less happy now than at 8 or 9, compared with 8 per cent of the group as a whole. Thirty-one per cent of Negroes think life will be worse when they reach 21, against 25 per cent in the entire group.

Yet 26 per cent of Negroes believe their generation has "more freedom" than other generations, vs. 22 per cent over-all. One-third of the Negro youngsters think racial discrimination will still be a problem for their generation, compared with 44 per cent in the over-all sample.

Most striking is the Negroes' attitude toward college. Forty-one per cent feel "certain to go to college." While 18 per cent of the entire group say their parents exert "a lot of pressure" on them to go to college, the figure rises to 38 per cent among Negroes, suggesting more parental pressure for higher education among Negroes than among any other geographic, chronological or economic group in the country.

In Watts, the Los Angeles slum district torn apart by Negro violence last year [1965], a 16-year-old Negro boy—call him Bruce (not his real name)—attends Jordan High School, almost entirely Negro except for a few Mexican-Americans. Subdued, bored ("There's nothin' to do. There's no place to go"), he has never been out of Los Angeles and has no car to get him out. A smile comes to his face when he talks of the riot. "Yeah, I was in it," he says happily. "I didn't do none of the burnin' but I was lootin'."

Bruce is a "B" student but isn't sure he can get into college. He wants a good summer job and can't find one. On winter weekends he earns extra money shining shoes at a downtown parlor. He is "scared" by his future. Yet even Bruce, with nothing going for him but his own determination and the sun through the smog, has not given up. He still believes white employers will treat him fairly if he is "qualified." He is not bitter. "I'm not gonna drop out. If I can't get into college I'll probably go out and get a job." Bruce's parents share his timid hope. "If he is prepared," his mother says, "he will have an equal break."

Still other teen-agers are not merely hopeful outsiders. They are outlaws, the violent minority, Negro and white, with vast capacities for destruction and a need to turn these capacities to action. Teen-age crime rates are rising. Over the last decade they have risen more than 100 per cent while the corresponding population increase has been 45 per cent. Children 13 to 17, 9 per cent of the total population, account for 18 per cent of all arrests. Most are for larceny and auto theft, though 15 per cent of their infractions are violations of curfew and loitering laws.

This is the segment of America's teen-age population that dwells on the dark side of a waxing moon, that gets the headlines, terrorizes the gentry and lives in terror itself. In Boston, a juvenile delinquent with a prison record talks into a tape recorder in the Streetcorner Research program organized by Harvard's Ralph Schwitzgebel: "Whenever I get in a fight or anything I'm shaking like a leaf . . . I'm just plain scared . . . scared to walk the streets, scared to go out of my house, scared to stay there."

"The long-term problem is failure," says Wayne County (Detroit) Probate Judge James H. Lincoln. "The doorways of opportunity have been pretty much slammed in everyone's face unless they have first walked through the doors of education."

Nevertheless, Lincoln believes there is "too much stress on the behavior problems of juveniles. We should talk more about achievement." Any juvenile "can get into trouble. Most do, but they will work out of any problem if they have any degree of success in their lives."

Slow to Rebel. In contrast to the troubled minority, most teen-agers seem docile indeed. They criticize themselves sternly: drinking, smoking, long hair, hot rods, eye make-up, net stockings, eccentric clothes. In Salt Lake City, Mormon teen-agers seem uniformly to abhor beards, connecting them with left-wing politics, liquor, licentiousness and dope. Brigham Young wore a beard, but at the right time.

Teen-agers prefer heroes to political issues. Fifty-eight per cent consider John F. Kennedy a "great" President. ("He gave us a young attitude.") LBJ ranks "fair" with 39 per cent, "good" with 41 per cent and "great" with only 9 per cent (though "great" with 25 per cent among Negroes). President Johnson, a New York City boy complains, "goes around dragging cars, cutting across fields, things the President shouldn't do."

Political apathy is the rule among adolescents, with a generally hawkish stance in their attitude toward Vietnam, but tiny pockets of revolt are visible. The cause célèbre is rarely international, usually local, but the significant thing is that the youngsters take action. Teenagers marched around the Memphis courthouse last week protesting a judge's campaign to close three teen-age "Go-Go" clubs because they supposedly had gone-gone too far toward dim lights and smuggled-in booze.

Last December four students at Detroit's Cass Technical High School were "temporarily excluded" for wearing black arm bands to protest the school's observance of "Military Day." One demonstrator was Barry Biesanz, 17, a semifinalist in the National Merit Scholarship competition. He had also been suspended for long hair. "I got my hair cut," he says, "but now they're regulating ideas and I can't get my ideas cut. I'm keeping them." Teen-agers, Barry's mother says, "are not always easy to live with, but by golly, they stimulate you."

With hair and politics intertwined, increasing numbers of teen-agers sense the immediacy of the war in Vietnam. The boys are faced with the draft, which worries not only them but the girls they may marry. A 17-year-old Ohio girl protests "the unfair way they take boys into the service."

The effects of the current campus rebellion may take time to trickle down to many high schools. Overt rebellion is easier for the college student than for the high-school student still within parental purview. Nonetheless, many sources of discontent are similar. The modern teenager is subject to pressures he cannot comprehend, and carries a heavier load than the sousaphone player in the marching band.

Pressures. High schools, once melting pots, are pressure cookers. Even on the playing fields youngsters feel a deep need to excel. Coach Blaine Crowther of Los Angeles's povery-ridden Roosevelt High says: "There's a lot more emphasis on getting an athletic scholarship or in signing to play pro ball." Moreover, sports are still an alluring way for underprivileged Negroes to better themselves socially and economically.

Adolescents "seem to be forced into a more regimented life," says Francis Mastropieri of Boston, a father of three. "I think they're the losers. People used to have time of their own when they could sit and daydream, sit and think, rather than be on the go all the time."

On the go, they are also under the microscope. Even relatively small rural schools are forced, by the demands for information made on them, to emulate the cities' massive educational bureaucracies. At Southeast Polk Junior-Senior High School in Iowa, where records in the 1890s listed grades and number of times tardy, student dossiers now include grades, attendance, birthplace, parents' background, phone, social-security number, all manner of achievement test scores,

IQ scores, extracurricular activities, rank in class, grade average, personality and mental maturity tests, insurance claims, pupil profile charts, health records, immunization records, reams of conduct records and discussions with guidance counselors. "We try and keep personal contacts," says principal Donald P. Kiester, "but we're getting away from it."

Inside school and out, students undergo a ceaseless commercial barrage. Advertisers compete for space in *Scholastic* Magazine. Television, movies and the press seduce the adolescent spender. Disk jockeys, whom the youngsters listen to but hold in low esteem, assault them between records with frantic exhortations to Send For! Try! Buy! Enjoy! Telephone Now! and Order Today! An occasional youngster with a highly developed nose for venality resents being pandered to; but inevitably, given the glitter of the good life's lures, most are extremely willing victims.

WHO'S IN CHARGE?

Newsweek asked, have your parents tried to run your life too much?

	%
Have run life too much	**12**
Haven't run life too much	**86**
Not sure	**2**

Newsweek survey by Louis Harris

Teen-Age Ghetto. Youngsters endorse the broad outlines of adult society and adults smile wryly over the Dictatorship of the Teen-ager. Yet the coin has a less shiny side. In the opinion of prominent educators and psychologists, the teen-age population, instead of riding roughshod over helpless adults, is actually being segregated, shunned, manipulated, discriminated against and forced to live in a deluxe ghetto where tastes and mores of a distinct subculture flourish only for lack of meaningful integration into a stable adult society.

"These youngsters," says Frank Brown, principal of the adventurous and widely admired Melbourne (Fla.) High School, "feel that nobody listens to them, that they have no friend at court. Certainly they're not listened to in the schools, because the schools are in a serious state of intellectual disrepair." Adolescents are "discriminated against by the parents, by the schools, by all of society." Social institutions, Brown contends, "have always been against young people."

Many major U.S. cities and suburbs have teen-age curfew laws which assume a youngster guilty as soon as he appears on a street without a "responsible adult" after the witching hour. Other cities, such as Richmond, New Haven, Cleveland, Omaha and Hallandale, Fla., have curfew laws on the books but do not enforce them. Why? "We just thought we ought to have one," one mayor says.

Spies and junior informers infiltrate teen-age nightclubs. Pedagogues dictate hair styles and anathematize granny dresses. Adolescents beg for responsible work in the adult world and find little or none. "I think life is rotten," says a 17-year-old in South Bend. "Man has to have a place in society but some of the places I just couldn't take." Adults, agrees sociologist Coleman, "have shut him out of the job market, have told him, in effect, to go off to school and not bother them."

PARENTS & PUNISHMENT

Newsweek asked, what "punishment" do you feel works best?

	% Boys	% Girls
Grounding—such as taking away car keys or confining to home	**31**	**31**
Taking away telephone or television	**18**	**20**
Talking over problem	**13**	**23**
Scolding	**7**	**8**
Spanking, the strap	**8**	**4**
Restricting to room	**9**	**3**
Cutting allowance	**3**	**2**
Restricting dates	**2**	**2**

Newsweek survey by Louis Harris

Until they reach 18, teen-agers have almost no civil rights. Courts act both as their prosecutor and protector. Teen-agers, says John A. Schulz, associate professor of psychology at Portland (Ore.) State College, are excluded from the family and forced to create a culture of their own. Different patterns prevail abroad. "I'll never forget the shock of walking into a Dutch tavern," recalls Schulz, "and seeing an entire family enjoying a beer together."

California's Friedenberg is a leading authority on adolescents and one of their most spirited defenders. His iconoclasm ranges far and wide. He compares the role teachers play to that of a doctor who might enter a home to treat a patient and begin to criticize the wallpaper in the patient's bathroom. Friedenberg also thinks teen-agers don't get enough money. "Kids still have very little to spend. They should have money. They should have cars. It's the one basis of their social order. Cars are important. They are for all America. There's no other privacy."

Looking Ahead. Shunned or sheltered, adjusted or manipulated, teenage America carries on. *Newsweek's* survey finds the youngsters optimistic about ameliorating disease, urban problems, college crowding and depressions, confident that creative talents will be used better in the future and that outer space will successfully be explored.

They are rather less optimistic about poverty, the threat of war, highway accidents, racial discrimination, moral standards and crime. But their own attitudes and openness to new ideas may be more potent than they think.

Nearly half their parents in a previous *Newsweek* survey, for instance, said they would object to a Negro family as next-door neighbors, but just over a quarter of the teen-agers feel the same way. Overwhelming majorities of the youngsters have no objection to sharing classrooms or churches with Negroes. Even in the South 62 per cent have no objection to sitting next to a Negro in school.

Enthralled by the marvel of themselves, the young know not what the future holds, but they think they know who holds the future. Some of the shaggier types will be shorn of their locks and will not, like Samson, lose too much strength. Steadily they will expand to keep pace with their expanding universe, tasting, trying, flying or falling, getting to do what they are now only yearning to do. On the last page of Chicago's Senn High School 1965 yearbook, a poem by Karen Miyake concluded:

Oh how
I want to be a Bob Dylan, a Pete Seeger, a Peter, Paul and Mary, an Illya Kuryakin, a Peter O'Toole, a Seymour Glass, a City seeker, a gate builder, a lemon flower, an umbrella mender, a roof beam raiser, a ball in the valley, a free, whole human.
I think I'll go eat a bananafish
It's a hard rains a-gonna fall.

And this year a 17-year-old New York City boy, Steve Anderson, looks into the future and beyond. "I hope there is a hereafter because it's something else to do."

Fitness Report: Good

Not only are there more young Americans in sheer weight of numbers—there is more *of* them in sheer physical bulk. Thanks to better nutrition, U.S. youngsters stand taller and heavier than their parents. Thanks to antibiotics and vaccines, they enjoy an unprecedented freedom from infectious diseases. And thanks to new educational techniques, they learn more at an earlier age than their elders. According to Dr. Robert Nichols, research director of the National Merit Scholarship Corporation, today's teen-agers score higher on the NMS tests than their counterparts ten to fifteen years ago. Teen-agers nowadays even seem to have clearer skins and sturdier legs than the adolescents of the last generation.

But this picture of adolescent health has another side. Growing up has always been a time of stress and change, and in the urbanized, pressurized U.S., the process seems to have accelerated. The teen-age boy, says Dr. Peter B. Jenney of McLean Hospital, Belmont, Mass., "gets up every morning and sees somebody different in the mirror. For some, it's a frightening process."

The draft-rejection statistics also contribute to the gloomier view of U.S. youth. Superficially, at least, they seem to show that the health of teen-agers is on the decline. Since the Korean War, the proportion of draftees rejected for service in pre-induction and induction examinations rose from 34 per cent to 58 per cent in 1964. But statistics based on draft physicals are misleading because they omit many of the healthiest young men—the reservists, enlistees, officer candidates. Among 3.6 million men examined for military service between 1953 and 1958, the rejection rate was 39 per cent for draftees, but only 7 per cent for volunteers.

Screening: Even so, over-all rejection rates have climbed—from 22.7 per cent in World War II to 23.6 per cent during the Korean War to an estimated 35.2 per cent in 1964. But military statisticians note that a good part of the increase stems from more discriminating mental testing. During World War II, for instance, the Armed Forces Qualification Test was given after induction. Since Korea, the AFQT has been used as a screening test before enlistment and induction.

Bernard D. Karpinos of the Army Surgeon General's office, believes the statistics, if anything, suggest better fitness of U.S. youth. The recruit of today, he notes, is 1.2 inches taller and 18 pounds heavier than the recruit of World War I, and half an inch taller and more than 7 pounds heavier than the inductee of World War II. The average Yale freshman was 5 feet 7-1/2 inches tall and weighed 136 pounds in 1885 and only about 5 per cent of the class stood more than 6 feet. By 1957, the average Eli freshman was 3 inches taller and 20 pounds heavier and 29 per cent of the class was over 6 feet. Young women at Vassar and Smith were almost 2 inches taller and 10 pounds heavier in the 1950s than they were at the turn of the century. Girls also are maturing earlier: The average age for the onset of menstruation has dropped from 14 in 1900 to 12.8 years.

These examples of earlier maturity and accelerated growth are, in part, a reflection of better nutrition for today's pregnant women and their children. Yet poor eating habits ("hamburger and French fries, heavy on the ketchup"), dietary faddism (particularly skipping meals) and chronic sweet tooth are common. Of 6,200 junior- and senior-high-school youngsters surveyed in Greensboro, N.C., for example, 15 per cent skipped at least one meal. The high consumption of sweets, most dentists suspect, may account for what the American Dental Association calls the "appallingly bad" state of teen-agers' teeth. In one group surveyed, 84 per cent needed fillings and more than a third needed to have teeth extracted.

Pediatricians estimate that from 10 to 15 per cent of U.S. teen-agers are too fat. But interestingly, obesity stems not so much from overeating as it does from physical inactivity. Dr. Jean Mayer of the Harvard School of Public Health found that obese girls consume 300 fewer calories per day than classmates of normal weight. He demonstrated the importance of physical inertia, however, by photographing the girls playing tennis. The fat girls, he found, tended to remain motionless 50 per cent of the time. "If the ball comes near them," says the Harvard nutritionist, "they whack it. If it doesn't, they don't run after it."

More Stamina: Alarmed over lax physical standards among U.S. youth, John F. Kennedy established the President's Council on Physical Fitness in 1961. There is some evidence that the council is getting results; a comparison of physical tests given to some 8,500 public-school youngsters in 1958 with the performance of 9,200 youngsters who took the test last year shows that the stamina and skill of U.S. teen-agers are improving. Among other feats, 14-year-old boys had trimmed 24 seconds off the 600-yard run, and 16-year-old girls averaged 28 situps in 1965, compared with 20 in 1958. In part, the improvement can be traced to better phys-ed programs in the schools. More than half the public schools surveyed by the association reported that they had increased the time allotted for physical education since 1958.

As the physical fitness of U.S. teen-agers improves, the emotional health of adolescents has come under increasing scrutiny. "Our heaviest load is just helping adolescents with the emotional problems of growing up," says Dr. Catherine Richards, newly appointed special counsel on youth for the U.S. Children's Bureau. "The major problem of all adolescents is getting squared away."

Superficially, the evidence indicates that today's teen-agers are having a good deal of trouble squaring themselves away emotionally. Some experts note a steady increase in the number of teen-agers in mental institutions. According to the National Institute of Mental Health, there were nearly 7,000 adolescents in public mental hospitals last year; and if current admission rates continue, the number will have climbed to 11,000 by 1970.

Enlightened Judges: But despite the headlines and the headshaking about "crazy, mixed-up kids," much of the increase may be artificial, a reflection of better adult attitudes rather than of deteriorating youth. Enlightened jurists, for instance, are more apt to channel disturbed youngsters to psychiatric facilities than to reform schools nowadays.

Juvenile delinquency has also risen sharply, further suggesting that U.S. youngsters are unable to make an emotional adjustment to society. The U.S. Children's Bureau reported last week that 686,000 delinquency cases were handled in juvenile courts last year, a 14 per cent increase over 1963.

Many U.S. sociologists read these figures as signs that the social tethers that helped keep teen-age behavior in check generations ago have disappeared. They cite, for example, the disintegration of the family unit and of religious values. Drs. Sheldon and Eleanor T. Glueck, who have been studying the causes of delinquency for 40 years, decry the absence of the "extended family," in which a child grew up amid grandparents and aunts and uncles as well as his mother and father. "There are a growing number of one-parent families," notes Mrs. Glueck. "And you don't have the old close neighborhood ties that could exercise some control."

Mobility—plus the decline in family ties—makes the school the center of the adolescent's life. The school, psychologist Robert Shellow notes, is "the only arena in which a kid can operate and get a sense of being worthwhile. If it doesn't provide satisfaction and a place for him, we are only heading toward more trouble."

The Normals: Obviously, the teen-agers who get into trouble get most attention. But in an unusual study, Dr. Daniel Offer of Chicago's Michael Reese Hospital undertook an in-depth psychiatric evaluation of 84 suburban high-school boys deliberately chosen because they were normal. About 23 per cent of the boys had been caught in at least one delinquent act, ranging from overturning garbage cans and breaking Coke bottles on a highway to stealing. Offer doesn't know whether the figure is high or low, but he emphasizes that the acts were seldom repeated. "They learned from their experience," he says, "and that was it." In the suburb studied, the police release first offenders with a warning. Half of the parents never knew of the misbehavior.

Teen-age sex in the suburbs makes good copy, but Offer's sample, at least, still knew how to blush when asked about girls. At the end of their junior year, a quarter of the boys had never been out on a date with a girl.

Just as in the *Newsweek* survey, almost all the boys in Offer's study accepted the moral values established in the home. Typically, the boys felt emotionally closer to their mothers, with whom they found it easier to discuss their problems. But they did not "over idealize" their mothers, and, for the most part, had good "positive identification" with their fathers.

If Offer's boys are at all typical of the "normal" American teen-ager, then their appearance of physical health is matched by a high degree of emotional well-being.

Six Faces of Youth

'I Never Want to Get Automated Out of a Career'

Thirteen-year-old Bruce Curtis lives the vanishing rustic life—hunting, fishing, camping out and raising his own livestock on his father's 116-acre farm 3 miles outside Newton, Iowa. Yet his exposure to television, newspapers and books has kept him remarkably tuned in to the world outside the small central Iowa community (population: 15,381). Bruce frets not only about his sheep and rabbits but about the poverty program. "It's a shame to let the poor go so low," he says. "But now that they're there, what do we do about it? It isn't always the person's fault, but those that are lazy or don't want to work—I don't know. Should the anti-poverty program help them?"

Last month Bruce watched the televised Senate hearings on Vietnam. He was particularly impressed by former Lt. Gen. James M. Gavin: "It was good that everybody got a chance to see how he viewed the problems. I learned something from him." But Bruce has his own views. "I believe it's going to end in a nuclear war, the way we're going now, anyway," he says. "I imagine the only way to get all this stopped is to use the H-bomb. Russia and China don't know as much about it as we do. I figure we could win it."

Bruce reads five or six books a month from the public library. Recently he finished "The Witnesses," *The New York Times*'s 634-page account of the Kennedy assassination. "The testimony really gave you an insight into what was going on," he says. "The assassination was the greatest tragedy the country ever had." He feels Kennedy was a great President because "he kind of stuck out his life for other people." As for LBJ: "Johnson is now trying to set his own example. He's doing the best he can with Vietnam and all that."

Bruce's day begins about 6 A.M. Before fixing his own breakfast, he feeds the resident animal life—30 Angus cattle, 24 Southdown sheep, twelve rabbits, eight cats and one dog. At Newton's Central Junior High School, his favorite classes are in new math ("It's really easier than the old math") and art ("Op art is great").

Making the Right Moves: Bruce plays trumpet with the school band, sings with the school's 54-voice mixed chorus and works out with the wrestling squad, 112-pound division. "Wrestling appeals to me," he says. "You can take on a guy 30 pounds heavier and still beat him with the right moves."

After school he is picked up by his father—52-year-old Carol Curtis, who is chief plant engineer at the Maytag Co. in Newton (Bruce's mother died when he was 2). Back at the farm, he attacks the evening chores—plowing, hauling hay bales and feeding and bedding down the animals. Last year, showing his stock at Iowa fairs, he earned $492.90—and plowed most of it back into his livestock business, putting the rest aside for college. "I never want to get automated out of a career," he explains.

He has never heard of Soupy Sales or the surfing set. On TV he likes sports and public affairs, nature shows and "The Man From U.N.C.L.E."

"There must be some truth to the spy shows," he adds. "Maybe this is really the type of thing that is going on."

Although Bruce is pessimistic about Vietnam, he is not about himself. "Lots of others have gone through wars," he says. "If they hadn't, we wouldn't be going to school and learning things. I don't think it will foul up my future too much. There's plenty of time to do things."

'Sometimes I Feel Like Dropping Out'

Blond and copper-toned, 16-year-old Jan Smithers of Woodland Hills, a section of Los Angeles, orbits between the worlds of the Surf and the Strip. At Malibu Beach she and the other bikini-clad "golden girls" take their places in the sun, switch on their transistors and lie back to watch the members of the Malibu Surfing Association riding the 10-foot "curls" into shore. The chatter seems to support the Hollywood version of teen-age life in southern California as one long beach party. But the scene, like a picture of Jan herself, is provocative but misleading. The swinging parties are usually held by older youths and, although 16-year-olds like Jan sometimes are invited by college friends, mostly they stick to homework and TV.

On weekend nights, Malibu girls pull on their purple bell-bottoms and ribbed sweaters, hop on the backs of motor cycles, and throttle off to the Strip—a 2-mile-long stretch of Sunset Boulevard that currently reigns as the teen-age nightclub capital of the U.S. Here the kids may make the circuit a dozen times in one night—starting out at Ben Frank's, an all-night snack bar, then over to the Fred C. Dobbs café and finally ending up at Canter's, an all-night delicatessen. Most of the action, however, centers on The Trip, a vibrating folk-rock haven whose name was inspired by the ecstatic state induced by LSD. Admission is legally denied those under 18, but Jan and hundreds of others under the age limit can get in by flashing borrowed or forged ID cards.

Giant Hunts: The Strip is relevant not only as a weekend nightclub circuit for Jan and her friends but also as a magnet for hundreds of disenchanted teens—girls such as 16-year-old Bobby, who ran away from her upper-middle-class home. Bobby did what Jan sometimes thinks about: She took LSD and other psychedelics; she cadged sleeping space in different pads; she went along on teen-age "giant hunts" in the Sierra Madre canyon at 2 A.M. Last month, police rounded up Bobby and hundreds of other teen-agers for violating Los Angeles's 10 P.M. curfew for kids under 18. She was returned to her family.

For all her tangential contact with the Surf and Strip scenes, however, Jan is solidly anchored. Mornings, her mother drives her to Taft High School, which recently went on a staggered, two-shift schedule to accommodate its 4000 students. An art major, Jan takes the 7:10 A.M. to 12:30 P.M. shift. "It's so fast," she says. "You just go and then you're home. I'm not a big school fan," she confesses. "Sometimes I feel like dropping out—but I know I won't."

Jan finally passed geometry after three attempts and, while racing home to show her mother her report card, plowed her car into a telephone pole. The accident broke her jaw, leaving behind a small scar on her chin. "After the accident, I went back to an old boy friend," she says "I don't know why—I guess I thought I'd be ugly and better find somebody."

Confused: Beneath the Fluoristan smile, Jan worries. "Sometimes when I'm sitting in my room I just feel like screaming and pounding my pillow," she says. "I'm so confused about this whole world and everything that's happening. My friends just sit back and say, 'Wow, it's happening'." But she wants to understand why. "Most of the guys I know are *ugh*. All guys are the same. All they've got on their minds is sex, I swear. Most girls don't have sex on their minds."

Although there are only a few Negroes in her entire school, Jan emphatically supports civil rights. "Negroes are not freaks and I don't see how people can be so cruel to them. I would date or even marry a Negro if I liked him."

Of adults, she says emphatically: "They're so stupid. They're so untrustful—you know, don't trust anyone. They think they've just got to clamp down."

The magic age of 25, marriage and a family loom, in Jan's mind, as the crossover point into adulthood. "I'm not planning what I'm going to do after I'm married," she quickly points out. "Teen-agers are out for fun. When you're young you might as well take advantage of it. And even if I become old and saggy, I'm still going to be young."

'Most Kids Avoid Discussions With Adults'

"I've always disdained the word 'teen-ager'," says Christopher Reed, a 17-year-old New Yorker who attends the Browning School, a private prep school for boys 5 to 17, located off Park Avenue. "It's a word adults have coined to mock young people. It has hostile connotations. People think anyone who's a teen-ager is automatically a delinquent."

Chris need never worry about people thinking that of him. Tall, lanky, conscientious about his schoolwork, careful in his speech, he rarely smokes ("The other kids might think I'm trying to be tough"), stays away from bars ("I feel unnatural in them"), has yet to visit a discothèque ("but I'm open to the idea, I do the new dances"), has no interest in cars ("All I know is they have a steering wheel") and doesn't have a steady girl ("I'm looking: going out with a girl is an ideal way to spend a day").

Currently living with his divorced mother and two younger brothers in an Upper East Side town house, Chris moves between his private school (tuition: $1,500 a year) and a grimy community center on the Lower East Side where he teaches remedial reading to underprivileged youngsters for five hours every Saturday. "I even made my first visit to a tenement down there," he says. "I felt frightened at first but then I sat down and talked to an old Negro man for a while. I really enjoyed it."

The Urban Type: Chris divides the remainder of his time between piano lessons (two hours a day) and the diversions of the urban teen-ager—visiting museums, art galleries and the theater, and playing "roof league" hockey with school chums atop Browning's roof, which doubles as a concrete softball diamond during the spring. "I'm sort of the urban type," says Chris. "I like everything near to me—the drugstore, the record store. The wide-open spaces are so spread out, and everything's so far apart." But his affection for New York extends beyond its conveniences. "I have an uncle who's an architect," he says. "He used to work on the Landmarks Preservation Commission, and I worked with him one summer. We sketched the fronts of Greenwich Village buildings."

When speaking of teen-agers, Chris always refers to them as "they" instead of "we." "I don't feel I'm a member of the vast portion of kids my age," he explains. Indeed, he observes with equal degrees of amusement "the kids who stand around on corners waiting all day for nothing to happen" and "the out-of-town prep schoolers who try to be very cool and stud in their white Levi's and loafers." Yet he is gentler in his assessment of adults. "Most kids avoid discussions with adults," he says. "They'll say to me 'Oh, you talk with your mother?' Many of them just aren't looking adults in the eye."

Kennedy Image: Chris feels he may have influenced his parents to vote for John F. Kennedy in 1960. "During the election," he says, "I had this urge to work, and I really felt it was important. But then, when Kennedy was President, I was indifferent to him, I think. Only after his assassination did I begin thinking of him all over again. Not that he was 'youth's representative,' as he's been called. In office I believe he did more for youth, but also for old people who'd been neglected and pushed aside."

On Vietnam, he says he would quietly accept military service, "although reluctantly." An honors student at Browning, he has applied to Harvard, Columbia, Johns Hopkins and the University of Michigan, but has yet to choose a career. "It might be law," he says guardedly, then quickly adds, "but not for any specific reason." In many ways, Chris remains committed and troubled. He took on Saturday tutoring sessions, for example, because a friend requested it of him and "I sort of felt I should." And, although he believes that "God is dying out," he participates in weekly group discussions at a local Episcopal church.

"Everyone is always talking about the big problems of today's teenagers," he says. "But do they really have any? They have the same problems as other older people—the world's problems."

'Motors Are So Exciting . . . You Feel Like You Own the Road'

Hondas are very big at Houston's Lanier Junior High where 14-year-old Laura Jo Davis goes to school. "Motors are so exciting," says Laura Jo. "They give you so much freedom. You feel like you own the road. In a car you feel trapped." Sometimes the boy-girl customs give her a trapped feeling too. "Kids start dating and petting so early that by high school they've already done everything they can do," she says, "and they go on and on."

This, however, is about the only potential problem Laura Jo sees in her future. "I rarely think about the Bomb," she shrugs. "Its a stupid thought. I guess I feel like it will never happen to me." Politics also turns her off. "My friends and I rarely talk about politics because when we do we sometimes get into arguments," she says. And although Laura Jo is a Presbyterian and an officer of her school's Devotional Club, she doesn't take religion too seriously. "We usually stay up so late on Saturday night that I feel too groggy the next morning to make church," she explains "I mean, I believe and everything like that, but it's not a major portion of my life."

Laura Jo lives in the modest suburb of Southampton. She is a cheerleader, volleyball player, waterskier and horsewoman. At Lanier, she usually gets A's and B's, and is conscientious enough about her grades to cry when she does poorly on a test. But not too conscientious. "I feel if I dropped some of my other activities I'd do a lot better in schoolwork," she observes. "But I don't intend to."

'Smoking is Repulsive': Like many of her classmates, Laura Jo has experimented with alcohol (beer and Daiquiris) and cigarettes. Nonetheless, she insists that "smoking for kids my age is repulsive" and she strongly disapproves of too much teen-age drinking. As for going steady, she reports that she's been asked three times but has refused each time. "The object of going to school is to meet a lot of people and to find out what you want in life," she says. With all her activities, Laura Jo finds scant time to read (Emily Dickinson, occasionally) or watch much television. When she does, her favorites are "Batman," "The Red Skelton Show" and "Where the Action Is."

Once a week she serves as a "candy striper" (nurse's aide) at a local hospital and she once learned some sign language in order to communicate with several deaf students. Nor is she totally isolated to the world beyond Lanier. While there are no Negro students at the school, Laura Jo says: "As far as I'm concerned, they're just everyday people. Some of them are wonderful and some of them—well, we have white trash, too. Down at the bay we fish with colored people all the time. They treat us like something great and we fish right alongside of them."

Laura Jo confidently expects her future "to fall into place"—college, job, marriage. At present her ambition is to become a dress designer, a model or a fashion coordinator for a department store. (She occasionally models at teen-age fashion shows at Neiman-Marcus's Houston store.) "I'm not some poor, lost, bewildered girl," she says with just a trace of self-satisfaction. "I don't have any emotional problems. But I want to see what life is all about.

'Education Counts More Today Than It Ever Did. . .'

Negro boys in Chicago's South Side ghetto divide themselves into Ivy Leaguers, Gousters and WWIG's. Ivies wear button-down collars and V-neck wool sweaters, and plan on going to college—or at least finishing high school. A Gouster—the word may come from the Spanish Gaucho, the South American cowboy who wears baggy pants with chaps—proclaims his toughness by wearing pleated, baggy pants and shirts with high, pointed collars. A WWIG, the word is an acronym for "Wear What I Got," puts on anything that's available and will often blend the two styles—not only of dress but of living.

One WWIG, 15-year-old Tommy Brewer, follows a path that lies almost midway between the worlds of Ivy and Gouster—and between the larger worlds of Negro and white. His family of eight lives in a housing project (where Tommy's father, a steelworker, pays $67.25 a month for the five small rooms). Yet Tommy's ambitions are Ivy; he hopes to go to college and study architectural engineering. While many of his Gouster friends roam the streets at night in gangs, Tommy studies at home or plays Ping-Pong at a friend's house. "I'm friendly with most of the Gousters," says Tommy, who is a solid 5 feet 7 inches. "They don't pick on people they are friends with, though I'm not with them as much as I used to be. And they don't want to pick on someone they couldn't beat up."

Tommy travels 6 miles via two buses and an El to attend Lindblom Technical High School (52 per cent Negro). "Lindblom offers better opportunities for the jobs of the future," he says, explaining his reason for attending a tech school rather than his neighborhood high. It has science labs, electronics courses, and woodworking and metalworking shops. "If teen-agers have the right education, they won't have any problems. Education counts more today than it ever did because we're entering a new age of exploration," he says. "The gang members were taught this but it just didn't sink in. They only think about tomorrow. When they get to be 18 and it's time to get a job, then they find out that they need a good high-school education to land one. So crime is the easiest way out. There's no pressure like there is in school."

Mostly A's and B's: At Lindblom, Tommy is taking algebra, English, world history, "foundry" and physical training. His grades are mostly A's and B's and next fall he plans to enroll in the more advanced honors program. "My ability to learn fast gives me a big advantage," he says. "Most of the stuff we're learning now I've already been over."

Two nights a week Tommy picks up clothing and date money by checking coats at the Oakenwald Social Center nearby. This $3.30 a week, plus an allowance of $3, allows him to buy records and extra clothes. "Clothing is the most important thing," he says, "except for a car and a license."

Tommy has a clear idea of where he wants to go. Men who marry young, he feels, are not financially ready to support a family. "They turn to drinking and crime," he says. "I won't get married until my middle twenties. I would like to have a home in the suburbs and plan for my kids and be able to send them to college. The number of children I would have would depend on how well I could plan for their education. I think if people would take time to do this, the crime rate would go down."

Tommy divides his reading between *Look* and *Ebony*. He listens to WVON, a Negro rock 'n' roll station, and his favorite groups are the Temptations and the Miracles, but he hurries home from the social center on Friday nights to watch "The Man From U.N.C.L.E." His heroes are Willie Mays because "he likes to help people even though he makes a lot of money," and Robert McNamara because "Johnson gives the order but it's McNamara's idea."

"Most of the reason for prejudice is because we know very little about each other " he says. "Our neighborhoods are different and so we have little contact. Every time some of us move into an area they move out. Eventually we have to communicate because they are running out of places to move to." From reading the Black Muslim newspaper Tommy has picked up enough knowledge about its philosophy to disagree with it. "They want the two races to be completely separate," he explains. "At one time that might have been possible, but now it's impossible."

Unlike Negro friends who are two or three years older than he, Tommy feels no bitterness about race nor militancy on civil-rights issues. (As one YMCA social worker put it: "At 15 they don't know they will be angry young men when they are 17.") "Most young people don't feel racial prejudice," he says. "We don't see the importance of civil rights yet. We believe in what Martin Luther King does, but we don't idolize him the way we do a baseball player."

'I Could Never Join the Mainstream of Society Now'

When 17-year-old Laura Hausman started high school in Boston, she recalls, all of her friends talked about only two subjects—dates and clothes. "They were a bunch of perfect, first class . . . finks," she says. Last year Laura switched to Berkeley High School across the bay from San Francisco and now, she reports, all her friends talk about five subjects—the Bomb, Vietnam, civil rights, marijuana and sex. "I really fit in here," she says.

"Being raised under the Bomb is one of the things that has made teen-agers ask questions," says Laura. "It's so completely stupid to have 'overkill' or to just be able to push a button and destroy the world. If that kind of thing doesn't make kids ask questions, nothing will. As for Vietnam, my solution is simply to get out. We're supporting a government that is completely corrupt. The people don't want it."

About civil rights, Laura says: "The problem is not just with the whites but with the Negroes as well. They generally don't want much to do with whites." As for marijuana, she contends that "pot should be legalized because it's nonaddictive. It's sort of like taking whiskey, only it doesn't cause cirrhosis. It's better than cigarettes because it doesn't cause cancer." And she vociferously endorses a campaign to legalize homosexuality, led by the San Francisco-based Sexual Freedom League. "You know, there's really nothing harmful about it," she says. "Laws are just going to make it worse."

Laura implements some of her beliefs with action. Last summer she worked for Venture, a privately financed program aimed at assisting Negro children in the Haight-Ashbury district, and she has joined in a "women-for-peace" march on Oakland's Army Induction Center. At Berkeley High, she belongs to the Student Committee of Concern—a high-school counterpart of the Vietnam Day Committee (VDC) at the nearby University of California. The SCC, Laura says, claims 30 members and some 200 supporters out of the school's 3,500 students. "It's a sort of free-speech movement," she explains. "We want to get the kids together on the same ideas that moved Cal last winter."

"School is just a place where I go to shake my head to stay awake," she says. "The lectures are usually boring and unstimulating, particularly in history. We get this barrage against Communism and somebody is supposed to fall for it."

'You've Got Long Hair': Aside from her mother, a secretary in the philosophy department at Cal, Laura holds little love for the older generation. "You rarely find a daughter who's a so-called beatnik who can discuss things with her parents," she claims. "They just say, 'Oh, no, you've got long hair and you hang around with the wrong people and I'm going to ground you for three months for doing this or that'."

After school, Laura puts on the activist uniform: sandals, wheat denims and turtleneck sweater, and sips Cokes and talks politics at the Forum—a teen-age hangout on Telegraph Avenue—or passes out antiwar literature around the VDC's card table at Sather Gate on the Cal campus.

For recreation, she paints, plays classical guitar, and listens to baroque music ("American rock-'n'-roll groups are so amateurish"). The gaudy Mexican book bag that swings from her shoulder usually contains a book by her favorites—Kafka, Dostoevski, Camus, James Baldwin and Sigmund Freud. "This summer I started reading Freud because I met a psych major at Cal who could analyze anybody," she explains. "I thought that was pretty cool."

Laura envisions herself in ten years as about the same as she is now—only more aware of herself and her world. She expects to be just graduating from college then; she's in no hurry. "Just why is everything being made to go faster and faster?" she asks. "You have to have this new math bit by the time you're 5. That's funny. And this great shift to stuffing people with education early so that by the time you get to college you see this world as a big, vast . . . *textbook*!"

I could never join the mainstream of society now," she concludes. "If you've been made aware, then you can't suddenly bury yourself. So society is just going to have to accept us. Either that or this darned society is just going to collapse. You can't have a society full of unaware people."

Pleasures of Possession

Pert, blond Susan Maletich is a 16-year-old New York high-school student who hasn't decided whether to go to college or straight into an acting career. In the last year, from funds supplied by two part-time jobs and the seemingly limitless indulgence of two fond parents, Susan has bought, among other things:

An ankle length muu-muu ($25), three pairs of sandals ($26), big bug-eyed sunglasses ($15, she already owns Ben Franklin glasses), leather boots ($22), a bright green and blue op-art dress ($16), English Leather men's cologne ($6.50, "Everybody who's in wears it"), a bold index-finger ring and two sets of earrings for her pierced ears ($10), a new bikini ($25), false eyelashes ($5), fishnet stockings ($5), a black-and-white check suit ($26), two pairs of round-toed, low-heel shoes ($16), a pair of sheer black tights ($5), a poor-boy sweater ($8), a skunk-fur hat ($16, "It was a fad downtown"), and a yellow feather hat ($10, "It was different . . . but I don't have the nerve to wear it"). All this, of course, was in addition to outlays on the standard clothing items, cosmetics, Peter, Paul and Mary record albums, movies, paperback books, snacks and soft drinks.

Multiply Susan Maletich by the 17.9 million other girls and boys between 13 and 17 and the result is a very neat set of figures, indeed. The high-school set has graduated from the ice-cream, soda-fountain and bicycle circuit into the big leagues of U.S. consumption. Most studies, in fact, estimate that rising allowances and swelling incomes from part-time and summer jobs this year will put a whopping $12 billion into the jean pockets of the nation's high-school boys and girls. This about equals the total output of South Africa and adds up to an income of $670 per teen per year.

La Différence: What's more, with basic food, housing and clothing provided by their parents, most of this money is available for recreational, luxury and impulse spending. And spend it they do. "The key is distinctive teen style—different from the adult world," analyst Louis Harris concludes on the basis of his *Newsweek* survey. "High-school-age Americans," he adds, "have never known drastic economic depression or wartime shortages—they're happy now and believe the future can only get better."

For the whole economy, the impact of this direct spending is immense; teens buy everything from typewriters to toothpicks. And for many industries the buying is decisive. The sports equipment, musical instrument and motorbike industries would be dwarfs without teen-agers. Eugene Gilbert of Gilbert Youth Research estimates that high-schoolers buy some 16 per cent of all cosmetics, about 45 per cent of all soft drinks, 24 per cent of all wristwatches, 81 per cent of all single phonograph records, 20 per cent of all radios, 30 per cent of all low-priced cameras. On clothes alone, the girls lay out at least $2 billion a year.

Flat Out: Teen-agers also influence their parents' buying decisions. An impressive percentage of high-school teen-agers, for instance, own autos (chart, page 70), and they buy about 4 per cent of all new cars sold annually and about 7 per cent of all used cars. But studies by the auto companies revealed that teen-agers often had a decisive influence on the model of car their parents bought; largely as a result of a 1962 survey, Ford Motor Co. moved body styles away from sedan models to sporty hardtops and fastback designs. Ford went ahead with its highly successful Mustang sports car only after extensive testing showed that teen-agers approved. "Gentlemen," Ford division manager Donald Frey told a Chicago business meeting recently, "78 million of our 196 million citizens haven't yet reached their twentieth birthday. The sheer weight of numbers makes the youth of this country a factor that just cannot be ignored . . . Frankly, we are going all out."

Department stores, cosmetics companies and other industries heavily dependent on teen-agers have mobilized to exploit the expanding youth boom for a decade or more. But in the last few years such unlikely groups as life-insurance companies, razor-blade firms and the tea and coffee industries have jumped on the bandwagon with special promotions. Most recently, the airlines, led by American Airlines, set out to capture young passengers by offering youths aged 12 to 21 half-price flights on a space-available basis.

For the Tea Council, which will send a rock-'n'-roll group and teen queen on a tour of dances, amusement parks, church meetings and fairs for two months this summer, it's a matter of getting in on the ground floor and changing the idea that tea is for "little old ladies." "Teen-agers are thirsty," Thomas J. Lipton president W. Gardner Barker says briskly. "The tea industry certainly can't stand by and allow this thirst to be quenched by competitive products." For American Airlines and other carriers, it's a matter of killing two birds with one stone: They establish the air-travel habit early and fill seats that would otherwise be empty. "It's practically pure profit for us," said American Airlines vice president Walter Rauscher last week. "We're getting about 1,000 kids a day and 90 per cent of them would never have flown if it weren't for our plan."

Whatever its success, any industry trying to crack the high-school teen market faces one formidable problem it meets nowhere else. By definition, teen-agers are changelings, intent on creating their own distinct style while taking on some of the trappings of the square adult world. As a result, many teen buying habits are incredibly more volatile than even the kaleidoscopic grown-up markets of the U.S. "It's an endless market with an unending stream of merchandise," sighed Leonard Hankin, vice president of New York's Bergdorf-Goodman, which joined the growing department-store trend last month when it set up a special teen-age boutique for far-out fashions and gifts. "You learn," adds Hankin, "from this world of instant change minute to minute."

To keep up with the go-go spenders, companies have adopted a variety of strategems. Firms that are small enough simply jump from one product to a new one as it catches fire. A couple of years ago, Los Angeles's Ed (Big Daddy) Roth, 34, was a reigning high priest of hot-rod customizing and titan of a craze for sweat shirts decorated with pictures of half-human fiends driving drag-strip cars. Both those lines have since "gone down the tubes" for Roth, and last week Big Daddy's seventeen-man factory force was working full blast turning out replicas of World War II German Army helmets. Roth has sold 20,000 of the replicas, which were apparently first paraded publicly by the Hell's Angels and other California motorcycle gangs. Why are they selling? "It burns up adults," shrugs Roth. "Teen-agers wear them to be set apart."

Big enterprises can't shift gears overnight. So they have a battery of instruments they use to monitor the teen-age pulse. Market surveys are continuously made as a matter of course, department stores almost all employ teen coordinators, who in turn maintain teen-age advisory boards selected from nearby schools and run frequent teen fashion shows to keep in touch.

Market-Wise: Perhaps the most sophisticated market-intelligence system is maintained by Bobbie Brooks, Inc., of Cleveland, Ohio, a sharp, teen-oriented clothes manufacturer whose sales have doubled since

1961 to $105 million a year. Every three weeks, Bobbie Brooks' marketing staff polls 100 new girls in ten cities for their views on colors and styles. The company then cranks this information—together with reports from salesmen, stores and its own designers—into its IBM computer and asks the computer to predict what colors and styles will sell the best. One recent bit of computer intelligence: Bikinis will be big among the high-school crowd, but the girls don't like the name. Presumably, Bobbie Brooks president Maurice Saltzman and his assistants are now tackling the problem of a new name.

Many companies, making products mainly for adult markets, can concentrate their ingenuity on long-term promotion. And here, the variety of pitches tossed at teen-agers is limitless. Home-economics teachers are bombarded with free samples, instructional materials, and offers of help by food companies and interior-decorating departments of stores. Sterling silver, china, diamond-ring and home-furnishings companies fill the pages of teen magazines with ads that depict teen-age girls dreaming happily about marriage. (A *Seventeen* magazine study shows that 13 per cent of all brides marry before they are 18, two-fifths are married before they are 20 and hope chests sometimes start filling up after a girl's sixteenth birthday.) Teen-age beauty and talent contests, sponsored by companies ranging from Dr. Pepper (soft drinks) to Eastman Kodak, are as common as corsages at a prom.

Many of the biggest and most important teen-age promotions tie in with a public service. Chicago's giant mail-order and retailing firm of Montgomery Ward, whose current catalogue opens with a 77-page section on girls' fashions and is entitled "Young America in Action," is a longtime sponsor of a 4-H Club home-economics program that currently has an enrollment of 1.2 million teen girls. San Francisco's Bank of America, the nation's largest bank, helps encourage teen saving (the high-school set saves 8 or 9 per cent of its spendable income) by handing out $211,000 a year in achievement awards to California high-school students. And the nation's auto companies achieve a fine blend of public service and self-interest by arranging for dealers to lend thousands of cars annually to high-school driver training programs. The lessons are well learned: The Automobile Manufacturers Association says that seven out of ten consumers generally buy the make of car in which they learn to drive.

Drawing Card: Teen-age fairs tie nearly all these efforts together. Several groups are now promoting them. A Los Angeles TV host named Al Burton, with partners Bart Ross and Frank Danzig, started the first one in a Santa Monica amusement park back in 1961. This year's version has drawn 300 individual company exhibitors, will tour nine U.S. and Canadian cities, stopping ten days in each between April and September, and will probably draw more than a million high-school-age visitors.

The shows have become a kind of World's Fair for teen-agers, with companies offering contests and prizes, dozens of rock-'n'-roll groups and other attractions to draw teen-agers to their booths. Once there, the teen-agers try out the products on display with no salesman in sight—highly important, in the view of Burton and other experts, because teen-agers are extremely pragmatic shoppers and like to taste, touch or use a product before they buy. One new fashion Burton is sure will click this year is "jellies," a ruffled, feminine version of the long, baggy bathing trunks (called "jams") that teen boys in southern California popularized last summer.

WHAT TEEN-AGERS OWN

	% Boys	% Girls
Records	**75**	**90**
Transistor radios	**75**	**72**
Record players	**50**	**72**
Encyclopedia	**64**	**60**
Car	**18**	**8**
Weights	**34**	–
Guitar	**27**	–
Motorbike	**20**	–
Perfume	–	**96**
Patterned stockings	–	**67**
Hair drier	–	**65**
High boots	–	**56**

Way to Grow: A great many social critics—and parents—wonder aloud if all this overwhelming commercial pressure on teen-agers is good. The answer, in the best of all possible worlds, might well be no. But one of the revealing discoveries of the *Newsweek* survey is that, even without the commercial push, teen-agers would probably be lusty spenders anyhow. When asked how they felt when they were shopping, the teen-agers responded, "mature, independent, good and happy, glad it was their choice, responsible and important," in that order. In other words, they are buying, not so much material things, but adulthood; in their way, they are trying to be like grownups.

WHAT THEY WANT NEXT

Car	44	37
Motorbike	9	–
Musical instruments	7	2
Record players	4	8
Clothes	4	11
Private phone	1	8

Newsweek survey by Louis Harris

Rites, Styles, Passwords

The Mule started out as a Madison Avenue special—a dance craze created, packaged and promoted like a new product. A leading vodka distiller, bent on putting some kick in its sales, hired New York dance master Killer Joe Piro ("King of the Discothéque") to fashion the Mule's steps and Skitch Henderson to compose music for it. The dance, teamed up with a new vodka drink also named the Mule, was launched last spring by a $2-million publicity campaign employing television, magazines, newspapers and billboards. And, just in case anyone had missed the word, the dance turned up on the Ed Sullivan and Johnny Carson shows.

The Mule, of course, never got off its hind legs. It died of neglect: The teen-agers wouldn't buy it—and without their endorsement, no adult would shake a leg either. Indeed, the Mule's demise is one more indication that businessmen can no longer manufacture a new craze as easily as a Davy Crockett cap. Most of today's fads, whether they be the skateboard, the granny dress or the jerk, are being originated by teen-agers. Says Jerry Mander, a San Francisco advertising man: "If the kids don't initiate it, it never happens."

Self-Defense: The explanation for this shift in initiative is related to the reason adolescents pick up fads in the first place. To the majority of girls and boys answering the *Newsweek* survey, their knee-high boots and Prince Valiant bobs symbolized, first, a declaration of identity with their peer group and, second, a declaration of rebellion against adult authority. The poll showed that nearly half the girls and almost one-third of the boys bought certain clothes against the express wishes of their parents. Also, more than half confessed they disapproved of boys' wearing long hair; yet when their parents criticized long hair, the majority defended it. In other words, nothing can solidify a fad faster than adult opposition. As Robert Shellow of the National Institute of Mental Health explains it: "Teen-age fads are carefully calculated to scandalize adults."

How does a fad get going? Sociologist Rolf Meyersohn, co-author of

"Notes on a Natural History of Fads," contends that a number of persons in various parts of the country—for a variety of reasons—will begin to do the same thing at the same time. "If this coincidence persists long enough," says Meyersohn, ". . . the phenomenon which had been statistical becomes a real fad." Put in simpler terms, a fad is started, according to an Atlanta high-school counselor, "by one of the popular, more intelligent kids."

Taking Off: Fads seem to evolve, according to University of California sociologist Edgar Z. Friedenberg, through two stages—the craft stage and the commercial stage. "It may start with something at which you have to be a kid to be pretty good at," says Friedenberg. "Hot-rodding and surfing started this way. Then the companies move in at the juncture when the article can be distributed more widely by mass production." Publicity follows—and the fad takes off.

Granny dresses, for example, initially went through a "craft" period; last summer California girls began hand-sewing them, possibly in imitation of the ankle-length, frontier dresses they saw at Disneyland. When *Women's Wear Daily* ran an item, the dress manufacturers moved in and grannies became "commercial." And the popularity of pea jackets and bell-bottoms as fashion items can be traced to economy-minded teen-agers who took to rummaging through Army-Navy stores in search of offbeat bargains. *Glamour* and *Seventeen* magazines then commercialized them. During its commercial phase, however, a fad meets sudden death if it is picked up by too many of the "wrong people" (translation: adults). "When anyone can walk into a department store and buy a granny dress or a pea jacket," says a Los Angeles girl, "we drop them quick."

A recent NIMH study of teen-age dancing habits, psychologist Shellow reports, reached a similar conclusion. According to Shellow, Washington teen-agers stopped doing the twist within a month after Mrs. John F. Kennedy gave a White House party at which twist music was played. The commercial exploitation of surfing may be causing a similar disenchantment, at least in California. "The new word for square on the coast is 'surfer'," reports Gloria Stavers, editor of *16* magazine, a monthly read by more than 800,000 teen-agers.

These days, at least, the inspiration for new fads seems to come from pop entertainers, Negroes, a few television shows and certain tuned-in disk jockeys. In fashion, for example, rock-'n'-roll groups now function as the templates for innovation. Jim McGuinn, the 23-year-old lead guitarist of the Byrds, started wearing tiny, rectangular glasses on stage because they protected his eyes from the spotlights. The popularity of the glasses among teen-agers kept pace with that of the Byrds, and today "Ben Franklin" glasses pop up everywhere. In Boston, teen-agers who normally wear glasses are getting their prescription lenses fitted into Ben Franklin frames, thereby making a fashionable virtue out of necessity.

Herman: Similarly, heavy, man-sized watches began appearing on American teen-age girls shortly after the Beatles' girl friends started wearing them in England a year ago. Other innovators of teen-age fashion include the Rolling Stones (plaid and checkered pants); Sonny and

Cher (wide, hip-hugger belts); Paul Revere and the Raiders (Paisley shirts and leather vests) and Herman's Hermits (round-toed boots).

The twist, which quickly became the favorite indoor exercise for the young, originally worked its way up from South Philadelphia's Negro neighborhoods. It was introduced by a then-obscure Negro singer named Chubby Checker. White teen-agers picked it up and danced it on Dick Clark's televised "American Bandstand"; within months the twist moved 100 miles northeast to New York's Peppermint Lounge, where it caught on with the jet set.

Parental Surrender: Why the twist and its variations? Part of the appeal, of course, stems from the contagious joyousness of the movements. But some experts see another dimension. "Teen-agers have a natural need to rebel," says Donald Barr, headmaster of the Dalton School in New York. "Parents surrender at the first sign of revolt, frustrating the rebellion drive and so teen-agers have to identify with minority groups in rebellion."

Lexicographer Bergen Evans of Northwestern University sees a similar kinship between Negroes and teen-agers, particularly in their slang. "The function of any slang is to give secrecy to the users, to prevent their being understood by outsiders," says Evans. "Both Negroes and teen-agers are subject groups, helpless, defiant of established authorities and at the same time afraid of them."

Evans' secrecy theory would explain the mercurial nature of adolescent slang. As their passwords are picked up by the enemy, teen-agers must constantly invent new ones. At last report, for instance, the word "cool" has been replaced by "boss," "spiffy," "tough," "groovy" and "bitchin'." What was once "real cool" is now "dead instant" or "out of sight."

New York disk jockey Murray Kaufman popularized the phrase "It's what's happening, baby," now heard everywhere. Television may also inspire phrases, provided the show carries the teen-agers' seal of approval. Soupy Sales, who is currently viewed by an estimated 20 million teens, has popularized "You really know how to hurt a guy"; "Batman" has scored with "My fine-feathered finks" and "Holy popcorn!" and "Get Smart" has promoted the tagline "Sorry about that, chief. . . ."

Today the most important relay stations for teen-age fads are London and Los Angeles. From model Jean Shrimpton and from fresh young designers like Mary Quant and Jean Muir, London has exported the "total look": the boots or little-girl shoes, white stockings, thigh-high skirts, long straight hair and Liverpool cap now seen in nearly every U.S. city. (Appropriately, the cap was also copied from a Non-U group—British blue-collar workers.) "All my friends are so proud that America was once part of England," says a 16-year-old New York girl. "I think they're sorry we broke away."

Los Angeles exerts a different kind of appeal. Last year, the sheriff's office rounded up more than 1500 teen-age runaways from other parts of the country—probably because of the city's image as the capital of celluloid glamour, surfing, hot-rodding and the teen-age nightclub. "It's where the action is," explains one Chicago girl.

Time Lag: Southern California fads seem to take about six months before they reach young people back East. Granny dresses are already "hokey" in Houston and are just beginning to show up on East Coast streets (three teen-age daughters of a Cornell University researcher were suspended by their high-school principal last week when they wore the dresses to class).

Other fads remain regional in scope. Kids in Orlando, Fla., make their own rings by filing down the necks of Coke bottles; in Salt Lake City, it's very "boss" to wear sunglasses upside down. In Bellevue, Wash., teen-agers contribute to the bail of local "fringies" (bearded, older kids tangled with the law) by paying 50 cents for a "fringie" button. "I just bought a fringie button to help spring a singing group called the 'Daily Flash'," says 17-year-old Jeanne Thompson. "They have real talent and they couldn't use it in jail." And New Yorkers are beginning to do a restrained version of the monkey called the Boston monkey—which is completely unknown in Boston.

Teen-age fads and fancies would seem to be ephemeral by definition. "They're teen-agers for such a short time," says sociologist Meyersohn, "and they always have new mascots." Yet today a curious new trend—the adoption of teen-age fads by adults—threatens not only to perpetuate the fads but the adolescent mentality as well. Housewives are stepping out in little-girl shoes, white stockings and short-short skirts while some of their spouses are beginning to affect the Mod look—from Dutch-boy caps to Chelsea boots. In the discothèques, both struggle to imitate the latest teen-age dance. "I have to get up early in the morning to get to my closet before my mother," says Diantha Douglas, a 15-year-old junior at Chicago's Hyde Park High. "She steals all my clothes." The adult generation "is really a teen-age generation," says a Boulder, Colo., boy. Age is now wasted on youth.

Adolescence Forever? How do the kids look on all this? "They don't like the competition it sets up," says psychologist Janet Greene. "They want parents to be parents and not to be members of their own peer group." Other observers suggest that the "youth cult" may be leading the real youths to wrong conclusions about how they should act as adults. Teen-agers of today, they suggest, may grow up to imitate tomorrow's teen-agers—thereby setting up a cycle of permanent adolescence.

More likely, today's teen-agers will join tomorrow's PTA meetings, executive training programs—and picket lines—in roughly the same proportion as the generation they succeed. "Our parents had their crazy fads once and they grew up all right," says a 15-year-old boy from Clifton, N.J. "We'll come out of it all right, too."

Perhaps, too, they will then look upon their own teen-age children—mercurial, bewildering, caught up in unimaginable crazes—and repeat the same refrains their parents sing today.

Values and Our Youth

Gordon W. Allport

What is your definition of values? Are they taught or "caught"—caught, perhaps, from adult example? Each generation is dissatisfied with its predecessor, yet values change slowly; and youth has tended to recant its own idealism in favor of a pragmatic, more success-oriented adult standard. Allport explores the phenomenon of adolescent values as introduced by the parent and (more importantly?) the teacher. Are the studies cited an accurate reading of young adult attitudes of right now? If you feel there have been shifts in ideals, is Allport's premise nevertheless valid?

One aim of education is to make available the wisdom of the past and present so that youth may be equipped to solve the problems of the future. If this is so, then we have good grounds for a feeling of consternation concerning the adequacy of our present educational procedures. The reason is that in the immediate future, the youth of today will have to live in a world very unlike the world of the past from which our store of wisdom has been drawn.

Some Prospects

Think of the vastly changed nature of life in the future, for which we have little relevant wisdom from the past to call upon:

1. The new generation of students will have to face an ever increasing domination of life by science, by technology, and by automation. (One thinks of the story of two cows grazing along the roadside. An immense milk truck passes with the painted legend: Pasteurized, Homogenized, Vitamin B Added. One cow turns to the other and says, "Makes you feel inadequate, doesn't it?")
2. The new generation will have to recognize the impossibility of living any longer in a state of condescension toward the colored peoples of the world (about three-quarters of the world's population). Centuries of comfortable caste discrimination and segregation are from here on impossible to maintain.
3. The coming generation will have to deal with a population explosion whose predicted magnitude staggers our imagination.
4. It will need a completer understanding of world societies and their marked differences in values. In the past, we could be politely ignorant of such places as Africa, Latin America, and Asia in a way that is no longer possible.
5. It will have to create a world government or, at least, an effective confederation to forestall the threat of thermonuclear war.

6. As if a planetary world view were not difficult enough to achieve, the coming generation may have to develop an interplanetary point of view. (I find this prospect especially alarming because we seem to be solving the problems of outer space before those of the inner space of mind, character, and values.)

It is no wonder that this preview of problems confronting our youth throws us educators into a state of self-scrutiny bordering sometimes on panic. Where can youth find the needed equipment? Are they sound enough in mind and morale?

Sometimes our dismay finds an outlet in gallows humor. They tell of the benevolent lady who saw a depressing specimen of the very young generation sprawled on the curb of a city street, swilling down cans of beer. Greatly shocked, she asked, "Little boy, why aren't you in school?" "Cripes, lady," he replied, "I'm only four years old."

And they tell the story of the London bobby. London police, we know, are well trained for social work, even for psychotherapy. This bobby's beat was Waterloo Bridge. He spotted a man about to jump over and intercepted him. "Come now," he said. "Tell me what is the matter. Is it money?" The man shook his head. "Your wife perhaps?" Another shake of the head. "Well, what is it then?" The would-be suicide replied, "I'm worried about the state of the world." "Oh, come now," said the bobby. "It can't be so bad. Let's walk up and down the bridge here and talk it over." Whereupon they strolled for about an hour discussing the state of the world and then they *both* jumped over.

Humor helps us put our dilemma into sane perspective, but it does not solve the problem. The vague apprehension we feel has led to certain empirical studies of the values of today's youth, with results, alas, that are not reassuring.

Assessing Values

Not long ago, Professor Phillip Jacob undertook to survey (5) all available studies concerning the values held by college students. He found a marked uniformity among them. Fully three-quarters of the students were "gloriously contented, both in regard to their present day-to-day activity and their outlook for the future." Their aspirations were primarily for material gratifications for themselves and their families. They "fully accepted the conventions of the contemporary business society as the context within which they will realize their personal desires." While they will not crusade against segregation and racial injustice, they will accept nondiscrimination when it comes as a "necessary convention in a homogenized culture." They subscribe to the traditional virtues of sincerity, honesty, and loyalty, but are indulgent concerning laxity in moral standards. They normally express a need for religion, but there is a hollow quality in their beliefs. They do not desire to have an influential voice in public policy or government. Their sense of civic duty stops at the elementary obligation of voting. They predict another major war within a dozen years, but they say that international problems give them little concern and that they spend no time on them. Only a minority value their college education primarily in terms of its intellectual gains. They regard it as good because it gives them vocational preparation, social status, and a good time. Such is the flabby value-fibre that Jacob discovers among college students of today.

The picture becomes more vivid when viewed in cross-national perspective. James Gillespie and I, in a comparative study (3) of the values of college youth in 10 nations, asked students to write their autobiographies of the future ("My life from now until the year 2000") and also gave them an extensive questionnaire. The instrument was translated into nine different languages.

In comparison with youth of other nations, young Americans are delightfully frank and open, unsuspicious and cooperative. Their documents had no literary affectation (and, I may add, little literary quality). But the most important finding was that within these 10 nations American students were the most self-centered the most "privatistic" in values. They desired above all else a rich, full life for themselves, and showed little concern for national welfare or for the fate of mankind at large. The context of their outlook was private rather than public, passive rather than pioneer. The essential point is made clear by two excerpts, the first drawn from the autobiography of a Mexican girl 18 years of age, and the second from a Radcliffe student of the same age:

> Since I like psychology very much, I wish, on leaving this school, to study it, specializing in it and exercising it as a profession. I shouldn't like to get married right away, although like any woman I am desirous of getting married before realizing all my aspirations. In addition, I should like to do something for my country—as a teacher, as a psychologist, or as a mother. As a teacher, to guide my pupils in the best path, for at the present time they need solid bases in childhood in order in their future lives not to have so many frustrations as the youth of the present. As a psychologist, to make studies which in some way will serve humanity and my beloved country. As a mother, to make my children creatures who are useful to both their country and all humanity.

Now follows the Radcliffe document. Its flavor of privatism is unmistakable:

> Our summers will be spent lobster fishing on the Cape. Later we'll take a look at the rest of the country—California, the Southwest, and the Chicago Stockyards. I want the children, when they get past the age of ten, to spend part of the summer away from home, either at camp or as apprentices to whatever profession they may show an interest in. Finally, I hope we will all be able to take a trip to Europe, especially to Russia, to see what can be done about Communism.

Many critics have called attention to the same American value predicament. Our current social pattern, they say, is almost completely geared to one objective alone, namely a profitable, expanding production. To insure expanding production, there must be more and more consumption. Hence comes the expensive glamor of our advertising and its control of our mass media. The sole objective seems to be to stimulate the accretion of goods. Self-respect and status, as well as comfort, are acquired in this way. Someone has called our national disease "galloping consumption." Half a century ago, William James saw the peril and was much worried by what he called "the American terror of poverty." He saw there was truth in the jibes that other countries direct at our "materialism."

Hope in Uneasiness

Now a high standard of living is not in itself an evil thing. All the world wants what we already have. But the single-minded pursuit of production and consumption has brought a dulling of other values. One consequence is symbolized by the scandal of rigged quiz programs. These were in the service of advertising, which in turn was in the service of a profitable expanding economy. Another consequence is the accumulated froth of our TV, radio, and movies. Another is the widely discussed conformity of the organization man, as well as the futile rebellion of the beats. An especially peppery critic, Paul Goodman (4), has shown that the starved lives of juvenile delinquents and of young people caught in the organizational grind are at bottom much alike. Both are attracted to the cult of easiness and aspire to nothing more than amiable mediocrity. Both styles of living fail to prepare youth for the problems that lie ahead for themselves and for the nation.

A somewhat vulgar story seems to me to summarize all this mordant criticism. Moses, a stalwart leader of the old school, said to the Israelites in Egypt, "Load up your camels, bring along your asses, and I'll lead you to the promised land." By contrast, the modern American prophet seems to urge, "Light up your Camels, sit on your asses, and I'll bring you the promised land."

All this familiar criticism is irritating; yet the fact that it flourishes is a hopeful sign. We suspect it may be too harsh. I am inclined to think so. It is rash indeed to indict a whole generation. At worst, Jacob's gloomy picture held for three-quarters of the college students studied, but not at all for a vital and far from negligible minority. And even though the gloomy generalizations have some truth in them, are the assets given fair attention? I myself have some favorable impressions, although one man's view is not reliable. But youth today appears to enjoy a certain freedom and flexibility that was not common in the more rigid days of our parents and grandparents. I even have the impression that there is less neuroticism among students now than among those of a generation ago. What is more, young people, I find, are not blind to the world changes that are occurring. Their apparent repression of the challenge is due largely to their bewilderment concerning proper paths to take. (And one has the feeling that our own statesmen in Washington are no less bewildered.) All in all, these are hopeful signs that should not be overlooked.

Values and the School

Another hopeful sign is the fact that many teachers are asking, "What can we do to be helpful?" They know, and we all know, that the ability of the school to give training in values is limited. For one thing, the home is vastly more important. A home that infects the child with galloping consumption, that encourages only canned recreation and has no creative outlets, can only with difficulty be offset by the school. Another limitation lies in the fact that the school is ordinarily expected to mirror current social values and to prepare the child to live within the existing frame. It is an unusual school system and an unusual teacher who even *wish* to transcend the current fashions of value.

But assuming that we have an unusual school system and an unusual teacher, what values shall they elect to teach? If they do not choose to follow the prevailing fashions, what standards shall they follow? The ancient Romans were fond of asking, "Who will judge the judges?" and "Who will guard the guardians?" Can the guardians turn perhaps to standard discussions of "the aims of education"? Such discussions are numerous, abstract, and often dull. Their weakness, I feel, is their effort to formulate absolute goals, vistas of abstract perfection. The result is often a series of platitudes or generalizations so broad as to be unhelpful. Of course we want to develop "good citizenship"; we certainly want to "free the child's intellect." These and all other absolutes need to be reduced to concrete, stepwise processes before they can guide us in the strategy of teaching values.

The teacher must start with the situation as he or she finds it and in concrete instances sharpen the value-attributes of the lesson being taught. To a considerable extent, these value-attributes can be drawn from the codified wisdom of our nation. We cannot neglect the value of profitable production and high living standards, for all our vocational and professional education contribute to this end. But the codified wisdom of our unique society extends far beyond the obsession of today. Our values include also such matters as respect for civil liberties. Does the school accent this value? They include approval for individual initiative, for philanthropy, for compassion. And they imply much concerning civic duties that are the reciprocal of civic rights. What must we do to deserve our precious cornucopia of freedom? Vote? Yes. But voting does no good unless the voter is informed above the stereotyped level of the mass media. He must also pay taxes willingly. Do schools and colleges teach the young to pay a glad tax? I wonder. To me the most disturbing finding in *Youth's Outlook on the Future* lay in the elaborate talk about one's right to a rich, full life and in the almost total silence regarding one's duties.

I am saying that in the first instance teachers should choose the values they teach from the whole (not from a part) of our American ethos. Deep in our hearts we know, and most of the world knows, that our national values, derived, of course, from Judeo-Christian ethics, are about the finest mankind has yet formulated. In no sense are these values out of date, nor will they go out of date in the world of tomorrow. Yet many of them are badly rusted. Unless they are revitalized, however, our youth may not have the personal fortitude and moral implements that the future will require.

The Larger Anchor

Excellent as the American Creed is as a fountainhead of values, it does not contain them all. It says nothing explicitly, for example, about intellectual curiosity. And yet surely schools exist to augment this value The most severe indictment of our educational procedures I have ever encountered is the discovery that a sizeable percentage of graduates of our colleges after completing their formal education never afterward read a single book.

There are other important values that are not spelled out in our American Creed. I am thinking of those details of human relationships that make all the difference between boorishness and brotherhood in the human family. As our population increases, it becomes more and more important to teach the elements of the new science of human relations which go far toward smoothing the roughness of common life by leading us to respect effectively the integrity of the other fellow. I recall a teacher of English whose class was studying *The Merchant of Venice.* She turned a wave of incipient anti-Semitism in her class to a sound lesson in values. Shylock, she explained, was like the resentful, self-seeking portion of every person's nature. We are all potential Shylocks. But while self-love is prominent in all of us, we are so constructed that it need not be sovereign in our natures.

To return for a moment to the relation between home and school —the former, as I have said, is far more important. Recognizing this fact, some people say, "Well, let's leave the teaching of values to the home and to the church. Schools can't do much of anything about the matter."

This position is untenable. If the school does not teach values it will have the effect of denying them. If the child at school never hears a mention of honesty, modesty, charity, or reverence, he will be persuaded that, like many of his parents ideas, they are simply old hat. As they grow toward adolescence, children become critical of the teaching of both parents and the church. They are in a questioning stage. If the school, which to the child represents the larger outside world, is silent on values, the child will repudiate more quickly the lessons learned at home. He will also be thrown onto peer values more completely, with their emphasis on the hedonism of teen-age parties or on the destructiveness of gangs. He will also be more at the mercy of the sensate values peddled by movies, TV, and disk jockeys. What is more, some homes, as we have said, give no fundamental value training. In such a case, it is *only* in the school that the child has any chance at all of finding ethical anchorage.

This brings us to the hardest question: How does the teacher, the instructor, the professor, handle his assignment in the classroom? How is it possible to teach values, including the value of intellectual curiosity?

The Meaning of Value

Before tackling this question, we must pause to define what we mean by value. You will recognize that I am using the term psychologically, not in its objective philosophical sense. Values, as I use the term, are simply *meanings perceived as related to self.* The child experiences value whenever he knows that a meaning is warm and central to himself. Values, to borrow Whitehead's term, are "matters of importance" as distinct from mere matters of fact.

So much for definition. Now the hard-pressed teacher is given a solid substantive curriculum to teach The curriculum in its original state consists of mere matters of fact. And on the number of facts absorbed the pupil's standing depends. It takes virtually all of a teacher's time to convey factual information and grade the pupil on his achievement. There is little time left to transmute these matters of fact into matters of importance, let alone teach all of the moral and social values we have thus far been discussing.

The curriculum itself is not, and should not be, a direct aid. Prescribed instruction in values would be laughed out of court. We have recently been bumped by Sputnik headforemost into core subjects. Get on with science, mathematics, language! Away with courses in folk-dancing, personal adjustment, and fudge-making! I agree that value-study has no place in curriculum planning, but not because it in a frivolous subject—rather, because it is a subject too hard and too subtle for curriculum makers.

Education for values occurs only when teachers teach what they themselves stand for, no matter what their subject is. If I were to write a treatise on the teaching of values, I would give most of my emphasis to the moral pedagogy that lies in a teacher's incidental comments, to the *obiter dicta.* The hard core is central, but the hard core has a penumbra of moral significance. I mentioned the teacher of English who made a value-lesson out of Shylock. I recall also my college professor of geology who paused in his lecture on diatom ooze to say to us, "Others would not agree with me, but I confess that when ever I study diatoms, I don't see how anyone can doubt the existence of God because the design and behavior of these protozoa are so marvelous." Is it not interesting how we all recall the *obiter dicta* of our teachers, the penumbra of value they point out to us, surrounding the hard-core data? We remember them better than the subject matter itself.

Why does the student remember them so well? No current theory of learning seems able to tell us. I suspect it is because values, being matters of importance to the self, are always warm and central and ego-involved and therefore claim priority on our attention. The child, being value-ripe, cannot help being impressed when the teacher betrays excitement and enthusiasm for a mode of thought or for the content of the subject being studied. True, the youngster does not, and should not, adopt the teacher's values ready-made; but the teacher's self-disclosure leads the student to self-discovery.

What wouldn't we give if we could develop intellectual ardor in every child for hard-core subjects? Why is it that for most pupils arithmetic, spelling, physics, remain forever dull matters of fact and never become a meaning perceived as related to the self? One reason, I think, is that the weary teacher fails to convey his own sense of the importance of the subject to the student. If he did so, he would, as I have said, at least fix attention upon the value-potentiality of the subject.

Another reason perhaps is that not all of a teacher's *obiter dicta* are wholesome. Some, indeed, may be deeply damaging, though the teacher may be innocent of any such intent. Sometimes we hear incidental (but still attitude-forming) remarks like this one: "All right now, children. You have had a good time playing at recess; now settle down to your English lesson." Play is recognized as a matter of joyful importance. English, the teacher is saying in effect, is a mere routine matter of fact.

Values and Learning

I think our educational psychology has been mostly wrong about the process of learning—or perhaps not so much wrong as woefully incomplete. At the beginning of his learning career, a young child cannot, of course, be expected to feel adult enthusiasm for the intellectual content of his studies. He does his work in the first instance to avoid a scolding or because he has a habit of obeying instructions. Soon he finds added incentive. The teacher—really in the role of mother—gives praise and love ("Susan, I am proud of you"). There is a great deal of such dependency in the learning situation. Love and social reward (as well as some fear of punishment) sustain the processes of attention and retention. When the child puts forth intellectual effort, he does so in order to obtain a gold star commendation, or other symbols of love.

All these incentives are extraneous to the subject matter. The youngster does not learn it because it is a matter of importance. When he leaves school or college, he loses these extraneous supports. He finds his love relations directly; they are no longer a reward for intellectual effort. Hence, intellectual apathy sets in, and, distressing to say, no further books are read.

In such a case at this, intellectual curiosity was never tied to independence, only to extraneous supports. At some point in the schooling—and the earlier the better—intellectual activity should become not a second-hand but a first-hand fitting to the sense of self. At the beginning, all learning must be tied, perhaps, to specific reinforcements; but if the dependency is long continued, authentic curiosity fails to develop.

It would be going too far to put the blame for intellectual apathy onto our current teaching of educational psychology. Yet I am inclined to feel somewhat punitive about this matter. Psychology has not yet settled down to the problem of transforming matters of fact—whose acquisition current learning theories explain fairly well—into autonomous matters of importance—which they do not explain at all.

Our emphasis has been on learning by drill and by reinforcement.

Such "habit acquisition" receives all the emphasis. But the learning theory involved postulates a continuing dependency relation (extraneous reinforcement). When the relation terminates, the habits of study simply extinguish themselves. I am surprised, therefore, that stimulus-response psychologists do not see this consequence of their own theory. Insofar as teachers employ an educational psychology of this order, they are not likely to break the dependency relation, which belongs properly only to the earlier stages of schooling.

Matters of importance, I strongly believe, are not acquired by drill or by reinforcement. They are transformations of habits and skills from the "opportunistic" layer of personality into the ego-system itself (1). Once inside the ego-system, these habits and skills turn into true interests and utilize the basic energy, the basic spontaneity, that the organism itself possesses. They are no longer sustained as "operant conditionings" by outside rewards. The interest, now being the very stuff of life itself, needs no outer supports.

Functional Autonomy

I have called this process of transforming means into ends, of changing extrinsic values into intrinsic values *functional autonomy*. Concerning this concept, I am often asked two questions: How do you define "functional autonomy, and how does functional autonomy come about?"

For a definition, I offer the following: Functional autonomy refers to any acquired system of motivation in which the tensions involved are no longer of the same kind as the antecedant tensions from which the acquired system developed.[1] To answer the question of how functional autonomy comes about requires a more extended and technical discussion. I can only hint at the direction of my answer. Neurologists are gradually discovering a basis for what I would call "perseverative functional autonomy." I refer to the "self-sustaining circuits," "feedback mechanisms," and "central motive states" that are now commonly recognized to exist in the nervous system. This line of discovery, I find, provides a partial answer to the question. But I believe we have to go further and call on the concept of self. Values, we have said, are meanings perceived as related to the self. Functional autonomy is not a mere perseverative phenomenon; it is, above all, an ego-involved phenomenon. Besides admitting an opportunistic layer to personality, which is the exclusive concern of most current theories of learning, we have no choice but to admit also a "propriate" layer. It is in this layer that all matters of importance reside.

The goal of the educator, then, is to shift the content of the subject he teaches from the opportunistic (matter of fact) layer to the propriate. But there is no sure-fire, mechanical strategy to use. The best general rule, one that John Dewey saw clearly, is to strive ceaselessly

[1]If this definition seems too technical to be immediately helpful, see Ch. 10 of *Pattern and Growth in Personality* (2) for a more extended treatment of functional autonomy.

to integrate routine matters of fact into the growing experience system of the child himself. It would take a long treatise to specify various detailed strategies of teaching that help achieve this goal.

Let me focus on only one aspect of this topic, upon a common mistake that teachers make. I myself am a continual offender. It is to present students with our own carefully thought out conclusions when they themselves lack the raw experience from which these conclusions are fashioned.

This particular error is inherent, for example, in the lecture system. Instead of lecturing on comparative religion, for instance, it would be much better to require all students to attend services of worship that are unfamiliar to them. If raw experience is present, then perhaps a lecture may be effective. Much of the intellectual apathy we complain about is due to our fault of presenting conclusions in lieu of first-hand experience. To us, our well-chiseled conclusion, summing up a long intellectual struggle with a problem of knowledge or of value, seems like a beautiful sonnet. To the student, it may be gibberish.

The fallacy of giving conclusions holds both for subject matter and for values. A lad of 15 cannot profit from the fully fashioned philosophy of life of a man of 50. To register at all, a statement about values must fall precisely on his present growing edge.

Teaching, then, is not the art of offering conclusions, however hard won and valid they may be. No teacher can forcibly enter the students' proprium and plant a functionally autonomous motive. He can at best open channels of experience and, by his *obiter dicta,* sometimes lead the student to see the value-potential in the experience.

The theory of personality that we need to guide a more fully developed educational psychology will teach us something important about our basic verb "to educate." It will show us that only at the outset of learning is it a transitive verb. By drill, by reward, by reinforcement, the teacher does indeed educate the child—in matters of fact. But true maturity comes only when the verb is reflexive. For in matters of importance, where values lie, the growing individual alone can educate himself.

References

1. Allport, G., *Becoming.* New Haven: Yale Univer. Press, 1955.
2. Allport, G., *Pattern and Growth in Personality.* New York: Holt, Rinehart, & Winston, 1961.
3. Gillespie, J., & Allport, G. *Youth's Outlook on the Future.* New York: Random House, 1955.
4. Goodman, P., *Growing Up Absurd.* New York: Random House, 1960.
5. Jacob, P., *Changing Values in College.* New York: Harper, 1957.

Physical Changes During Adolescence

Gerald D. Winter

St. John's University

The physical changes that signal the onset of puberty are universal. However, so much time is devoted to the psychodynamics of adolescence that we tend to overlook the importance of the physiological aspects of this stage of development—perhaps because of a lack of understanding of the physical dimensions of human growth. If this is not so, why are such important changes relegated to an overlooked position?

Students of adolescence often become so involved in psychodynamics that they tend to overlook or relegate to less importance the physical changes of that period of life. This tendency is unfortunate in that physical factors of human development are inseparably interrelated with those of the psychological and sociological; physical changes preceeding and accompanying adolescence play a major role in precipitating behavioral changes and difficulties of adjustment.

The following is a list and brief description of the major physical changes in body systems that one must consider when studying adolescence. How these occur in the life of each individual will determine, to a great extent, the character of his "adolescenthood."

Digestive System

The organs of the digestive system undergo considerable growth during adolescence. The stomach increases in size and capacity, accounting, in part, for the marked increase in appetite during this period. In order to maintain normal metabolism the adolescent's protein requirement is three times that of the adult. Because of increased capacity and nutritional needs, digestive upsets are the rule rather than the exception for the teen-ager. He is not usually known for his consumption of a balanced diet, and his stomach is often overloaded with a conglomeration of food that would run down adults with so-called "iron constitutions."

Respiratory System

The lungs, which have grown slowly during childhood, undergo rapid growth during puberty, particularly in boys. The lungs of girls, compared to boys during this period, tend to be smaller because of their relative inactivity. The lungs of an adolescent have the elastic capacity of an adult although they have not yet reached adult volume. They tend to develop in size according to the demand made of them. Abnormal development of the lungs is unusual unless they are affected by disease.

Cardiovascular System

During adolescence, the heart increases in size and muscle mass or thickness. It pumps a larger volume of blood with an increase in stroke volume. The systolic blood pressure rises and the pulse rate slows in proportion to the rise in pressure. The pulse rate of a girl is generally 10 beats per minute faster than that of a boy; her pressure is approximately 10 points lower.

Nervous System

In gross size, the nervous system develops very little during adolescence. It is probable that the complexity of the brain is greatly increased early in this period, including a marked increase in length, thickness, and expanded contacts of the fibers.

Glandular System

Skin Glands

There are three types of skin glands: the *apocrine sweat glands*, which are located in the armpits and the mammary, genital, and anal regions; the *merocrine glands*, which are located over most of the skin area of the body; and the *sebaceous glands*, which are the oil-producing glands of the skin.

The *apocrine* and *merocrine* glands become active early in adolescence. Their secretion has a definite odor and is one of the main causes of body odor. The menstrual cycle causes an increased secretion from the *apocrine* glands. The *sebaceous* glands increase in size during adolescence and are a major source of skin trouble in teen-agers. Though the size of the gland increases the duct does not increase proportionately, with the result that it may become clogged with dried oil, exposure of which to air turns the residue black, causing "blackheads." The glands continue to function, though blocked, causing pimples and irritations on the surface of the skin. Although it has been suggested that a balanced diet is important in the control of "acne," other factors in development are of equal importance. The best medication for the control of acne is soap and water applied often during the day.

Ductless Glands

1. The *pituitary* gland is located at the base of the brain and controls growth. It sets off physical changes in adolescence and helps to stimu-

late growth of some secondary sex characteristics as well as male gonad development. Overactivity of the pituitary gland from birth will cause giantism; underactivity from birth will cause dwarfism.

2. The *pineal* gland is also located at the base of the brain and contributes to general growth, but there is no direct connection between its function and emotional problems in adolescence.

3. The *thyroid* gland is located in the front of the throat and regulates metabolism. It is often a source of difficulty in adolescence. Underperformance of this gland will cause a low level of activity, as well as overweight, constipation, coarse and brittle nails, and tough skin. Overactivity of the thyroid will cause body functions to accelerate. Rapid pulse, overstimulated nerves, irritability, too rapid digestion, digestive upsets, overreactive emotions, and frequent fatigue are all signs of an overactive thyroid.

4. The *parathyroid* gland is located in front of the throat and controls the level of calcium in the blood and the body, which is vital for skeletal development. It has an effect also on the sustaining of nerves and blood clotting.

5. The *thymus* gland is located in the chest and contributes to general growth, but there is no direct connection between its function and emotional problems in adolescence.

6. The *adrenal* glands are located in the abdomen. They affect the development of secondary sex characteristics in males and stimulate the body for action during periods of emotional stress and anxiety.

7. The *pancreas* is located in the abdomen and contributes to general growth, but there is no direct connection between its function and emotional problems in adolescence.

8. The *ovaries*, among the female sex organs, produce eggs for fertilization. They grow from 10% of their normal adult size prior to puberty to full weight at approximately age twenty-one.

9. The *testes*, among the male sex organs, produce sperm for fertilization of ovum. They grow from 3% of their normal adult weight prior to puberty to full weight at approximately age twenty-two.

Skeletal System

The bones of the body grow in length, thickness, and width during childhood, but the characteristic development during adolescence is the lengthening of all the long bones and ossification of cartilage. The degree of skeletal ossification is the best indicator of physical development. Often an X ray of the hand and wrist are used to ascertain degree of development and maturation.

A person has 27 or 28 of his 32 teeth at age 13. The second molars erupt at the onset of puberty and the third molars (wisdom teeth) generally make appearance after age 17. The cutting of molars is generally painful and is often characterized by general bodily upset and emotional disturbances. The eruption of the second molars is taken as a definite sign of the advent of puberty.

Muscle System

The development of the muscles of the body is closely related to the degree of sexual maturity. Rate of growth of muscles in boys is related to the functional status of the testes since the secretion of the testes stimulates muscle growth. Growth of muscles in girls is less and slower than with boys. This occurs, primarily, because girls exercise less than do boys and because muscle development in girls is not directly related to the production of secondary sex characteristics as it is with boys.

Reproductive System

The *uterus*, the female sex organ, is 45% of adult size at birth. It immediately shrinks and doesn't recover birth size until age five. It grows slowly during childhood, rapidly increases in size during adolescence, and reaches adult size and weight at approximately age twenty. The *penis*, the male organ of copulation, grows rapidly during the first four years of life and then slowly until puberty. Rapid growth begins again with the onset of puberty and continues until the penis reaches adult size at approximately age twenty-one. The maturing of the sex organs and glands is the most important development during the stage of adolescence.

Changes During Adolescence by Sex

Girls	*Boys*
Growth of pubic hair	Growth of pubic hair
Growth of hair under arms	Growth of hair under arms
Light growth of hair on face	Heavy growth of hair on face
Light growth of hair on body	Heavy growth of hair on body
Slight growth of larynx	Considerable growth of larynx
Moderate lowering of voice	Considerable lowering of voice
Eruption of second molars	Eruption of second molars
Slight thickening of muscles	Considerable thickening of muscles
Widening of hips	Widening of shoulders
Increase in perspiration	Increase in perspiration
Development of breasts	Slight temporary development of breasts around nipples
No change in hairline	Receding hairline at temples
Menstual cycle	Involuntary ejaculations
No change in neck size	Enlargement of neck
Growth of ovaries and uterus	Growth of penis and testicles

Discussion Questions for Chapter 1

1. What is your position with regard to the general need for the study of adolescence? Is the period called adolescence functionally distinct from childhood and adulthood?
2. Is the psychology of the female considered different from that of the male? If so, does this reflect yet another aspect of our society's double standard for sexual behavior?
3. If values are caught rather than taught, what does this suggest to the teacher? the counselor? the parent?
4. What is adolescence? Is it a mystique or is it another adult defense against youth? Who are the victims of adolescence—the adolescents or the adults?
5. How do you account for the apparent differences in point of view with regard to the nature of adolescence as described in this section?
6. Why is there a tendency to de-emphasize the importance of the physical aspects of puberty in favor of the sociological and psychological?

Chapter 2
Sex: The Adolescent's Personal Dilemma

Sex—a basic fact of human life, yet perhaps the most difficult of all subjects to discuss.

In America today, attitudes toward sex range from deep concern over alleged "excessive" sexual freedom to the view that sex is fun and should be enjoyed by *everyone* capable of performing. At one pole we have the "Let's Eliminate the Devil Sex" group, at the other extreme the "Let's Have Fun with Sex" set.

Perhaps most young people take a less radical position; however, many persons, young and not-so-young, admit to confusion and uncertainty when asked to describe what they consider appropriate sexual behavior.

Sex is a dilemma for the American adolescent primarily because human biology and human culture are incongruent. Neither recognizes the sovereignity of the other. What the body desires, society does not permit or at least will not condone.

Concern and confusion in sexual beliefs and behaviors tend to inhibit and distort our thinking about the implications of sexual practices. For example, with regard to illicit sex, taboo is but one important consideration. Venereal disease, premarital pregnancies, and illegitimacy are problems that need, and seldom receive, society's best thought and effort.

In this section, the authors explore and interpret the current sex scene in America. They suggest a new approach to the morality debate, and they offer concrete solutions to sex problems. One article describes a rather dismal picture of venereal disease on the rampage in adolescent America.

The apparent inability of a modern society to offer physically and psychologically healthy modes of sexual behavior for its young is altogether disturbing. It is embarrassing to note that most "primitive" societies did better. However, through improved communication, education, and awareness, perhaps the present generation will have greater success in this regard than did those which have preceeded it.

The New Morality

Esther Lloyd-Jones

Is adolescent society in a state of moral anarchy, or is it simply confused —or both? Do scientific data suggest that there is, indeed, moral rebellion among adolescents? Or is the adult view of adolescent immorality motivated by hypocrisy, jealousy, and/or fear?

The author presents her observations on these questions and offers possible causes of moral confusion in modern culture. How would you characterize her theories of dealing with moral confusion, and what concrete means of implementing them might you suggest?

Thoughtful people all over the world are deeply concerned today with morality and our lack of it. This is by no means the first time, of course, that the human condition has been viewed with alarm. One can always find some in any age in every part of the world who habitually wear their eyebrows lifted or their faces set in expressions of horror. Throughout history, however, there have been times when moral crises of a general and sweeping nature have prevailed; times when standards—not only specific standards, but standards and norms in general, orderliness and admiration of excellence—have been dangerously threatened and even temporarily lost. We are again, perhaps, being precipitated into one of those times.

Webster says, "Morals are characterized by excellence in what pertains to practice or conduct; springing from, or pertaining to, man's natural sense or reasoned judgment of what is right and proper." Morals deal with or are concerned with "establishing and disseminating principles of right or wrong in conduct or behavior." We may have lost in a very real and dangerous sense our concern for excellence, for establishing and disseminating principles of right or wrong in conduct or behavior.

Dean Samuel Miller of Harvard's Divinity School says we do not have any image today of moral excellence. At a World Conference of Educators called by the International Red Cross which I attended in August, delegates from every country were discussing our plight. Mr. Stephen Mossai, Maharaj of Trinidad and Tobago, said, "Young men all over the world are uncertain and vulnerable. They cannot see how to live life in view of multiple pressures." I would add that I think this is even more true of young women than it is of young men.

England is vigorously concerned about morality and spirit in that country. Writers—particularly since the Profumo affair last summer

Originally presented at the New York State Dean's and Guidance Counselor's Conference, November 3, 1963. Reprinted by permission of the author, retired Head of the Department of Guidance and Student Personnel Administration, Teachers College, Columbia University.

—have agreed that much in English life today suggests decadence and dissolution. "Popular morality," says psychologist G. M. Carstairs, "is now a wasteland, littered with the debris of broken conventions. Concepts such as honor, or even honesty, have an old-fashioned sound, but nothing has taken their place."

Many writers suggest that Britain may not be a moral wasteland, but rather a battleground in which a more realistic, less hypocritical generation is attempting to win legal and social recognition of the facts of everyday life.

With the loss of empire and the decline of the Church as an influence in society, Britons have tempered their old moral certitudes. Author James Morris fears that his compatriots are becoming "congenitally incapable of disregarding the opposite point of view, and are constantly groping toward some general synthesis of *everybody's* point of view on *everything.*

But the stir created by the Profumo case suggests to me that there is still a lot of power left in the "moral machinery" in Britain.

Bernard Hollowood, editor of *Punch*, said in a *New York Times Magazine* article, dated June 30, 1963, "Queen Victoria would not have been amused (by the Profumo affair) nor are we. The proof, surely, of Britain's underlying decency is that it *has* been deeply shocked and wounded by the Profumo revelations. The time to start worrying about a nation's decline and fall is when the public conscience has been anesthetized into apathy by repeated doses of scandal. One Profumo would not have inspired Gibbon."

On September 14, 1963, a report was issued in England of a document called the Marlow Declaration. This Marlow statement grew out of a meeting of church leaders, educators, industrialists, trade unionists, and civic leaders who, like an increasing number of Englishmen, seem to want to retrieve lost ideals and achieve a higher standard of behavior than has been apparent in Britain recently.

The central statement of the Marlow Declaration is that "The cardinal emphasis of the British way of life must be on individual responsibility, established on a framework of high moral values and integrity. This is the stuff of success and international respect." The Archbishop of Canterbury, Dr. Michael F. Ramsey, called the declaration the spontaneous upsurge "of a great desire to have something of a breakthrough in the moral situation." Dr. Ramsey said that industry is in special need of a new orientation, but he added that the need extends to the whole field of personal relationships. We need a breakthrough here in America, too.

Robert Oppenheimer says:

> I have been much concerned that in this world we have so largely lost the ability to talk with one another. In the great succession of deep discoveries we have become removed from one another in tradition, and in a certain measure even in language. We have had neither the time nor the skill nor the dedication to tell one another what we have learned, nor to listen, nor to welcome its enrichment of the common culture and the common understanding. Thus the public sector of our lives, what we have and hold in common, has suffered, as have the illumination of the arts, the deepening of

> justice and virtue, the ennobling of power and of our common discourse. We are less men for this. Our specialized traditions flourish; our private beauties thrive; but in those high undertakings where man derives strength and insight from the public excellence, we have been impoverished. We hunger for nobility; the rare words and acts that harmonize with simplicity and truth. In this I see some connection with the great unresolved public problems: survival, liberty, fraternity.

Harold Taylor complained in a recent issue of *Saturday Review* (May 18, 1963) that in our universities:

> The purpose of education is seldom conceived to be anything more than providing the academic materials by which the student can achieve a degree, with all its material rewards and possibilities. Faculty members take as their task the manufacture, refinement, and distribution of knowledge to those who come by the hundreds before them; rarely are the big questions of truth, justice, beauty, and human destiny raised. Philosophy, the love of wisdom and the pursuit of ultimate conviction, is put in a department of the university where information about systems of philosophy is dispensed at the rate of three credits per student.

Robert Oppenheimer blames our situation on the great succession of deep discoveries that have been made so recently. And one could make a good case for science as the cause of our moral crisis. Science has given us the computer—which threatens to deprive the individual of the opportunity to work and thus robs him of the one most important way of finding significance for his life. Science is automating the processes of production; some economists predict that in ten years we will be able to produce all life's material necessities without a single man on a production line. Without work and its discipline to teach us industry and how to stretch our abilities, without work to give us the satisfaction of coming closer and closer to excellence—what will life mean? How can man be shaped up into something strong and beautiful and worthwhile without the effort that work demands?

Science has given us the bomb with which we could easily kill three times all the people now on earth. Murder has taken on new dimensions.

Science has given us oral contraception which could seriously damage man's traditional sense of responsibility. Furthermore, if J. B. S. Haldane was right, the great experience of conception and birth could become matters of glass tubes and incubators in scientifically contrived laboratories.

At the World Conference of Educators in August, we talked of the many causes that we thought were contributing to moral confusion and even apathy: the dizzy acceleration of history; the pile-up of the generations, with many women grandmothers in their 30's, great grandmothers in their 50's, great, great grandmothers before they are 70; the explosions of population all over the world with, perhaps, a consequent cheapening of the value of each human life; the explosion of knowledge, without enough time and effort spent on evaluating the worth of the knowledge in terms of some carefully thought-out, ultimate criteria, the push into the worlds of the developing countries with their revolutions of rising expectations, and refusal to defer rewards; the greater and greater segregation of youth from adults—truncated age groups isolated together in larger and larger educational institutions; segmented families.

Certainly there is overwhelming evidence that we live in desperate times from a moral point of view, and we can understand many of the reasons why we are in this condition. The big problem is what to do about it.

I am convinced that in this country a very large measure of responsibility for doing something about it rests on student personnel, deans and counselors. While the young in every culture learn their basic social and moral attitudes and behavior in their families, still it is abundantly clear that a great many families confidently look to the schools and colleges to stamp in more firmly the basic values that they have tried to teach at home. Most parents want their children's schools and colleges to help their children to become strong, competent men and women. A problem we are struggling with at Teachers College this year in our special Institute program for counselors is just how far counselors in the school can and should go in attempting to mold, modify and change the aspirations, expectations, attitudes, value systems and behavior of the high school boys and girls in New York City with whom we are working who come from homes that are culturally and socially "different" and/or deprived. We recognize our obligation to work closely with the parents of these children, and this we are attempting to do insofar as possible, but just how far are we justified in attempting to implant new values in these youngsters? How firmly are we, perhaps, obligated to attempt to do so? If deans and counselors are to fulfill their responsibilities in this time they are going to have to face up squarely to some serious inconsistencies in their present professional stance. For at least 20 years it has been not merely acceptable but almost compulsory for counselors to be accepting, nonjudgmental and nonmoralistic in their relationships with students whom school counselors have misleadingly and incorrectly called their "clients." This position has been beautifully rationalized by phenomenological psychology, which has powerfully influenced the guidance-personnel field. The very title of "dean" has been derogated and abolished in countless places because it was tarred with suggestion of firmness instead of permissiveness, discipline instead of acceptance.

Now, as we begin to perceive again the need there is in schools and colleges for wise and skillful valuational leadership, deans and counselors, it seems to me, must face up squarely, not only to the need, but also to the fact that they are the ones to supply this need. After all, the pose of valuational neutrality and incompetency is only 20 years old. Back of that there lies a long and noble tradition.

The historian, Arnold Toynbee, warns us that "It is getting more difficult in our highly organized society for the individual conscience to break through," but, as I know this professional group, I have every confidence they can and will accomplish it. I am especially confident because I see our professional field turning away from phenomenological psychology that says, in effect, that choice and decision are mirages, that man is the victim of the forces of his social field, to an existential philosophy as expounded by Rollo May and Adrian Van Kamm that holds that man is both free and responsible. Values and decisions are central in the philosophy of the existentialists. In his *Systematic Theology* of 1951, Paul Tillich defines responsibility and ties it to the freedom of self.

> Freedom is experienced as deliberation, decision, and responsibility. The etymology of each of these words is revealing. Deliberation points to an act of weighing (librare) arguments and motives. The person who does the weighing is above the motives; as long as he weighs them, he is not identical with any of the motives but is free from all of them. To say that the stronger motive always prevails, is an empty tautology, since the test by which a motive is proved stronger is simply that it prevails. The self-centered person does the weighing and reacts as a whole through his personal center, to the struggle of the motives. This reaction is called "decision." The word "decision," like the word "incision," involves the image of cutting. A decision cuts off possibilities, and these were real possibilities; otherwise no cutting would have been necessary. The person who does the "cutting" or the "excluding" must be beyond what he cuts off or excludes. His personal center has possibilities, but it is not identical with any of them. The word "responsibility" points to the obligation of the person who has freedom to respond if he is questioned about his decisions. He cannot ask anyone else to answer for him. He alone must respond, for his acts are determined neither by something outside him nor any part of him but by the centered totality of his being. Each of us is responsible for what has happened through the center of his self, the seat and organ of his freedom.[1]

For some time I have been concerned with what I perceive as an unwillingness and failure on the part of deans and counselors to undertake valuational leadership. We have dealt with problems *ex post facto*, but have done little to keep the problems from happening. We recognize it as our duty to try to help unmarried, pregnant girls and putative fathers, for example, but, like the man who continued to fish drowned bodies out of the river, we never go upstream to find out where and why they are falling in.

Concerned with this problem, I began, over a year ago, to plan a Work Conference on Current Sex Mores, co-sponsored by the National Association of Women Deans and Counselors. It was held this past August.

The American Guidance and Personnel Association and the National Association of Student Personnel Administrators, who also were invited to co-sponsor this conference, said it was probably something that very much needed to be done, to let them know what happened, but that they preferred not to co-sponsor.

The Work Conference enrolled 35 men and women deans and counselors from Alaska, Oregon, California, Utah, Mississippi, Florida, Maine and points in between, as well as a young Catholic priest who is counselor to students at a university in Chile. We had 14 lecturers and

---

[1]Paul Tillich, *Systematic Theology*. Chicago, Illinois: University of Chicago Press, 1951, Vol. 1, p. 184.

consultants many of whom came a day or more before their day on the stage and came back for one or more days afterward. A young man and a young woman student participated in the group. Everyone who attended the conference seemed to think it a worthwhile undertaking and a good use of two precious summer weeks.

The reason that made me determine to hold that conference was the repeated statement by deans and counselors—as well as by parents—that the kids were certainly confused in the area of sex mores, but that they thought they were just as confused as the kids. They just plain felt they did not know. They were clearly in no position to give valuational leadership.

I cannot begin to tell you of all the excellent thinking that was contributed to that conference, but I do want to tell you of one formulation of value systems that I thought especially valuable.

Dr. Isadore Rubin, who has a comprehensive and critical grasp of the literature in the area of sex mores, categorized for us the six value systems he has identified in the vast literature he has examined. I think every one of us at the Work Conference could see the value that it would be to young people, as they struggle with one of their most important developmental tasks, if they could have the skillful help of their dean or counselor in fashioning a framework for thought and decision for this critical area of their lives. These are the six value systems which Rubin says now exist side by side in what is clearly a transitional period in morality. These are the value systems which contend for supremacy in the minds of high school and college students today.

1). "Traditional repressive asceticism," which maintains that sex is essentially bad and shameful, but, unfortunately, necessary. All of us are familiar with this value system—through reading nineteenth-century literature, if not in contemporary life. Most people today in our culture pass this value system by with what they consider appropriate sneers.

2). "Enlightened asceticism" holds that society has always had to maintain a delicate balance between freedom and responsibility. David Mace is one who sets forth this value system coherently. He believes that the selfish pursuit of pleasure based on the exploitation of others is not an *inevitable* consequence of increased sexual opportunity, but that the possibilities to exploit others certainly becomes greater as sexual opportunities are eased and increased. Mace also believes that the thesis that all great civilizations have ultimately gone into decline following the slackening of the sexual code "may have more substance than our contemporary mood is ready to admit." Mace has been an ardent exponent of the need for stating and weighing the issues involved in the various systems of human relations; he speaks emphatically of the need for an open forum. Mace does not hold sex to be shameful or bad, but he does believe it to entail serious responsibilities, both for persons and for society, which cannot be tossed off lightly.

3). "Humanistic liberalism" is the name that has been given to a system of values that is being developed by the Society of Friends in England, and, also, in this country, outstandingly, by Lester Kirkendall. Dr. Kirkendall believes that the negative fear approach of ensuring moral conditions in the area of sex has rapidly lost its power and is destined to weaken still more. What is needed is a positive approach concerned, broadly speaking, with the fulfillment of human potentialities, one which can rest upon a liberal philosophy of human relations. He believes that a sexual morality geared to the use of reproduction alone cannot and should not stand. "Whenever a decision or choice is to be made concerning behavior, the moral decision will be the one which works toward the creation of trust, confidence and integrity in relationships. It should increase the capacity of individuals to cooperate and enhance the sense of self-respect in the individual." Kirkendall is searching for a value system that will help supply individual internalized controls which will stabilize family life and promote personal fulfillment even in the midst of conflict and change.

4). "Humanistic radicalism" is represented by the views of Dr. Walter R. Stokes, and probably by Morton Hunt. Stokes accepts the humanistic position of Kirkendall, but goes further in proposing that society should incline in the direction of making it possible for children to have biologically a completely natural sex life, and should steer away from the doctrine which many in the professional fields have upheld that we should teach that "sex is beautiful, etc., . . . but don't dare go near the water before marriage."

5). "Fun morality" has as its most consistent spokeman Albert Ellis. Ellis strongly, consistently, and without compromise upholds the viewpoint that "sex is fun" and the more sex fun a human being has, the better and psychologically sounder he or she is likely to be. Sex misdeeds, he holds, are only truly immoral or iniquitous when they involve one individual's deliberately and needlessly harming another individual.

6). "Sexual anarchy" has as its philosopher the French jurist Rene Guyon. Guyon bases his argument on the "legitimacy of sexual acts." He upholds the desirability of a variety of sexual experience, attacking chastity, virginity and monogamy. He calls for the suppression of all anti-sexual taboos, advocating complete sexual freedom and the disappearance of the notions of sexual immorality and shame. He holds that the only restriction that should be applied is the general social principle that no one may injure or do violence to his fellows. His thinking is based upon the Freudian notion that sex repression creates neuroses, that any sublimation of the sex impulse is impossible, and that, therefore, all repression is harmful and should be done away with.

All six of these systems compete to control the minds and behavior, not only of adolescents, but of all of us today. The following accorded to each of these systems differs by area of the country, socioeconomic status, religious beliefs, and probably by other factors which have not been reliably established. All of them are found in many situations today, existing in a veritable mishmash of contending, confusing beliefs and behaviors.

It is my view that it is as appropriate for guidance-personnel workers to give valuational leadership by helping young people and their parents achieve an intellectual understanding of these value systems of sex behavior as it is for guidance-personnel workers to help young

by social safeguards which made violations difficult. These safeguards were supplied by the nature of the culture itself. At the turn of the century methods of transportation were slow, and so young people were easily kept under the surveillance of their elders. The negative consequences of violating conventional patterns bore down upon the individual and his family with real force. Chaperonage was an acceptable practice. Sexual matters were very seldom discussed, and the controls of the super-ego were strong enough that while even then a choice was available, it never occurred to many young people that it was possible for them to make it. If the conventional standards were disregarded it seemed less a choice than it did a violation.

One by one the safeguards which supported chastity have been withdrawn or knocked into a cocked hat. The possible dangers of disregarding traditional standards have lost much of their threat. The frequency with which nonmarital pregnancies occur simply highlights the fact that they are not feared. Beyond that, young people know that practically foolproof contraceptives are available, and many of them think that they know how to use them. Quick available transportation enables most young people to be free from adult supervision and attain anonymity in a matter of minutes.

Chaperones in the 1960's are found only behind potted palms. Sexual matters and techniques of intercourse, even seduction, are discussed in the media of public communication and the entire spectrum of views and attitudes are available for all to read.

Young people are provided the circumstances in which sexual experimentation and experience may easily occur, yet their elders act as though things are as they were sixty years ago. We are reminded of the anecdote donated by a boy in one of the college conferences on sexual morality in which we participated recently. He was attending a school in which men and women were permitted limited visitation privileges in each others' dormitory rooms. The issue had been raised as to whether the visitation rules should be liberalized. The echoes of the debate had drifted back to this boy's parents who became quite exercised about the situation. Their strictures against the university and the youth who attended it were frequent and biting. One day in the midst of a warm exchange one of his parents made the assertion that no university should be in the business of providing students with bedrooms to use for sexual purposes. This was too much for the son who retorted, "Well, what do you think you did for me when you gave me an Impala for my high school graduation?"

If we are going to provide them with "Impalas" (of various kinds), we need to be realistic about the choices that go with them! Yet we still find it comfortable to pretend that these conditions do not exist.

Second, the approach to considerations of moral decision-making must be both rational and affirming (7). By rational, we mean an approach which is based upon reason. These reasons ought to go beyond the physical and the material realm, for human beings have an emotional nature and need love and a sense of belonging. But we are past the time when this can be handled in a purely metaphysical way. Neither can patterns be imposed by fiat. We have a society nurtured on scientific inquiry, we have been taught to ask for evidence, and young people have learned their lesson well.

In a group of college young people with whom we were working recently, this point stood out. The issue under discussion was the possible consequences of premarital intercourse and the youth were pressing for specific answers. At first some of the older persons in the discussion took the position that on the matter of premarital intercourse no answer was needed. "Isn't it enough just to say no?"

Anyone who has worked with young people knows that this isn't enough, and it wasn't in this case. Finally under further pressure one of the adults said, "Well, it corrodes the inner psyche."

The laughter which arose indicated the extent to which this answer was regarded as unacceptable. The speaker was well aware of the rejection with which her comment had been greeted. Yet this was unfortunate, for there is no question but that sometimes premarital intercourse (as well as some marital intercourse) does "corrode the inner psyche." The speaker's failure lay either in her inability to speak freely about sex, or in her incapacity to explain objectively and logically what the nature of the corrosion was and why the result was "corrosion."

By "affirming" we mean an approach to sex education which accepts the fact that sex can contribute to full and satisfying living as well as detract from it. Unfortunately we are hardly ready to discuss the former possibility; our concentration has been on the detracting features.

We have been impressed, from time to time, with the extent to which our teaching about the nature of sex and its use in relationships has the same overtones as our teaching about disease. We are preoccupied with the dangers of both, with ways of immunizing against them and with other avoidance techniques, and with detailed discussions of the threats they pose. Teaching in this negative context, we speak of both sex and disease with conviction and in detail; teaching in the positive context we have generally spoken of the positive meanings of sexual expression as we have good health, in very general, non-explicit terms.

We do, of course, find very positive but highly generalized statements about the positive place of sex in relationships, marriage, and the family. For example, we find Bertocci and Millard (8) saying, "What requires special note at the human level is that there is room for much experimentation and learning and therefore for much artistry in the expression of the sexual urge."

But we are mute when it comes to spelling this out in any way. In fact what probably happens is that children and youth are dealt with in such a way that by the time they reach marriage they will have much difficulty in attaining and practicing the "artistry" of which Bertocci and Millard speak.

The major objective of sex education then would seem to be to provide everyone, whatever his age level, with the knowledge and insights needed for successful decision making and responsible management of the sexual impulse. The educational concern would be the *integration of sex into a balanced and purposeful pattern of living*, rather than denying its existence on the one hand or making it the crux of all meaning on the other. All this is easily said but its accomplishment is obviously quite an order! What is "successful" decision making? By what criteria shall judgments be made? What is "responsible" management? What is "integration" and how is it achieved? And who among the teachers of youth sees sex in this context?

This kind of an objective obviously implies a value framework of some sort. It also implies enough knowledge of sex and its subtleties that one can be explicit and speak in detail about some of the ways in which it can and does work out given certain circumstances. This implies the need for much more research than has been done, and for much more freedom to discuss sexual matters than we presently have.

It also suggests a different group than we are prone to think of as the target for sex education. What is needed is sex education for adults! It is adults, much more than adolescents, who should be the recipients of sex education efforts in our culture. Both groups need it, but adolescents by their inhibitions and their neuroticisms are not blocking the efforts of adults to obtain it. The converse cannot be said. Actually, compared to adults, adolescents are pretty well off.

If this position is accepted the issues in sex education need to be approached from many sides. Usually when sex education for adults is mentioned, we envision adults obtaining information to pass along to children or youth. Let me say emphatically that we have much more than this in mind! We would like briefly to identify several reasons for the importance of sex education for adults. They need it

1. *For their own feeling of self-confidence, sense of well-being, and personal adjustment.* There is an erroneous assumption in our society that married adults through their experience in marriage naturally have acquired a great deal of knowledge about sex and the role it plays in life. Unfortunately this is not true. While lack of sexual adjustment is not considered to be the primary reason for divorce it is recognized that problems of frigidity, impotence, and other sexual maladjustments in marriage are frequently related to the lack of a proper foundation in sex education. The flood of letters from married and unmarried adults to the newspaper and magazine columns, the continued popularity of self-help books on sexual adjustment, the increasing number of sex education classes for adults support the contention that adults need and want help in integrating sex into their lives.

Neither can sex education for adults be accomplished in one session any more than it can be completed at one time for youth. It is a continuing process through each stage of life. At the adult level it will have to be self-education very largely. What is most needed is the feeling on the part of adults that it is respectable to pursue it.

2. *So that they may be effective in the sex education of children and adolescents.* When adolescents have been asked to describe the kind of person whom they felt could best provide them sex information their answers reveal that they are quick to perceive the inadequate knowledge of adults, and more important—they sense the adults' basic fear of sex. Adults with unresolved sexual problems lack the objectivity necessary to avoid saddling youth with their own fears and emotional reactions. Lack of understanding about the nature of the sexual impulse as a crea-

tive force in life not only makes it an embarrassing experience for adults to provide reproductive information but prevents them from being the kind of role model young people can emulate. Poorly informed and basically fearful of sex, adults have pulled sex out of context (9) and gotten themselves into a morass of contradictions (10) which makes most of them highly inefficient and ineffectual as sex educators. Their restrictive attitude toward sex makes it difficult for them to help young people deal with handling their normal sexual feelings; they are even likely to panic when facing the more difficult issues of child molestation, homosexuality, or other deviations. Until these difficulties can be overcome it is foolish to expect adults, whether parents, teachers, religious or medical workers to do anything effective as sex educators for children or youth.

3. *In order to work cooperatively in improving the societal attitude toward sex.* Observers from outside our culture (11) have commented on our American preoccupation with sex and our inability to deal realistically with social issues pertaining to sex. Our mass media testify to our society's neurotic compulsion toward erotic stimulation (12). Our so-called "openness" is not a healthy acceptance of sex and its place in social context, but merely a continual titillation of the mental erogenous zones. Only an informed, emotionally mature citizenry can change the punitive and antiquated sex laws of the land or decide how to disseminate the knowledge and devices which enable us to make reproduction a voluntary matter. It will take intelligent adults to develop educational programs for the school which will go beyond reproduction information and assist and support an educational approach which has as its central objective integration—and "artistry"—rather than merely repression. We need creative thought from our clergy about the church's position and teachings so that sex may be understood as a positive force rather than as an evil and danger which must be denied or suppressed. A revolution in the way adults think about sex is necessary if we are to change our image as a sex-saturated society.

4. *To improve their understanding of the moral issues facing us.* Advances in science and medicine have made it possible to reduce infant mortality, curb disease, regulate pregnancy, and extend the life span. Our technological revolution has changed the functions of marriage and the family, making the defining of sex roles much more difficult (13). The swiftness of these changes has left most adults unprepared to cope with their moral implications. There is an emotional reaction rather than a reasoned consideration of issues such as birth control, legalized abortion, interracial marriage, and premarital expression of sexual feelings. Mature adults who can understand the basic moral issues we face and will continue to face in the years ahead are urgently needed.

Granted that adults are the prime target for sex education, how do we proceed? Adult education programs become very important. Some beginnings have been made in the form of classes for parents and other adults (14).

Institutions for higher education should also play a major role in this effort. We must educate those who will be in a position to teach and influence others, e.g. doctors, lawyers, educators, counselors, social workers, clergy. Sex education programs should enable these professional people to gain insight into their own attitudes and to deal more creatively and objectively with the problems and challenges of human sexuality they encounter. Professional people from whom youth and other adults have a right to expect help and guidance are all too often hobbled and hemmed in by the same fears and misconceptions which afflict the uneducated.

"Sex education" (you will note that this phrase has now been put in quotation marks) viewed in this context becomes education for effective living with an understanding of human sexuality as an integral, inseparable part. The creation of satisfying interpersonal relationships rather than simply the exercise of sex is the ultimate goal. Because of its narrow connotation we are nearer an accurate description of what is needed if we speak of "education concerning human sexuality" than when we say "sex education."

Education concerning human sexuality involves the whole population and the total life span. Its expression goes far beyond genital behavior to include roles and intersex expressions of love and affection. It becomes involved with public and social as well as personal and private matters.

No small task this—to provide the kind of education about human sexuality needed in our modern scientific, free-choice, pluralistic society.

References

1. Kirkendall, Lester A., *Sexual Education as Human Relations.* Sweet Springs, Mo.: Roxbury Press, 1950.
2. Radler, D. H., and Remmers, H. H., *The American Teen-Ager.* Indianapolis, Indiana: Bobbs-Merrill, 1957.
3. Ramsey, Glen V., "The Sex Information of Younger Boys," *The American Journal of Orthopsychiatry.* Vol. 13, No. 2, April 1943.
4. Ehrnamm, Winston, *Premarital Dating Behavior.* New York: Holt, 1959.
5. Deschin, Celia S., *Teenagers and Venereal Disease: A Sociological Study.* American Social Health Association, New York.
6. Calderwood, Deryck, "Differences in the Sex Questions of Adolescent Boys and Girls," *Marriage and Family Living.* November 1963, 25: 492-5.
7. Kirkendall, Lester A., *Premarital Intercourse and Interpersonal Relationships.* New York: Julian Press, 1961.
8. Bertocci, Peter, and Millard, Richard M., *Personality and the Good.* New York, David McKay, 1963.
9. Endore, Guy, "War, Yes! Sex, No!!" *Etc.* 21:389. December 1964.
10. Duvall, Evelyn, and Duvall, Sylvanus, *Sex Ways: In Fact and Faith.* New York: Association Press, 1961. Pp. 118ff.
11. Gorer, Geoffrey, *The American People* (Revised Edition). New York: Norton Company, 1964.
12. Ellis, Albert, *The American Sexual Tragedy.* New York: Lyle Stuart, 1962.
13. Kirkendall, Lester A., *Sex and Our Society.* New York: Public Affairs Pamphlets, 1964.
14. Johnson, Warren R., *Human Sex and Sex Education.* Lea and Febiger, 1963.

Problem in Teen-Age Sex Education

Francis L. Filas, S. J.

Loyola University

Father Filas, a Roman Catholic theologian, suggests that adults are not fully aware of the seriousness of the social disease problem in our society. He discusses disease prevention through education and believes that schools, including Catholic parochial schools, should be responsible for sex education. His critics imply that his proposals are unrealistic in view of traditional religious attitudes toward sex.

As these lines are being written, newspaper headlines and news commentators are stridently calling attention to an epidemic of spinal meningitis at Fort Ord, Calif.—some 85 cases within a year, and 14 deaths. The tragedy is that an epidemic unbelievably more extensive exists and is growing daily in our midst, and yet hardly a ripple of public attention has been stirred because of it. This is the hard fact of the social diseases: as estimated *minimum* 100,000 annual cases of syphilis, and a million cases of gonorrhea, 25 per cent of which are infections of teen-agers (i.e., from the seventh grade or 12 years up to 19). This statistic does not carry its full impact until it is translated into day-to-day figures. Daily, 2,800 new gonorrheal and 280 syphilitic infections occur at a minimum, of which 750 affect teen-agers *per day.* Deaths from syphilis in the United States total 4,000 per year—more than ten daily; and almost ten babies are born every day who have contracted syphilis—3,000 per year.

As a final show of statistics, the 66 per cent of American youth who learn about the social diseases from their peers on the street usually get a batch of half-truths loaded with biological superstition and gross error on the methods of transmitting venereal disease and the chances for its cure. In this mass of shadowy half-truths, little or nothing is conveyed about proper means of prevention. The only genuinely effective method of preventing an increased spread of syphilis and gonorrhea is to avoid sexual promiscuity. The gang-in-the-gutter likewise knows little about the second elementary truth of venereal disease education: If infection has certainly occurred or is even suspected, a physician should be consulted so that the disease will not spread to possibly innocent victims.

Reprinted with permission from *America,* The National Catholic Weekly Review, 106 W. 56 Street, New York, N.Y. 10019. Fr. Filas has made three LP records dealing with problems of family life: "Sex Education of Children for Parents," "The Battle of the Sexes—Can It Be Avoided?" and "Who's Boss? You or Your Children?"

A program of venereal disease education from the U. S. Department of Health, Education and Welfare has been worked out with consummate prudence for use in the schools. This program (embracing the two aspects of avoidance of sexual promiscuity and frank submission for treatment) is not truly a part of that sex education which ideally and theoretically should always be reserved in the first place for parents at home. Moreover, so many parents are themselves ignorant of the technical facts about venereal disease—as known in 1964 and not 1934—that the schools must do this job of spreading the proper attitudes and information on venereal disease. A final problem occurs with regard to the inhibitions of parents who shrink from mentioning venereal disease, in the mistaken notion that "such things don't happen to nice people." The facts are that they happen in the nicest neighborhoods.

One of the reasons that have militated in the past against an approval of venereal disease education in the schools is the belief that such education necessarily implies something crude, shocking, vulgar and disgusting; or that the approach is on a strictly utilitarian basis, implying that "getting caught" with venereal disease is the sanction of a pseudo-moral order. More than this, the misunderstanding frequently persisted that venereal disease education meant a ridiculing of the God-given respect due to sex, so that it degrades sex as such. Even against venereal disease education in a thoroughly acceptable form, as outlined above, certain arguments recur that in many areas hinder a school program from going into effect. It will interest Catholics—and, let us hope, Catholic critics of parochial schools—to know that education programs have been introduced much more easily and with far greater co-operation in the Catholic parochial schools than in certain public schools. In these latter, the school boards or school administrators have feared to bring up the subject and have mistakenly thought that "religion" was against the idea.

There are a number of typical objections offered against this sort of program. One of them goes somewhat as follows: "*It is disgraceful to admit that our students need this. It implies that the character training in our schools has failed.*" If this argument comes from an educator, it betrays a disgraceful selfishness and lack of interest in the welfare of the students. For the strongest way to combat venereal disease is to teach young people to avoid sexual promiscuity and hold up the moral ideal of a strict respect for sexual intercourse, so that the desire for it is satisfied exclusively within the bonds of marriage. The school must also realistically admit that its character training cannot be counted on to reach each individual student, just as the Church's moral training will to some extent inevitably fail. There is simply no argument against the fact of the widespread increase of venereal disease among teen-agers. And this certainly indicates that character training, first in the home and secondarily in the school, has failed. Why should a first and possibly relatively inculpable failure be compounded into culpability by a refusal to take necessary and irreproachable action?

A second objection is based on a complete caricature of the proper education: "*The inclusion of venereal disease education units in a general science or social science curriculum implies that there is no immorality in the use of sex outside marriage, and that the only norm is: 'Don't get caught; and if you get caught, treatment is so easy and certain that you can keep doing this again and again with impunity.'"* Here again, the opponent forgets that the best prevention of venereal disease consists in teaching the moral standards of the proper use of sex in marriage. The use of this education in other departments of the curriculum does not mean an invasion of the sphere of theology and moral religious training. Venereal disease education properly prescinds, abstracts from, any explicit moral and religious judgment; it does not, however, contradict these. And as for the treatment being certain, though penicillin treatment can cure, this is hardly an infallible remedy. Moreover, the temporary disappearance of primary lesions of syphilis can lull the ignorant teenager into thinking that all is well. He or she does not know that a killing, crippling or mentally debilitating germ is latent until a later flare-up indicates that irreversible organic damage has occured.

A further objection: *"This will call the attention of innocent students to what they should not know and what they do not need to know."* The only answer to such a statement is a flat denial. Any health problem involving so many thousands of teen-agers is something the American student should know about.

"Our parents and grandparents got along without this; why can't our children?" Yes, our parents and grandparents got along without this — but how? With what shame and heartaches and further unnecessary spread of disease in their own day, under the hush-hush atmosphere of an era when reliable cures did not exist. Moreover, the times have changed. If the incidence of venereal disease had been as critical in our parents' and grandparents' times, they, too, should have been given education about it in their schools with the same critical imperativeness with which it is justified today.

"There is too much talk about sex already in the air. The less of it the better. Besides, our children in seventh and eighth grade and early high school are too young to hear it." It is thoroughly correct that too much undigested and improperly presented raw information about sex is being circulated. Much of this comes from 1) an openly prurient press, which seems to be almost beyond control because of court decisions on the legal meaning of obscenity; 2) from the respectable press and radio and TV, which none the less at times inject their "respectable" snide comments and sexy emphasis for the sake of circulation rises and ratings — and this often in the name of what must be called, for want of a better name, pharisaical concern for public morality. A double standard on sex openly exists: on one page, an editorial decrying juvenile delinquency, and for the next ten magazine pages, the latest pictures about the hottest sex kitten. But it should be remembered that venereal disease statistics begin in the seventh and eighth grades and early high school. Hence the need to start the education early.

"The Church is against such mention of venereal disease and the means of stopping it." This objection is a puzzling one, since no reasonable basis exists for it either in biblical theology or in official Church teaching — to speak at least for Catholicism. Papal documents on Catholic atti-

tudes toward sex condemn "pansexualism" as a philosophy of attributing all human ills to a uniformly sexual cause. The Church might also be listed against any coeducation of the sexes where male and female are treated as completely identical human beings. They have, indeed, identical human dignity; but they do not have the same talents, needs, potentials and approaches. The Church is truly opposed to any implication that the body of any man or woman is a purely animal entity that must have its sense desires satisfied whether or not they conflict with one of the laws of the Creator. The Church is opposed to any implication that sexual intercourse or sexual pleasure is an absolute necessity for mental and physical well-being. But proper venereal disease education offends against none of these approaches, and either does not touch on them or implicitly supports them.

"Venereal disease is the punishment of God. Let the culprits suffer." In the present context, this objection is the most raw and uncharitable expression one can imagine. Jesus admitted no excuse when He said: "He who is without sin, let him cast the first stone." The love that God expects us to show toward our neighbor means at the minimum that we should not callously wish evil even on those who seem to have brought such evil on themselves. The biblical dictum "Mine is vengeance, says the Lord" does not mean that God is vengeful, but that only the Creator knows the innermost sanctum of human free will; only He knows, satisfactorily and adequately, how blameworthy or how innocent any man or woman or teen-ager is. Even if we were to admit as true so bigoted an interpretation as that venereal disease was the divine punishment for sin and that those who received it must stay with it, we would then be forgetting that venereal disease can also strike those who are completely innocent. How about the child of a syphilitic mother, infected from her? How about the subjectively innocent, namely, the teen-agers who have not been given adequate character education at home, and who have been led astray by bad companions or temporarily blinded by strong passions, which confuse them and which they do not fully know how to control?

The main objections against such a program of education in schools can thus be met. It becomes obvious, then, that the real educative process must begin with school administrators and, through them, teachers. For unless they are persuaded, the program will not succeed. It cannot be too strongly stressed, in this connection, that a reverential attitude toward sex must always be maintained. In this way it can be made clear that the lawful use of sex—according to conscience and religious teaching—is not wrong; what is being decried is the abuse of sex and the disastrous effects that follow from it.

Of all the objections to venereal disease education, the one that needs refuting more than any other concerns what it tells students about treatment. It is a popular misconception that the program describes the treatment as so certain, so infallible, that anyone can indulge in sexual promiscuity again and again with no risk through re-infection. Education about venereal disease may indeed seem to imply that prompt application for medical treatment makes re-infection harmless. But no such implication is contained in current literature from reputable agencies interested in this field, for as we have noted, cure is by no means certain. Public misunderstanding on the point, however, may be an obstacle to wider introduction of a program badly needed in our schools.

Incidental Sex Education

Gerald D. Winter

St. John's University

Sex education is not ordinarily recommended for the month-old infant. Yet, the author of this article suggests that sex education actually does begin during the neonatal stage of development. Moreover, very early learnings about one's body are believed to have strong and lasting effects on later ones, especially those about sex and sexuality. While sex education during early life may be primarily incidental, the position described herein suggests the need to give it more than incidental attention. It may be that what one learns about sex prior to six greatly influences his sexuality at sixteen.

"Should we teach sex in the school?" "Who can impart the proper values to our children?" It's the church's job!" "I don't want anyone teaching my children any of that dirty stuff!" "The school has no right to interfere!" "Let's get experts to teach about sex!"

Though parents and educators have the best of intentions, and PTA's get involved in the discussion, often the most important aspects of sex education are overlooked. We somehow concern ourselves with the intellectual aspects of formal education and miss the obvious patterns that are set by people. When we say that "values are caught, and not taught," we believe it, but we do not often associate this idea with our thoughts about sex. We probably learn more incidentally than we do intentionally. "Incidental" means that which we obtain just by being aware of what is about us. You do not intentionally set out to know the color of your classroom walls, but you learn simply by being there. Often our nonverbal communication imparts more than does our verbal activity. A look or a gesture can sometimes imply more than can be contained in a treatise on the subject. A good deal of sex education falls into the realms of nonverbal communication and incidental learning from the environment.

The interaction between parent and child can have many effects on the child's later functioning. This interaction may either hinder or facilitate later sexual behavior at each of the three psychosexual stages of development. The big question is how?

Our aims in giving sex education are rather obvious on an intellectual level, but our emotional concern here is usually so great, and often so conflicting, that our motivations become confused. Our intentions are to aid the child in adjusting to a marital partnership when he comes of age—a partnership including love as a major ingredient. But how do we learn to love? What is involved in this type of relationship? Why do we become so easily confused? Why do we have so many conflicts about a subject that should be so natural? These are questions that I will attempt to answer to a modest degree.

At all ages, persons communicate their love for each other with their bodies. Long before sex education is considered, we give the infant his first experience in learning to give and receive love. At this stage, the infant responds with his entire body to the satisfaction of being fondled and caressed. We teach him, very early, that there is satisfaction from being touched and handled. When a baby cries, we pick him up and cuddle him and give him a feeling of security. The feeling of gratification that the mother feels is imparted to the baby in this manner. This then becomes the first step in sex education. Studies have shown that the child who does not experience this at an early age has difficulty in learning to give and to accept love. We note that children within orphanages who are deprived of this type of satisfaction have particular difficulty in adapting to a love situation and that the divorce rate for them is considerably higher than for most others. Often a mother rejects a baby for any of various reasons and doesn't give him the sense of well-being that can be established by fondling. This, too, may lead to adjustment difficulties in a later marital setting. Self-esteem tends to be regulated by the supply of satisfaction that the infant receives from the external world; this is not imparted with rejection. Of course, there is always the other side of the coin, the mother who doesn't know when to stop. This produces similar types of difficulty in adjustment but in another manner. Here a child may develop who can receive but not give or give but not receive.

At the same time that we are imparting ideas about physical contact, we are also conditioning the child to satisfaction that comes from oral stimulation. We feed him and he feels comfortable and relaxes. We fondle him to produce the same results and often use the combination of both to bring more lasting satisfaction.

The next step in the child's incidental learning takes place during toilet training. By our methods of training and expressions of disgust, we readily impart our notions of the genital areas. What comes out of the body is "dirty." We speak of diapers as messy. We show displeasure with "accidents." The proximity of the sex organs and the organs of elimination adds to the confusion of the child. Most of us have said that the body "down there" is dirty if it is wet or even moist. Adolescent girls often become frightened by any vaginal discharge, which is common, particularly after the menstrual cycle commences; they have the fear that they have somehow become sick. We talk of germs and disease with the same connotation as that of dirt. How can a child relate the dirty areas with clean, wholesome living? We begin, here, to cause confusion in later adjustment to sex. We instill within the child the idea that everything below the belt is dirty and unhealthy. Though this thought often disappears from the conscious mind, the association remains. Many children visualize intercourse as "going to the toilet inside the girl." The sexual act becomes a "dirty" and a contaminating act. It becomes a shameful thing that is to be hidden. With this notion in mind, the child separates love and sex because he has been taught that love is clean and that sex is dirty. How can we establish healthy attitudes about sex when we do so good a job in the opposite direction with the genital areas? Now we can begin to see why there is such difficulty in sexual adjustment. As if this were not enough, we add further to the process of confusion.

Many parents show anxiety when they use a rectal thermometer because they are worried that the child may be ill. Though the anxiety is not from the insertion, the child can easily make this type of association. We also give enemas in the same area. Children commonly develop fear fantasies about injury to the anus, penis, or vagina since at an early age they cannot separate these areas—they are all closely associated. After all, if the parents are so anxious this must be a possibility.

Perhaps the greatest problems are the spankings. What types of associations does the child derive from these? "Below the belt" is not only dirty but also an area of punishment and hurt. When we are bad we are spanked, we are forgiven. One way of receiving affection from the parent is to be spanked in the dirty area then forgiven. The possibilities of fantasies from this are unlimited. One way to love is to get hurt. Carried to a pathological extreme, this could create masochistic modes of functioning; and carried to a neurotic extreme, one must fight with a mate to be accepted and forgiven. Often a "grown-up child" recreates his spanking in married life.

During the oedipal stage of development, the child becomes aware of the mother's and father's going to bed together. He knows from his own experience that body closeness feels good. This causes many ambivalent feelings, particularly when he is not invited to join them. At this point body contact becomes a mode of rejection to him and he often resents one or both of the parents. Emotional attachments are intense at this point, but proper handling of the child may override any problems that may arise from the feelings of rivalry that present themselves.

Many of the fantasies that children have about sex and reproduction are direct products of formal communication on the part of the adult, and this too becomes part of incidental learning because the end results do not coincide with our beginning intentions. Unfortunately, many of us, in our attempt to explain the impending arrival of a new infant to our children, add to the problem rather than detract from it. For example, most of us tend to say to the young child, "The baby grew inside mommy's tummy," without further explanation. From a child's point of view, how does anything get into a tummy?—through eating, of course. If we added just one more line, we could avoid much confusion: " . . . but not in mommy's eating tummy. There is a special tummy for growing babies." This can help the child bridge the gap that may resolve itself in fantasy. Children often view the birth process as a bursting of the stomach. How else does a baby get out? Often, if a child has eaten too much and is uncomfortable, he can visualize himself as bursting just as mommy will when the baby is born. An explanation that there is a special place for the baby to come out will often help this type of situation.

We also attempt to have a child accept or feel responsible for a new baby and not left out by saying, "This is your baby, and you will have to take care of it." This sets off the fantasy machine in double time. This seeming responsibility overwhelms the child and may cause more resentment than had been bargained for. Another example of this occurs when the father dies and the mother says, "Now you are the man of the house and must take care of your mother." Instead of easing a situation, a resentment builds up toward the father for leaving and giving the child a job that he can't handle. This resentment can often be generalized, and a child will have difficulties in other areas. In the case of the responsibility of caring for an infant, the child may associate unpleasantness with the birth process or the results of the birth process because of new demands placed on him with the addition of another child to the family.

As the child becomes older he becomes more aware of the sexual process; by the time he is eight, he usually has a good idea, though a bit confused, as to reproduction. A child is aware that sex takes place between parents, and he often envies the intimacy of the mother and father every night. He is too old to receive satisfaction from the cuddling he received as a child and too young for the mature relationships of an adult. This may cause all types of jealousy and resentment. Children have been reported to say, "You and daddy sure made a lot of noise last night." We have to realize that children hear many things and that often, when we think that they are asleep, they are not. We also need to recognize that children may build fantasies that lead to fear and resentment. Parents do have sexual relationships. This is part of love and marriage. If we can attempt to place this in proper perspective, perhaps we can envision and anticipate the types of fantasies that a child will experience with his own realizations.

If we were to look at all the problems that the adult world imposes on the child in his later adjustment to sex, we would probably stand in awe and wonder of how the child is able to adjust at all. Is it any wonder that in our society there is much difficulty in the making of adjustments to sex? The average child starts out with two strikes against him.

If we analyze the problems of association that may arise from the fantasies of children, we will realize that much remains to be accomplished in sex education in order for a program to be successful. Something must be done to separate the concept of dirt, on the one hand, from those of sex and love, on the other; these often remain interrelated long after the initial associations are produced. We must attempt also to visualize the types of childhood fantasies that may evolve from our gestures and other communications concerning sex and sexual relationships. It may seem that I am asking for "hindsight" in advance; maybe I am, but some change is not impossible. Values and ideas are caught as well as taught; and when we realize that this applies as much to sexual matters as to others, we will set the stage for better adjustment in sex by setting the example for it.

Some Thoughts on the Sexual Revolution

Paul Woodring

Western Washington State College

If one examines the laments of past generations, it would appear that America has been the scene of a continuous sexual revolution from at least as early as the beginning of the eighteenth century. The author discusses the causes for a relaxation of sexual standards, and he suggests that a new code of premarital behavior—"one that can be accepted by young people"—is needed. He recommends guidelines for a sexual code built upon the realities of today's world rather than upon traditions that no longer have either meaning or utility.

For as long as I can remember—and my memory for such things goes back into the Twenties—we have been hearing about something called a "sexual revolution." Undergraduates of the flapper era, who identified themselves with the "lost generation," dated the revolt from World War I. Students of the Thirties believed that it began with the Depression, which made marriage impossible for many young people, who consequently looked for other sexual outlets. Those of the Fifties thought the revolution was an aftermath of World War II and began when returning veterans encountered patriotic coeds. Today's undergraduates firmly believe that the revolt started about 1960, when they were in junior high, and that it is somehow related to both the threat of nuclear war and the invention of the Pill.

All these views reflect the innocence of youth, because neither sexual activity nor the discussion of it is as new as many students believe. In 1721, Harvard undergraduates formally debated the question:

Reprinted by permission of the author and of *Saturday Review*, January 20, 1968.

"Whether it be fornication to lye with one's sweetheart before marriage." It is unlikely that there has ever been a generation to whom sex was not a major interest or which did not include many individuals who violated the rules laid down for them by their elders. It might well be argued that the sexual revolt really began when Eve tempted Adam with the apple. It requires no great knowledge of history to know that the sexual mores are no more relaxed today than they have been at many times in man's long past, and that the loosening and tightening of the restrictions on sexual activity go in cycles of irregular length which are related to a wide variety of social forces and social changes.

The present trend toward a loosening of restraints dates roughly from the 1890s. It is not so much a revolution as a growing reaction against the restrictive sexual morality that has variously, and somewhat carelessly, been described as "Puritanical," "Victorian," or "middle-class." The trend was accelerated by the invention of the automobile, improvements in the techniques of birth control, the two world wars which took young men away from the restraining influences of their home communities, and the dislocation of families resulting from the move from farms and small towns to cities. Freer sexual activity was made to seem more necessary by the careless reading of Freud, and more normal—at least statistically—by the careful reading of Kinsey. It both gave rise to and fed upon the literature, motion pictures, and television programs of the twentieth century.

Early in this century, young people discovered that a date in a parked car could be something quite different from one in the front parlor with Mother hovering in the background. Those who first made this discovery, and who now are grandparents, are shocked to learn that students now have dates in dormitory rooms while the dean of women looks the other way. Perhaps the activities in either case do not differ greatly from those that took place on back porches or in lawn swings in the Nineties—research psychologists report that there are as many virgins among today's coeds in at least a few selected colleges as there were a generation ago. But most people are convinced that a larger proportion of today's adolescents now participate freely in what has always been the favorite sport of the human race.

Whatever the change in frequency or kind of activity—and no statistics on such a subject can be highly reliable—there has been a vast change in the kind of advice given to young people. A half-century ago, the books of intimate advice for boys and girls told readers that any sexual activity outside of marriage was sinful, and that premarital sex precluded the possibility of a happy marriage because no man respected a girl who allowed what then were called "liberties." Girls were told that anything more intimate than handholding aroused the baser passions in a man and could lead to no good end.

Some of the books read by teen-agers today still frown upon "heavy petting" and advise against premarital intercourse, but the reasons given usually are practical or psychological rather than ethical. Most of the authors agree that a modest degree of petting and fondling is a normal way of showing deep affection and that such preliminary activities are a necessary prelude to good marital adjustment. And every teen-ager has read at least one book by a psychiatrist, psychologist, or possibly a minister who sagely pontificates that, while caution is advisable and love is important, no activity involving two consenting adults is necessarily harmful or really sinful. Any reader who has reached the age of sixteen is certain that he is an adult and that the consent can be obtained—if necessary, with the aid of the book, which can be discussed on the next date.

Today's students, though they seem excessively eager to conform to the standard of the peer group if they can discover what it is, are not willing to accept an absolutist view of what is right and wrong. They have read enough history, anthropology, and literature to know that sexual morality differs from one culture to another and from one period to another within a culture. They have learned enough psychology to know that whether one will feel guilty about any kind of behavior depends on what he has been taught and what he has learned from his own experience. They know that pregnancy can now be prevented by anyone willing to plan ahead, and they have more confidence than may be justified in their ability to do the planning.

They are not inclined to accept the restrictions which adults attempt to place on their activities, because they are aware of a conspicuous gap between the publicly announced morality and the actual behavior of men and women. They know that many "respectable" adults—including, quite possibly, their own parents—have at times violated the conventions and seem to be none the worse for it. They are convinced that the older generation hypocritically gives lip service to a code in which it does not really believe and which it does not always follow. And they are contemptuous of hypocrisy.

The dilemma faced by young people is clear enough. Human males reach their period of greatest sexual vigor and desire at a time prior to marriage, when the doors to socially approved sexual activity are closed to them. But these doors, which have never been successfully locked and barred, have now been set aside by a more permissive society. The dilemma faced by girls, though different, is no less perplexing. Though some girls have strong sexual urges, more of them are motivated more by the desire to be popular with boys or by the desire to please one particular boy. They do not want to be thought old-fashioned, moralistic, or "square." When they ask their elders "What are the permissible limits?" the usual answer is, "It all depends." Consequently, they are not likely to conclude that all sexual activity must be avoided until marriage.

In the absence of an effective and accepted code, each boy and girl must decide for himself where to draw the line. This places an enormous strain on each individual because, as Richard Hettlinger reminds us in *Living with Sex: The Student's Dilemma*, "There is no field of human activity in which it is so easy to deceive oneself and to be convinced by arguments which are in fact nothing but rationalizations of clamant desires." A young man or woman needs all the advice he can get from older people whose desires presumably have cooled a bit and who can take a longer view. But, being young, he is not likely to take it.

A new code of sexual behavior—one that can be accepted by young people—clearly is needed. In our pluralistic society, a code that is to be effective must be acceptable to Catholics, Jews, and Protestants of many denominations, as well as to the agnostics and atheists who are found in substantial numbers on most campuses, because all these groups exchange dates. The fact that this seems a large order probably explains why a new morality has been so slow to emerge; but, unless it does, we are faced with the prospect of moral chaos, because the older sexual morality, based as it was on a combination of religion, tradition, and fear of pregnancy and disease, is no longer effective with the younger generation.

The new code must be consistent with the knowledge now available from psychology, sociology, anthropology, and biology. It must be based on a clear recognition of the fact that most of the educated and enlightened people living today, whether young or old, look upon sexual desire as biologically, socially, and psychologically normal rather than as something evil, dirty, and shameful. And it must reflect the fact that the double standard is no longer acceptable to educated people, nor is the view that desire to produce offspring is the only legitimate motivation for sexual activities.

Unless a new code emerges, we are likely to see a continued relaxation of standards, a growing contempt for the traditions and laws governing sexual activities, and still more confusion on the part of young people as to what is and is not acceptable and moral. If our culture takes a downward trend, historians and archaeologists of the future who examine the remnants probably will conclude that a decline of sexual morality was a major cause of the deterioration. But if our culture continues to survive and flourish despite a greater degree of sexual freedom, tomorrow's historians may call attention to the fact that sexual freedom has been a characteristic of many of the greatest periods of human achievement. And they will find many examples to cite.

The Vicious Chain

Fred Warshofsky

CBS News

Although the idea of a "Venereal Disease Investigator" may seem far-fetched or overly dramatized, the following article might lend to it some credibility. This fascinating account of fast-moving syphilis infection (and an even swifter investigating team) reads like a detective novel, but it is soberingly factual and real.

It was a small room, barely larger than a broom closet. The walls were a pale green, the only furniture a large, scarred desk, a pair of wooden chairs, and a metal filing cabinet. On the desk was a telephone directory for the city of Newark, New Jersey.

This is the interview room in the Newark Venereal Disease Clinic. The room and the rest of the clinic occupy the entire second story of a half-block-long building at 102 William Street on the western fringe of downtown Newark. It is a two-story building, built in 1929 to house a factory. During the depression it passed into the hands of the city, served briefly as a soup kitchen, and finally was assigned to the Health Department. Its depressing exterior remains unaltered, the red bricks have been blackened, but not softened by the weather. The building carries no sign of designation, simply the numerals, 102.

In the interview room, facing each other across the desk were a young man and a teen-ager. The man is Tim Lindman, a 27-year-old ex-football player from the University of New Hampshire. He has one of the most important public health jobs in the United States. Tim is a venereal disease investigator for the City of Newark Health Department. He and hundreds of other young investigators around the nation are trained for this job by the U. S. Public Health Service and then assigned to various state and city health departments. More precisely Tim might be called an epidemiologist, whose specialized, vital task it is to trace the chains of venereal infection from patient to patient until all contacts have been unearthed and treated. It is a tough, demanding job that leads a man to bars, plush apartments, split-level houses, street corners, brothels, and, alarmingly, schools and playgrounds. It is a job that requires dedication, training, and intelligence—a job Tim Lindman does well.

Facing him across the desk on the 28th of June, 1962, was a young-

Reprinted with permission of the author and the Reader's Digest Association from *Today's Health* (August 1963).

ster I shall call Victor. Victor was 16, just old enough under New Jersey law to drop out of high school. The fact was not lost on the boy —he had already begun a thus-far unsuccessful search for work. But that was not the reason for his presence in the VD clinic. A blood test had revealed the unequivocal presence of reagin in Victor's blood.

Reagin is an antibody manufactured by the body in response to an invasion of *Treponema pallidum*, the bacterial cause of syphilis. The high reagin content in Victor's blood and other signs indicated to the examining physician that the youth was firmly clutched in the scabrous embrace of secondary syphilis. He was immediately treated with an initial injection of 2.4 million units of penicillin and sent to Tim Lindman.

Lindman represents the most vital part of the nation's venereal disease program, the contact interview. Syphilis is a wildly infectious disease that is spread by sexual contact. Until Victor entered the clinic, he had been roaming the city, possibly infecting many of those with whom he had been able to establish intimate relations. It was Lindman's task to find every one of these people who had been infected by Victor and who were themselves now capable of spreading the disease.

The interview began in matter-of-fact fashion. The VD investigators do not sit in judgement; their job is simply to obtain the necessary information.

"Victor, the doctor tells me that you have syphilis." Lindman paused for an instant to let the weight of his words sink in. "Now you may know it as bad blood, lues, syph, or some other term, but its medical name is syphilis. It is a venereal disease, and that means virtually the only way a person can contract it is by sexual contact with an infected person."

At this, the youngster leaned forward to object, but Lindman waved him into silence. "The germ that causes the disease cannot live outside the human body for more than a few seconds. It is therefore impossible to catch the disease from a toilet seat or a dirty drinking glass."

Victor muttered something, as if a basic tenet of life had suddenly been shattered.

"Now, we've started you on a course of treatment and you will be cured, but what about the person you caught it from? And you may have given the disease to a lot of other people before coming here. That is what I would like to talk to you about now."

The boy squirmed nervously in his seat. "Well," he began hesitantly, "I don't think I remember."

"Let's try it and see. You can recall last Christmas, can't you?"

"Yeah."

"Well, since last Christmas, how many different girls have you had relations with?" Lindman's choice of Christmas as a starting point was deliberate. First, it was a convenient memory jog and second, it was almost exactly six months earlier, a critical period during which Victor was in a highly infectious stage of the disease.

"I don't know," said the boy angrily. "I told you before I couldn't remember."

"Come on now, Victor, surely you can take a guess at the number of girls you've been with since Christmas. Was it 10, 50?"

The youngster grinned. "No, it was more like five. Yeah, maybe four or five, around there."

"All right, let's talk about those five girls and see how they figure in your infection. Now, just so I'll know who you're talking about, let's just use their first names or nicknames."

"Their names? What do you want their names for? I thought we were talking about me?"

"We are, but I won't be able to keep them straight if you just say she or her all the time. Now, just give me their first names."

"Well, okay, but you won't tell them I told you?"

"No, your name won't be mentioned. This interview is confidential, but we must know the names of all the people with whom you had contact so that we can help them before the disease permanently damages their health and before they can spread it to others."

"Okay. The first was Lila. That was the day after Christmas. We were at a party and . . ."

The interview continued for another half hour. Before it was ended, Victor had supplied 10 names—girls between the ages of 12 and 17, with whom he had had sexual relations.

The information provided by the youngster led Tim Lindman on a trail that eventually uncovered 96 other teen-agers, in all parts of the city and as far away as South Carolina. Eighteen of the youngsters named had syphilis, and were it not for the quick action of Tim Lindman, countless others might have caught the dread disease. For syphilis respects neither social position nor race, religion, or national origin. It is by far the most democratic of diseases, requiring no more than the sex act to spread explosively through all levels of the population.

Due to its mode of transmission, syphilis has been a taboo subject in the American home since the days of the Puritans. As a result, few people even today know very much about the disease. Yet each year syphilis kills 4000 Americans and in 1962 infected a reported 20,000 others, plus 4000 babies who contracted the disease from their mothers during pregnancy.

In spite of the massive campaign to find and treat everyone who has the disease, experts such as Dr. Leona Baumgartner, former head of the New York City Department of Health, estimate that fully 50 per cent of all the syphilis cases in the country go unreported. Some experts go so far as to claim that as many as nine million Americans have syphilis or have had it at some time in their lives. Further, expert opinion suggests that possibly 1,200,000 people are now afflicted with untreated syphilis.

The problem is compounded by the fact that public knowledge of the disease and the means of its spread is in woefully short supply. Despite all we do know of the disease, few of the nation's schools offer courses in sex education or VD education and a shockingly small number of parents are equipped to provide their children with the information they must have. Louis P. Thorp, in his book, *The Psychology of Mental Health*, pointed out that in many homes "discussions relating to sex were strictly forbidden. . . . The child is made to feel that all matters concerning sex are improper and shameful."

This basic lack of knowledge coupled with the tensions of today's life, where sexual behavior is becoming more casual among many groups, creates a climate in which venereal disease can spread like a raging fire over the land.

Syphilis is caused by a delicate, spiral organism known as *Treponema pallidum.* Amazingly fragile, the microbe must have ideal conditions of warmth and moisture to survive. Since exposure to the environment outside the human body kills it within seconds, the microbe passes from one person to another only through the mucous surfaces of the genital tract or mouth, or through any break in the skin, no matter how miniscule. It cannot, however, pass through unbroken skin.

Once beneath the surface of the skin or mucous membranes, the syphilis-causing germs enter the lymph capillaries and are gently floated to the nearest lymph gland. Here they roost, multiplying and growing. Within a short time the microbes continue the journey, passing into the blood stream, which whirls them to every part of the body. Eventually, the pale, flexing microbe has burrowed deep into the marrow of the bones. The attack is swift and secret, for not one outward sign of the disease's course has been displayed.

Now, firmly entrenched, syphilis commences its malignant, extensive, and prolonged destruction of tissue, bone, and organ. Within 10 to 90 days, but usually about three weeks after infection, the first sign appears—a chancre, or sore, at the point of contact. It is a round, ulcerous lump, with sharp, raised edges, but is usually not painful. Generally this is the only sign of infection and a blood test at this point will probably not reveal the presence of the *Treponema.* Only a microscopic examination of the lesion will uncover the destructive microbe. This then is the primary stage of syphilis.

About nine weeks later, the disease enters its secondary stage. Lesions and rashes pit the body, and syphilis is now in its most infectious state. Fever and malaise often accompany the more obvious skin eruptions. The total effect is a number of symptoms that singly or collectively may often resemble any one of a dozen other diseases. Lesions around the mouth look like the result of a vitamin deficiency, fungus infection, or any other bacteria-sparked eruption. The skin of the victim may become dry or scaly, indicating a condition known as psoriasis. A red throat, swollen lymph glands, and over-all weakness may suggest mononucleosis. A victim may experience alopecia, falling hair, as huge patches pull out with every combing.

And again the signs of syphilis vanish of their own accord, but the disease lies hidden and enters the final two stages—latent and late syphilis.

Now only a blood test will reveal the presence of the devastating microbes and the disease may slumber quietly within its host for many years. Then, with little or no warning it launches a debilitating attack, perhaps on the nervous system, destroying the body's psychomotor functions. It may mount the spinal column and erode the reasoning centers of the brain, causing insanity, or it will attack the optic nerve, pitching its victims into blindness. The *Treponema* may invade the cardiovascular system, inflaming the walls of the heart or the coronary arteries.

Many times death is the end result, masking as any number of fatal degenerations, but which can unquestionably be traced to a syphilis infection acquired 20, 30, or more years before. In actual numbers, late syphilis commits one in 50 to insanity, kills one of 15 by heart attack, and blinds one in 200 of its victims.

Although syphilis is not hereditary, it can be passed by a mother through the placenta to her unborn baby. This form of the disease is known as congenital syphilis and the results are tragic—blindness, death, deformity are all possible. But even as late as the fifth month of pregnancy, congenital syphilis can be prevented if the mother-to-be is treated. The baby, if it lives, can also be cured after it is born. As is the case with syphilis in adults, however, the damage that has already been done to organs, tissue, and nerves can never be repaired.

The origins of syphilis have been the subject of more controversy than any other disease. Although Hippocrates in 460 B.C. described hard and soft genital lesions which followed sexual exposures, it was not until 1530 that both a specific remedy and the name by which we know the disease were suggested.

Now the hunt for the guilty microbe was underway. It proceeded amidst a welter of confusion for almost 400 years, with some of the world's top scientific minds insisting that syphilis was hereditary and that it was the same disease as gonorrhea.

With the isolation of the syphilis spirochete in 1905, developments followed each other more rapidly. In 1907, August von Wassermann developed a complex test that would detect the presence of syphilis in the blood. The Wassermann test has been refined, improved, and simplified over the years, but its importance as a diagnostic tool has never diminished.

Armed now with a sort of medical radar, the researchers turned their efforts toward development of a weapon that would cure the disease. For 400 years, only one remedy had been used that was thought effective—mercury. The treatment was a highly volatile one, sweeping in and out of public favor, killing as many victims by poisoning as it seemingly cured of syphilitic lesions.

Finally, in 1910, a reasonably effective method of treating syphilis was discovered. Dr. Paul Ehrlich, a German biologist, methodically experimented with and discarded 605 compounds before discovering salvarsan, a preparation of organic arsenic. Salvarsan became a "magic bullet," which would, according to Ehrlich's passionate belief, cure syphilis with one injection.

The reaction was at first truly astounding—syphilitic lesions and rashes that had responded so slowly to mercury treatments cleared up magically with salvarsan. But after a year or so, all the supposedly cured patients suffered relapses. Two doses were given, then three, and finally 20 to 40 were being prescribed over a period of 18 months. The cure for syphilis was long and tedious, but it did work and the epidemiologists moved onto the scene demanding control programs to prevent the spread of the disease.

America's entry into World War I also indirectly aided the battle against syphilis. It was quickly learned that one of the leading causes of draftee rejection was syphilis. This fact shocked many officials and pointed even more sharply to the need for a control program. The U.S. Public Health Service immediately recommended a program which Congress passed into law in 1918. The bill required all states to report venereal disease cases, provide clinics to dispense free treatments, and investigate sex contacts. The government also seized the German patents for salvarsan, and American companies were soon manufacturing it by the ton under the name of arsphenamine.

Ehrlich's magic bullet was improved somewhat by alternate injections of bismuth—but the minimum course of treatment was still one injection a week for 72 weeks. Then, in 1942, the Public Health Service set up a number of specialized VD hospitals known as Rapid Treatment Centers. In them, treatment time was reduced to five days as arsenic was dripped directly into patients' veins 10 hours a day. The element of risk was high—one of every 200 patients died and one in 100 developed brain damage, but the nation was again at war and VD was considered a menace to the war effort.

A year after the RTC's were established, Dr. John Mahoney, a Public Health researcher working in a Staten Island, New York, laboratory found that penicillin completely routed the *Treponema* in experimental animals. Mahoney's discovery was quickly applied to humans and became the standard treatment for syphilis. Today the accepted course is 4.8 million units of penicillin injected in two doses over a period of two or three days.

To wield the new weapon most effectively, a new breed of public health worker developed—the VD investigator. Soon eager, well-trained investigators were joining the ranks of city and state health departments across the nation and the battle against syphilis seemingly entered its final stage. By 1954 an all-out educational, treatment, and investigation campaign sent the number of cases plummeting toward the elusive goal of complete eradication.

But since 1957, syphilis has made an alarming comeback. One of the reasons was stated by Dr. William Brown, chief of the Venereal Disease Branch of the Communicable Disease Center in Atlanta, Georgia. "As a program for the control of a disease approaches the end point, meaning eradication, it is not the disease, but the program that is more likely to be eradicated."

Funds for the program from federal, state, and municipal governments were sharply reduced and the disease made a stunning comeback. Against the rising tide of syphilis, epidemiologists such as Tim Lindman struggle to trace and break the chain of infection.

Lindman, of course, knew how swiftly the disease could be spread and he moved rapidly to round up the contacts named by Victor. Four of the 10 girls were infected and one could not be located.

"Her mother said she had gone down to visit her grandmother in South Carolina," Lindman noted. "I gave the information to Bob Wood in the State Health Department in Trenton and he phoned his opposite number in South Carolina. Within two days they had found the girl.

She was infected, all right, and they treated her down there. She named four sex contacts, all here in Newark."

Soon the young epidemiologist was juggling several dozen boys and girls in a chain of infection that seemed without end. "The five infected girls we got from Victor provided us with another 18 names. We were lucky, though—only two of that group were infected. It was really a pitiful situation. I visited each of the girls at home and since they were all under 21—the youngest was 12, the eldest 17—I needed their mother's consent to take them into the clinic. One of the girls was in the secondary stage and she was a mess. Her hair had come out in huge patches, giving her a terribly moth-eaten effect and she's begged and pleaded so much, her mother finally bought her a wig to wear to school."

Lindman then turned to the two infected boys. "They named another 11 girls with three infections. They in turn led us to 15 more contacts, but again we got lucky. Most of the boys had been with them just prior to the time they had picked up the infection and we got only one positive out of this group."

At this point, it was the end of August and the epidemiological chart that Tim Lindman was drawing began to take on the appearance of a huge, somewhat misshapen Christman tree. "I was beginning to hope we were nearing the end, for the boy I was at this point interviewing, Frank, was absolutely certain about the number of girls he'd had relations with during the infectious period—five. There's a sort of random susceptibility at work here as in most diseases and there is a slight chance that not everyone who is exposed will get it. Also, he could have been off on the dates of intercourse, which meant that one or more of the girls may not have been exposed to the disease."

Frank was No. 11 on the list of infections that could be traced to Victor. But now, for the first time, Tim Lindman had hopes that the infection might be halted right here. He located the five girls named by Frank and brought them to the clinic. Blood tests revealed only one infection.

"I had my fingers crossed at this point," recalls Tim. "If only Pauline—that was the girl's name—had not been too promiscuous, we might have stopped it right there."

Pauline shattered the hopes by naming seven contacts. Wearily, Tim went after the new crop. Six of them were free of the disease. The seventh was Victor.

"I lit out after him like a scared rabbit and brought him down to the clinic. The two of us sat in the interview room and sweated out the blood test. He'd finished his treatment the first week in July, and the date of exposure was the middle of August. Now, penicillin is absorbed by the blood and retained for about three weeks. There was a chance that there was enough of the stuff still in his blood stream to prevent infection."

The slim chance vanished—Victor's test was unquestionably positive. The chain of infection he himself had started had twisted around to re-infect him. What was more, he named five new contacts. For a moment Tim Lindman was stunned. Then, he rolled his head toward the door. "Out," he said resignedly. As soon as the boy had left, Tim followed him out onto the street. There were five new cases he had to investigate. They undoubtedly would name still more contacts and the chain would stretch on and on. Would it ever end, Tim Lindman wondered, as he headed for the first address.

An Interview With Christine Jorgensen

Norma L. Newmark and Irene von Cseh

Hunter College

Self-doubts about one's sexuality can contribute to deep psychological crisis and ineffectual social behavior. In American society today, it is important that one be certain about his maleness or femaleness if he is to avoid serious personality difficulties. Christine Jorgensen was once labeled a male by her society, yet she felt that she had a "female psyche" and in fact wished to be a female. Below is part of her story about how it feels to be recognized by one's society as belonging to the wrong sex and the difficulty that she experienced in making the transition from male to female.

"You are what you think you are, and what the world thinks you to be."*

What is male, and what is female? What is masculine, and what is feminine? What is masculinity, and what is femininity? How do we become male, or become female? Is it simply that the doctor says "Now, Mother, you have a lovely son," or "daughter," after a quick glance at the external sex organs, and the family's expectations, patterning, and conditioning then confirm the original sex designation? Or is it deeper in our genes and chromosomes, in the marrow of our bones, so to speak, from which we get our sex identification—our feelings that we are male or female, masculine or feminine, or the emotions that we are unable to reconcile with our outward selves? Do we feel that we are of a piece, or do we wish that we could be other than we are?

Great advances are being made in the biochemistry of sex, in the

---

Reprinted with permission from the authors; based on an interview with Miss Jorgensen arranged by the Tri-State Council on Family Relations in February 1968.

*Christine Jorgensen in her autobiography.

study of genes, and even in work on creating life. Much attention has recently been drawn to the chromatin test used to find the predominant sex of a person even in spite of his obvious sex characteristics. Athletes in the Olympic Games have been tested to make certain that no presumably female competitor had an oversupply of male chromatin that might give her more stamina and power than she would have as a truly feminine person, and indeed several were barred from competition.

In the attempt to further understanding of these and related problems, the Tri-State Council on Family Relations held a meeting in New York City in February of 1968 that was devoted primarily to an interview of Miss Christine Jorgensen. This article is based upon a transcript of that conversation.

Miss Jorgensen, born George Jorgensen, Jr., in New York City, was one of the first persons in the U. S. known to have had surgery to change her physical structure to confrom to her emotional feelings, her psyche. She had been aware from her earliest years that she was not truly a boy—she felt different from what she was told of how boys think, feel, and act. She lived in an isolated world, cut off from honest and deep communication with even her close family because she never felt that she could explain her emotional reactions to the world. Shy, delicate, feminine in appearance, her greatest fear was that she would be thought a homosexual, and this she knew she was not; the times she was approached by men were among her most traumatic experiences. In her recently published autobiography, she describes a simple but happy home in which she grew up alone, unhappy, and confused and then the long struggle to find her identity and build a new life as the woman she was completely certain she was. She became a transsexual, one who crosses from one sex to another by the surgical alteration of the sex organs. Miss Jorgensen has spent her life pondering masculinity-femininity on a personal basis. Having struggled with these concepts, she is probably in a better position than are many professional persons to define them.

Among the participants were Dr. Rita S. Finkler and Mrs. Lee R. Steiner. Dr. Finkler, endocrinologist of Millburn, New Jersey, has had a distinguished career and is now Chief Emeritus and Consultant in the Department of Endocrinology at Newark Beth Israel Hospital. She established the first endocrine department of a hospital in the East and has the distinction of being one of the few endocrinologists who has concerned herself with the social and emotional aspects of endocrine function. Mrs. Steiner is a clinical psychologist who for twenty years had headed the radio program "Psychologically Speaking." Through the years she and Dr. Finkler have carried many cases together and have observed the changes in both males and females that come about with the proper balance of hormones and with emotional therapy.

One of the first questions that Miss Jorgensen was asked was: How does a young child feel "like a boy" or "like a girl"? She responded that as a child her identification with a sex was rather in terms of blue for a boy and pink for a girl, a concept she feels she has changed only in the last twenty years, since her surgery. She did not feel like a little boy because of her identification of what a little boy should be and because of what she now considers a very elaborate misconception of what being male or female is, a misconception she thinks is not uncommon among young people even today.

Mrs. Steiner was anxious to pursue the other symptoms. She asked many questions about Miss Jorgensen's feelings during her adolescent years, questions such as: Were you often fatigued? Did you seem to have a wall around you? Were you isolated? Did you feel you were feminine in appearance? Were you a social recluse? Did you have an abhorrence of yourself? Mrs. Steiner pointed out that such feelings often reveal a schizoid child and that as Miss Jorgensen was obviously not schizoid, nor had ever been, perhaps what we know as schizoid is often endocrine in origin, as was Miss Jorgensen's problem. (This is, in fact, one school of medical thought. There are psychiatrists who find much value in chemotherapy.) Miss Jorgensen replied, "I would say offhand that most children—myself included—use the comparison basis of looking at . . . what I call so-called normal young boys. At that time, I thought everyone was normal except me, and I have since learned not to use the word normal because the norm happens to be average, but that has come only with learning over the years. At that time, I was confused as to my own identification because of my build, because I did not compare in the expected ways with other boys I knew who were growing up.

"Psychologically, I always felt feminine in my inclinations in comparison to my sister and other girls I knew. This was the only way I could determine what my feelings were, by comparing them with others, and with what I considered the established male-female, which were to me at that time opposite ends of the stick. But now I realize, of course, that they are not, that we are all integrated with about 80 per cent male or female, the highest percentage hormonally any person can be."

As she reached adolescence these feelings increased. Miss Jorgensen continued, "When I was very young, I just felt that I was a girl. I don't know why I felt that way, but then as maturity came, gradually I compared myself physically and I was immature—sexually, in musculature, visibly I was physically immature. I was always very pale, very thin, what I would say, feminine looking. Again today I feel that there are very many feminine looking men who do not have the psychological inclinations that I had, which I assumed at one time, when I first began to understand it, was a homosexual emotion, and it probably would have had to be considered so at that point because . . . I was identified within society as a male and felt inclined toward males. As Dr. Freud would say, my psychological love image was male. Then, at that time I would have to have been considered a homosexual or to be considered as having a homosexual emotion."

Miss Jorgensen was asked why she thought that she was not homosexual. She was reminded that she had fallen deeply in love with two men—at different times—and was asked why she thought that hers was a different emotional response from that of any other man who falls deeply in love with men. Miss Jorgensen responded, "The first time I fell in love, I was quite young. I was not aware of homosexuality. I was really quite immature, and I was probably living a very hidden life because of my own emotional instabilities, or my own emotional lack of acceptance of what I felt I was as a person. Consequently, to me homosexuality was relatively unknown. I did not know what this emotion was. I knew from what I had been taught through religious principles and so forth that it was not an established relationship of the male toward the female.

"Why I felt female, I do not know. I just did simply feel female, and . . . in my emotional relationships towards both of these men —one of them came with maturity—I felt I was female in my attitude. . . . I have since learned the difference between homosexuality and transsexualism emotionally because my own physical organs to me were the opposite of what I should have had, which may have been something I talked myself into—I am not sure—but that is the way I felt. That is the way I still feel. And I have since discovered that . . . the average homosexual is in love with his own organs. He enjoys being a male to a male or a female to a female. Consequently, the identification with the removal of organs, immature as they may have been, of sexually identifying organs, to me may be the very great difference between a transsexual and a homosexual. . . .

In 1946, just at the conclusion of World War II, Miss Jorgensen was drafted into the army, after three rejections for being underweight, and served her time as a clerk, although before her discharge she did have to go through basic training. Her description of her army life in her autobiography is a tale of a desperate attempt to become part of the social world around her, but of not succeeding. Shortly after her discharge she went to New Haven to study and there read the book she credits with saving her life—Paul de Kruif's *The Male Hormone.* All of a sudden Christine started thinking that her emotional problems might have a biochemical or endocrine base, that the basis of all her problems was deep in her body chemistry. She decided to investigate it. "I went," she says, "to one very interesting doctor who was doing hormone work. He was an endocrinologist in New Haven, Connecticut. I know he was fascinated by the idea, but I frightened him. I knew for him it was too revolutionary an idea for the era in which we were living, 1946.

"As I have discovered over the years—and I must honestly say it, now that we are progressing in this country—the thought process toward sexological problems is so far more advanced in Europe, particularly in the Scandinavias, than it is here, but we are catching up really quickly. We Americans are an amazing tribe. We will reject something for years and years and then have someone finally put it on a paper, as John Hopkins did with their announcement in November 1966 that they have begun to do the surgery, and suddenly all those illegitimate years of my being a charlatan have ceased to be illegitimate. Now we are running ahead, and there are about ten different hospitals in the United States doing the surgery which they wouldn't consider at all in 1946, not at all."

It was shortly after this, in 1950, that Miss Jorgensen went to Denmark to seek some help. For one and one-half years before surgery she underwent testing and the start of endocrine 17-Keto-steroid examination. At that time she was a guinea pig, because her physicians were studying ACTH, also. The chore of collecting two-hour urine samples every day, seven days a week, began. They gave her an injection every day and watched the results on her body chemistry. They were doing chemical castration, which is the chemical reduction of the testicular male hormones by the use of female hormones. Then they would watch the graph on the Keto-steroid and the ACTH and the endocrine, all of the endocrine hormones. Through these urine specimens, they were watching the progress of her biochemistry. When the doctors became convinced that her body was producing female hormones in greater quantity than is normal in the male, they performed the first surgery. After the male hormone source had been removed, they watched the balance of steroids again and found more evidence of the production of the female hormones by her body.

After the first surgery, George Jorgensen went to the American Embassy, spoke to Ambassador Eugena Anderson, told her story, and showed the documents from her doctors. Within ten days, a new passport arrived for Christine Jorgensen. That was the beginning of a new life, that of a transsexual who had left behind an unsatisfactory life and had become one with her emotions as a woman.

Dr. Finkler, who has devoted a lifetime to endocrinology and has seen many persons with confused sex feelings and organs, feels that endocrine study can bring order out of the chaos that confused sex patterns bring to a life. She described several types of patients. "There are certain special groups. There are hermaphrodites and pseudohermaphrodites. There are transvestites and there are transsexuals. There are those with Kleinfelter's syndrome and Turner's syndrome. In other words, there is a variety of sexual deviations with normalities in the sex build and with abnormalities in the sex build. But obviously they don't belong to the sex which they were notifed that they are in." Dr. Finkler said that she has seen children born with mixed sex, but that usually this becomes apparent only at maturity, as the glands begin to work. At this point, the deviations in personality and physical makeup become evident. She said that in the early years some tests were carried out, but that they were not many; things like 17-Keto-steroid, 17-hydroxicortico and pituitary gonatropin were not known then, nor was chromatin. Today we can readily recognize sex by chromatin studies.

Two questions that Miss Jorgenson answered must not be overlooked. The first (and haven't we all said so at one time or another?) was "What is male thinking, and what is female thinking?" The second asked what the role of her home was in her development.

Miss Jorgensen found this very difficult. To her, what she felt and considered to be male and female was an emotion. She said that she supposed that what is male and what is female is a matter of individual decision. Over the years Christine had found it more and more difficult to recognize a difference between male and female thinking and has not yet decided what it is. She said she had met what one would call total males, sexually, that have a great female way of thinking, and that yet this seemed not to be a sexual matter but entirely an emotional one.

To the question about her home life, Miss Jorgensen replied "That is a very interesting point because generally you find a lot of problems with over-mother-love and this type of thing. I examined my home life, and I do examine it rather carefully in the book, with the idea of trying to find out if there was an influence of that sort. I did not come from a wealthy home. I came from a very happy family. I did not have problems identifying with either my father or my mother, although I have come to the conclusion, since the death of my mother and father in the last two years, that if I were to write the book over, I think it would . . . bring in more of the possibility of genetic inheritance factors involved with a case like mine, which I didn't touch because my mother was still living until last July, and I felt this was not . . . a thing to add because I found great acceptance in them with the change. However, in conversations with geneticists, I have learned they truly feel there is probably a very strong genetic reason for much of what has happened to me and others like me, which I feel free to discuss now because no one can be hurt. I think my parents were rather typical of the era in which they lived and possibly typical even of today. My parents denied that they saw anything wrong with me, even after I came back from Europe. They came over and we met there, and they accepted the entire procedure.

"In one letter my father wrote to me, 'I don't want you to use any medical terms, and make it as simple as you can, but explain the whole thing in one page.' I said to him it was like explaining the history of the world on a pinhead. But they accepted me, and we did live together harmoniously in the latter years. But I don't think they ever really quite understood exactly all the genetics and other things that were involved. I never discussed genetics with my parents, although my mother, about three months before she died of cancer, when she knew she was dying, admitted that she was aware from early childhood that I had a deep-rooted problem of some sort.

"But they were typical parents; they were afraid to delve into it. How many parents do admit that something is wrong with a child even today, because if they do they must accept the fact that if there is something wrong, perhaps they gave birth to something less than a wonderful superchild. It then reflects on their establishment. In fact, I think it was harder on my father, much more, and this goes into the philosophy of what it feels like to be a male. The male is indoctrinated to such a degree that this 'rah, rah, male' cannot believe that he can give birth to anything but a superchild; whereas I am sure there isn't a woman who during her pregnancy hasn't said just let it have all its arms and legs. The father never thinks of that, but thinks in terms of his superior being having procreated, which is the established way of male thinking."

If one were to be asked the question, "What makes you think you are a man, or a woman?" what would be the answer? Mrs. Steiner said that since her meeting with Christine Jorgensen she had been pondering the question, but she felt that she had no answer, especially a psychologically sound one. "I have always taken for granted that I am a woman the way I take for granted my breathing; I had never really thought about it. I don't think we really know how to define the psychic femininity and masculinity. I would wager there are as many combinations as there are people. What makes a woman feel like a woman? I can't define it."

One suggestion was that the difference is simply to which sex you are attracted. When you see a man and he looks kind of nice, does that mean you are a woman? Or, when a man is sexually attracted to a good-looking woman does that mean he is a male? Another thought was that we have a built-in social expectancy that we learn as we go along; it is purely environmental. To which Miss Jorgensen replied, "Why do people like myself rebel, if it is purely psychological, against social acceptance? What is the chemistry that goes on inside? . . . I am convinced it is biochemistry. I think the same thing is true with homosexuality, that there is a rebellion against the society, the conformity of the society. But I think it is triggered by something which is deep-rooted within the cell structure of every human being. Most people do not have it; they rebel in a different way. It is always easier to conform."

Near the end of the interview, Miss Jorgensen was asked if she had ever taken the chromatin test. She had not but would like to do so. However, regardless of the results, it would cause no change in her thinking about herself. She is convinced that she is a woman. To Christine Jorgensen feeling sure about her sexuality is *the* most critical component of her self image. Isn't it for all of us?

Discussion Questions for Chapter 2

1. Visitors to America point up the discrepancy between what we say we want our adolescents to be and what we encourage them to become. It is said that we expect chastity, virtue, and integrity. Yet we support early dating, dancing, and petting, being at the head of one's class, and being successful above being respected. Do you agree with this charge of inconsistency? If the charge is true, how does it affect the adolescent?
2. Of the following approaches to sex for adolescents, which do you support and why?
   a. Complete sublimation of the sex drive.
   b. A combination of sublimation and masturbation.
   c. Heterosexual relationships leading to and including orgasm.
3. The Public Health Service believes that we can and must separate venereal disease education from sex education. Do you agree with this?

4. How much sense or nonsense is there in the statement that adolescent morals are degenerating? Haven't morals always been in a state of change? Reports from early society talked about the decadence of youth, just as we do today. Is the world going to pot or is it that we are talking about our problems more honestly and openly than ever before?
5. What are the implications of maleness without masculinity? Femaleness without feminity? How can adolescents who have doubts about their own sexuality be recognized and helped?

Chapter 3
Problems of Special Significance To the Adolescent

If we agree that "adolescenthood" is a stage of development we must also agree that this stage, like all others, has problems that are unique to it. The adult population is quite often critical of the adolescent and may be inclined to think of this stage not in terms of adolescent needs but rather in terms of the needs of the adult world. Perhaps if more were known about this critical time in growing up we would have less need to be defensive about it. This chapter deals with the problems that have special significance for the adolescent. If the problems are real, then both the adolescent and adult must be made cognizant of them. If the problems are imagined, what is their significance and what purpose do they serve for the young adult?

Some of the articles speak directly to the adolescent and some speak to the understanding of adults. Is it practical to approach the problem from these divergent points of view? Is it another step toward reality? Are the problems discussed superficial or do they get at the core that needs understanding?

Dropouts, Automation, and the Cities

Robert A. Dentler

Teachers College, Columbia University

Who drops out and why? Is the central issue the school and academic success or failure? Can automation be blamed or is it an inability to adapt and adjust to changing times that causes our difficulties?

The author suggests that the dropout problem is much more complex and subtle than is generally acknowledged. He discusses the educationally disadvantaged child who becomes the adolescent dropout and makes recommendations that could help to overcome these disadvantages. The view presented in this article is disturbing in that it points out a rather unpleasant picture of a class- and race-conscious America. It is promising, however, because it does offer concrete solutions to the basic problem of the school dropout. Solving the dropout problem is of critical importance to human development in America. Do the solutions offered herein seem to meet the need?

Many educators have asserted that the problem of finding ways to encourage youths to complete high school is one of the most crucial current issues in American education. The message has been repeated so emphatically that government has invested in programs to rescue old dropouts and to rehabilitate potential ones. The mass media have joined in, for the most part on the basis of tax-deductible advertising; to campaign for a return to high school. Social agencies have contributed an array of diagnostic examinations, casework and groupwork services, and clinical orientations that have helped to foster an image of The Dropout as a special type of character disorder.

Is withdrawal from high school a crucial issue? What aspects of the evidence are sometimes neglected? Is The Dropout perhaps a gloss for a more fundamental policy problem—the intensifying underemployment of youth? This paper explores these questions in the spirit of the policy scientist. The evidence and its interpretation are fitted to the larger forces of automation and urbanization toward the end of articulating a broader, more fundamental challenge than school withdrawal.

Neglected Evidence

An educational problem is first of all a matter of definition. Policy makers and educational practitioners concerned with school withdrawal

From *Teachers College Record*, Vol. 65 (March 1964), pp. 475-483. Reprinted by permission of the author and *Teachers College Record*.

like to fashion their rhetoric so that the extent of withdrawal seems large. They typically report that about one out of two children who begin elementary school in the United States finishes high school, and that only half of those who finish high school go on to college. On the surface, this is not too far from the facts. For every 1,000 students enrolled in fifth grade in 1951, 582 graduated from high school by 1959. And for the same cohort, 308 had entered college.

But this is only the surface. First, it is worthwhile to treat the rate of withdrawal comparatively. If we look at fifth-grade cohorts from 1920 through the present, and if we plot the rate for each year, we obtain a rather smooth curve that *declines* from about 80 per cent high school withdrawal in 1920 to about 40 per cent in 1960. If we follow the line of the resulting curve, we get the definite impression that in 1975, about 30 students per 100 will fail to graduate from high school, and that this may drop to 20 per cent by the end of the century. The main historical evidence is thus a pattern of eight decades of increasing levels of school retention, with a dramatic shift from a likelihood of .80 of withdrawal from high school to a likelihood of .80 of graduation.

This is still the surface. If we carve into the dwindling fraction of those who drop out of school, we identify some sizeable groups whose characteristics are obscured by the superficial evidence. There are students who change communities and schools without adequate transmission of records. There are mortalities, severe physical disabilities, and late-blooming mental retardates, as well as youth who suffer one or another of the several types of conditions defined as emotional disturbance and delinquency. These categories are extremely difficult to locate and measure. But if we follow the lead of researchers who have struggled to distinguish between voluntary and involuntary withdrawal on these bases, the rate of school withdrawal is reduced further. Applying the crude estimates of one of the best of these studies, my inference is that voluntary withdrawal has declined from about 70 per cent in 1920 to about 25 per cent in 1960. Using this curve, the voluntary dropout rate should level off more or less permanently at about 15 per cent by 1975.[1]

Those who argue that the dropout is a major national educational problem also neglect the question of absolute numbers. For example, we are seldom reminded that the high-school-age population expanded by 500 per cent between 1920 and 1960. It will probably increase by another 400 per cent between 1960 and 1975. The historical statistics suggest that the *number* of high school dropouts has remained relatively constant. For the period 1900 to 1930, it averaged about 500 thousand a year. From 1930 to 1950, the number averaged about 600 thousand annually. Since then, the yearly crop of high school dropouts has hovered in the range of 650 thousand. This absolute increase is very slight if our baseline is the absolute number of high-school-age youths.

[1]My data are drawn principally from tables in (*6*). For a careful treatment of the question of involuntary versus voluntary withdrawals, see Segal and Schwarm (*5*).

Mobility and Concern

Finally, those most concerned to promote new policies and practices for retaining youths in school tend to neglect the fluidity common to all communal, institutional, and occupational aspects of American life. We are seldom told, for example, that a dropout rate is usually based on a fifth-grade cohort examined eight years later. Census data reveal the substantial number of persons attending junior high schools and high schools, especially in metropolitan communities, who are 19 to 24 years of age. There are many who remain in school but take additional years to graduate. A recent survey in Syracuse revealed, as one aspect of this neglected pattern, that 10 per cent of all 1959-1960 high school dropouts returned to school to work toward graduation within the next two years. Another 15 per cent sought further educational instruction of other sorts in the same period (3).

The evidence suggests that, for the individual American student, the over-all odds of graduating from high school have improved substantially during each decade. In the abstract, this reflects the evolution of an educational system that corresponds in capability to the requirements of rapid technological change and population growth. Much of the improvement has resulted from changes in school promotion policies from a rule of success or failure grade-by-grade to a practice of social or age promotion. In turn, this change in policy is perhaps the glove on the fist of state laws prohibiting "premature" withdrawal from school and, most especially, the implementation of these laws. This change in the odds of graduating may be a mixed blessing, but surely one cannot have matters both ways. A legally sanctioned system designed to keep most youths in school for the longest feasible period is bound to alienate some youths in the process.

In the sizeable literature about school dropouts, there seem to be three main genres. One is exhortative. This largest group is not worth commenting upon, as it consists mostly of articles published to enhance the careers of educator-authors. A second group consists of descriptive statistical reports about rates for regions, states, school districts, and particular communities. These would be valuable if some uniform method that was roughly valid could be developed that would allow confidence in the statements about parameters. The United States Office of Education and various agencies and institutions are now struggling to achieve this uniformity.

None of the literature is explicit about assumptions, theoretical or normative, but the third group of papers—surveys of the social and educational characteristics of alleged dropouts—offers a point of departure. The characteristics reappear with such regularity that one is invited to generalize. The evident recurrence may be spurious, however. Educational researchers may merely imitate one another's questions. Very few studies attend closely, for instance, to the characteristics of the schools or the instructional staffs which make up the context out of which the dropout emerges. Nor are social and psychological differences between hypothetical types of dropouts emphasized.

Dropouts in Profile

The recurrent attributes common to high school dropouts are easy to catalogue. The modal dropout is a low school achiever, usually below grade for his age. He is a member of a low-income family in which his parents have low educational attainment. And he participates infrequently in the extra-curricular life of his student peers. Some studies strain toward greater depth in tapping these attributes. Clinically oriented researchers tend to find character disorders. They hedge toward delineation of a disease or disability syndrome. Sociologically oriented researchers tend to find disorganized families and associated evidence of poor early socialization. These emphases draw our attention away from the school, its program, and its staff. They direct us toward developmental failures.

Given the high positive intercorrelations between low educational, low occupational, and low economic attainment of parents, racial minority group membership, and marital and family disorganization, we may lump the surface attributes of the dropout together and view him as *deprived.* This concept may have relevance for theories of cognitive and emotional development (although this remains an empirical question), but it raises new difficulties. For example, the dropout is not *culturally* deprived. The standard of culture advanced by the school is but one standard among many; and in our society, schools are supposed to buttress some degree of cultural pluralism. In the same sense, social deprivation is ambiguous.

If we work with the connotation of deprivation, we make better headway. We can then conclude that the high school dropout is *educationally disadvantaged.* If he wants to live by the rules of the school game, his chances are reduced by counterpressures from his home and his environment outside school. If he is uncertain about the merits of staying in high school and graduating, his "background" and the response of educators to their own internalized assumptions about that background may reduce his ability to remove that uncertainty. In this event, the disadvantaged student is one who is vulnerable to determination from without. Finally, if he defines himself as a dropout in advance of legal age for withdrawal, this self-definition can be selectively reinforced by home, neighborhood peers, and the school itself. The dropout is educationally disadvantaged because, at any one moment, his behavioral setting includes forces that constrain him to quit school. That setting contains self, family, peers, and the school.

The survey literature supports strongly the impression that the *relation* between disadvantage (socioeconomic, ethnic, and—reciprocally—school experience) and voluntary withdrawal from school was as marked in 1928 as it was in 1958. The psychosocial correlates of withdrawal are durable as well as strong and readily identifiable. Because of this, a specious sort of timelessness enters interpretations of the dropout. The correlation coefficients remain the same; therefore, the interpretation of the meaning of disadvantage goes unchanged.

Logic and Fact

Suppose we exercise our logic and our knowledge of social trends, however. Let us assume that the proportion of economically impoverished American households has declined rather steadily since 1910, and that because of improvements in the organization of education and changes in laws affecting withdrawal, the high school dropout rate has declined just as steadily. Finally, let us assume that the correlation between economic level of the household and withdrawal from high school remains high and constant.

TABLE 1 Hypothetical Cross-Tabulation of High School Graduates and Dropouts Versus Status*

Year: 1940

Status	*Dropout*	*Graduate*	*Total*
Low†	40	20	60
Other	0	40	40
Total	40	60	100

Year: 1960

Status	*Dropout*	*Graduate*	*Total*
Low	25	15	40
Other	0	60	60
	25	75	100

Year: 1980

Status	*Dropout*	*Graduate*	*Total*
Low	15	15	30
Other	0	70	70
	15	85	100

*Years chosen to illustrate changing trends in holding power of schools and in socioeconomic mobility in population. Figures reflect rates per 100.

†Taken as composite of sources of relative environmental deprivation, *e.g.*, low income, educational attainment of parents.

The data in Table I were invented to examine the effects of these assumptions. The logic in the results is clear. The over-all chance of being both disadvantaged economically and of dropping out *declines* from .40 in 1940, to .25 in 1960, to .15 in 1980. More intriguing and disturbing is the logical conclusion that the likelihood of graduating if one is disadvantaged declines over time. It appears that low economic status was less handicapping in 1940 than in 1960 or 1980. Twenty per cent of the disadvantaged students graduated in 1940 in contrast to 15 per cent anticipated in 1980.

The intent here is to amplify the demographic process. As the society changes economically and educationally, the dropout who is economically disadvantaged becomes a clearer object for concern. When his numbers were relatively legion, he was understandably less visible. Surely these changes in the larger context induce changes in what it means to be a dropout in each decade. As the various probabilities change, and if they change in the directions suggested by the imaginary data, the dropout will be perceived as educationally more problematic. Similarly, the high school graduate becomes less impressive. His diploma fails to command selective attention on the job market as it becomes common property.

It is in this sense that the research literature on the dropout is misplaced. Educational and psychological surveys are conducted on the one hand. Population, income, and educational statistics accumulate on the other. No one connects the individual with the society.

The literature and, therefore, the problem are fuzzily conceived in another way, too. The attributes involved in what I have summarized as a "disadvantage" are not only aspects of the same pattern of stratification; they are a circular statement of what is involved in withdrawal from school. They tell us that a socioeconomic disadvantage is the equivalent of an educational disadvantage, which is in turn productive of poor school performance, disinterest, and withdrawal.

Employment and Automation

The main key to socioeconomic advantage in our society is secure employment. Is graduation from high school a key to membership in the labor force, let alone to secure employment? A sound analysis of national survey data by the Bureau of Labor Statistics challenges the affirmative answer offered by most commentators on the dropout question.

Keep in mind when examining Table 2 that the average national adult level of unemployment from 1959 through 1961 was about six per cent. Young adults who graduated from high school between 1955 and 1958 were generally employed by at least the fall of 1961. *White* young adults in this group achieved an employment level identical to the entire older national labor force. White young adult dropouts in the same cohort were only slightly less fortunate. About 94 per cent of the graduates, compared with 88 per cent of the dropouts in this group, were employed.

TABLE 2 **Job Fates of Recent High School Graduates and Dropouts, Excluding Those Continuing School, by Color***

	Per cent unemployed in 1961 (Oct.) among graduates				Per cent unemployed 1961 (Oct.) among dropouts		
Year Last in School†	Total	White	Non-white	Year Last in School†	Total	White	Non-white
Prior to 1959	7.4	6.3	17.8	Prior to 1959	12.7	11.9	15.5**
1959	8.3	7.2	16.7	1959	17.0	16.5	18.4
1960	11.6	11.0	17.9	1960	17.2	16.1	21.4
1961	17.9	16.3	31.0**	1961	26.8	29.1	18.0

*Adapted from Jacob Schiffman (*4*), especially detailed Tables A and B.
†Data are from three-year panel survey of youths 16 to 24.
**Small-base *N* makes per cent *less* reliable in these cells.

There is an evident occupational handicap involved in dropping out, but the handicap of race, of being nonwhite, is far greater. About 12 per cent of the white *dropouts* were unemployed among those who had a few years to secure work, but nearly 18 per cent of the nonwhite *graduates* in the same age group remained unemployed. Racial "minorityship" is a correlate of socioeconomic disadvantage. Thus, a high school diploma is an economic advantage to those who have the socioeconomic advantage in the first place. It has little apparent job benefit to offer the youth stigmatized through discrimination.

The data in Table 2 suggest something else. Each year, the high school graduate and the dropout both manage to find a way, however limited, into the labor force. They get jobs, although for many there is a lag between age 17 and the year of first real employment. This lag is greater for the dropout. For graduates, unemployment shakes down within three years after high school to about the level common to the entire civilian labor force. But the *major* youth problem is neither socioeconomic disadvantage nor failure to obtain a high school diploma. *It is, rather, a steady relative breakdown in this absorption of the young noncollege graduate into the work force* as a result of the upgrading of occupational requirements through automation and the relation of this change to changes in the young adult population.

Labor Force in Flux

The net growth of the labor force from 1960 to 1970 will be about 13 million, an increase of more than half over the net growth from 1950 to 1960. Suppose that new jobs are generated at the pace set during the last five years. At this rate, unemployment will amount to about eight per cent of the labor force by 1970 in contrast to six per cent in 1960. Most of the increase in job seekers will be due to increases in the number of young adults entering the labor market—more than 40 per cent of the increase, at least (*1*).

The President's Advisory Committee on Labor-Management Policy reported in 1962 that

> It is clear that unemployment has resulted from displacement due to automation and technological change. It is impossible, with presently available data, to isolate that portion of present unemployment resulting from these causes. Whether such a displacement will be short-run depends to a considerable extent on our ability to anticipate and plan for programs involving technological change and to make better use of various mechanisms for retraining and relocating workers who find themselves unneeded . . . (*2*).

The absolute number of high school dropouts will remain fairly constant, even across the coming period of expansion of the young adult population, because of the increased rate of school retention. But the total number of young adults will increase so over the next decade that competition among noncollege graduates trying to enter the labor force in any capacity will prove to be more severe than in any recent period except the Great Depression. Against this backdrop, high school graduation or the failure to graduate *will not* differentiate the employed from the unemployed.[2]

The social and educational outcomes are those of incompatible rates of change between technology and the occupational structure, or between automation (broadly conceived) and structural unemployment. The dropout rate is pertinent, but it has in fact declined steadily, while more pertinent factors have not kept pace with the change in technology.[3]

Within education, adjustment to changing rates of automation is complicated by our inability to articulate general education prior to job training with changing work requirements. Ancillary educational enterprises in adult education, vocational preparation, and career counseling have lacked fiscal support and have failed to cope adequately with the tremendous complexities inherent in massive, rapid change when they have secured support. We have only begun to learn how to "retrain" young adults from unskilled to technically skilled workers, for example.

The dimensions of reorganizing education have been well explored for years. While the discussion goes on, considerable slack is taken up outside schools by industry and government, where employers have the resources to train, to counsel, and to retrain individuals when the need for net returns dictates the importance of "classrooms in the factory" (*1*).

Central City Leverage

Is there a *root* educational task in this thicket of changes and strains, however? Can priorities be assigned, not against a moral standard but in terms of adaptations between institutions? The main root, perhaps, is the predominant response within education—increased holding power in higher education as well as in high school. The energies of the educational establishment have been invested for decades in widening the base for higher education. Thus (using the indicator of fifth-grade cohorts), the rate of entry into college increased from 12 students per 100 in 1931 to 32 per 100 in 1960.

A prior task involves the residual group of youth from low status backgrounds, the dropouts and the high school graduates who do not enroll in school beyond the 12th grade. For the generation currently in elementary and secondary schools, we have little to offer here beyond remediation and retraining. Current federal proposals involve primarily only vocational training and make-work programs through updated, probably worthwhile variants on the Conservation Corps of the Great Depression.

---

[2]My argument rests on the premise of no substantial change in the rate of national economic growth. With increased growth and with extra prosperity, automation could generate new employment in the ten-year short term as it does in any case in the long term.

[3]Among the noneducational factors in this problem, one might give first priority to insufficient economic growth, periodic recessions, imbalance in economic changes from area to area with resulting chronic distress in some localities, limitations on labor force mobility, and incompletely developed and far from adequate unemployment insurance and related social security provisions—all, of course, in relation to rapid population growth.

A positive program for the noncollege and the disadvantaged group must be stronger tactically and more transformative than this effort, however. The best possible point of departure is the search for excellence in early instruction in *central city* schools.

The youth problem that is symbolized so superficially by the dropout issue comes to its head in the central cities. The low-income families, the rural households from the Deep South and from the distressed areas of the mountain states, the racial minorities, and the small-town families of low educational attainment—all will continue their massive relocation into the nation's biggest central cities during the next 15 years. Underemployment on the surplus of marginal farms, dwindling sources of rural nonfarm employment opportunities for unskilled workers, intensified conflict between racial groups in the South, and many other social and industrial forces continue to stimulate this old but intensifying movement.

Moreover, sociologists have recently verified their suspicion that earlier dichotomies between privileged suburban and deprived city families are breaking down as this cityward migration persists. For in addition to growing numbers of lower status families in the *outer* ring of every large city, an increasing number of disadvantaged groups are beginning to cluster at points throughout the suburban and exurban but nonfarm areas beyond the city.

Cities initiate technological change; they are also more vulnerable to its effects than are other types of communities. Increasing unemployment and the underemployment of noncollege educated youths will share in this dualism. Youth unemployment is already felt most sharply in the largest cities. The transformative capability of metropolitan communities is the ability to muster skills and to foster action. In the case of this problem, I think the main attack should be on *improvement in the quality of early general elementary education.*

As the Seeds Are Sown

It is the urban production of well educated children which constitutes the primary and, to date, most neglected challenge. Higher Horizons, Mobilization for Youth, the Ford Gray Areas Projects, and other energetic demonstrations inaugurated during the last ten years have made contributions to the salvaging of human resources. Few demonstration projects in any of our cities have been evaluated systematically; we are not sure what parts work best, how they work, or why. But we have learned much of practical relevance about the provision of *rehabilitative* social and educational services.

What cities need most now are health, education, and welfare programs that address the exigencies of the newest generation, the one- to five-year-olds who will pour through the urban schools, agencies, clinics, and hospitals in increasing numbers during the years from 1965 to 1980. Current rates vary from city to city, but calculations from census data suggest that, on the average, the nation's 30 largest central cities now house from one in seven (for Los Angeles and San Francisco) to two in five (for New Orleans) children who are educationally disadvantaged when they enter elementary school. These are children from economically impoverished or deprived households, an increasing proportion of which are nonwhite.

The missing component in a program of preparation for social and educational accommodation to the rapid changes that lie ahead for our urban society is a platform of excellence in the first, second, and third grades. It is this platform, not later rehabilitation, that will make fluid adjustments to a changing occupational structure possible. We presently know more about the vocational rehabilitation of a disabled adult, I suspect, than we do about teaching disadvantaged children how to read or divide numbers. It is this platform of improvement of instruction in early cognitive skills that can provide the noncollege youths of the 1970s with the means of something better than a choice between a life of make-work and a life of enforced idleness. We do not now *know* how to achieve this excellence. Our best energies, after all, have gone into identifying and reinforcing the gifted and into patching up the disadvantaged during adolescence.

But urban educators can come alive in response to this opportunity. The issue of early low and declining achievement among low-income children, especially Negro children, is not deep below the surface of the issue of racial imbalance. Early school learning is intimately related to problems of system organization and teacher-management conflicts, though these issues have not yet been well enough articulated.

To relate all this to the issue of the dropout: The determinants of voluntary withdrawal from high school are imbedded in the transactions between children and schools in the first years. We need an elementary system of such a caliber that the seeds of withdrawal are less and less likely to be sown in the first place. But even when we have accomplished this, we need excellence in urban elementary education of a kind that will equip the youth who stays on for a high school diploma with the cognitive skills necessary for continuous adjustment to change.

References

1. Clark, H. F., *Classrooms in the Factory.* New York: New York Univer. Press, 1958.
2. President's Advisory Comm. on Labor-Management Policy, *Automation: The Benefits and Problems Incident to Automation and Other Technological Advances.* Washington, D.C.: U.S. Govt. Print. Off., 1962.
3. Saleem, Betty L., & S. M. Miller, *The Neglected Dropout: The Returnee.* Syracuse: Syracuse Univer. Youth Dev. Cent., 1963.
4. Schiffman, J., Employment of High School Graduates and Dropouts in 1961. *Month. Labor Rev.,* 1962 (May), Special Labor Force Report No. 21.
5. Segal, D., & O. J. Schwarm, *Retention in High Schools and Large Cities.* Washington, D.C.: U.S. Off. Educ., 1957.
6. US Dept. Health, Educ., & Welfare, *Annual Health Education and Welfare Trends,* 1961. Washington, D.C.: U.S. Govt. Print. Off., 1962.

The Fourth R—The Rat Race

John Holt

Fayerweather Street School, Cambridge, Massachusetts

Why should there be a rat race? Is it the school's fault, or does the school merely reflect society's values and expectations? We consistently blame a system for many of the problems that we help to create. What solutions do we have for this artificial situation? Can we realistically solve it or are we deluding ourselves because of a snowballing effect of the problem? Holt's suggestions may or may not be applicable. Is he, as a teacher, too involved to give a detached view?

Most of what is said and written about the tremendous pressures for high grades that burden so many young people today implies that schools and colleges are not really responsible for these pressures, that they are the innocent victims of anxious and ambitious parents on the one hand, and the inexorable demands of an increasingly complicated society on the other. There is some truth in this, but not much. Here and there are schools that have been turned, against their will, into high-pressure learning factories by the demands of parents. But in large part, educators themselves are the source and cause of these pressures. Increasingly, instead of developing the intellect, character and potential of the students in their care, they are using them for their own purposes in a contest inspired by vanity and aimed at winning money and prestige. It is only in theory, today, that educational institutions serve the student; in fact, the real job of a student at any ambitious institution is by his performance to enhance the reputation of the institution.

This is true not only of colleges and universities. I have heard teachers at secondary and even elementary schools, in reply to the just claim that students were overworried and overworked, say that if students were less burdened, their test and examination scores would go down and the reputation of the school would suffer. I can still hear, in my mind's ear, the voice of a veteran teacher at a prestigious elementary school saying at a faculty meeting that if the achievement-test scores of the students did not keep pace with those of competing schools, the school would have to "close its doors"—and this in spite of the fact that it had a long waiting list of applicants. I know of a school in which, at least for a while, the teachers' salaries were adjusted up or down according to the achievement-test scores of their classes.

From *The New York Times Magazine*, May 1, 1966.

Not long ago, I went to an alumni dinner of a leading New England preparatory school and there heard one of the faculty, in a speech, boast about the percentage of students who had been admitted to the college of their first choice, the number who had gone directly into the sophomore class at college and so on. The tone was that of a manufacturer bragging that his product was better than those of his competitors. Conversely, when the faculty of the school meets to discuss the students who are not doing well in their studies, the tone is likely to be that of management considering an inferior product, one not worthy of bearing the company's name and which they are about to drop from the line. There is sometimes concern and regret that the school is not doing well enough by the child; much more often there is concern, and resentment, that the child is not doing well enough by the school.

I do not think it is any way an exaggeration to say that many students, particularly the ablest ones, are being as mercilessly exploited by ambitious schools as they are by business and commerce, which use them as consumers and subject them to heavy and destructive psychological pressures.

In such schools, children from the age of 12 or 13 on are very likely to have, after a long day at school, two, three or more hours of homework a night—with more over the weekend. The load grows heavier as children get older. Long before they reach college, many children are putting in a 70-hour week—or more. As Paul Goodman once put it, children have not worked such long hours since the early and brutal days of the Industrial Revolution.

One of my own students, a girl just turned 14, said not long ago, more in a spirit of wry amusement than of complaint, that she went home every night on a commuter train with businessmen, most of whom could look forward to an evening of relaxation with their families, while she had at least two or three hours more work to do. And probably a good many of those men find their work during the day less difficult and demanding than her schoolwork is for her.

Schools and colleges claim in defense that they are compelled to put heavy pressure on students because of society's need for ever more highly trained men and women, etc., etc. The excuse is, for the most part, untrue and dishonest.

The blunt fact is that educators' chief concern is to be able to say, to college-hunting parents on the one hand, and to employee-hunting executives on the other, that their college is harder to get into, and therefore better, than other colleges, and therefore the one to which the best students should be sent and from which the best employees and graduate students can be drawn.

In a recent private talk with some of the teachers at a men's Ivy League college, I said that the job of our universities was not to provide vocational training for the future holders of top positions in business, government, science and the learned professions; it was to help boys and girls become in the broadest sense of the word, educated adults and citizens. In return, I was asked a most interesting and revealing question: If a college does not turn out future "leaders," where in future years, will it get the money for its alumni fund, the money it needs to stay in the prestige race? Where indeed? A difficult problem. But not one that should be the primary concern of educators, and certainly not one that justifies the kind of pressure for grades that is now bearing heavily on more and more children.

What are the effects of these pressures? They are many—and all harmful. They create in young children an exaggerated concern with getting right answers and avoiding mistakes; they drive them into defensive strategies of learning and behavior that choke off their intellectual powers and make real learning all but impossible.

On older children, like the teen-agers I now teach, the effects are even wider and more harmful. This is perhaps the time in a growing person's life when he most needs to be free of pressure, when he needs the most time, leisure, solitude and independence. It is at this period in his life that he becomes most sharply aware of himself as a person, of the need to know who and what that person is, and of the fact that he can and will to a large extent determine who and what that person becomes. In short, it is at this time that he begins not only to know himself but also consciously to create himself, to feel intuitively what Thoreau meant when he said that every man is his own masterpiece.

A person's identity is made up of those things—qualities, tastes, beliefs—that are uniquely his, that he found and chose and took for himself, that cannot be lost or taken from him, that do not depend on his position or his success or other people's opinion of him. More specifically, it is the people that he admires; the books, the music, the games, the interests that he chooses for himself and likes, whether or not anyone else likes them, or whether or not they are supposed to be "good" or "worthwhile"; the experiences that he seeks out for himself and that add to his life.

An adolescent needs time to do this kind of seeking, tasting, selecting and rejecting. He needs time to talk and think about who he is and how he got to be that way and what he would like to be and how he can get there. He needs time to taste experience and to digest it. We don't give him enough.

In addition, by putting him in a position where he is always being judged and where his whole future may depend on those judgments, we require the adolescent to direct his attention, not to who he is or ought to be or wants to be, but who we think he is and want him to be. He has to keep thinking about the impression he is making on us—his elders, the world. Thus we help to exaggerate what is already, in most young people, a serious and crippling fault—an excessive concern with what others think of them.

Since our judgments are more often than not critical, unfavorable, even harsh, we exaggerate another fault, equally serious and crippling—a tendency to imagine that other people think less well of them than in fact they do, or what is worse, that they do not deserve to be well thought of. Youth ought to be a time when people acquire a sense not just of their own identity but also of their own worth. We make it almost certain to be the very opposite.

In this competition into which we have driven children, almost everyone loses. It is not enough any more for most parents or most schools that a child should go to college and do well there. It is not even enough for most children themselves. More and more, the only acceptable goal is to get into a prestige college; to do anything else is to fall. Thus I hear boys and girls say, "I wanted to go to so-and-so, but I'm not good enough." It is outrageous that they should think this way, that they should judge themselves stupid and worthless because of the opinion of some remote college admissions officer.

The pressures we put on our young people also tend to destroy their sense of power and purpose. A friend of mine who recently graduated with honors from a prestige college said that he and other students there were given so much to read that, even if you were an exceptionally good reader and spent all your time studying, you could not do as much as half of it.

Looking at work that can never be done, young people tend to feel, like many a tired businessman, that life is a rat race. They do not feel in control of their own lives. Outside forces hurry them along with no pause for breath or thought, for purposes not their own, to an unknown end. Society does not seem to them a community that they are preparing to join and shape, like the city of an ancient Greek; it is more like a remote and impersonal machine that will one day bend them to its will.

My students ask, "How can I defend myself, the real person within me, against society?" Having asked the question, they gloomily decide that it cannot be done. This is, I think, what Paul Goodman meant when he said that we have imposed on the elite of our younger generation a morale fit for slaves. We have not given them a sense of mission and vocation, but of subjection and slavery. They do not seek more knowledge and power so that they may one day do great work of their own choosing; instead, they do their tasks, doggedly and often well, only because they dare not refuse.

Along with their sense of mission, we destroy to a very considerable extent their sense of joy, both in work and in leisure. Thoreau once wrote: "The truly efficient laborer will not crowd his day with work, but saunter to the task surrounded by a wide halo of ease and leisure." The man is badly cheated who has never felt that he could not wait to get back to his work and so feeling, hurled himself into it with fierce joy. Not only is he cheated; he probably has never done much work worth doing.

Nor do our young people, on the whole, get much more joy out of their pleasures. They are not much re-created by their recreation. We, their elders, say that this is because their amusements are trivial; but even when this is true, it is so to a great extent because we have left them so little time or energy for anything more serious. A member of the Boston Symphony told me not long ago that the music programs of even our best suburban schools do not compare with those he knows in the Midwest, simply because the college pressure leaves so few students time for serious practice.

Even the songs the young sing for fun have little fun in them, but are mostly tragic, bitter, angry, defiant. They seem to sing them, as they do most things that they do of their own choice, as a way of shaking their fists under the noses of their elders. No fad is more sure to succeed among the young than one they think the adults won't like.

I think of a student of mine, years ago, kept on campus weekend after weekend for not having his work done—presumably so that he could use the time to get it done. On one such weekend I found him working on one of his hobbies, a small printing press. In exasperation I said to him, "If you'd just do the things you have to do and get them out of the way, then you could be free to do the things you want to do."

With tired wisdom, much greater than mine, he said, mildly: "No you can't. They just give you more things you have to do."

It is truer now than it was then. Schools cannot bring themselves to say, "That's enough." No matter how high they raise the hoop, if a child manages to jump through it, they take it as a signal that they must raise it still higher.

The gross effects of these pressures are painfully evident. Along with an increase in psychological disturbances we have increases in suicide, in the use or overuse of alcohol and in drug-taking. We also read of a great increase in all kinds of cheating, not among unsuccessful students, but among superior students whose grades would be very good even if they did not cheat. It is no small thing that large numbers of our young people, supposedly our ablest and best, are becoming convinced that they must cheat in order to succeed; that success is so important that it justifies the cheating.

But the broader and more general consequence of the pressure for grades is that it has debased and corrupted the act of learning itself. Not by what we say but by what we do, by the way we hand out rewards and prizes, we convince many young people that it is not for the joy and satisfaction of understanding that we learn, but in order to get something for ourselves; that what counts in school and college is not knowing and understanding, but making someone think you know and understand; that knowledge is valuable, not because it helps us deal better with the problems of private and public life, but because it has become a commodity that can be sold for fancy prices on the market. School has become a kind of racket, and success in school, and hence in life, depends on learning how to beat it.

Can schools and colleges be persuaded to do away with, or greatly reduce, their demands for high grades? There are many reasons for thinking they cannot.

First, they do not seem aware of the harm that their competition for prestige is doing to American youth and American education. In fact, they take quite an opposite view, talking about higher standards and upgrading education.

Second, they would say that they have found from experience that it is the students with high test scores who have the best chance of staying in college. But this is because so much of their teaching is based on getting high test scores; if they reduced the importance of exams and marks, they would reduce the need for getting only those students who were good at taking exams.

Third, the colleges would say that unless they make entrance difficult by demanding high test scores, they will have too many applicants to choose from. But they have too many as it is, and must ultimately make many choices on the basis of criteria other than test scores. Why not make these criteria more important, and if they still have too many applicants, choose from them by lot? Under such a system, a student applying to a popular college would know that his chances of being admitted were slight, but would feel, if he was not admitted, that it was chance that had kept him out—not that he was no good.

Perhaps a number of prestige colleges could be persuaded to agree to say jointly that they would admit some fixed percentage of applicants each year, despite low test scores, if the applicants had other important qualifications. If they found, as I believe they would, that such students were on the whole as useful and valuable as students getting very high scores, they could raise the percentage. Such a policy would encourage primary and secondary schools and teachers to work for goals other than high test scores, and it would give hope to at least a number of very talented young people who are not good at taking exams.

But if the colleges cannot be persuaded to give up, or moderate, their competition for prestige and for high-scoring students who will enhance that prestige, then the schools should resist them. A good place to begin would be by attacking the notion that only at a prestige institution can one get a good education.

I have known, and know, students at prestige colleges who are not interested in their courses and for whom college has not been an exciting or stimulating experience. I know other bright and able boys and girls who have been, and are being, very much excited and stimulated at institutions that have much less prestige, or none at all.

It may well be true that a nonprestige institution has fewer first-rate scholars or teachers, but it is probably true that such as there are have more time for and interest in their really able and curious students. And the students, themselves under less pressure, have more time for them.

Most important of all, the schools and their teachers must do all they can, by word and deed, to destroy the notion that education is a race against other students to win the favor of someone in authority. They must put in its place the idea that what is important—and here I use the words of the late President Griswold of Yale—is "the desire and the capacity of the individual for self-education; that is, for finding meaning, truth and enjoyment in everything he does."

The Affluent Delinquent

Gerald J. Pine

University of New Hampshire

For generations we have deluded ourselves by stereotyping delinquents. Our society tends to attribute "good" to the middle group and "bad" to the lower. Pine systematically attempts to puncture some of the commonly held ideas with the truth as he sees it by pointing out that delinquency is not exclusively a lower-class trait. Do you agree with his premises? With the contributing factors set forth? What changes do you anticipate in society's attitude toward delinquency?

At one time or another nearly everyone has assumed the role of delinquency expert. Public and professional comment on juvenile delinquency seems never to die or fade away. Like sex, religion, sports, politics, and the weather, delinquency can always provide a subject for discussion. One dimension of the delinquency problem which has been a good conversation piece of late is the occurrence of delinquent behavior in the middle and upper classes. Statistics released by the Federal Bureau of Investigation and other governmental agencies, the growing number of newspaper accounts describing the antisocial and aberrant behavior of privileged youth, and the frequency with which delinquency in suburbia is discussed during cocktail *tête-à-têtes* attest to an apparent rising incidence of affluent delinquency.

This paper examines the relationship between delinquent behavior and social class status. Its pivotal concerns are reflected in the following questions:

1. What is the extent of delinquent behavior in the middle and upper classes?
2. How is delinquent behavior treated in the middle and upper classes?
3. Are there any forms of delinquency which are more peculiar to one class than another?
4. What is the relationship between social class mobility and delinquency?
5. What are the factors which generate the affluent delinquent?

In attempting to answer these questions, I have expressed my notions in a series of propositions anchored so far as possible in research findings, in theory, and in my personal experience as a school counselor in an affluent suburban community.

From *Phi Delta Kappan*, Vol. 48, No. 4 (1966), pp. 138-143. Reprinted by permission of the author and Phi Delta Kappa.

Proposition 1.

There is a significant relationship between an increase in a country's economic growth and a rise in delinquent behavior. There is evidence that a significant increase in the gross national product of a nation is accompanied or followed by a significant increase in delinquent behavior. Teen-age crime, once little known in France, is up 400 per cent over a decade ago. Prosperous West Germany is becoming concerned about crime by children, especially in the 14 to 18 age groups. Sweden, Denmark, Norway, Holland, and Switzerland all report increased teen-age criminality. Japan, which is enjoying the fastest rate of economic growth in the world, is also experiencing one of the most rapid escalations of delinquency.[1] Such trends offer a sharp contrast to the comparatively low rates of delinquency which appeared in the United States during the depression years.[2]

An increase in economic growth triggers a great deal of social and spatial mobility. The by-products of mobility and their role in delinquent behavior will be discussed in the propositions to follow.

Proposition 2.

There has always been a considerable amount of delinquency in the middle- and upper-class segments of our society. Several investigations have attempted to ascertain the frequency and nature of delinquent behavior in the middle and upper classes by using samples vaguely defined as middle- and upper-class in terms such as: "upper-income group," "children of the professional class," "college students," and "group from relatively more favored neighborhoods." In contrast to the evidence based on official records, these studies, notwithstanding the general definition of class, indicate delinquent behavior is more equally dispersed among the various social classes than the average American citizen realizes.

In 1946 Austin L. Porterfield[3] compared the offenses of 2,409 cases of alleged delinquents in the Fort Worth, Texas, area with the admitted conduct of several hundred students at three colleges of Northern Texas. He found that many college students had committed one or more of the "delinquency offenses" but seldom had been so charged as in the case of their less fortunate counterparts.

Wallerstein and Wyle[4] distributed to an upper-income group a questionnaire listing 49 offenses under the penal code of the state of New York. All of the offenses were sufficiently serious to draw maximum sentences of not less than a year. Replies were received from 1,698 individuals. Ninety-nine per cent of those questioned answered affirmatively to one or more of the offenses.

---

[1] *Boston Sunday Globe* (UPI), August 22, 1965, p. 53.

[2] Negley K. Teeters and David Matza, "The Extent of Delinquency in the United States," *Journal of Negro Education,* Summer 1959, pp. 200–213.

[3] Austin L. Porterfield, *Youth in Trouble,* Texas: Leo Potishman Foundation, 1946.

[4] James S. Wallerstein and G. J. Wyle, "Our Law-abiding Lawbreakers," in *Probation,* 1946, pp. 107–112.

In response to a questionnaire which Bloch gave to 340 college juniors and seniors during the period from 1943–1948, approximately 91 per cent admitted that they had knowingly committed offenses against the law, both misdemeanors and felonies. The groups sampled came from considerably better-than-average middle-class homes. Women students were as glaringly delinquent in this respect as men, although the volume of major offenses which they admitted to was somewhat smaller than that for men.[5]

In another study Clinard discovered that of 49 criminology students at a Midwestern university, 86 per cent had committed thefts and about 50 per cent had committed acts of vandalism.[6]

Exploring the implications of "white-collar criminality" in regard to delinquent behavior, Wattenberg and Balistrieri compared 230 white boys charged with automobile theft with 2,544 others in trouble with the Detroit police in 1948. They found the automobile theft group came from relatively more favored neighborhoods and had good peer relations.[7]

An investigation was conducted by Birkness and Johnson in which a group of delinquents was compared with a group of nondelinquents. Each group included 25 subjects. It was found that five times as many of the parents of delinquent children (in contrast with the nondelinquent children) were of the professional class. Almost twice as many parents of the nondelinquents were classified in the manual labor status in comparison with the parents of delinquents.[8]

A study carried out by Nye in the state of Washington revealed that there was no significant relationship between one's position in the social class structure and the frequency and severity of delinquent behavior, i.e., the middle- and upper-class adolescent was involved in as much norm violating behavior as the lower-class adolescent.[9]

In summary, during the past 20 years there has been an accumulation of evidence to demonstrate that delinquency is not the exclusive property of the lower class; it appears to exist to a significant degree in all strata of our society. But if this is the case, why have we only now become so deeply concerned about the affluent delinquent? Certainly if we have been concerned we have not been "publicly" concerned to the degree that we are today. Perhaps the answer lies in the fact that within our social structure there is a protective shield which hides the affluent delinquent and which up to now has served as a curtain of silence making privileged delinquency socially invisible. Nearly 30 years ago Warner and Lunt, in their classic work *The Social Life of a Modern Community*, observed that the disparity in number of lower- and upper-class arrests is not to be accounted for by the fact that criminal behavior is proportionately higher among lower-class juveniles or that there are

[5]Herbert A. Bloch and Frank T. Flynn, *Delinquency: The Juvenile Offender in America Today*, New York: Random House, 1956, p. 11.

[6]Marshall B. Clinard, *Sociology of Deviant Behavior*, New York: Holt, Rinehart & Winston, 1957, p. 165.

[7]W. W. Wattenberg and J. Balistrieri, "Automobile Theft: A Favored Group Delinquency," *The American Journal of Sociology*, May 1952, pp. 575–579.

[8]V. Birkness and H. C. Johnson, "Comparative Study of Delinquent and Nondelinquent Adolescents," *Journal of Educational Research*, April 1949, pp. 561–572.

[9]F. Ivan Nye, *Family Relationships and Delinquent Behavior*, New York: John Wiley & Sons, 1959.

more ethnic groups whose children have been imperfectly adapted to city life. It must be understood as a product of the amount of protection from outside interference that parents can give members of their families.

Proposition 3.

Official delinquency data have been and are biased in favor of upper- and middle-class youth. Delinquency is usually considered primarily as a lower-class problem. However. the research reporting significant relationships between delinquent behavior and lower socioeconomic status has been characterized by a built-in bias, i.e., the use of official delinquency statistics that do not reflect a considerable amount of upper- and middle-class delinquent behavior. Middle- and upper-class children are less likely to become official delinquency statistics because their behavior is more frequently handled outside the sphere of formal legal institutions. The middle and upper classes control various means of preventing detection, influencing official authority, and generally "taking care of their own" through psychiatrists, clinics, and private institutions, thus avoiding the police and the courts—the official agencies.

In the following telling and graphic descriptions, Harrison Salisbury[10] describes the classic middle-class way of dealing with antisocial behavior:

> If sixteen-year old George and three of his friends "borrow" a nice-looking Pontiac convertible from the country club parking lot and set off on a joyride and are caught speeding by the county police they are taken to the station house all right, but nothing goes on the blotter. The parents come down, there is much talk, the fathers bawl the daylights out of the kids, the boys promise to be good, the owners wouldn't think of making a charge, and by two o'clock in the morning everyone is back home, peacefully sleeping. There's no case, no records, no statistics, "no delinquency."
>
> When 17-year-old Joan gets pregnant after letting 18-year-old Dennis "fool around" at a beach party one summer night, she isn't sent to the Youth House. Nor is Dennis confronted with the dilemma of marrying the girl or facing a charge of statutory rape. There is an angry dispute between the two families. Joan's family blames Dennis. Dennis's family blames Joan. In the end Joan's father finds a doctor who takes care of Joan for $750. Joan is a month late starting school in the fall because, as her mother explains to the principal, she had a severe reaction from the antibiotics they gave her at the camp up in New Hampshire where she went in August.

In addition to the built-in bias of official delinquency data, studies reporting on the relationship between social class status and delinquent behavior are characterized by another critical shortcoming: a paucity of empirical material on a significant dynamic of social class—social mobility.

[10]Harrison E. Salisbury, *The Shook-up Generation*, New York: Harper & Bros., 1958, pp. 107–109.

Proposition 4.

A significant factor related to delinquent behavior in the upper and middle classes is the dynamic of social mobility. What bearing does movement from one social class to another class have on delinquent behavior? What are the implications of vertical movement between classes in regard to norm violations? The question of social mobility has an important place in the study of social class and its impact on delinquent behavior for two reasons:

1) Social mobility introduces a dynamic feature of possible change into a class system, and 2) it can alter the structure and patterns of class relationships as the consequences of mobility introduce changes into those close relationships.

Here I would like to share with you the results of a study designed to determine the significance of the relationships between social class status, social mobility status, and delinquent behavior.[11] The study was conducted to determine the significance of the relationships between social class, social mobility, and delinquent behavior. Data were collected from a population of 683 pupils (grades 9–12) attending an urban high school. Information regarding delinquency was gathered by using a 120-item anonymous "delinquency inventory." The chi-square technique was employed to analyze the data, which showed that, in general, there is no significant relationship between social class status and delinquent behavior. A very strong relationship exists between social mobility status and delinquent behavior. Adolescents moving downward in the social structure are more heavily involved in delinquency; adolescents moving upward are least involved.

The primary conclusion made in this study is that delinquent behavior is less a function of the class an individual is in at the moment and much more a function of the class to which he aspires or toward which he is moving. In examining the relationship between social class and delinquent behavior, it is not only important to know what class an individual is in but perhaps more important to know if he is securely located in the class, if he has just managed a toehold in the class, or if he has just moved down from a class.

The findings indicate delinquent behavior is not a lower-class phenomenon. However, one aspect of the question of class differential in delinquent behavior which invites further investigation is the relationship between value system and delinquency. Social class status may be more accurately measured in terms of value systems than in terms of economic factors such as occupation, housing, residence, and income. The lower-class boy moving upward into the middle class may be guided in his behavior by a middle-class value system and, therefore, might be more accurately described as a member of the middle class.

The behavior of the middle-class boy moving downward in the social structure may be influenced primarily by lower-class concerns, hence

[11] Gerald J. Pine, "Social Class, Social Mobility, and Delinquent Behavior," *Personnel and Guidance Journal*, April 1965, pp. 770–774. See also: Pine's "Occupational and Educational Aspirations and Delinquent Behavior," *The Vocational Guidance Quarterly*, Winter Issue, 1964–1965.

he might be more accurately described as lower class. It is quite possible for a child to live in a lower-class neighborhood and in the midst of a lower-class culture and still be considered middle class.

An explanation of the strong relationship between downward mobility and delinquent behavior may be found in Reissman's hypothesis[12] regarding the psychological consequences of "downward mobility." He suggests that these consequences can be channeled away from the individual to avoid injury to self-conceptions and self-respect. The individual imputes to others the blame for his or his family's descent in the social structure. His frustration and his failure are poured into an explanation that implicates society or society's institutions as the cause of it all. Hostile and negative attitudes toward others and toward authority develop.

If the intensity of the psychological consequences of "mobility failure" is in proportion to the degree of failure, then it is not difficult to understand the strength of the relationship between downward mobility and delinquent behavior. Certainly, downward mobility represents the greatest failure in the mobility process. For, in a culture which highly esteems the success value, what constitutes a greater failure than the failure to at least maintain one's status quo in the social structure?

Proposition 5.

Successful social mobility is a breeding ground for the development of delinquent behavior. The research evidence presented in Proposition 3 indicates there is a statistically significant relationship between downward mobility of adolescents and delinquent behavior. Paradoxically, the downward movement of the adolescent may be the consequence of the successful mobility of his parents. Psychological tension and conflict often accompany successful movement in the social structure and may be expressed in delinquent behavior.

Successful mobility necessarily involves a major adjustment by the individual. He must reject the way of life of the group he has just left and assume the new way of life of the group he has just entered. It is a process of class "acculturation." Depending upon the change required, the reorientation of the individual can be enormous; depending upon the recency of the change, the reorientation can involve a great deal of insecurity.

"Successful mobility places the individual, for some period of time, in a marginal social position. The individual's former friends and associates may find him threatening; his success is a mark of their failure. His newly created friends and associates produced by his successful move may find him too 'different,' too 'raw,' and too recent to be accepted as a bona fide member. The individual thus finds himself suspended in a 'success limbo.' The insecurity he feels may produce reactions the same as those exhibited by failure."[13]

---

[12] Leonard Reissman, *Class in American Society*, Glencoe, Ill.: The Free Press, 1959, p. 369.
[13] *Ibid.*, pp. 371–372.

Not only does the individual experience the results of success or failure but his family does also. Whyte[14] found that the individual's family must become implicated in his success just as they do in his failures.

On a larger scale, our society must experience the consequences for its emphasis upon social mobility, upon seeking and achieving success. Tumin[15] sets forth the following as by-products of the stress placed on social mobility in American society:

1. A "diffusion of insecurity" as more and more people become involved with trying to get ahead rather than developing any lasting and sure sense of the group and its needs. Traditional beliefs and values of society become threatened as behavior is more and more oriented toward "status acceptance and prestige ranking."

2. A "severe imbalance" of social institutions as a result of rapid mobility of the population as religion, education, and the family become tied to the struggle for economic success.

3. "Fragmentation of the social order" as more and more individuals become rivalrous with each other. Competition does not always lead to the greatest good for the greatest number.

4. "Denial of work" as the emphasis shifts from the importance of work and striving to the urgency of appearing to be successful. Preference is given to the open portrayal of *being* successful, as measured by the power and property which one openly consumes.

5. "Rapid social mobility" generates in the older portions of the population a cranky and bitter conservatism and worship of the past; and in the new mobile segments a vituperative contempt of traditions.

It is the accumulation and the complex interaction of these social by-products which fertilize the soil for the growth of affluent delinquency.

Proposition 6.

The female-based household is a by-product of successful mobility and an important variable in the development of delinquent behavior. Success and the striving for success in the middle and upper classes is frequently the incubator of the female-based household. A number of studies have identified the female-based household as a characteristic of lower-class society and as an influencing factor in the development of delinquent behavior. And yet anyone who has worked with middle- and upper-class youth is keenly aware of the large number of female-dominated families in suburbia. In order to insure and maintain his success, father often becomes a "weekend briefcase-toting visitor" who is either absent from the home, only sporadically present, or when present only minimally or inconsistently involved in the raising of the children. Mother becomes "chief cook and bottle washer," assuming both the maternal and paternal roles.

---

[14]W. H. Whyte, "The Wives of Management," *Fortune*, October 1951; and "The Corporation and the Wife," *Fortune*, November 1951.

[15]Melvin C. Tumin, "Some Unapplauded Consequences of Social Mobility in a Mass Society," *Social Forces*, October 1957, pp. 32–37.

It is not too difficult to understand how female-centered families in the middle and upper class can produce delinquents, particularly in the male adolescent population.

Because of the inconsistent presence or involvement of an adequate masculine model in the home with whom the suburban boy can identify, many teen-age males develop uncertainties about their masculine identity at a time in their lives when identity is a crucial matter. For the adolescent male who feels insecure about his sex identification, delinquency represents a demonstrative vehicle for asserting his masculinity.

Proposition 7.

The emphasis on success in our culture has led to the elongation of adolescence, a contributing factor in the development of delinquent behavior. Another consequence of success in the middle and upper classes is the extension of adolescence as a period of growth and development. The emphasis on success in suburbia is epitomized in the pressures exerted on youth to get into college. For the vast numbers of young boys and girls who do go to college one fact is very clear: Adolescence doesn't end at 18 or 19; it probably ends at 21 or 22, and perhaps even later. Thus for a large number of our privileged youth at least four years have been tacked on to the process of growing up and four years can be a long time to wait to prove yourself—to demonstrate that you are a man or a woman. Four more years of that social limbo we call adolescence are very conducive to intensifying the already existing feelings of anxiety, tension, restlessness, and rebellion so common to high school youth. Adolescence is becoming an "existential vacuum," a social process lacking purpose and meaning. To the degree we elongate the process of adolescence without providing purpose for its existence, to that degree should we anticipate more frequent socially aberrant and rebellious behavior.

Proposition 8.

A middle- and upper-class "sheepskin psychosis" nourishes norm-violating behavior. In the middle and upper classes there is tremendous pressure placed upon youth to succeed. These pressures emanate from the dominating concern of parents for achieving and "getting ahead," and the feeling in youth of an ensuing sense of discrepancy between aspiration and achievement. "This strong focus in the middle-class milieu may induce the whole perfectionist-compulsive syndrome, in which children have impossible ideas of what they should accomplish; the result for some individuals is a combination of neuroses built around the individual's inability to achieve internalized goals of various types, e.g., learning to read, being on the honor roll, or getting into the college of first choice. . . . The stresses imposed through the conflict over aspiration and achievement wake a wide variety of symptoms. One of these symptoms may take the form of norm-violating behavior."[16]

Proposition 9.

Middle-class values which once served as behavior controls are weakening. One of the identifying characteristics of the middle class is the tradition of deferring immediate gratifications for long-range goals. For years this tradition helped to instill in middle-class youngsters a capacity for self-denial and impulse control. However, there is mounting indication today that the strength of this tradition of focus on achievement, of directed work effort, and deferment of immediate pleasures is diminishing in a number of middle-class sectors. Impulse buying and installment plan financing are very representative of the "have-it-now" pattern of the lower-class culture. Concomitantly, compulsory education and a continuous promotion policy act to keep all youngsters in school regardless of effort, achievement, or future goal. These trends have tended to lessen the view of middle-class youth that success is achieved through deferred gratification, frustration tolerance, directed effort, and self-control. If delinquency is on the rise in the middle class, it may be attributable in part to a diminution in the classical middle-class tradition of "hard work today and rewards tomorrow."

Proposition 10.

Middle-class youth behavior reflects lower-class values. Currently, lower-class concerns and values are being sold to and bought by the middle-class consumer. Mass media and the advertising world have dipped deeply into the lower-class culture. Lower-class focal concerns such as force, duplicity, chance, excitement, trouble, autonomy, and "present pleasure" have been mined over and over again for use on the screen, the air waves, the picture tube, and the printed page. The effect of this cultural saturation has been the borrowing of lower-class concerns by middle-class youth. Adolescent fads, jargon, music, and behavior seem to mirror a number of lower-class behavior patterns. It would seem that the interaction of these recently assumed lower-class concerns with the other social and psychological by-products of social mobility constitute a powerful generative force in developing affluent delinquency.

[16]William C. Kvaraceus and Walter Miller, *Delinquent Behavior: Culture and the Individual*, Washington, D.C.: National Education Association, 1959, pp. 99–100.

The Unhappy Mother

Louise E. Simons

Following is a discussion of the emotional needs and problems of the pregnant unwed adolescent. Do you believe that the "pill" may be the answer to this type of problem, and is it likely that American society can accept birth control to this extent? The problems stated here are real. The role of an unwed teen-age mother is one of the most difficult to face. Among the possibilities are removing the stigma of being an unwed mother or using contraceptives universally and having children only when it's considered proper or thought desirable. Do you think that one or both of these could be the answer, or are there other proposals to be made? Will the problem be faced or shall we continue to be involved with difficulties that the author describes?

It is likely that in sociology and psychology few subjects are currently more discussed or more disagreed upon than that of the unwed mother. Certain facts, however, are more or less accepted by those studying the subject: 1) The number of illegitimate births is increasing, if for no other reason than that there are more unmarried women than ever before; 2) Changing mores and social practice are putting more and more pressure on young girls to enter into premarital sexual relations, while still censuring the natural result of such relations, i.e. premarital pregnancy;[1] and 3) Emotional and psychological factors play a large part in bringing about pregnancy in the unmarried woman.[2]

Whatever her emotional state prior to her pregnancy, it may be assumed as an initial and rather obvious hypothesis that every unmarried mother has some degree of emotional difficulties as the *result* of her pregnancy. A corollary hypothesis is that the teen-aged unmarried mother has additional emotional problems by virtue of the very fact that she *is* a teen-ager. Furthermore, these problems are often synergistic, resulting in a state of emotional disequilibrium greater than the sum of problems of adolescence and out-of-wedlock pregnancy in themselves.

Just what are these emotional needs of the unmarried, pregnant teen-ager? First of all, let us consider those of any adolescent. Most important, perhaps, is establishing his identity. "Who am I, really?" is an ever present, all pervasive riddle for every adolescent. "Am I a child? Am I an adult? Am I *really* a man? A woman?" His answers to these questions change from day to day, and the times when he most needs a stable and satisfactory self-concept are likely to be those times when his own appraisal of himself has hit rock bottom.

Reprinted by permission of the author.

[1]Clark E. Vincent, *Unmarried Mothers* (New York: The Free Press of Glencoe, 1961), p. 7.

[2]Leontine Young, *Out of Wedlock* (New York: McGraw-Hill, 1954).

In attempting to establish his sexual identity, it is the sensitive, self-analytical adolescent who may most doubt his masculinity or femininity, yet who, because of his internalized values, may be least able to prove it to himself. If he is expected to attend college and, perhaps, graduate school, he not only has greater pressures upon him for academic performance, but he realizes that his situation regarding sexual gratification is not likely to change for quite some time.[3] The ability to postpone gratification of desires is a second developmental task common to all adolescents; most, however, find it an exceedingly difficult aspect of the transition from childhood to adulthood. By gratifying his immediate desires, the teen-ager attempts to preserve the security of childhood while, simultaneously, attempting to establish his manhood. This dichotomy re-emphasizes his basic lack of identity: "Who am I? Child, or man?"

A third emotional task which must be undertaken by every adolescent is that of establishing his independence. Independence cannot come overnight; it does not grow spontaneously. It must be planted and carefully cultivated over a long period of time. It must be inseparably linked to a sense of responsibility—of being responsible for one's actions, *not* simply a matter of "fending for one's self."

These three tasks, then, may be said to constitute the primary emotional needs of the adolescent: establishing his identity, adjusting to the necessity for postponement of the gratification of his desires, and establishing his independence.

What of the emotional needs of the pregnant woman?—not only the teen-ager, or the unmarried mother, but every woman with a new and unique individual developing within her body—what does she need? First of all, she needs approval and reassurance. To give life to a person is to be responsible for that person; how many women feel truly capable of meeting such a responsibility? A child must be fed, protected, "trained," and given security . . . disciplined, educated, and taught responsibility. Can any mother feel that she is qualified to do all this? And what about her husband? Can she be *sure* that he really wants this child? Even in the best of all possible circumstances, when parents love each other and desire a child, it can be staggering to consider the responsibility involved.

Therefore, the pregnant woman needs constant reassurance that what she is doing is right and that she is doing it well. She needs acceptance as a mature person who will be a good mother to her child. She needs her husband's assurance that she is, and will continue to be, attractive to him and a good wife to him. She needs her parents' approval and support at this time when she is taking the drastic and irreversible step from being a *child* to being a *mother*; without such approval and support she may feel intense guilt at assuming this new status, usurping their authority, as it were.

The expectant mother also needs to be treated with great dignity as she becomes more and more awkward and misshapen. If she is happy

[3]A. C. Kinsey, W. B. Pomeroy, and C. E. Martin, "Social Level and Sexual Outlet," in *The Unwed Mother*, ed. Robert W. Roberts (New York: Harper & Row, 1966).

to be pregnant and confident of her ability to be a good mother, her very shape can be a source of pride and evidence of her accomplishment. If, however, she is *not* happy or secure in her pregnancy, her physical appearance may become abhorrent to her and may threaten her already precarious emotional balance.

Every pregnant mother feels occasional twinges of apprehension concerning her unborn child: "Will he be all right? Have I unconsciously done anything which may harm him?" If she has a basic doubt about her right to bear a child, this doubt, and the resultant guilt feelings, may intensify her concern about the fate of the child. She may consciously or subconsciously try to wish him out of existence; this can only increase her lack of confidence in her ability as a mother, and the cycle continues. It is only by open lines of communication that the pregnant woman can give voice to her fear for her child; even then, it may be so deeply buried that she cannot express it as such. However, an understanding, accepting attitude by those around her can help her examine her fear and be reassured.

Finally, she has a great need to share this entire experience with someone. The subjective changes which she notices day by day, the tremendous implications of her condition, the hopes and dreams, the eventual personality and accomplishments of the individual now growing within her—all these are things which she needs to discuss, not on a factual, professional basis with a doctor or nurse, but on a wonderfull, awe-full, joy-full basis with someone she loves.

These needs of the pregnant woman—for reassurance, approbation, acceptance, pride in personal appearance, and open lines of communication—are all quite compatible with the primary needs of the adolescent. Indeed, we can assume that a pregnant teen-ager who could meet these secondary needs while, simultaneously, establishing her identity and independence and maturing in her ability to postpone gratification of her desires might pass through a pregnancy with no greater emotional problems than are experienced by the older woman.

However, the teen-ager who is unmarried at the time of her pregnancy may well be unable to fulfill the emotional requirements of *either* the adolescent *or* the pregnant woman. At this time, when she most needs reassurance, approbation, acceptance, and open lines of communication, she is offered none of these; quite the contrary, these are withdrawn from her, and negative experiences are substituted for positive. Her need for pride in her personal appearance is incompatible with her need for secrecy. Her search for a sense of identity is blocked, and she becomes still more confused as to who she is. Her struggle for independence collapses in the face of her suddenly increased, almost total dependence on either her parents or some other adult. She must now have help in almost every aspect of her life: physical care, financial assistance, shelter, guidance in making tremendously difficult decisions; she becomes increasingly incapable of taking care of herself. She is now *forced* to postpone those things which she wants most—the end of her pregnancy, a return to her family or to school, her slender figure—and the very fact that she has no choice in the matter may well delay her ability to postpone gratification voluntarily.

It seems that the case of the unmarried, pregnant adolescent may be unique in the degree to which it eliminates the possibility of meeting the normal developmental tasks of the individual involved. In the case of the girl who unconsciously chooses pregnancy as a means of solving a problem, the problem is frequently intensified. The welcome security of obvious biological maturity is short-lived in the girl who sought to assert her independence; all too soon she realizes just how young and immature she is. The girl who is concerned about her femininity and even possible homosexual feelings may wish to prove that she is "normal" by "having a baby." However, the conditions of her illegitimate pregnancy may so preclude the development of any maternal feeling for the child, often causing feelings of disgust and rejection instead, that the mother may end her pregnancy with even graver doubts about her femininity than when she began it.

In addition to these emotional requirements common to every adolescent and every pregnant woman, the unmarried teen-aged mother has still further needs: understanding, a sense of worth and dignity, a positive, meaningful relationship with an adult authority figure, insight into her behavior, direction and guidance, and opportunities for rehabilitation.

While there is less stigma attached to premarital pregnancy than there was a generation ago (perhaps simply because of its greater incidence), the degree of understanding for each *individual* girl depends on her *individual* situation. Her parents may realize the intense stresses placed upon the present-day adolescent, with society's implied permission for premarital intercourse, the threat of nuclear war, the increased use of drugs, and the general restlessness and revolt of the young people of today, or they may simply see that their daughter has disgraced, not herself, but them. Fortunate indeed is the girl whose parents can accept her and support her through this crisis. It is even possible, with parental understanding, for a premarital pregnancy to become a learning and maturing process, calling attention to the girl's problems and providing an opportunity for solving them. If, on the other hand, she receives no understanding or support within her home, she must turn to the community or to private organizations for whatever help she can find.

One natural consequence of acceptance is a sense of worth and dignity; it does not, however, follow inevitably, as this sense of personal value comes only from active, positive relationships, and never from a negative or passive "acceptance." Where there is genuine, warm understanding and concern, miracles can happen; it is only then that a meaningful relationship with an adult authority figure can be established, and only then that the girl can begin to gain insight and accept direction. Her experience with adults prior to this time may have been anything but conducive to the establishment of such a relationship; her parents are likely to have been either too strict or too permissive, rejecting or possessive. The luckier girl in such a family setting may reach out, of her own volition, and set up a positive relationship with a teacher, a spiritual advisor, or the parent of a friend; but the "unlucky" girl, the one who is most likely to become an unwed mother while still in her teens, has seldom had such a relationship with anyone whose authority she could accept. It is little wonder, then, that many of these girls are suspicious of everyone who tries to help them, doubting their motives, dreading their criticism or contempt, attempting only to wage a solitary battle against the world, as they have been accustomed to do.

Thus, the emotional needs of the unwed, pregnant adolescent are many, complex, and often incompatible with each other. Unfortunately, all too little is being done to meet these needs, and some well-meant efforts seem only to compound the problem. In our attempts to provide privacy and prevent exposure, we may so insulate these girls that we cut them off from all communication. They come to the hospitals to deliver their babies, and, with the kindest of intentions, the staff studiously avoids mentioning their problems, as if unaware that such problems exist. Every mother about to give birth should have the opportunity to talk about it if she wishes to do so, to express her feelings about her pregnancy, and to discuss her baby with someone who cares about her as a person. *If a mother has greater needs because she is an unwed adolescent, then she must be afforded greater opportunities to meet these needs because she is an unwed adolescent.*

It is highly probable that the unmarried mother about to deliver did not consciously choose to be in this position. However, regardless of the emotional problems which may have contributed to her pregnancy, and regardless of her chances for rehabilitation and her eventual role as a "productive" individual,[4] she is, at the time of giving birth, fulfilling her unique function as a woman. To rob her of a sense of dignity and accomplishment at this time is inexcusable.

The miracle of birth will always be just that. But it is only when the fundamental emotional needs of both adolescence and pregnancy have successfully been met that the birth of a child is likely to become a source of lasting fulfillment and joy.

---

[4]Philip M. Sarrel, M. D., "The University Hospital and the Teen-Age Unwed Mother," *American Journal of Public Health,* August 1967.

The Dangerous Drug Problem—II

The Medical Society of the County of New York

Much misinformation is bantered about with regard to barbiturates, amphetamines, tranquilizers, and hallucinogens. This article is a policy statement, with recommendations for legislation, on the abuse of LSD and other non-narcotic drugs. The medical point of view is difficult to argue with since it describes statistics and physical reactions, and the suggestions for legislation are contrary to many of the expressed desires of youth. Yet, parts of the suggestions could have been made by youth. Are these recommendations realistic? If not, what would be?

I Introduction

In January 1965 the Subcommittee on Narcotics Addiction of the Public Health Committee of The Medical Society of the County of New York issued a position paper outlining current problems in the treatment of narcotics addicts and offering a series of recommendations which were adopted by the Society.

During the last two years the renamed "Committee on Drug Abuse" has focussed its attention on the ever widening scope of abuse and illicit use of non-narcotic drugs such as marihuana, amphetamines, tranquilizers and hallucinogens.

This report constitutes a revision of the Society's paper, "The Dangerous Drug Problem," formulated by the Subcommittee on Narcotics Addiction of the Committee on Public Health and approved with amendments by the Society on March 28, 1966, and issued on May 5, 1966. This revision attempts to clarify our position in some areas and to update information and recommendations on the problem of drug abuse.

II Background and Current Problems

Products of the ubiquitous hemp plant, Cannabis sativa, are referred to by the generic name Cannabis. Cannabis preparations include marihuana (U.S.A.), dagga (South Africa), kif (Morocco), ganga and charas (India).

Reprinted by permission from the January 1968 issue of *New York Medicine.*

A. Marihuana:

Several features of marihuana use should be noted.

1. There is evidence that marihuana use is increasing among young middle and upper income groups, especially those on college campuses. Recent articles show that an average of 7-15 per cent of college students use marihuana on one or more occasions during a four-year collegiate career. In certain colleges the incidence is substantially higher (20-40 per cent).

2. There is no statistical evidence that marihuana use is associated with crimes of violence in the United States.

3. Marihuana is not a narcotic nor is it addicting. It is a euphoriant and mild hallucinogen. However, it can produce all the untoward effects attributed to more potent hallucinogens. It should be emphasized that marihuana users frequently have impaired judgment in certain areas, particularly in skilled activities, such as driving.

4. The continued linking of marihuana with opiates and cocaine potentially results in excessively harsh penalties at both federal and state levels. According to federal law, conviction for possession of marihuana may result in a 2- to 10-year sentence for the first offense, and 5 to 20 years for a second offense. In 62 per cent of the states, the penalty for marihuana possession is a minimum of 2 years imprisonment. The maximum possible sentence in 44 states ranges from 5 years to life. Conviction on a second possession offense may incur a sentence of a minimum of 5 years in 37 states.

5. Part of the confusion concerning the dangers of marihuana can be resolved by identifying the potency of the cannabis preparation used. Indian ganga and hashish are highly potent. Habitual and heavy use of these forms of cannabis has been associated with criminality, violence, and psychosis. The marihuana used in the United States, the kif used in North Africa, and the bhang drunk in India are perhaps one-fifth the strength of hashish and are less dangerous. Acts of violence have not been statistically correlated with use of less potent forms. Although anecdotal reports indicate that in a given individual marihuana may unleash aggressive tendencies, the many psychoses induced by kif in Morocco occurred mainly among those who used large amounts over long periods of time. However, cannabis is an unpredictable drug and is potentially harmful even in its mildest form. Even occasional use can produce (although rarely) acute panic, severe intoxication, or an acute toxic psychosis.

6. The statement that marihuana users frequently progress to heroin needs careful scrutiny. The lack of correlation between marihuana use and subsequent heroin addiction was authoritatively reported by the New York City Mayor's Committee on Marihuana in 1944. Experience suggests that many individuals use marihuana only once or at infrequent intervals. Most individuals who eventually become heroin addicted or use LSD previously used a variety of drugs including marihuana. However, use of marihuana may initiate the individual into the morass of drug abuse and this may result in subsequent use of other drugs such as LSD or heroin.

B. Barbiturates, Amphetamines, and Tranquilizers:

Approximately one-half of the estimated 13 billion pills and capsules of these agents produced yearly in the United States are diverted to the illicit market, selling for $.10 to $1 per single dose. The consumption of these drugs has increased markedly in the last 30 years. In 1936, for example, 231,167 pounds of barbituric acid were produced in the United States. By 1960 this had risen by 250 per cent to 852,000 pounds. In the same period the population had increased by only 25 per cent. Between 14 and 18 per cent of all physicians' prescriptions are for sedatives or tranquilizers. The profits in the illicit market are enormous, the estimate ranging between 250 and 500 million dollars annually.

Barbiturates such as Phenobarbital, Pentobarbital, Secobarbital, Amobarbital (amytal), and the combination of Secobarbital and Amobarbital (Tuinal) are the most abused drugs in this category. Every year there are about 3,000 deaths due to accidental or intentional overdose of barbiturates, but a far more common problem is habituation and addiction. Barbiturate addiction, defined by physical dependence, is characterized by intellectual impairment, self-neglect, slurred speech, tremor, defective judgment, drowsiness, emotional lability, bizarre behavior, and ataxia. Those who treat it consider it a "nasty" addiction, often characterized by excessive activity, agitation, and by aggressive, sometimes paranoid behavior. Withdrawal, if abrupt, may produce nausea, vomiting, weakness, tremulousness, insomnia, fever (up to 105 degrees F), delirium, hallucinations, convulsions, stupor, and coma, which may be fatal.

A survey of six state and two city hospitals with narcotic detoxification units reveals that heroin addicts are currently having withdrawal problems, not because of the opiate but because of concomitant addiction to barbiturates. They can easily be withdrawn from the opiate but the barbiturate withdrawal is prolonged and trying. Over half the heroin addicts use multiple drugs, and according to a careful study at Lexington, Kentucky, 22.8 per cent are also physically dependent on barbiturates (JAMA 189:366, 1964).

Of the plethora of nonbarbiturate sedatives and tranquilizers on the market, several, such as glutethimide, have been found to be addicting. The addiction and withdrawal manifestations of these drugs are similar to those observed with barbiturates. Physical dependence on these may develop and, on some occasions, abrupt withdrawal has led to convulsions. Death has been reported during withdrawal from some of these drugs.

Amphetamines are habituating and dangerous. Judgmental and intellectual impairment, aggressive behavior, incoordination, and hallucinations all may occur during habituation. A variety of symptoms may also occur during withdrawal. Furthermore, amphetamines are being implicated in increasing numbers of automobile accidents. The use of amphetamine-like stimulants, such as methedrine or desoxyn, intravenously has been associated with a remarkably high incidence of paranoid psychoses. Such intravenous administration of amphetamines has increased markedly in recent years, especially among so-called hippies and among opiate users.

Tranquilizers, sedatives, and stimulants are not only dangerous in themselves, but if taken in combination, their potential harm is markedly augmented. This applies not only to combinations of these three but also to concurrent use with ethyl alcohol.

C. Hallucinogens:

In somewhat arbitrary fashion the commonly used hallucinogens can be divided into 3 groups according to potency. These can be summarized as follows:

1. Mild Hallucinogens: Airplane glue, gasoline, nutmeg, marihuana (American type), Freon, and morning glory seeds.
2. Moderately Potent Hallucinogens:
   dimethyltryptamine (when smoked)
   psilocybin (sertonin-related)
   bufotenine
   peyote, mescaline } (epinerphrine-related)
   more potent preparations of cannabis (marihuana) including Indian hashish and ganga.
3. Highly Potent Hallucinogens: LSD (d-Lysergic acid diethylamide), intravenously administered dimethyltryptamine, and STP (variously described as a phenylethylamine or a combination of mescaline and amphetamine).

LSD, an indol derived from lysergic acid, was isolated from the fungus *Claviceps purpurea* in 1938 by Hofman, together with ergotamine and ergonovine. Its hallucinogenic properties were discovered inadvertently 3 years later. Since that time it has been studied extensively by the medical profession; more recently it has become the center of an increasingly vitriolic controversy.

Discussion:

In the United States the use of dimethyltryptamine, STP, morning glory seeds, psilocybin, nutmeg, and mescaline are minor problems. Glue sniffing remains a persistent and disturbing problem among children at school age. The major hallucinogenic abuses are related to the use of marihuana (American type) and LSD-25.

LSD currently is licitly unavailable except for experimental investigations sanctioned by the National Institutes of Health.

LSD has been reported to be of benefit in the treatment of psychoneuroses but until additional, careful, long-term studies are performed, the precise role of LSD in the treatment of psychoneuroses will not be clear. It has also been claimed by several investigators that administration of LSD to alcoholics on 1 to 3 occasions has resulted in 6- to 12-month abstinence rates of 20 to 60 per cent. These investigations, although optimistic, suffer from lack of adequate controls and prolonged follow-up. It should be noted that in those recovering, substantial adscititious therapeutic measures were also initiated. Furthermore, there is a marked decrease in sobriety found between the 3rd and 6th months of the follow-up period.

LSD has also been said to be useful in the treatment of frigidity and sexual perversions, and in the study of psychoses, but the data are inadequate and conflicting. It appears to offer some promise in the treatment of autistic children.

LSD has also been recommended for the treatment of severe pain in patients with terminal illness such as cancer. It should be emphasized that LSD given experimentally by trained physicians and psychiatrists is usually used in relatively small dosage, under which conditions untoward reactions are less likely to occur.

There are then at present no indications for use of LSD except in a strictly controlled experimental setting. Although LSD's medical use is confined to valid experimental projects, its more prevalent use is illicit in the form of LSD-coated sugar cubes, in capsules, or dissolved in water or soft drinks. The LSD used for such purposes is obtained from "amateur" chemists, from organized criminal operatives who either manufacture LSD here or import it from abroad, or from legitimate companies in foreign countries who sometimes ship batches of lysergic acid to unauthorized persons who request it on legitimate-appearing letterheads.

Once obtained, 100–600 mcg. of LSD are ingested. This is called "taking a trip"—a "trip" is infrequently taken more than twice a week. The cost of the individual cube varies from $1 to $10. The cubes once saturated with LSD may remain potent for a period of several months. The illicit user has no way of telling the exact amount in the cube or drink.

After the cubes, containing 100–600 mcg. each, are ingested, a startling series of events occurs with marked individual variation. All senses appear sharpened and brightened; vivid panoramic visual hallucinations of fantastic brightness and depth are experienced as well as hyperacusis. Senses blend and become diffused so that sounds are felt, colors tasted, and fixed objects pulsate and breathe. Depersonalization also occurs frequently so that the individual loses ego identity; he has a feeling of unity with other beings, animals, inanimate objects and the universe in general. The body image is often distorted so that faces, including the user's, assume bizarre proportions and the limbs may appear extraordinarily short or elongated. The user is enveloped by a sense of isolation and often is dominated by feelings of paranoia and fear. If large doses are ingested (over 700 mcg.) confusion and delirium frequently ensue. During LSD use, repressed material may be unmasked which is difficult for the individual to handle. Although the duration of the experience is usually 4–12 hours, it may continue for days.

There are some sociologists and psychologists as well as a substantial number of interested lay people who insist that LSD has a miraculous capacity to induce an ecstatic religious and mystical experience permitting a person to expand his mind to understand God, the universe, himself, love, and the hereafter. Some of those persons advocate the unrestricted use of LSD-25 by all who so desire it. However, there is no clear evidence that valid transcendental experiences have taken place as a result of LSD.

The members of the Subcommittee on Drug Abuse, noting that the legitimate uses of LSD have not yet been clearly defined, are deeply concerned over reports of adverse effects observed in persons to whom the drug is administered in a nonscientifically controlled setting.

In an 18-month period between 1965 and 1967, over 130 persons were admitted to the psychiatric division of Bellevue Hospital with acute psychoses induced by LSD. Prior to that time, LSD intoxication was rarely observed in that hospital. One hundred and fourteen of the hospital charts were available to the committee and were scrutinized. All 114 took LSD in a nonscientifically controlled setting.

Of the 114 patients 88 per cent were white and 68 per cent were male. These figures contrast with those available for heroin; among heroin addicts over two thirds in New York City are from lower socio-economic minority groups (Puerto Rican or Negro). The average age was 23 years with a range of 15-43 years. Seventy-three per cent had taken LSD on only 1-3 occasions. The predominant manifestation in 13 per cent was overwhelming fear, and an additional 12.3 per cent experienced uncontrolled violent urges. Others were found running or sitting nude in the streets. Homicide or suicide was attempted by 8.6 per cent. One third of the 114 appeared to have underlying psychoses or schizoid personalities. Approximately half of these were actively psychotic prior to LSD use while the others either had been treated in psychiatric institutions in the past but were adequately integrated into society until given the LSD or had no prior known psychoses but clearly had schizoid personalities.

Interestingly, although visual hallucinations usually predominate in LSD psychoses, one third had prominent auditory hallucinations, including one patient whose "voices" told him to jump in front of a subway train, which he did (without serious injury).

Most of those with acute LSD psychoses recovered rapidly, becoming oriented and "normal" (for them) in less than 48 hours. In others the psychoses resolved in less than a week. In 15.8 per cent, however, recovery did not take place during their Bellevue hospitalization and they had to be referred for long-term hospitalization; half of these had no history of underlying mental disease.

The data from the literature and the Bellevue experience indicate that apparently normal, well-adjusted persons can undergo an acute psychotic break under the influence of LSD, and those with unstable personalities may experience prolonged LSD-induced psychoses. Thus, Grinker noted in 1963 (Arch. Gen. Psychiat. 8:425) "Latent psychoses are disintegrating under the influence of even single doses."

The question remains unanswered whether "normal," well-adjusted persons given LSD can suffer prolonged (as contrasted to transient) psychoses. Reports of children accidentally ingesting single doses of LSD indicate that severe personality disturbances and recurrent hallucinations may persist for weeks or even months.

The dangers of LSD have been summarized by many others including Levine and Ludwig (Comp. Psychiat. 5:314, 1964, JAMA 191:92, 1965), by Cohen and Ditman (JAMA 181:161, 1962) and by Frosch, Robbins, and Stern (New Engl. J. Med. 273:1235, 1965). These include (1) acute or prolonged psychoses, (2) acting out of sociopathic character disorders, (3) acting out of homosexual impulses, (4) suicidal or homicidal attempts, (5) uncontrolled aggression, (6) convulsions, and (7) reappearance. The last named is an intriguing phenomenon in which the manifestations of LSD intoxication, including hallucinations, reappear weeks, months or even to two years after LSD use when the user finds himself in a stressful situation.

Grinker (Arch. Gen. Psychiat. 8:425, 1963; JAMA 187:768, 1964) notes, "The drugs are indeed dangerous even when used under the best precautions. There are increasing numbers of reports that temporary or even permanent harm may be induced despite apparently careful pretherapeutic screening of latent psychosis and careful precautions during the artificial psychosis." Here again is the story of evil results from the ill-advised use of a potentially valuable drug due to unjustified claims, indiscriminate and premature publicity and lack of proper controls.

Clearly, the danger is far greater in nonmedical hands. The ease of manufacture, the potential profits in the illicit trade, the gaudy publicity, and the activities of certain proponent groups all have contributed to hallucinogenic drug abuse.

In addition to the aforementioned dangers, the recent studies on chromosome change appear convincing. Eighty to 85 per cent of those using LSD manifest both an unusually high incidence of chromosomal breaks and chromosomal rearrangement. Similar chromosomal abnormalities have been found in some offspring of women who took LSD during pregnancy. Thus, the spectre of genetically induced damage in the users or their progeny is raised. The actual significance of these chromosomal findings await additional genetic and epidemiologic studies. (Of the studies on humans available at this writing, two show chromosomal aberrations, whereas in four studies, chromosomal defects were found.)

Recommendations:

1. No hallucinogen (LSD, mescaline, STP, psilocybin, or dimethyltryptamine) should be administered except by a physician trained in its use, and this should apply even if current studies show LSD to be of value in the treatment of psychoneuroses, sexual perversions, frigidity, alcoholism, or other illnesses. We stand unalterably opposed to any expansion of the use of psychedelic drugs beyond their use by physicians. Even use by trained physicians should continue to be limited to carefully controlled experiments.

2. Appropriate educational materials should be made available to the public emphasizing the potential dangers of the more potent hallucinogens as well as the amphetamines and barbiturates.

3. The local and state medical societies should prepare adequate

educational materials for physicians so that hallucinogenic (and also barbiturate and amphetamine) toxicity can be readily recognized.

4. In regard to barbiturates once severe habituation or addiction has been diagnosed, withdrawal should be performed in the hospital because of the dangers of convulsions and coma. Most barbiturate addicts require psychiatric treatment.

5. Persons using LSD who have adverse reactions should be promptly referred by physicians to a psychiatric institution or to a psychiatrist trained in its manifestations and treatment. If a patient is severely ill because of LSD use, treatment given prior to referral for psychiatric help should consist of intramuscular chlorpromazine. It is important to emphasize that oral chlorpromazine is often ineffective in this situation and may even exacerbate the illness. The recent abuse of STP has complicated the treatment problem, since chlorpromazine will accentuate STP mania. It is therefore crucial that the physician know exactly what the patient has taken before prescribing.

6. Marihuana should at long last be relegated to its rightful position as a mild hallucinogen, and should be removed from the opiate-cocaine category. New York State should take the lead in attempting to mitigate the stringent federal laws in regard to marihuana possession. However, we would make it clear that we condemn marihuana use and do not recommend changes in the marihuana laws related to illicit sale or smuggling for sale.

7. The dangers of LSD and other potent hallucinogens such as mescaline, psilocybin, STP, and dimethyltryptamine are so great that penalties for their illegal manufacture, distribution, or sale should be increased both at federal and state levels; these crimes should be made felonies with severe penalties. (The current laws in New York State are satisfactory in this regard but they must be revised in other states.)

8. The intentional administration of LSD, mescaline, psilocybin, dimethyltryptamine or STP to any person without that person's knowledge is a heinous act and should be categorized as a felony.

9. A special advisory body made up of pharmacologists and physicians should be instituted by county medical societies to continuously advise the Mayor of New York City, and a similar body should be established at the State Medical Society to continuously advise the Governor of New York on those drugs (especially new ones) which are dangerous or addicting and might have to be controlled by legislation.

10. There should be increased flexibility in modifying laws governing the abuse of dangerous drugs in accordance with newer knowledge and the advent of new drugs so that penalties can be modified with relative ease.

11. A special committee composed of legislators, pharmacists, and physicians should be formed to evaluate the effects of recently enacted laws on the abuse of stimulants, depressants, and hallucinogens. If the committee is formed now and engages in a continuing study, recommendations concerning any needed modification in the laws could be ready for the legislature by 1969.

12. We urge that physicians exercise great care in prescribing sedatives, tranquilizers, and stimulants, limiting the use of these drugs

to those in whom there are clear indications that such treatment is beneficial.

13. A mandatory reporting system should be initiated through the New York City Department of Health and the State Department of Mental Hygiene so that accurate data can be collected on the incidence of hallucinogenic abuse.

14. The treatment of established drug abuse is far more difficult than its prevention or arrest at an early stage. As a result, a massive educational campaign must be conducted in our schools and colleges. Additionally, it is imperative to undertake extensive research and epidemiological studies to determine what traits or personality constellations underlie drug abuse. It is especially important to determine why one individual in a given environment subjected to certain stresses turns to drugs and another individual under identical circumstances does not. An understanding of such factors may allow early detection of the drug prone individual and permit initiation of effective preventive measures.

LSD and the Drugs of the Mind

Newsweek

Newsweek attempts an unbiased report on LSD and similar substances. Can this type of reporting truly be unbiased? It attempts also concisely to give Leary's point of view. Can this be done without passing judgment on that which is considered "not mature"? It would seem to be an impossible task to please everyone on a topic as controversial as this. When there is such a degree of emotional involvement, any stance taken would be considered, depending on the critic, too lenient, too strict, or too middle of the road. How do you view this topic?

"As I was lying on the ground, I was looking up at the sky and I could sort of see through the leaves of the plant and see all the plant fluids flowing around inside it. I thought the plant was very friendly and very, very closely related to me as a living thing. For a while, I became a plant and felt my spine grow down through the bricks and take root . . . and I raised my arms up and waved them around with the plant and I really *was* a plant!

"But toward the end I was watching Lois and I thought I saw the drug take hold of her in a bad way . . . Suddenly I was afraid. I looked down and Lois was miles and miles and miles beneath me sort of as if I were looking at her from the wrong end of a telescope."

The man who thought he was a plant is a 29-year-old Yale graduate. And he was indeed looking at his wife through the wrong end of a telescope: his perceptions had been altered by a chemical called d-lysergic acid diethylamide.

"Inner Space": Largely unknown and untasted outside the researcher's laboratory until recently, the hallucinogenic drug LSD has suddenly become a national obsession. Depending on who is doing the talking, it is an intellectual tool to explore psychic "inner space," a new source of kicks for thrill seekers, the sacramental substance of a far-out mystical movement—or the latest and most frightening addition to the list of mind drugs now available in the pill society being fashioned by pharmacology. "Every age produces the thing it requires," says psychiatrist Humphrey Osmond of the New Jersey Neuro-Psychiatric Institute in Princeton. "This age requires ways of learning to develop its inner qualities."

The new LSD subculture, for the moment at least, is mainly American and young. It has its own vocabulary: on college campuses, in New York's Greenwich Village, Los Angeles's Sunset Boulevard and San Francisco's Haight-Ashbury District, the drug is called "acid" and its devotees "acid heads." Users "turn on" and go on LSD "trips." Some of the trips are contemplative affairs; but on others, hippies take off their clothes and turn on orgiastically. And as the young world turns on, the adult world—shocked and bewildered—turns off.

The LSD culture also has its own leader, former Harvard psychologist Timothy Leary. To 45-year-old Leary, LSD is a "cerebral vitamin." Instead of the term hallucinogenic drug, Leary promotes the less invidious phrase "psychedelic (from the Greek: mind-manifesting) experience." "I get revelations from my cells," says Leary, "which are wiser and older than my mind."

And the new LSD culture has its own special horrors. Last month, a 5-year-old Brooklyn girl, Donna Wingenroth, accidentally swallowed an LSD-impregnated sugar cube, became hysterical and was hospitalized for six days. Her 18-year-old uncle told police he had bought the cube in Greenwich Village at the going rate of $5. A week later, Stephen Kessler, a 30-year-old former medical student, was arrested in Brooklyn for killing his mother-in-law with a kitchen knife. Kessler told police that he had been "flying for three days on LSD." Patients have been entering New York's Bellevue at a rate of about two a week. Seemingly, an LSD epidemic was raging in the nation's largest city.

Bootlegging: Amid great hand-wringing, politicians and law-enforcement officers have rushed before TV cameras to call for new drug laws and stiffer penalties. Alarmed by reports that college students were making LSD in chemistry labs or buying it from bootleggers, U. S. Food and Drug Administration director Dr. James L. Goddard recently wrote to college administrators asking them to report the use of LSD and other hallucinogens to his agency.

But the first to feel the heat of the political blast was the only legitimate LSD distributor in the U.S. Reacting to the unfavorable publicity, Sandoz Pharmaceuticals of Hanover, N.J., which distributed LSD supplies to U.S. researchers working on government-approved research, abruptly withdrew the drug and asked for return of laboratory supplies. The action made no dent in the black market, since the LSD bootlegged on campuses and city streets is obtained from manufacturers abroad or, in many instances, home-brewed and then dropped onto sugar cubes. With police on the lookout for the cubes, the newest dodge supposedly is to coat the glue on an envelope flap with LSD so that it can be licked off.

"Uppies" and "Downies": In truth, however, LSD lives up to neither the scare headlines nor the glowing tributes of the believers. The number of Americans who have ever tasted LSD, mescaline, psilocybin and the other hallucinogens is small compared with users of such other mind drugs as the amphetamines ("uppies") that provide users with psychic energy, the barbiturates ("downies") that put them to sleep and the tranquilizers that allay their anxieties and fears. "Every other prescription written in this country," says Dr. John D. Griffith, a Vanderbilt University psychiatrist, "is written for a drug that affects the mind." Last year, 24 million prescriptions for amphetamines and 123 million for sedatives and tranquilizers were filled in the U.S. (the total bill: $508.2 million). Moreover there is also a huge bootleg market for such drugs. An estimated 13 billion amphetamine and barbiturate pills are manufactured each year—enough to supply every man, woman and child in the U.S. with almost six dozen apiece—and at least half are distributed through illegal channels.

Such drugs, of course, all have important legitimate uses. Amphetamines are prescribed to treat depression and for weight control because they curb appetite. Tranquilizers have revolutionized the care of the mentally ill and emptied hospital wards; properly prescribed, they have helped normal people face crises in their lives. But these mind drugs have been more widely abused than any other type of medication. Many of the barbiturates and amphetamines legally distributed are carelessly prescribed. The barbiturates—and a number of tranquilizers—can become addicting; and overdoses can seriously depress the nervous system. Each year some 3000 deaths are blamed on the overuse of barbiturates alone; many of the victims are menopausal women.

New Law: Such cases have led to the Drug Abuse Control Amendments to the Federal Food, Drug and Cosmetic Act. The amendments, which went into effect last February, require manufacturers, wholesalers and pharmacists to keep records of drug shipments and sales for FDA inspection, limit prescription refills to five within a six-month period (after that another prescription must be written), and provide a $5,000 fine and two-year prison term as a maximum first-offense penalty for giving such drugs to minors. LSD and other hallucinogenic drugs will now come under its provisions.

Yet, if the number of Americans who have taken a trip at one time or another is relatively small—Leary estimates 1 million, possibly a high figure—the potential health hazard is great.

LSD can be used almost at will, since it produces few toxic side effects, even in high doses, and it isn't addicting. It is powerful: just 1 ounce of the drug can provide enough doses for 284,000 full-scale trips. Finally, it is colorless, tasteless and odorless when dissolved in a glass of water. (These attributes gave rise to the story that a pound of LSD dumped into a city's water supply by an enemy agent would render the community helpless. But a Pentagon expert asserts that such a plan couldn't come off.)

On top of this potent chemistry, an alluring patina of pseudo-intellectuality and adventure coats the LSD pill. The combination has proved particularly attractive to certain affluent members of today's pop society—students from multiversities, young professionals in the big cities, artists and self-proclaimed creative types, and fringe people of all kinds.

Drugs of Distinction: Psychiatrists, for example, have already noted a distinct difference between the mind-drug takers and the "hard" narcotics addicts. Most of the LSD users admitted to Bellevue have been white, while two-thirds of New York heroin addicts are Negroes and Puerto Ricans. According to Dr. Donald Louria, chief of the New York County Medical Society's subcommittee on narcotics, "the reason is not racial, but social, economic and cultural." Heroin addiction goes with a sense of social, economic or personal inferiority. The addict typically is not a beat but the beaten—he seeks euphoria as an escape from the squalor of his circumstances and his sense of inadequacy. The users of LSD and pot (marijuana), which is technically a hallucinogen rather than a narcotic, may live in high rises and split levels rather than slum tenements. "The LSD people I know," says Jack Margolis, a 31-year-old Hollywood scriptwriter, "are doctors, lawyers, psychiatrists. Talk about trips. Well, taking LSD is more enriching than going to Europe."

Finally, the psychedelics are also supposed to provide deep religious insights and break down the barriers of communication between individuals, creating a deeper love of mankind. These themes surround the psychedelic experience with an aura of sexuality. Yet, contrary to widespread belief, the hallucinogens don't necessarily increase sexual desire or prolong the act of intercourse. "All of these drugs," says Dr. Nathan S. Kline of New York's Rockland State Hospital, "tend to dull sexual capacities." But, he adds, they may lower sexual inhibitions. "Under drugs like pot you tend to feel that you love everyone and the world is a great place," Kline says. "And if anyone wants to go to bed with you, it's just one more great experience to share. Pregnancy becomes the most frequent serious side effect of pot."

In such highly charged circumstances it is not surprising that the public discussion of LSD has blurred the fact that the drug first made its appearance in the laboratory and was used as a research tool.

The drug was synthesized by Dr. Albert Hofmann of Sandoz Ltd., a Swiss pharmaceutical firm, from ergot, a fungus that attacks rye, in 1938. (LSD and atomic energy, Leary likes to point out, were developed in the same decade.) Five years later, the chemist discovered LSD's ability to alter mental perception when he accidentally inhaled some of the whitish powder. "Objects, as well as the shape of my associates in the laboratory," he wrote in his notebook, "appeared to undergo optical changes . . . Fantastic pictures of extraordinary plasticity and intensive color seemed to surge toward me."

Because the distortions produced by LSD resembled those of schizophrenia, Hofmann's discovery was soon used to produce "model" psychoses in the laboratory. But although hallucinogens may be useful in studying mental illness, psychiatrists aren't convinced that the LSD experience exactly mimics schizophrenic distortions. Schizophrenics tend to have auditory hallucinations, while LSD effects are usually visual.

The discovery of LSD also gave a boost to the theory that mental illness, particularly schizophrenia, involves a disturbance in body chemistry. Chemically, LSD resembles a substance called serotonin, which aids in the transmission of impulses between nerve cells. The hallucinations of schizophrenia, therefore, might result from an excess of serotonin in certain brain centers.

Unblocked: The mechanisms of mental illnesses might be easier to understand if scientists knew now just how LSD acts on the brain. Some researchers believe the drug acts on the cells of the reticular activating system and parts of the limbic system lying deep within the brain; in these subcortical centers, the level of awareness is regulated and the impulses of rational thought are integrated with the senses and emotions.

Some psychiatrists believe hallucinogens can help break down the unconscious roadblocks of patients undergoing psychoanalysis. A New York psychiatrist, Dr. Harold Abramson, cites a patient who couldn't remember his father at any time in his life prior to the age of 8. With the aid of an LSD-like compound, the patient recalled being beaten by his father, while his mother stood by saying, "Give it to him! Give it to him!" The patient vividly recalled what he was wearing at the time, and remembered it had happened when he was 4.

Psychiatrist Osmond, who administered Aldous Huxley's first dose of mescaline, believes the drugs should be further explored as an aid to creativity and expansion of awareness—but in the right setting, supervised by a competent physician. "One needs to have a technically qualified person there," he says, "a psychiatrist who really knows something about the drug." A patient's bad reaction to LSD, for example, can be stopped quickly by administering a potent tranquilizer such as chlorpromazine.

Strangely, there is no known lethal dose of LSD. In fact, the only known victim of LSD was an elephant at the Oklahoma City zoo, given an unintentional overdose during an experiment.

Over the Line: The real hazard of LSD lies in the personality of the person taking the drug, the dose, and the setting in which it is administered. Even the most normal "normal" may have a bad reaction. And the drug may push a latent psychotic over the borderline into a full-blown break. "There are a sizable number of these individuals," says Nathan Kline. "Unfortunately, these are the people who usually go seeking this type of experience."

Even the most perceptive psychiatrist may have trouble picking safe subjects for research. "At present," says Harvard psychiatrist Graham B. Blaine, Jr., in his new book *Youth and the Hazards of Affluence* "there is no known method of predicting for whom such an experience will consist of one short episode, and for whom it may mark the beginning of a lifetime struggle against a crippling and terrifying emotional illness."

Many psychiatrists believe hallucinogenic drugs are far more dangerous than narcotics in their potential effect on overt behavior. "Your ego or central control mechanism falls apart," says Kline. "It's not that the drugs themselves induce anger or violent behavior, but that they loosen the controls over impulsive behavior." Violent reactions to LSD are rare—but when they happen they are memorable. One of the Bellevue LSD patients, responding to "voices," hurled himself in front of a subway. Others have jumped out of windows or hurtled down stairs, thinking they could fly.

On and Off: LSD may have more subtle as well as violent effects on the psyche. Dr. Sidney Malitz of the New York State Psychiatric Institute is convinced that a number of people who have taken hallucinogens habitually have undergone distinct personality changes. "They become very self-centered, very grandiose and feel their own standards are the new standards of the world," Malitz says. Some psychiatrists have suggested biochemical changes may occur in the brains of habitual users of LSD.

Leary began experimenting with psychedelic drugs five years ago. And by his own account he is so conditioned that he turns on without drugs. Naturally enough, he doesn't agree that changes brought about by the drug are necessarily bad. Yet there is a poignancy about Leary's present position. He considers Fellini's masterful film "Juliet of the Spirits" an LSD movie because "you never know when the heroine is hallucinating and when she's not." Critics think the same seems to apply to Leary. But he recently advised his young followers to relinquish psychedelic drugs for a year. "The psychedelic battle is won," he said. His next piece of advice: "turn on" parents and teachers "by the messages you have learned."

In point of fact, the battle hasn't been won—even on the hip campuses. In one large Eastern university, where up to 50 per cent of the undergraduates reportedly used marijuana, a careful faculty investigation revealed that only about 1 per cent of the students had ever smoked pot. But at San Francisco State, an estimated 35 per cent of the students have used LSD at least once. In fact, George Harrison, a 26-year-old graduate student in psychology, has started a kind of "LSD Users Anonymous" to help those who have had bad trips. One of the cases Harrison saw involved a couple who went to Golden Gate Park after taking LSD. "They got separated and the girl called me, panic-stricken," Harrison recalls. "We found the boy sitting and watching the buffalo herd they keep in the park."

Some of the replies the FDA is now receiving from Goddard's letter to college administrators provide another measure of the amount of tripping going on. An Ivy League university official called it a "problem of great concern," and asked Goddard to send an FDA man to counteract the favorable publicity LSD has gotten.

Future Trips: Where do LSD and the trippers go from here? First of all, law enforcement will be tightened; the FDA has already sent undercover investigators to some of the bigger campuses to find out who is distributing LSD. According to one San Francisco pharmacologist, the major California supply comes from Mexico, where it can be sold legally to drug distributors.

Second, legitimate research will go on, but quietly. Despite Sandoz's action, the National Institute of Mental Health has enough to supply current projects for years. Third, tripping for kicks will continue. Most psychiatrists believe LSD is here to stay. Osmond suggests LSD is now part of the battle between older and younger generations, between those in authority and those in rebellion. Stricter drug laws may only make drugs more fascinating, Osmond notes, just as Prohibition made drinking more adventurous and appealing.

Many teen-age trippers are quick to cite their parents' drinking habits when reproached for their own misbehavior. And statistics from non-psychedelic sources suggest that alcoholism remains a bigger mental crutch and health hazard than cerebral vitamins, goof balls, pep pills and tranquilizers combined.

Psychiatrists themselves disagree on whether society's growing dependence on mind drugs is good or bad. "The notion that we can be in this world without stress and conflict is one of the major errors of our time," says Dr. Sidney Cohen of UCLA. And critic Marya Mannes asked young people last week: "Why do you need drugs to give you excitement and revelation, when the real world, if you really bothered to examine it, is so full of both?"

Whatever the answer, LSD and the current mind drugs are only the curtain-raisers for the brave new world taking shape in the lab. Learning drugs are next. Researchers at Albany Medical College have tested a drug called magnesium pemoline and have found that it improves the memory of rats; they are now testing it on humans. Others are working on drugs to improve concentration. Researchers studying the chemical cyclazocine to block effects of heroin also found the drug may increase sex drive.

All these experiments in the lab—like LSD trips that began in laboratories only a few years ago—may seem beyond the fringe today. But for doctors, educators, parents—and for the young—they will raise basic questions. When "learning pills" become available, what value can be placed on artificial intelligence? What fulfillment for lovers in chemical sex? And what worth for anyone in synthetic human experience?

The Growth of a Mystique

Timothy Leary says he is in trouble with the world because—through the use of mind-expanding drugs—he has unlocked the "Rosetta stone of consciousness" and threatened the established order. Actually, he is in trouble with U.S. narcotics agents and the Dutchess County, N.Y., sheriff's office. He has been arrested twice on marijuana charges.

To listen to Leary is to listen to an evangelist, to a minister—or scout master—of some swinging sacrament. Instead of bread and wine, Leary offers the taste of LSD and the hypnotic sight of an Oriental mandala, a circular symbol of the universe. Through these his dedicated disciples think they achieve communion—not with God, but with a superreal awareness rarely, if ever, attained in everyday life. As any hipster can attest, it's consciousness-expanding, man. Says novelist Ken Kesey, who foresees an entire nation of turned-on converts: "We've got a great organ we can play if we can find where all the keys are."

"God's Flesh": Men have been searching for those keys for centuries. The ancient Persians believed they had found them in *soma pulari,* a potion that made the imbiber "like a god." Herodotus recorded the Scythians' fondness for hemp seeds. Later, Eurasian nomads chewed a crimson mushroom for its capacity to induce fantasies, and the Indians of the New World ritualized the use of fungi ("God's flesh" to the Aztecs), peyote, cohoba and the potent caapi vine.

Though several scholars (William James and Havelock Ellis, among others) experimented briefly with mind drugs in the late nineteenth century, the psychedelic mystique didn't seize the popular imagination until the 1950s. Leary traces its true beginning to Aldous Huxley, the visionary who constructed a drugged society in his 1932 novel *Brave New World* ("A gram is better than a damn"). By 1953, nature was imitating art. Huxley took the hallucinogen mescaline and wrote "The Doors of Perception."

Huxley reported he saw "what Adam had seen on the morning of his creation—the miracle . . . of naked existence." Cars poking along Hollywood's Sunset Boulevard in the evening sun became "a Red Sea of traffic," and "brick chimneys and green composition roofs glowed in the sunshine, like fragments of the New Jerusalem."

Religious motifs also appear in the writings of ex-Roman Catholic Leary, 46. Raised near Boston, Leary briefly attended West Point, then turned to psychology. But in Mexico in 1961, he tasted psilocybin (a mushroom derivative) and proclaimed a new religion. Back at Harvard's Center for Research in Personality, Leary and co-worker Richard Alpert dispensed 3,500 doses of psilocybin to 400 subjects in the next two years. But Harvard authorities accused Leary and Alpert of breaking their promise not to involve the undergraduates in their experiments, and in 1963 both were dismissed from the faculty.

Leary now pursues his studies under the auspices of the Castalia Foundation, an organization of his own creation. At his 4000-acre retreat near Millbrook, N.Y., surrounded by dogs, cats and children (including his 16-year-old son), Leary plays host to an assortment of visitors ranging on any given day from psychiatrists and Hindus to wide-eyed kicksters.

The Millbrook estate (rented from Manhattan banker William Hitchcock for $500 a month) is a strange mutation of Thoreau's Walden and a Tantric Buddhist temple. The surrounding woods are dotted with statues and shrines. Tibetan symbols are scattered about the grounds, and near the manor house there is a "Bavarian baroque" hut "where people go for days and weeks at a time and meditate and fast."

In the drafty hall of the main house, part of a grand piano sits on its side, its strings waiting to be plucked. The floors are rugless. The rooms are furnished with legless tables, bedless mattresses and mandalas on which the eye of the true believer is supposed to "lock" during drugless exercises.

Precellular: In rediscovering the rituals of the Orient, the psychedelists, in fact, have converted many of the bearded beats of the '50s. The poet laureate and guru of the beats, Allen Ginsberg, was long a sidewalk spokesman for legalized marijuana ("Pot Is Fun"). Now he sings the praises of LSD. "It's only a catalyst to what's natural and human," says Ginsberg. "Everyone's been turned off by McCarthys and the cold war . . . and even the smog of Los Angeles."

The breviary of both the old Zen beats and the new psychedelists is "The Tibetan Book of the Dead," a guide to the death and rebirth of the ego ("The transformation is into the All-Performing Wisdom . . ."). From Tibet, too, Leary has lifted what he calls the five levels of consciousness. The first is sleep, or stupor, the "blindfolds" attained through alcohol or narcotics. Level Two is the waking life, the world of words and external symbols. Next is the level of sensory consciousness, which may be reached with marijuana; then comes cellular consciousness where the LSD-borne mind reaches beyond its senses into the world of pure matter. And finally, Level Five—"that precellular flash," says Leary, "for which we have no word but which I'll call soul."

Evolution: Because of his run-ins with the law, Leary has expansively invoked a one-year moratorium on using LSD and is now polishing up a technique for "turning on" without drugs. The method, he says, involves yoga-like breathing exercises, stroboscopic light projections on the ceiling, and the use of psychedelic music.

"Psychedelic music avoids harmony," Leary explains. "John Cage's music is classically psychedelic . . . and Indian music . . . When I listen to Beethoven when I'm turned on, it makes me want to say, 'Oh, *come on*, Ludwig, get off it'." Leary calls Dali an LSD artist, "although he doesn't *take* LSD."

In the LSD subculture—and its acceptance by some students and intellectuals—Leary somehow manages to see not so much a revolt against "the stable world that used to be" as an evolutionary process. In fact, he believes "we may be at another one of those wrenching transition points in intellectual history when the accepted ontological and mythological fundaments of society and of man's view of himself comes into uneasy collision with new concepts." Huxley also examined this idea. "Which is better?" he asked. "To have Fun with Fungi or to have Idiocy with Ideology?"

Leary and his followers have made their choice. But any man who can transport himself through five levels of consciousness should be able to find another choice—involving neither Fungi nor Idiocy—in the real world.

Cool Talk About Hot Drugs

Donald B. Louria

Bellevue Hospital

Dr. Louria, considered an outstanding authority on drugs and their use, attempts to describe the more popular drugs that are reportedly in use by adolescents. He attacks many of the popularly held nonuser's beliefs and substantiates many others in an attempt to set the record straight. Can his attempt at realism be criticized because of his expected bias or has he presented the facts that need to be known?

Three drugs in illicit use have captured the public imagination. They are heroin, LSD and marijuana. Each has had built up around it layer upon layer of popular belief about its chemical nature, psychological tie-ins, sociological implications, criminal outcomes, and so on and so on. This article is an attempt to peel away, as with an onion, some of the misconceptions about the Big Three drugs of the nineteen-sixties.

It has been underemphasized that we are not now in a period of burgeoning heroin abuse. In 1900, when various opiates (of which heroin is one) were incorporated in many patent medicines that were sold without prescription, about one in 400 persons in this country—a tremendous proportion—was addicted, whereas the current figure is about one in 2000. Our problem is not that we have more heroin addiction than we used to, but that we have been unable to make a dent in the number of heroin users over the past dozen or so years.

Heroin is not a problem of college campuses and high schools. There is virtually no heroin in any of our colleges. Heroin is a problem of the high-school dropout. It is a problem of the areas of decay within our large cities. Some 65 per cent to 70 per cent of those who use heroin are Negroes, Mexicans or Puerto Ricans. And, of course, it is well known that New York City has more than 50 per cent of the addiction in the country.

There is not one whit of evidence that heroin users are given to violence. It is true that addicts commit homicide slightly more often than the general population, but this excess is almost uniformly the result of some violence between the addict and his pusher, rather than between the addict and an innocent bystander. In New York City, some 20 per cent to 30 per cent of crimes against property are committed by heroin addicts; the figure that is usually given is that they steal about $1 billion worth of goods a year to support their habit. But they do not ordinarily commit crimes of violence.

It is widely believed that one shot of heroin inevitably leads to addiction. This simply is not true. There is a sharp distinction between habituation (chronic use of the drug) and addiction (physical dependence), and there are many weekend users of heroin, or people who take two shots a day, who never increase the amount and never become physiologically addicted. If heroin is discontinued suddenly for these individuals (the so-called cold-turkey treatment) they recover without any of the symptoms—nausea, vomiting, chills, fever, diarrhea and muscle aches—popularly associated with withdrawal.

What has happened is that the criminal element engaged in selling drugs has cut the heroin inordinately, so that the addict gets a progressively weaker mixture—now usually in the range of 1 per cent or 2 per cent. One per cent is not very much heroin. Five years ago, if an addict came to us at Bellevue Hospital with a $15-a-day habit, we knew that he would have withdrawal symptoms and so we would give him a substitute drug, such as methadone, a synthetic which is itself addictive but which makes it impossible to feel the effects of heroin. As of now, if a patient has even a $30-to-$40-a-day habit, we usually do not give him a substitute because we know that $30 or $40 worth a day of today's heroin may not addict an individual physiologically. (Of course, if a patient does show signs of withdrawal symptoms, we treat them.)

For example, a woman with a $40-a-day habit who came to Bellevue recently told us she had tried to get off three or four times, but had never been successful. We just cut off her drugs—cold turkey. The first night, we gave her a sedative. The next day, she was improved. The day after that, she was completely well. Afterward, I talked to her at some length and asked her—since she had wanted to get off—why she had not just stopped.

Her answer was interesting. She said she had been told that if she stopped her heroin abruptly she would have withdrawal symptoms characterized first by a runny nose and then by a terrible complex which could result in her death. Every time she started to withdraw, her nose got itchy and she felt it was running a little, so she would take more heroin. In point of fact, she could have stopped cold at any time and nothing would have happened.

Addiction is a curable disease. When addicts reach the age of 30 or 35 they often suddenly lose the need for heroin, withdraw by themselves and never go back to the habit. It is called the maturing-out process. Why this should be no one knows—the cured addicts themselves cannot explain it—but it is ridiculous to assume that this disease is in any way incurable and that therefore these people must be maintained indefinitely on narcotics. Our problem is to keep them from dying of heroin addiction before they get to be 30 or 35, and to replace their 10-year to 15-year period of drug abuse with years of useful activity.

About 1 per cent of the addict population in New York dies each year of overdose—an enormous incidence. It can happen, for example, if the addict has just been released from jail after a period of enforced abstinence. He takes the same amount of drug that he did before incarceration, but his body has lost its tolerance. Sometimes, if a pusher wants to get rid of a troublesome addict, he gives him pure heroin; the user takes it, thinking he is getting his usual weak dose, and he dies. Or some neophyte may see other people use two bags of heroin; not realizing that they have been doing this for months or even years, he takes two bags, and for him it is a lethal dose.

No user knows what he is getting when he buys a packet. He may be getting milk sugar; he may be getting quinine; he may be getting baking soda; he may be getting one-tenth of 1 per cent heroin; he may be getting 75 per cent heroin. Anything above 30 per cent is likely to be fatal. It can kill very quickly. The New York Medical Examiner's office has photographs of people who have died without time to pull the needle from their vein.

An overdose produces virtually immediate lung congestion. When addicts see the symptoms in a companion, they first slap the victim, hoping to wake him that way, then try to make him walk it off. The treatment is actually quite effective.

Another medical complication that claims a fair number of lives is hepatitis—the result of unsterile needles. Recent studies suggest that as many as three out of every four apparently healthy addicts have chronic liver infections—a fantastic percentage. It will be interesting to see whether these addicts develop chronic liver disease (cirrhosis) 10 or 20 years from now.

Treatment is one of the most misunderstood aspects of the heroin problem. To be effective, a rehabilitation program must reach addicts in their teens or early twenties. The user tends to be an immature, self-centered, non-goal-directed person, incapable of rehabilitating himself without outside help. Yet once he becomes addicted he becomes a pariah. He spends his whole time getting heroin. Very soon, his circle of friends has dwindled until there is nobody left except heroin users. He may go to a hospital and get off drugs temporarily. After a brief period, he returns to his community without a job and without any meaningful follow-up. He goes back to the only people he knows, and they are still on heroin. Very soon he is hooked again.

Britain allows a doctor to prescribe drugs, perfectly legally, for an addict. This does not mean that the British endorse maintenance as initial therapy. The doctor must first try to get the addict off drugs, but once he is convinced that the patient is truly addicted he can issue repeated prescriptions for heroin or cocaine. They are very inexpensive.

One assumption was if there was no illegal traffic in high-priced drugs. addicts would not be forced to become criminals and would be restored to social usefulness. But addicts, not pushers, are the greatest recruiters of new addicts. London's addicts congregate at certain well-known pubs and devote their main activity to increasing the number of members of their subculture. In the last five years the number of British addicts has doubled—and the number of youthful heroin users has increased sixfold. There have been scandals at Oxford, for example, and at the University of London.

Lady Frankau, the London doctor who was once the most enthusiastic proponent of this system, told me recently that she now refuses to treat any addict unless he gives a flat guarantee that he will go back to work and eventually be withdrawn. She is tough enough to make such promises stick, but the British system has failed—egregiously. Britain is now planning to impose more restrictive regulations.

There are three major approaches in the United States. One is civil commitment, which both New York and California employ. Until this year, the New York program was largely voluntary. Now, if a user is arrested, he can choose either to stand trial or to sign up for rehabilitation—with a three-year follow-up period. If he chooses to go to trial and is found guilty, he is likely to be put in the rehabilitation program anyway. Previously, after-care was voluntary, and more than 80 per cent of discharged patients disappeared within a month. Now, after-care is compulsory—authoritarian but benign, New York's program—with its emphasis on education, job rehabilitation and careful follow-up—seems to me the potentially most effective of any yet undertaken.

The second is the methadone maintenance program, such as the one being conducted in New York City under the supervision of Drs. Vincent Dole and Marie Nyswander. Preliminary results are indeed very encouraging, but it is important to stress certain caveats: The patients are very carefully selected, highly motivated volunteers (50 per cent of the applicants are rejected during the screening process). They remain addicted, with methadone merely substituted for heroin. And the program includes an extensive panoply of schooling, job training and other rehabilitative activities. These are an essential part of the program, and it might be that they would be as effective *without* methadone. In any event, the program is at least three or four years away from being considered for public-health policy.

Finally, there are the group-therapy programs, typified by organizations such as Synanon and Day Top. These are primarily voluntary. Synanon has fewer than 100 people in the community in seven years. Day Top, which is a Synanon offshoot, does return its people to the community. Results so far are encouraging but tentative.

None of these programs, however, deals with the real problem. Heroin abuse is a symptom; poverty, under-education, inadequate housing, prejudice, lack of job opportunities are the underlying culprits. Unless we stop just treating the disease after it has occurred and do something more about prevention by eliminating urban decay and deterioration, we will not succeed in minimizing the heroin problem.

No one knows the prevalence of use of LSD, though four separate recent studies suggest about 1 per cent among young people. The evidence is that it is increasing on the West Coast while diminishing in Chicago and New York. At Bellevue, for example, admissions for LSD psychosis have dropped 50 per cent in the past five months.

There are potential medical uses for the drug—treatment of chronic alcoholics and schizophrenic children, the relief of patients in terminal disease, for example—that should be explored much further under medical control. But its major use, of course, is for hedonistic purposes, though these are often disguised under pretentious claims.

Advocates of LSD say that it increases creativity. There is no evidence that this is so. In one study, accomplished pianists were tape-recorded while playing under the influence of LSD. They insisted they had never played so well before, but when the tapes were played back later almost invariably their reaction was: "How could I have been that bad?"

Another claim is that it makes one a better person, or that it helps in achieving self-understanding. That for the most part is erroneous. The level of understanding is usually childishly superficial. One boy was brought into Bellevue after taking 3000 micrograms of LSD—an enormous dose. When he came out of his trip, which was after substantial time, he said it had been a great experience. We asked him why, and he said: "Well, I understand myself now." We said: "Well, that's jolly. What do you understand?" And he said: "Through this experience I have learned that I am basically egotistical." That's a lot of LSD to take to learn that you are basically egotistical

The claim that angers me most, because it is egregiously spurious, is that LSD is an aphrodisiac. *Playboy* magazine quoted Dr Timothy Leary as saying such things as: "There is no question that LSD is the most powerful aphrodisiac ever discovered by man," and "A woman will inevitably have several hundred orgasms under the influence of LSD."

It is true that an LSD hallucination may have highly erotic content but the drug is, if anything, an antiaphrodisiac. In the course of a debate at Muhlenberg College, I asked Dr Leary how he could justify his statements in view of the known facts. He replied that he had been misinterpreted; that what he had meant was that LSD is an aphrodisiac in the sense that it infuses one with love for his fellow man, but that it has nothing to do with sexual gratification. Yet surely, some people are deliberately promoting the drug on the basis of the false claim.

There is no other drug used promiscuously under uncontrolled circumstances that is as dangerous as LSD. It is absolutely unpredictable.

In the 114 cases hospitalized in the past 18 months at Bellevue (a large number for a single hospital), the average age was 23 years. Thirteen per cent entered the hospital with overwhelming panic. There was uncontrolled violence in 12 per cent. Nearly 9 per cent had attempted either homicide or suicide, none successfully. Of the 114, one out of seven had to be sent on from Bellevue to long-term mental hospitalization, and half of those had no history of underlying psychiatric disorder.

LSD has another kind of toxicity which I think has not been adequately emphasized. A small but growing number of people who take LSD repeatedly withdraw from society into a totally solipsistic existence. In essence, they engage in perpetual introspective orgies live a totally drug-oriented life, and become negativistic and unconstructive. These people are beginning to worry even some of the proponents of LSD. If the group were ever to become much larger it could conceivably be a substantial danger to society as a whole.

I think the laws concerning LSD should be made tougher than they are. Manufacturing or selling it illicitly should be a felony, and illicit possession a misdemeanor. These laws should also apply to other drugs now in the psychedelic wings, such as dimethyltryptamine, bufotenine, psilocybin and the recently described STP.

Marijuana is the campus drug. It is a relatively weak form of the hallucinogen known generically as cannabis. (In other countries kif and bhang are cannabis preparations of similar strength; more potent variations are ganga, charas and hashish.)

The number of marijuana users in the United States undoubtedly numbers in the hundreds of thousands. It is estimated that about 15 per cent of college students experiment with its use, but most try it on no more than one to four occasions. Even among chronic users in the United States, average consumption rarely exceeds three cigarettes a day.

Is it dangerous? The answer is a qualified yes. For one thing, an individual under the influence of marijuana tends to lose his coordination, and yet often has a feeling of omnipotence. A marijuana smoker behind the wheel of an automobile *is* dangerous. He is in a sense more dangerous—because less liable to detection—than a drunken driver. Until some way is found to measure marijuana levels in the blood, legalization to me is unthinkable.

Those who would legalize marijuana often quote the so-called LaGuardia report of a New York City study made in 1944. One section they do not quote records that—depending upon which set of statistics is used—either 8 out of 72 subjects or 9 out of 77 developed acute psychoses when given marijuana experimentally. Admittedly, these subjects were given an extract equivalent to something between two and eight cigarettes at one time. But the report also records: "One subject smoked one cigarette and became restless, agitated, dizzy, fearful of his surroundings, afraid of death, and had three short attacks of unconsciousness." That is not my definition of an entirely safe drug. I think it only fair to emphasize that such reactions, though well documented, are infrequent and far less extreme than with LSD..

Marijuana does not inevitably lead the user to experiment with "hard" drugs such as heroin, nor, in the strength smoked in the United States, does it cause addiction or physical deterioration.

But it does often start an individual in the morass of drug abuse; whether he moves on or stops depends upon him and his environment. There also is evidence from Morocco, where kif is commonly smoked in excess of 10 cigarettes a day, that heavy consumption is associated with a marked increase in mental derangement. And studies in India indicate that excess use of the more potent forms, such as ganga and charas, is associated with criminal, often violent, behavior.

The arguments for legalization of marijuana are based on pure hedonism—the proponents want the legal right to use the drug because it gives them pleasure. Faced with the data on the potential dangers of its unrestricted use, they rely on the argument that marijuana is no more dangerous than alcohol There are six million severe alcoholics in the United States. If marijuana were to be legalized as an escape mechanism to supplement alcohol, why should not amphetamines, cocaine and heroin be equally condoned?

The major criterion for legalization of any drug should not be a comparison with the dangers of alcohol, but rather the inherent dangers in indiscriminate use of the drug. Otherwise, there would be a proliferation of drugs dispensed merely for pleasure, and if each of these carried the risks presented by alcohol—and cigarettes—the number of persons damaged would inevitably increase strikingly. Surely, society has an obligation to limit the distribution of potentially dangerous and medically useless drugs.

Yet though I am implacably against legalization of marijuana, I feel that the federal and state laws (in some 25 states) which make no distinction between marijuana and heroin should be mitigated in terms of the penalties for possession of marijuana. I do not favor amelioration of the laws regarding the sale or smuggling of marijuana.

My idea of a realistic penalty for, say, a college student caught with marijuana would be to have him work on weekends in the poverty program for a given period of time, thus making the penalty constructive. If he persisted in disobeying the law, there would be no alternative, or course, to imposing a jail sentence. As it is, young people are having their lives ruined for mere possession of marijuana. I am against their smoking it, but I do not think we should over-react.

This nation is clearly kicks-oriented. Some of the drugs used, such as banana scrapings, provide—if anything—a mild psychedelic experience. Others, such as gasoline and glue, codeine cough syrups and marijuana, have limited though clearly present dangers. Still others, such as LSD, heroin, cocaine and amphetamines, are capable of causing serious or permanent psychic or physical damage.

If we are to minimize the prevalence of drug abuse, we must involve our children early in constructive activity and in the problems of our society, for those who are so committed tend not to use drugs. For those who are susceptible, the prevention of drug abuse will depend on a judicious mixture of education, reduced supply, and laws.

Discussion Questions for Chapter 3

1. Our society has been described as having many ills. How does this chapter approach them? In your opinion, has there been overemphasis in some areas? Are there considerations or problems that have not been dealt with? Explain.
2. Many of the articles in this chapter blame the school for much of our difficulty. Is this realistic? Whether it is or not, can the schools help us to solve many of these difficulties? What is the role of the school in our society?
3. Does Pine expose some of the prejudices surrounding delinquency? Why should such a stereotype arise and how should it be handled?
4. In the three articles on LSD, are the approaches divergent enough to present all points of view? What are the similarities among the three?

5. Why do adolescents feel the need to become involved with the use of drugs? Do you feel that we tend to over- or underestimate the use of these drugs?
6. Is it possible that too much is made of the problems of young adults? Some critics maintain that adolescence is just another phase of development and that youngsters become responsible adults in spite of all the vicissitudes of early life. What do you think?

Chapter 4
Adolescence in Cross-Cultural Perspective

If one defines culture as the sum of a society's attempts to meet its needs, it follows that cultural differences can account for behavioral variations among groups as well as personality differences among individuals. For example, if Society *A* provides much needs-fulfilling activity for its adolescents, one might expect to find that adolescent behavior in that society will vary from the adolescent behavior in Society *B*, where very little needs-fulfilling activity is possible. Is it not useful, then, to compare societies in this manner, and in so doing, to understand better how well a society has done and what it yet must do to effect optimal development of young adults?

This chapter discusses several of the tools used by the anothropologist to examine culture. It looks at adolescence in a number of societies ranging from the primitive to the modern, industrialized. The reader may conclude that the United States has no monopoly on adolescent problems. However, he may also find that progress, as Americans tend to describe it, is a mixed blessing with regard to the nurture of the adolescent.

The Adolescent and His Education in Cross-Cultural Perspective

Gladys A. Wiggin

University of Maryland

There is general agreement that formal education contributes to the development of the human characteristics by which a society is known. How the schools function to create inter- and intra-societal differences among adolescents is the focus of the author's thesis. The processes by which a society changes its culture are extremely complex and often not visible to the untrained observer. While keeping the adolescent in perspective, Dr. Wiggin discusses these processes and, in so doing, develops conceptual tools useful to the understanding of cultural change, including that of youth.

If 14-year-old Gamal from Istanbul and 14-year-old Frederick from Milwaukee were to meet on a UN tour, sooner or later they might get to discussing their more serious concerns.[1] There would be many areas in which their problems would sound similar. But there would be one area of Gamal's concern which to Fred (if he were not a fundamentalist) might sound strange. For Gamal would confess that he spent considerable time "thinking about heaven and hell," and that he was "afraid God" was "going to punish" him. The total pattern of Fred's beliefs and behaviors would be rather different from (but not necessarily better or worse than) Gamal's.

This reference to difference in patterns of behavior serves to introduce the dual intent of this chapter. It is first to explore the complexity and variability of culture which is in turn a way of explaining human behavior . . . . But second, the present chapter will deal, albeit briefly, with the interrelationship of the adolescent's schooling and his culture.

An Exploration of Culture

The nature of the differences which characterize cultures can be illustrated with further detail on Turkish youth as seen through a study of potential elites in Turkey.[2] In societies where only a very small proportion (perhaps no more than 10 per cent) go to a secondary

---

Reprinted by permission of the author.

[1]An extrapolation from Hasan Tan, "A Survey of Student Problems with the Mooney Problem Check List in a Secondary School in Istanbul, Turkey" (Unpublished Master's Thesis, University of Maryland, June 1953).

[2]Andreas M. Kazamias, "Potential Elites in Turkey: Exploring the Values and Attitudes of Lise Youth," *Comparative Education Review*, Vol. 11, No. 1 (February 1967), 22–37.

school, that population is ordinarily socially and economically selected and is a potential governing (elite) group.[3]

There has been speculation as to whether this group has modernized its attitudes, a necessary prerequisite to modernizing the society. Kismet (a predetermined fate) is a Moslem belief which must be questioned if youth are to think of themselves as active agents in social change. Kazamias finds that beginning lise (secondary school) students have a greater belief in fate than do those who are graduates. Schooling apparently increases the confidence of the youth in his ability to direct his own destiny. Kazamias concludes, however, that though there have been attempts to change traditional values, lise youth still retain attachment for authoritarianism (superior-inferior) in human relations of all kinds, a narrow interpretation of various kinds of personal relationships, a distrust of people and the world, and a fear of taking chances. The reverse of these attitudes would be typically found among United States secondary school students.

A second illustration of culture difference can be found in a similar contrast in adolescent beliefs emerging from a study of Buenos Aires and Chicago adolescents.[4] The study population consisted of 13- and 16-year olds from the upper middle and upper lower classes in two urban societies which are very similar in socioeconomic structure. Nevertheless, the investigators found that cross-national differences were more pronounced than those related to such other variables as sex, social class, and age. Hence these differences between the two geographic groups take on real meaning. The Chicago youths in contrast to those in Buenos Aires are more self-assertive, autonomous, resistive to authority, instrumental (as opposed to expressive), active, and interested in heterosexual relationships. In illustration of one of these traits, a Chicago youth sees his parents as equals, and displeasure with father is a function of the father's relationship with the youth himself. Buenos Aires youth, much like Turkish youth, see parents as superior to and apart from themselves: Parents' faults are in the parents themselves rather than in relationships with their children.

The contrast between Turkish and American, and between Buenos Aires and Chicago, youth not only emphasizes differences but highlights a problem of all societies. It is that the typical attitudes and behaviors of any given society may well stand in the way of the society's accomplishing the tasks it needs done. This concept will be found prominently in the examples given under the section on culture and schooling. But at this point a more formal discussion of the meaning of culture is in order.

A Definition of Culture

A culture is a complex of learned behaviors: spanking children, speaking French, belching at the dinner table (a polite gesture in some

---

[3]See also Andreas M. Kazamias, "Potential Elites in Turkey: The Social Origins of Lise Youth," *Comparative Education Review*, Vol. 10, No. 3 (October 1966), 470–481.

[4]Robert J. Havighurst *et. al.*, *A Cross-National Study of Buenos Aires and Chicago Adolescents*, Bibliotheca "Vita Humana," Fasc 3 (Basel, Switzerland: S. Karger, 1965).

cultures). Sometimes we say that a culture is made up of behaviors, and beliefs and attitudes. But a belief or an attitude is only an inference from behavior. Fred says that (talking is a behavior) he believes his parents are too restrictive, and he acts as though he believes it. Hence his attitude about his parents is an inference from what he says and does.

Fred's saying and doing is learned behavior Unlike animals that act on instinct, we act as we do because our parents, teachers, peers, and neighbors have taught us from birth on to act, feel, believe in ways termed right, good, or proper. Furthermore, all these ways of acting, believing, feeling interact with one another to create a culture which is uniquely different from any other culture in the world. This uniqueness pervades and infects the several parts, so that a familiar-seeming institution may, on investigation, turn out to be quite different from a previous conception of it. All of us, for instance, know what it means to be in the process of being educated. This is happening presently to the readers of this text, in colleges and universities over the land. But quite a few of the world's peoples are educated for their life roles without benefit of schooling of any kind. Now what does *being educated* mean?

Multiple Cultures in the Same Society

The reference to schooling versus education presumes a dichotomy between the schooled and the unschooled, and thus suggests two cultures in a given society. In actuality this is a too simple reading of the situation. First, every sizeable society has something approximating a national or country-wide culture to some of which beliefs and behaviors most citizens adhere. But second, the reference to *most* rather than *all* of the citizens is made advisedly. There are some newly developing countries which are called *plural* because rural and urban cultures exist side by side with virtually no contact between the members of the several cultures. Third, beyond these urban and rural cultures there may be other subcultures such as those fostered by membership in a particular class or substrata of a society.

A study of school problems in Lebanon provides some inferences as to how subcultures may be promoted in a society.[5] The study employs a ranking of families into four distinct classes in one modest-sized town. Members of each of these classes undoubtedly share with others many behaviors in the Lebanese culture, and possibly in a local culture. But each class also has its own set of behaviors, as indicated by the fact that all the 13-year-olds in the top status families (eight in number) are sent away to school in Beirut or Tripoli. The culture these adolescents will acquire (with links to an outside world) will be rather different from that they would have assimilated if they had attended the local secondary school Furthermore, the behaviors which Class II and Class

---

[5]George H. Weightman and Zahi Rihani, "Social Stratification and Adolescent Academic Performance in a Lebanese Town," *Comparative Education Review*, Vol. 11, No. 2 (June 1967), 208–216.

IV youth will learn in the same school will be different because both grades of youth and their pass-fail status are significantly related to their position in the class structure. There may well be three subcultures in this one modest secondary school.

Lest we think of multicultural societies as being exclusively foreign, let us remember that a society as heterogeneous as the United States spawns a rich set of subcultures. We are literally an imported people: imported, except for our Indians, within the last two and a half centuries and especially within the last 85 years. Thus in the Chicago of 1968, adolescents grow up in varied cultural patterns which are a mixture not only of a United States, an urban, and a Chicago culture, but the remnants of an African culture (over 22 per cent of the population is Negro), and along with that a Southern rural culture, a Czech-American culture (a radio station broadcasts in Czech), an Italian-American culture, a Polish-American culture, and so on. In the last few years, sociologists have been talking about the emergence of a youth society, and hence, we might conclude, a youth culture also must exist in Chicago. Thus the Chicago scene is a cultural kaleidoscope.

Interaction of Schooling and Culture

A phenomenon of the nineteenth and more particularly the twentieth century is the speed with which cultures are changing and hence the multiplication of problems for human beings whose behavior is being challenged by various social institutions which attempt to disrupt or replace behavior termed good and right. In the midst of this process is the school, largely unevaluated as to its effect in culture change.

Despite the lack of evidence as to the precise effects of the schooling, the interaction of school with culture in the process of culture change can be readily observed in the newly developing nations. In many of these there has been a deliberate use of schools, both by a former imperial master and by a newly native elite, to change the culture.

Process of Culture Change

One of the more complicated intermeshings of cultures comes when a technologically highly developed people (usually a European group) asserts its will over a people of another culture and sometimes another skin color. The native culture may survive in places, almost untouched. In other areas a new culture, that of the conqueror, is introduced. But this is not necessarily the culture in its generalized form but rather a special version of it. The British in Nigeria, for instance, were said to be a bit more haughty, a bit more imperial, a bit more demanding than persons of their same status in England. This new culture may be temporarily resisted even in urban areas where it is most available. Then it will be assimilated by a portion of the population, and a wedge will be driven between the new elites (the natives acceptable to the conqueror) and the untouched or untouchables in the rural culture.

In the process by which the invader changes certain aspects of the native culture, he uses schools. These may include elementary schools for urban or rural children. But they are more apt to be secondary schools for a select group of adolescents, accompanied by a university education for a smaller group through a new university or through sending the native elite youth back home for higher education. Providing formal education is for the conqueror an investment in the future of the country, in that there will be a native population readied as to behavior, when the society demands new occupational skills. And it is with this education for preferred jobs that the native elite take on a new culture.

When finally the society achieves its independence, there will be instituted a search for something called a native culture, some particulars of which such as language will be pressed on schools. But if the society is to modernize, some elements of a universal culture must be taught. In the meantime the upward-striving youth and their families remain enamored of the educational route by which native elite achieved status under a colonial regime. Thus the native value system of the masses and the acquired value system of the native elite vie for supremacy and complicate the stabilization and modernization of the new nation.

The School as an Agent in Culture Change and Maintenance

What role schools play in promoting, sustaining, or eliminating various kinds of behavior is not clear, as has been said. Certainly newly constituted governments in newly independent countries are inclined to believe that "education is the central agent in social change."[6] Teachers are probably not as powerful as parents in conveying basic ideas of right and wrong and setting the life behavioral pattern. But schools undoubtedly support other agencies in sustaining particular value systems and assist in changing those values. They certainly act as brokers (links) between superordinate and subordinate cultures.[7] Their graduates in turn are brokers in the society. Whatever else it is, it serves as a tool of the dominant class in society, and to the extent that it can, it communicates a universal culture.

Illustrations of culture change and maintenance and of the school as agent are legion. For sake of familiar overtones let us start with the American Indian who was as surely conquered as were the Africans or the Indonesians or any of the others of the developing countries. One of these Indian groups was the Seminoles of Florida, who were the victims of nineteenth-century wars and 50 years of "American removal tactics."[8] Unlike their counterparts in colonial areas, these people re-

[6]J. E. Anderson, "The Kenya Education Commission Report: An African View of Educational Planning," *Comparative Education Review,* Vol. 9, No. 2 (June 1965), 203.

[7]For a discussion of the role of the school, see Joseph P. Farrell, "Education and Pluralism in Selected Caribbean Societies," *Comparative Education Review*, Vol. 11, No. 2 (June 1967), 160–181.

[8]James Clyde Stull, "Seminole Rejection of American Education" (Unpublished Doctoral Dissertation, The University of Toledo, 1967).

sisted American education for some 80 years, says Stull. One of their reasons appeared to be unrelated to schooling. It was that when white Americans and Seminoles had met, there had always been violence and hence there was a large backwash of hatred. But the second reason was based on what the Seminoles apparently know to be very deep-seated differences in their culture and in that which the American school was designed to teach. The Seminoles lived in the present (not the future as do most Americans), with only a desultory sense of time. They put little emphasis either on hard work or on monetary saving. The reverse of all these values is what they realized their children would learn in the white man's institutions. Only when the physical environment altered in such a way that they were forced to learn new behaviors did they in the 1960's turn to formal education as a medium of survival.

In 1946 Margaret Mead pointed out that if members of primitive societies were to learn world mobility and participation in the span of one generation, account must be taken of striking differences between native and universal cultures.[9] She noted that in societies based on caste, as an example, the order in which skills are learned may be crucial. Is it status-enhancing to learn a skill first? Does a skill lose its value if a lower caste person acquires it? These and other cultural uniquenesses must be considered in relation to the six necessary factors for a successful schooling for the present. These factors, according to Mead, include: (1) a world language in which one may find the world's most recent riches; (2) teaching how to live in a contract as opposed to a status economy; (3) communicating a cross-cultural sophistication; (4) changing certain attitudes about the natural world from those of folklore to those of science; (5) facilitating a change in time perspective which includes both past and future; and (6) helping the individual to live in a culture other than the one in which he was born and brought up, and without "crippling nostalgia." These might well be used to evaluate a school in a developing nation.

With these criteria for a maximum culture-changing institution, it might be well to look at some specific instances of schools in developing cultures.

The Case of Ceylon

Sometimes the conquering nation can graft a set of values and institutions onto native systems in such a way that old values will be reinforced to the doubtful advantage of a country which is to seek its independence. This happened to Ceylon when the British took over.[10]

When the British entered Ceylon in the nineteenth century, they instituted a system of government and mission schools of which the latter were the better institutions. The most acceptable of these schools carried on instruction in English. Side by side but usually inferior were vernacular schools.

---

[9] Margaret Mead, "Professional Problems of Education in Dependent Countries," *The Journal of Negro Education*, Vol. 15, No. 3 (Summer 1946), 346–357.

[10] Unless otherwise indicated, the account of Ceylon is taken from Bryce Ryan, "The Dilemmas of Education in Ceylon," *Comparative Education Review*, Vol. 4, No. 2 (October 1960), 84–92.

This dichotomy in formal schools gave rise to a "distinctive Westernized elite." Through the preferred system the British educated a special native group who would be Ceylonese by birth and drawn to England through education. They perhaps inadvertently produced the first Ceylonese as opposed to Sinhalese or Tamil (the two leading ethnic groups).[11]

The preferred system at the same time reinforced many values in the old Sinhalese culture. The latter was replete with the importance of caste and royal honors. Physical work other than agriculture was degrading. So also was business enterprise, says Ryan. For others education was a refuge from caste, an antidote for economic insecurity, a way of fleeing an unrewarding village life, and a means by which to progress to higher economic levels.[12] Advancement in economic terms came through political attainment (as in some Latin American societies) rather than through economic enterprise.

The English-medium system promoted an education of white collar government workers. It took advantage of the distaste for physical labor and other Sinhalese values and added security through the pension plans as well as the dubious honor of rubbing shoulders with the dominant English group.

With the reinforcement of a native culture by the invaders' school, the Ceylonese penchant for equating government service with a status and honor was reinforced. In a survey of village children, for instance, it was found that on a scale 0–100, a government doctor was rated 81 and a private physician only 61. Concomitantly in a preference ranking of 38 occupations the government doctor was 2nd and the private practitioner, 8th. These youth ranked a chief government clerk fourth but an insurance clerk, 17th. In another survey of youth in four provinces 75 per cent of the boys preferred government service and had no clearly defined choices beyond this. In Ryan's study of occupational choices for their sons, 90 per cent of the village fathers selected government service. Two-thirds of the adolescents entering the University of Ceylon anticipated government employment, with others selecting professions in terms of their relationship to government, whereas only two per cent showed interest in business. In addition Green reports that in 1961 and in face of the drive to increase scientific interests, twice as many students at the University of Ceylon were in arts and Oriental studies as were enrolled in the sciences.

Now that Ceylon is independent, a pressing problem is changing the value system in response to occupations which were preferred under British rule. Green points out that presently formal education aggravates "the problems of vocational ambition which under social pressures lean heavily towards 'white collar work'."[13] Ceylon, which is still largely rural, probably needs scientific agriculturists who can demonstrate in overalls more than it needs government clerks. How can the

---

[11] T. L. Green, "The Problem of Expanding Education in a Plural Society—Ceylon," Chapter 13 in *The Education Explosion*, The 1964 World Yearbook of Education (New York: Harcourt, Brace & World, Inc., 1965), pp. 371–386.

[12] *Ibid.*, p. 374.

[13] *Ibid.*, p. 381.

culture be modified through education to help youth to perceive agriculture as a status occupation?

The Case of Indonesia

As in Ceylon, the imperial power, the Dutch government, saddled a rigid Dutch curriculum on Indonesian schools and along with it a dual system of education which gave preference in secondary and university education to the traditional aristrocracy.[14] The academic secondary education again fostered a preparation in large part for the government service.

At emancipation after World War II, schooling became generally available, but the cultural seeds had been sown in the colonial period. Hence the reason why larger numbers of youth seek academic secondary education is because they and their parents equate it with education of the aristocracy and for civil service. Business and vocational-technical education and science education, which is desperately needed for a largely village (peasant) society, is not pursued by large numbers of "diploma-hungry Indonesians."

Thus secondary education reinforces a value system among youth and adults which emphasizes contempt for manual labor and any occupations connected with it, and produces a surfeit of graduates culturally biased toward government clerkships. With this situation government employment has enormously expanded: 140,000 in the colonial period as against 900,000 to one million in the 1950's.

The best brains in some areas are being drained into government service through education, and yet they yield no new returns for the Indonesian economy which is made the poorer for having to absorb diplomaed graduates. The process highlights the cultural differences between the U.S. and Indonesia, which makes for a dynamic as against a stagnating culture. A former Minister of Education in Indonesia said that in the U.S. there is a continuous search for "new facts, traditions, and values," whereas in Indonesia there is instead "a rediscovery and a streamlining of 'ancient facts'."[15]

Assessing the School as Agent

It would be presumptious to evaluate formal education in developing countries on the basis of no more evidence than can be contained herein. Any analysis must be, at best, suggestive.

The most striking departure from Mead's World Language is to be found in Ceylon as reported by Ryan in some detail. Nationalism in its narrowest sense has taken over, and Sinhalese and Ghuddism have become the watchwords of the new society. The language used by less than seven million people is being forced on elementary and secondary

---

[14]Justus M. van der Kroef, "Social Disfunctions of Indonesian Education," *Comparative Education Review*, Vol. 2, No. 2 (October 1958), 15–20.

[15]*Ibid.*, p. 19.

schools, as well as on the university. Where is a Sinhalese literature to be found for the medical school? In view of Sinhalese dislike for technical fields and a consequent takeover by Tamils, who is to "teach engineering in Sinhalese, and to what students?"[16]

Along with this self-defeating move toward nationalism has come an enhancement of the Ayurvedic physician whose skill is rooted in tradition rather than in science. With a paucity of literature and a return to native medicine, the schools may well communicate the antithesis of the attitudes Mead believed were mandatory.

Both Indonesian and Ceylonese schools are educating for status rather than modern economic societies. Schooling is making inroads into traditional religious views of Turkish youth, but the latter are not overcoming attachment for traditional hierarchical human relationships. Indonesians (and thus probably their schools) are streamlining ancient facts (as have been many of the Latin American universities) rather than acquiring Mead's scientific attitudes.

Withal, few schools, including those for American Indians, have grappled realistically with native cultures. Instead, they have ignored them and thus left inconsistencies unreconciled or agony widespread; or they have paid their ado to superstition as in present-day Ceylon.

Summary

This then has been a very brief introduction to the idea of culture (learned behavior) as a way of explaining the very obvious differences among the world's adolescents. Some attention has been given to the number of overlapping cultures in which most of us live, as well as to the process by which cultures are changed and maintained. The schools as an agent of culture change and maintenance have been briefly explored. Central questions, however, remain largely unanswered here and elsewhere. Two of these might well be: Can culture change proceed without social disorganization? and Can the schools for adolescents communicate a universal culture within the framework of a multicultural society?

---

[16]Bryce Ryan, *op. cit.*, p. 91.

Adolescence: An Anthropological Approach

Abraham E. Knepler

University of Bridgeport

In this article the author applies the tools of the cultural anthropologist to the study of the nature of adolescence. His comparative evaluation of American society with primitive societies suggests several specific causes of the high-level stress that seems characteristic of American adolescence. Notable among these factors discussed by the author is the cultural phenomenon known as the *rites de passage.* While the picture of how children become adolescents in America is somewhat grim, it is at the same time hopeful. For it strongly implies that the major difficulties associated with adolescence are not phylogenetically determined but culturally determined—thus controllable, rather than inevitable.

The contribution of anthropology to the study of adolescence is based upon its furnishing of data that may provide:

1. an understanding of what adolescents are like in other societies (especially preliterate or primitive societies);
2. a comparison of adolescents in various societies or cultures, with a view to learning and explaining differences and discovering similarities, in the development and behavior of adolescents.[1]

Essentially the sources of such data, and the methodological procedures for obtaining such data, are the concerns of cultural anthropology. In obtaining data, cultural anthropologists must often take into account two sets of variables—man's biological equipment, and the particular societies of "historical forms" within which this biological equipment has been given expression through the patternings of social relationships.[2] An important task of the cultural anthropologist is to attempt to sort out what might be essentially a culturally determined set of traits from those traits which are fundamentally phylogenetically determined features of man.

An example of such an approach is to be found in the testing of the biogenetic hypothesis of G. Stanley Hall, early American psychologist (1844–1924), that adolescence universally is a period of "storm and stress," or, in the German, *Sturm und Drang.*[3] According to Hall, the

---

Reprinted by permission of the author.

[1]For an example of a newer type of anthropolical-sociological study employing sophisticated research techniques and involving "inter-cultural variability," or the differences between cultural groups across national boundaries, see R. J. Havighurst *et al., A Cross-National Study of Buenos Aires and Chicago Adolescents,* Bibliotheca "Vita Humana," Fasc 3 (Basel, Switzerland: S. Karger, 1965).

[2]Margaret Mead, "Anthropological Data on the Problem of Instinct," in Clyde Kluckhohn, Henry A. Murray, and David M. Schneider, eds., *Personality in Nature, Society, and Culture,* 2nd ed. (New York: Alfred A. Knopf, 1953), pp. 115–118.

[3]G. Stanley Hall, *Adolescence,* 2 vols. (New York: Appleton, 1916). See especially chapter on "Feelings and Psychic Evolution."

adolescent's emotional life is naturally one of contradictory tendencies and turmoil—including rebellion against authority and the flowering of idealism. Hall viewed adolescence as a phenomenon due chiefly to the phylogenetic nature of adolescent development, and hence a stage little influenced by environmental factors.[4]

How might one go about testing such a hypothesis? Since it was not possible to submit human beings to a test of the hypothesis under controlled conditions in a biological laboratory, the alternative was to utilize the anthropological method of studying human beings in another part of the world, under different cultural conditions, and preferably in a relatively uncomplicated society. Samoa was accordingly selected as the field laboratory in which a brilliant young woman of 23 set out to find the answers to the questions, "Are the disturbances which vex our (American) adolescents due to the nature of adolescence itself or to the civilization?" and "Under different conditions does adolescence present a different picture?"[5]

Margaret Mead, the young anthropologist who undertook the investigation, found the Samoans to be a people who were relatively casual, easygoing, unhurried, blessed by a comfortable climate and a not overly demanding economy, with a culture in which children could easily escape from displeasing home conditions by moving into another household, where work detail and age-sex roles, relationships, and taboos were clearly understood by all, where baby tending was largely the responsibility of small girls—where consequently authority and affection were diffused rather than intense, localized, and concentrated. The "facts of life" regarding birth, sex and reproduction, and death were common knowledge at an early age.

The most carefree period for Samoans was during adolescence, when the coincidence of work chores, which were least burdensome, the heterosexual stirrings of youth, the freedom of movement and association of young people, the absence of deep emotional involvement, and the pleasantness of the climate, enabled most young people to enjoy a number of years of casual sex and lovemaking before they married and settled down to raising a family.[6]

Thus, to the question as to whether adolescence was a particularly difficult period, a period of conflict and stress for Samoan youth, Dr. Mead's answer was in the negative. At least such was the finding regarding the adolescent girls who were the focus of Dr. Mead's study.[7] Compared to her sister who had not yet reached puberty, the adolescent girl differed in only one principal respect, in "certain bodily changes . . . which were absent in the younger girl." Nor were there any important differences between the girls in adolescence and those who had preceeded them in adolescence by two years.[8]

Mead reviews the question, if the claim as to the universal nature of adolescent *Sturm and Drang* is not supported by the findings in Samoa,

---

[4]Rolf E. Muuss, *Theories of Adolescence* (New York: Random House, 1962), pp. 14, 17.

[5]Margaret Mead, *Coming of Age in Samoa,* Mentor Book edition (New York: The New American Library of World Literature, 1949), pp. 13–17.

[6]*Op. cit., passim.*

[7]*Ibid.,* pp. 108, 130–31.

[8]*Ibid.,* p. 131.

then what explanation is there for the stressful experiences of American adolescents? Or, to put it another way, "What is there in Samoa which is absent in America; what is there in America which is absent in Samoa, which will account for this difference?"[9]

Two sets of background factors are suggested to account for the difference: those factors which are unique to Samoa, and those which are characteristic of primitive societies.

Some reference has already been made to characteristics of Samoan life that contributed to the general atmosphere of casualness. As Mead phrases it, "No one plays for very high stakes, no one pays very heavy prices, no one suffers for his convictions or fights to the death for special ends." From infancy, as the child's needs are attended to by one or another person, the individual experiences an atmosphere where, ordinarily, no one cares deeply or gets deeply involved with another person.[10] Hence, one's emotions get blunted or become shallow. "Love and hate, jealousy and revenge, sorrow and bereavement, are all matters of weeks."[11]

The uniqueness of a society in which adolescents as well as others need not feel deeply dependent emotionally on others is reinforced by the characteristics which Samoa shares[12] with so many other primitive societies. They tend to be homogenous or fairly so in population, with members of a society sharing a fairly uniform set of beliefs, values, regulations, expectations, and ways of doing things. Roles[13] assigned to members are usually clearly prescribed, with few ambiguities. Primitives of such and such an age and sex, and of such a relationship to another, are rarely in doubt as to how to act in a given situation in their own culture. Since technological development is not complex in such societies, division of labor and specialization of function also are not very extensive. Members of such a society tend to be generalists, "jacks-of-all-trades," rather than specialists. Given one's sex and age range, one person can either do pretty much what the others do, or at least can readily understand another's role or limited specialty. In such a society, the range of career choices or of other kinds of choices is likely to be very limited.[14] Under such conditions, life tends to be not only fairly uncomplicated but also relatively integrated and coherent.[15] One aspect of the simpler society's culture, in other words, "meshes

---

[9]*Loc. cit.*

[10]*Ibid.*, p. 132.

[11]*Ibid.*, p. 133.

[12]Present tense is characteristically employed in anthropological writings, even though the conditions described may no longer prevail.

[13]A role may be regarded as "a set of mutually expected behaviors, within a known reference group, around a more or less clearly defined situation, such as family or school." The author of this fairly standard conception of role indicates the need to add the idea of "*development* that leads to a consideration of the function of any given role as preparation for later roles. Adolescent role behavior may therefore be described partly in terms of immediate expectations of all persons involved in situations and relationships in which adolescents participate. In addition, roles assumed by the adolescent may also be seen in terms of their functional preparation for adult roles anticipated by self, others, and the community." Martin B. Loeb, "Social Role and Sexual Identity in Adolescent Males: A Study of Culturally Provided Deprivation," in George B. Spindler, *Education and Culture: Anthropological Approaches* (New York: Holt, Rinehart, and Winston, 1963), pp. 284–300.

[14]Ina Corinne Brown, *Understanding Other Cultures*, A Spectrum Book (Englewood Cliffs, N. J.: Prentice-Hall, 1963), pp. 31–54. See also John W. M. Whiting, *Becoming A Kwoma* (New Haven: Yale University Press, 1941), pp. 8–14, 65–72, *et passim*.

[15]Margaret Mead, "Adolescence in Primitive and in Modern Society," in Theodore M. Newcomb and Eugene L. Hartley, eds., *Readings in Social Psychology* (New York: Henry Holt and Co., 1947), pp. 6–14.

in" with another, and tends to reinforce a central set of values and goals for the culture more readily than would be the case in a more complex society.

This does not mean that all primitive societies are lacking in pressures upon young people. Even in Samoa, despite the relatively carefree period of adolescence, a girl is normally concerned with whether she will eventually marry and, if so, whom she will marry. Apparently boys, too, give considerable thought to the question of mate choice. Perhaps the important factors here are that such considerations in Samoa occur in a cultural setting in which the range of choices is not wide, in which few choices, if any, are so significant and preoccupying as to drain the energies of a person through indecision, regret, or grief for a sustained period of time, and in which the self-image is seriously threatened by questions regarding one's success or failure in a central role.

In some societies, as among the Manus, the pressures and crises experienced by girls and boys may occur, but not necessarily at puberty or during adolescence. Such is the case, to some extent, among Samoans. Among the Manus, the pressures occur at different times during development. For Manus girls, the pressures and demands of society may or may not be distributed in time from early childhood (if engaged then to a boy), to the early years of marriage. Viewed in the light of the generally repressive nature of the Manus society and the taboos against sex and freedom of action, stress is likely to be experienced irrespective of adolescence.

Dr. Mead, therefore, does not discount the existence of pressure in puberty or adolescence. Rather, her point is that adolescence is "not necessarily" a stressful period and that stress and strain, when they do occur, are traceable to "cultural anxieties" or to culturally produced anxieties [16]

To understand further those factors which are characteristic of primitive societies and which are relatively absent in the United States, one must consider the accompaniments of a technological civilization. Modern technological societies tend to be much less integrated and coherent.[17] American youth, living in a highly industrialized, urbanized, and heterogeneous society, face a variety of choices as to career and career preparation, friends, associates, lovers, recreational activities, the uses of money, religious and ethical behavior, and so on.

The choices are the more difficult to make because they are reflective of the diversity of values to be found in a pluralistic society.

Furthermore, given such a plethora of choices, yet beset by so many different, and at times conflicting, value systems, American youth are likely to experience conflict in making what they may regard as appropriate choices. Even if they were more confident as to the appropriate choices, they might find themselves unprepared to execute the choices effectively.

---

[16] *Ibid.*, p. 12.

[17] Walter Goldschmidt, *Exploring the Ways of Mankind* (New York: Holt, Rinehart and Winston, 1960), pp. 72–73.

Continuities and Discontinuities

The late Ruth Benedict has posed the problem of adequate preparation to execute choices effectively in terms of "continuities and discontinuities in cultural conditioning." By comparison with a good many primitive societies, Benedict sees American society as emphasizing considerable contrast between the child and the adult, and consequently as making for serious discontinuity in the life cycle. For example, in American society, while "the child is sexless, the adult estimates his virility by his sexual activities; the child must be protected from the ugly facts of life, the adult must meet them without psychic catastrophe; the child must obey, the adult must command obedience."[18]

The great dilemma, the major discontinuity, in the life cycle is in the fact that the child will eventually become the father, and by then will be expected to reverse the behavior to one appropriate to his adult role. In American society the roles of father and son are strongly differentiated. To perform his adult role, after having been conditioned differently as a child, will require considerable, and possibly embarrassing or painful, unlearning and relearning.

Three contrasts in our culture that make for discontinuity are examined by Dr. Benedict, in the light of practices and expectations of other cultures:

(1) responsible vs. nonresponsible status role;
(2) dominance vs. submission;
(3) contrasted sex role.[19]

In selecting these three areas, Benedict does not imply that primitive societies have no areas of discontinuity, or that American society has no areas of successful cultural conditioning. Indeed, Benedict cites the conditioning of Americans to eat three meals a day and to achieve modesty through the wearing of clothes in public, as examples of continuity.

However, to obtain a clearer understanding of American child-adult contrasts, a look at the training of children in primitive societies for the assumption of responsible status roles is warranted. In primitive societies adults commonly encourage children from an early age to become familiar with the nature of adult roles, and to become increasingly more adept at these roles.

Even before he can walk, a child might be carried along in the mother's shawl, as the mother goes to work in the field; later on the child will assume tasks on his level of ability to perform. Some of these tasks may not relate directly to specific work assignments in adulthood, yet may be related to adult responsibilities. The instance is cited by Dr. Ruth Underhill of observing a Papago Indian father in Arizona, sitting with a group of other elders, who asked his three-year-old granddaughter to close a heavy door. The child tried unsuccessfully. As the little girl tried several more times, her grandfather encouraged her

---

[18]Ruth Benedict, "Continuities and Discontinuities in Cultural Conditioning," in Clyde Kluckhohn, Henry A. Murray, and David M. Schneider, *Personality in Nature, Society, and Culture,* 2nd ed. (New York: Alfred A. Knopf, 1953), p. 523; article reprinted from *Psychiatry,* I (1938) 161–167.

[19]*Ibid.,* pp. 524–528.

with, "Yes, close the door." No one moved to assist the girl, nor did anyone prod her. When she finally succeeded, she was thanked. She had carried out a task that apparently the adults thought she could perform successfully at this age. In the course of her doing so, her conditioning toward gradually increased and responsible participation in the society was reinforced.[20]

The teaching of the young in the arts of warfare and of getting food have been vital areas of continuity in cultural conditioning for primitive children. A nineteenth-century student of American Indian affairs, Henry R. Schoolcraft, reported that boys in Indian tribes of the East and Southeast generally were given, at a very early age, miniature bows and arrows as playthings. As the boys acquired strength, they received encouragement to shoot at birds, squirrels, and small game. Praise was given at the first evidence of success, and a ceremony was usually conducted to mark the occasion.[21]

A still earlier observer of southeastern American Indian tribes, George Henry Loskiel, noted that as the boys grew older, they began to hunt larger game, with the first success again being celebrated. The boy was now ready to be counseled by elders in the tribe regarding the chase and his own future, and also concerning the respect and obedience to be accorded the senior members of the tribe.[22]

The early training of a prominent Cherokee Indian, Major Ridge, included long and rigorous experiences in patience, exposure, fatigue, approaching a grazing animal, and so on, as part of the process of his becoming an expert hunter who could procure food from stream or forest at all seasons. By the age of twelve, young Ridge felt ready to move on to another level of training—that of becoming a warrior. An impressive rite formally dedicated Ridge's future life to the career of a warrior. When fourteen, the boy volunteered in an expedition against a fort of whites in Tennessee.[23]

Indian girls, too, were progressively instructed in the variety of tasks devolving upon the adult woman. From serving as assistants in the work of housekeeping, they proceeded to learn the agricultural and other duties which were expected of them. And, as the boys learned the traditions of the Cherokee people from the old men, so did the girls learn the tribal customs from the old Cherokee women.[24]

Erikson describes a similar pattern of conditioning of Sioux boys and girls. Boys were conditioned by "every educational device" toward achieving a maximum level of self-confidence, and through attaining a sense of mastery (despite a long period of indulgence by the mothers) as "a hunter after game, woman, and spirit." To counter the expected aggressiveness of the male youths toward them, girls were taught to assume responsible roles through appropriate defensive attitudes and

---

[20]*Ibid.*, pp. 524–525.

[21]Henry R. Schoolcraft, *Information Respecting the History, Condition and Prospects of the Indian Tribes of the United States,* II (Philadelphia: Lippincott, Grambo & Company, 1851–57), p. 50. Cited in Abraham E. Knepler, "Education in the Cherokee Nation," *Chronicles of Oklahoma,* 21:383 (December 1943), 378–401.

[22]George Henry Loskiel, *History of the Mission of the United Brethren Among the Indians of North America,* Christian I. LaTrobe, trans., I (London, 1794), 63. Cited in Knepler, *loc. cit.*

[23]Knepler, *op. cit.* pp. 383–384.

[24]*Ibid.*, p. 384.

maneuvers. But, of course, the girl was also taught the skills and the attitudes important in being a helper to a hunter-husband and a mother to a future hunter.[25]

Dominance-submission, the second of Benedict's categories, is an area of perhaps even more marked contrast in the United States as against a primitive society. As suggested in the reference to the universal problem of the child growing up to be the father, the dilemma exists in the fact that the set of behavior patterns and attitudes to which one has been conditioned as a child must give way in the individual to an opposite set when he becomes an adult.[26]

But is not this the case everywhere? Indeed not. In societies in which conditioning is more continuous, "approximately identical reciprocal behavior tends to be the more characteristic pattern." In some primitive societies, the terms of address employed by such reciprocal pairs as father and son, grandfather and grandson, or uncle and nephew, with one another, are the same, in the sense in which we may exchange the same appellation with a cousin. Thus, a father and son will throughout life use the same term in relation to each other, and the son will in turn employ the same term with *his* son as his son will with him. Such relationships extend beyond terms of address. For example, they may include a child's right to reciprocate his maternal uncle's banter or teasing or practical jokes with like behavior, or to have access to his uncle's belongings in the same manner in which his uncle may have access to his.[27]

As a further example of continuity in conditioning, Benedict describes a Crow Indian situation in the nineteenth century, when a father who had been scorned or mocked by his small son boasted of his son's intractability. Proudly the father remarked, "He will be a man."[28]

The contrasted sexual role assigned to American children and adolescents on the one hand, with the expectations that they refrain from sex play as children and remain virtuous as adolescents, and the role assigned to adults in marriage, [that] they make good sexual partners, constitute a major form of discontinuity in our society.

Accompanying such contrasting cultural expectations as to behavior are expectations as to attitudes. Historically fostered attitudes toward sex in American youth have been characterized by a stress on sinfulness and danger. For the girl a positive ideal has been the coming to the wedding as a virgin—an ideal reinforced by the symbolic white of the wedding gown. As husband and wife, a couple should be responsive to each other sexually. For a married couple to achieve such cultural expectations in marriage, after exposure to culturally negative attitudes toward sex before marriage, requires some considerable unlearning for a great many Americans. But many cannot unlearn such negative attitudes impressed upon them in more formative years.[29]

Even in societies with more continuity in cultural conditioning, bi-

---

[25]Erik Erikson, *Childhood and Society*, 2nd ed. (New York: W. W. Norton and Co., 1963), pp. 143–144.
[26]Benedict, *op. cit.*, p. 526.
[27]*Loc. cit.*
[28]*Ibid.*, p. 527
[29]*Ibid.*, p. 528.

ology must be contended with. Maturationally speaking, the development of the individual's reproductive equipment comes late. If children are kept, and actually remain, ignorant of sex until puberty or even until marriage, Benedict sees no particular harm done—provided that nothing has been taught to the individual that must now be unlearned. Or if, as among the Zunic, a child has impressed upon him the wickedness of premature sex, no particular harm is done to subsequent adjustment. For the Zunic, sex is wicked not in itself, but below a certain age. Here is where Benedict sees the significant contrast with our society in the attitudes which are impressed on the child.

It is evident from what has been said that a society such as Samoa's provides a minimum of discontinuous conditioning and a maximum of continuous conditioning. The Samoan child experiences a highly continuous growth pattern, assumes graded levels of responsibility in caring for children or in other work, and assumes progressive degrees of dominance over younger children while still being under the domination of older ones—a domination which is alleviated somewhat by a child's ability to move into another household and under the domination of someone else, while still dominating younger children, but a domination which is alleviated also by a progression in status with age. As a youth gets older, there are fewer to regulate or discipline her or to "rebel" against. Hence another factor helps to explain the relative absence of "emotion-loaded conflict between dominance and submission that often erupts during adolescence in our society."[30]

In the area of preparation for sexual adjustment in marriage, the Samoan youth's continuity of cultural conditioning starts well before adolescence—as the girl or boy becomes aware of physical developmental processes through everyday observation and of the sexual proclivities of adolescents through hearsay and spying, and of the sexual practices of adults because of the lack of privacy within Samoan houses.[31]

Puberty and Adolescence

At this point some differentiation should be made between two terms that are often used synonymously—puberty and adolescence.

Puberty is a shorter period of time than is adolescence, and refers essentially to the physiological changes during which the sexual organs of boy or girl become mature. Cole and Hall suggest that for girls, puberty is a period of scarcely over six months in time, but for boys may be as long as two years or more. While puberty begins pretty much at the same time as adolescence, Cole and Hall regard adolescence as lasting for about eight years and as including such nonpubertal changes as "developments in intellectual capacities, interests, attitudes, personal adjustments, emotional adaptations, vocational and academic interests, aptitudes, and religious and moral attitudes."[32]

---

[30]Muuss, *op. cit.*, p. 65.

[31]Mead, *Coming of Age in Samoa*, pp. 93–95.

[32]Luella Cole, with Irma Nelson Hall, *Psychology of Adolescence*, 6th ed. (New York: Holt, Rinehart and Winston, Inc., 1964), p. 3.

Yet Mead would quarrel as to whether even the beginnings of puberty and adolescence need necessarily coincide. Among the Luiseno, a tribe of California Indians, the ceremonial observance of a girl's first menses (the menarche) had become so much of a socialized affair that an entire group of girls were included in the rite, yet only one of the group was at the actual physiological period of first menses.[33]

Nevertheless, for a great many peoples, Cole and Hall's definition applies. But while Cole and Hall, and other authorities, recognize so many additional features in adolescence beyond the pubertal, one of the central characteristics differentiating adolescence from childhood is the nature of adolescent sexuality.

Whether or not children identify strongly with their own sex, whether or not they have curiosity about sex, whether or not they are interested in the opposite sex, it is not until the arrival of puberty, with the biophysical changes involving hormonal secretions and bodily form, and the psychological accompaniments of such changes, that the maturation of a distinct quality of sexual stirring occurs.

How such urges achieve expression is to a considerable extent dependent upon cultural factors. Basic to the patterns of permissiveness and restrictions is the particular culture's view of the fertility potential of adolescents, and the culture's readiness to accept the idea that pregnancy may occur. Consequently, how the sexual interests and stirrings of adolescence achieve expression is to a considerable extent dependent upon cultural factors.

But such cultural factors affect not only direct sexual expression. They may also affect the presence or absence of strong frustrations related to sex. However, this does not mean that severe cultural restrictions on direct sexual expression will necessarily produce severe symptoms of emotional disturbance, or that the relative absence of restrictions will in itself produce an idyllic existence in adolescence. As Ausubel points out, "there is no simple relationship between degree of overt freedom in sexual expression and the development of stress in adolescence."[34]

Among the Manus, for example, the restrictions upon the social life and repression of sexual interests and sexual expression are so thorough for girls that there is an absence of conscious acknowledgment of sex feelings. Furthermore, there is no discernible evidence of anxiety or of other emotional distress as a consequence of such sexual repression during adolescence.[35] Yet the feelings, upon marriage, of shame and disgust toward intercourse suggest previously held unfavorable views by girls regarding sex.

Boys, on the other hand, are recognized in Manus society as having powerful sex drive, yet expression of the drive outside the institution of marriage is strongly tabooed. Homosexual practices and other peer group activities nevertheless provide some outlet for the expression of male sexuality.[36] Whether the adolescent male's sexual urges are weak-

[33]Margaret Mead, "Adolescence in Primitive and in Modern Society," in Newcomb and Hartley, *op. cit.*, p. 7.
[34]David P. Ausubel, *Theories and Problems of Adolescent Development* (New York: Grune and Stratton, 1954), pp. 16, 404.
[35]Ausubel, *op. cit.*, pp. 19–20.
[36]*Ibid.*, p. 20.

ened, deflected, or intensified by the competitiveness, aggressiveness, and exploitativeness of adult Manus society is difficult to determine, but such a world should be mentioned as one into which the Manus boy is suddenly projected upon reaching adolescence. Without a transitional period, and without any appreciable assistance from others, the Manus boy enters this adult world after a rather easygoing and pressureless period of childhood.[37]

Rites de Passage

Reference has already been made to ceremonial rites or observances which mark the attainment of a certain stage of chronological, physical, or social development by a primitive boy or girl. Such ceremonial observances, or *rites de passage* (rites of passage) as A. Van Gennep[38] termed them, celebrate the transition from one stage or status to another in the life cycle of individuals in a given society. Most commonly observed are the life crises, the crucial physiological stages of birth, puberty, and death, although other stages may also be observed.[39]

What purposes do such rites of passage serve? Along with calling public attention to the individual's arrival at a new status, the rituals serve to enhance the initiate's awareness of that new status and its accompanying roles, responsibilities, and possible privileges.[40] Drucker comments that an underlying concept in such observances is the belief that "the person at the moment of change was in a peculiar condition of ritual uncleanliness offensive to supernatural beings, and simultaneously imbued with magical power capable of causing good or evil."[41] Drucker cites the case of the North Pacific coast people who blame the coming of a glacier over two hundred years ago on the actions of a pubescent girl. Confined during her long initiation into puberty, she became bored, peeked at a glacier through an opening in the wall of her place of confinement, held up some dried salmon from her meal for the glacier to see, and spoke to the glacier as she would to a dog. Given the ominously magical power of her physical state, the glacier reacted as might "an obedient dog, with disastrous results."[42]

In the example provided by Drucker, we note the obvious state of the entire society in the puberty rites and their strict observance. When the puberty or other rites involve the whole community, "rites of intensification" serve to strengthen the individual's sense of belonging and to intensify group ties, expecially since these rites have obvious religious implications.[43]

As already noted in the discussion concerning continuity-discontinuity, puberty or adolescence is not necessarily the first stage after birth

---

[37]Margaret Mead, *From the South Seas* (New York: William Morrow, 1939).

[38]A. Van Gennep, *Les Rites de Passage* (Paris: Noury, 1909).

[39]*Ibid.*; also Philip Drucker, *Cultures of the North Pacific Coast* (San Francisco: Chandler Publishing Co., 1965), p. 98.

[40]Walter Goldschmidt, *Man's Way* (New York: Henry Holt and Co., 1959), p. 177.

[41]Drucker, *loc. cit.*

[42]*Loc. cit.*

[43]Goldschmidt, *Man's Way*, p. 178. See also John J. Honigmann, *The World of Man* (New York: Harper and Brothers, 1959), pp. 514–516.

subject to observance. A series or number of "first" ceremonies often distinguish the progression of the individual from childhood to young adulthood.[44] A "first" for a small girl among the Yuit in Alaska, for example, would usually be the picking by her of her first berries, whereas for the boy it would be the killing of his first bird.[45]

Most dramatic usually are the "firsts" or the rites of passage relating to puberty or to the broader aspects of adolescence. Not all primitive societies celebrate puberty or the approximate time of puberty. For example, among the North Pacific coast peoples in America, there were no puberty rites for boys, although among some of the groups, a rigorous routine of training for strength, resistance, and fortitude, involving the taking of a daily bath in the chilly rivers or seas of the area, began well before puberty, and among other groups at about the time of puberty.[46]

Girls on the North Pacific coast, however, did engage in puberty rites. At the beginning of her menstruation, the girl was secluded. Except for the elderly female relatives who attended to her needs, she could not see or be seen by other people for an extended period of time. Then both a private or semiprivate rite of purification, and a public rite of symbolic purification, were held. The girl was now considered a woman and eligible for marriage.[47]

In a contrasting type of setting, among the Gururumba, in New Guinea, girls are secluded also, upon the first menstruation, and must follow certain procedures to avoid contamination of others, herself, and the community. Among the Gururumba, too, the girl eventually emerges and a final purification rite is performed. Significantly, the Gururumba girl, while being made aware that menstrual blood is dangerous, is also made aware that menstruation itself is a positive sign. A new, vital energy has come into being that produces children—and gardens.[48]

For the Gururumba male as well as for the female, initiation rites at puberty are concerned with sexual potency and physical growth. However, whereas the girl's puberty rites celebrate the attainment of reproductive power as well as growth of the body, the boy's initiation rites are intended to induce bodily growth and reproductive power. Boys at initiation time are not considered to be sufficiently potent to cope with the vital power of the girls' sexuality.[49]

The initiation of the Gururumba boy involves two phases, the first of which provides for an introduction to the secret of the manipulation of sacred flutes. All of the boys between the ages of ten and fifteen are gathered together into the men's house, once every several years, to live together for a number of months. Through a series of initiation steps, the boys are prepared for the physical and other assumption of adult male responsibilities. An important part of the initiation is learn-

---

[44]Knepler, *op. cit.*, pp. 383–384; Wendell H. Oswalt, *Alaskan Eskimos* (San Francisco: Chandler Publishing Co., 1967), pp. 200–201.
[45]Oswalt, *loc. cit.*
[46]Drucker, *op. cit.*, p. 101.
[47]*Ibid.*, pp. 99–101.
[48]Philip L. Newman, *Knowing the Gururumba* (New York: Holt, Rinehart and Winston, 1965), pp. 76–78.
[49]*Ibid.*, p. 80.

ing to play the sacred bamboo flutes, since the flute playing will make the boys strong physically, sexually, behaviorally.[50] After experiencing a series of purification rites and observing a number of taboos that free the youth from female influences which may contaminate him or make him weak, the young man emerges with the techniques for developing healthily and for maintaining his strength and other capacities as an adult. The boys who have shared the series of initiation experiences constitute a group of age mates who subsequently address each other by a special term.[51]

While not all primitive peoples celebrate puberty for boys, Goldschmidt states that puberty rites for girls are "probably universal."[52]

Cohen,[53] however, contends that the kinds of puberty rites which have been discussed thus far—initiation ceremonies—are found in fewer societies than other kinds of ceremonies relating to puberty. He refers to initiation ceremonies as the *second* stage of puberty.

The first stage of puberty corresponds to the period of "latency," when biochemical and hormonal changes are taking place internally, beginning with the production of androgens and gynogens.[54] For the child, according to Cohen, this stage is very confusing, since the child senses that something new is happening inside his body, yet he cannot see what is occurring. In the second stage of puberty, by contrast, the emergence of the outward and observable secondary sex traits produces somewhat less confusion for the individual.[55]

"Why," asks Cohen, "is so much attention given to the *rites de passage* of the second stage, when in fact they are of less importance than the more neglected events of the first stage?"[56] He notes that the second stage is celebrated in a much more colorful and impressive manner than the first, and often involves the efforts of many members of the group. The first stage "seems drab and prosaic by comparison."[57]

Thus far mention has been made of the developmental physiological state which occasions the first stage ceremonies, but no mention has been made of the ceremonies which appear so "drab and prosaic." Two ceremonial aspects are involved, either or both of which may be practiced by the same people: the first is *extrusion*, the second *brother-sister avoidance.*

Extrusion refers to the physical removal of the child from his or her household during this "latency" period or "first stage of puberty." The particular form of physical dislodgement varies from society to society. The child may spend the day with his family, but may have to sleep at another location at night, or may return to sleep on the roof of the house at night, or may be informally adopted by friends or distant relatives. The basic rule operative in extrusion is that the child is not allowed to sleep under the same roof as his father and mother.[58]

---

[50]*Ibid.*, pp. 66–67.
[51]*Ibid.*, p. 68
[52]Goldschmidt, *Man's Way*, p. 177.
[53]Yehudi A. Cohen, *The Transition from Childhood to Adolescence* (Chicago; Aldine Publishing Co., 1964), pp. 50, 101.
[54]*Ibid.*, p. 46.
[55]*Ibid.*, pp. 49–50.
[56]*Ibid.*, p. 101.
[57]*Loc. cit.*
[58]*Ibid.*, p. 55.

In some societies, boys and girls are assigned to separate "bush schools," where they may be kept for periods of time that may last until marriage. Here the young people may undergo initiation rites, learn tribal rituals, and acquire certain skills, myths, and group values.[59]

In connection with the earlier discussion of continuity and discontinuity, it should be observed that the practice of extrusion is likely to constitute a marked form of cultural discontinuity. Children or youth are separated from much that is familiar to them, undergo training or other activity under the direction of adults who ordinarily are strangers, or at least not members of the family or household.[60] The practices consequently impose sharp breaks in the continuity of the child's patterns of associations and activities.[61]

The application of the rule of brother-sister avoidance prohibits physical contact, speech, or other direct interaction between brother and sister, and usually takes effect after the older sibling has attained the first stage of puberty. Usually the prohibition extends to touching or looking at one another, or to being alone under the same roof. In most instances, the avoidance regulations end when one or both marry.[62]

Basic to both extrusion and brother-sister avoidance is the incest taboo. Since the sexuality of children usually first becomes a serious concern of parents during this first period of puberty, when most children are likely to be somewhat aware of sexual connotations of marriage and may themselves soon have the ability to act upon their sexual feelings, the danger exists of the children directing their sexual feelings toward parents or siblings. The safest way to cope with the problem is to remove the children from close contact with other members of the family before the children become fully capable and inclined to express their sexuality and until the children are about to marry.[63] The alternative is to prescribe patterns of avoidance, especially between brother and sister, when at least one of them has reached puberty —stage one or two.

While the practices of extrusion and brother-sister avoidance take place with relatively little fanfare or none, they are likely to produce a considerable impact on the eight-, nine-, or ten-year old child, and to have much more crucial significance for the child and for the society, Cohen notes, than do the initiation rites of the second stage of puberty.[64] For one thing, the rites of the first stage come when the child is so young. For another, they last much longer, as a rule.

The second stage of puberty, involving the more dramatic and often physically painful initiation ceremonies, nevertheless comes at a time when the youth's labor value to his society is important. Hence, initiation ceremonies rarely last more than several months, lest the economy

---

[59]John J. Honigmann, *The World of Man* (New York: Harper and Brothers, 1959), pp. 572–573. See also the youth houses described in Bronislaw Malinowski, *The Sexual Life of Savages* (London: Routledge and Kegan Paul, Ltd., 1932).

[60]Cohen, *op. cit.* passim; Honigmann, *op. cit.*, p. 573; C. W. M. Hart, "Contrasts between Prepubertal and Postpubertal Education," in Robert Endleman *Personality and Social Life* (New York: Random House, 1967), pp. 281–284.

[61]Cohen, *op. cit.*, p. 104.

[62]*Ibid.*, pp. 57–58.

[63]*Ibid.*, pp. 53, 57.

[64]*Ibid.*, p. 101.

suffer. A briefer, although perhaps a more intensive, experience ensues for the adolescent than is the case of the child in the first stage of puberty. It is difficult to imagine, according to Cohen, that the briefer and later ceremonies (of the second stage) could have as great an impact on the child's personality development as the earlier-starting and more extended practices of extrusion and brother-sister avoidance, which begin to have their effect when the child, already confused, is also much more impressionable.[65]

Cohen does point out, however, that the initiation ceremonies of the second stage of puberty, differing in degree rather than in kind from those of the first stage, are more likely to involve extended separation and seclusion from familiar persons, physical mutilation—usually genital, a shift in social position, and all coming at a developmental period of "some psychological vulnerability." Furthermore, occurring as the second-stage puberty rites do, in a painful setting in which the nuclear family can no longer serve as protector, the rites nevertheless help deflect emotional identification and a sense of "anchorage" from the family (a process perhaps already started by the practices of extrusion and brother-sister avoidance) toward the more extended Kinship group.[66] Despite the painful nature of the situation or perhaps because of it, Cohen suggests that the complex process of emotional arousal associated with a possible "critical period in development"[67] and the fact that the initiation rites are shared by a group of age-mates, many of whom are kinsmen, may help to weld a sense of solidarity among the initiates.

Whether we consider the puberty rites of the first stage or those of the second or both, it is evident that many societies provide more or less clear means of defining a child's or adolescent's status and roles. The very procedures employed for defining such status and roles tend to provide also certain psychological satisfactions such as those of belonging to a peer group or age-grade group (this would be the case in extrusion, where the child ordinarily sleeps with other members of his own age group, as well as in the group of older initiates, but would not be the case in brother-sister avoidance),[68] as well as to provide the means for transferring young people from one status to another, and to prepare them for future statuses.

By contrast, American society as a whole provides little guidance to the preadolescent or the adolescent. For neither boys nor girls in our society are there formal means of recognizing the physiological, psychological, or social changes that a boy or girl experiences at puberty, nor are there *rites de passage* to provide for the American youth's transition to another status in society.[69] Whiting and colleagues acknowledge that the changing status of American boys from childhood to

---

[65]*Ibid.*, pp. 107–109. Another writer, however, refers to "initiation procedures, beginning around puberty or a little later and lasting from six months to fifteen years" (C. W. M. Hart, *op. cit.*, p. 286).

[66]*Ibid.*, 108–110.

[67]Cohen cites the review of the studies on this topic by Scott (J. P. Scott, "Critical Periods in Behavioral Development," *Science*, 138:949–58, 1962).

[68]Cohen, *op. cit.*, p. 112.

[69]See Margaret Mead, "Adolescence in Primitive and in Modern Society," *op. cit.*, pp. 11–14; John W. M. Whiting, Richard Kluckhohn, and Albert Anthony, "The Function of Male Initiation Ceremonies at Puberty," in Robert Endleman, *Personality and Social Life*, pp. 294–295.

adulthood might get some cursory notice, as when they shave for the first time, or might be noted by a series of minor events rather than by any one major and memorable ceremonial or initiation rite. But such events as graduation from elementary or secondary school or the obtaining of a driver's license cannot be considered as ceremonial demarcation points for youth in our culture in the same manner as is a *rite de passage.*[70]

The point might be argued that in American as in other western cultures or subcultures, the customs of particular groups, such as the Bar Mitzvah among Jews, provide an example of a *rite de passage.* While the Bar Mitzvah (literally, "Son of the Commandment") ceremony has traditionally marked an important milestone in the religious life of the Jewish boy (usually on or near the boy's thirteenth birthday) and formally marks the entry into the adult religious fellowship of Jewry, it is not quite a full or true pubertal or adolescent *rite de passage.* The Bar Mitzvah ceremony as commonly observed today in the United States is, of course, essentially religious in its orientation, even though in many less religious Jewish circles the social aspect tends to be heavily emphasized. In addition, a considerable amount of time and attention are given to training for the Bar Mitzvah. Theologically speaking, the boy's status does change—for example, he is now responsible for his own actions and he can be counted as a member of a *minyan* for the formal conduct of a religious service.

The crucial aspects in which the Bar Mitzvah is not a true *rite de passage* relates to the group factor—it is essentially an individual rather than a group ceremony[71] (although some synagogues may have to schedule more than one Bar Mitzvah on the same Sabbath and arrange for the sharing of services and other aspects of the Bar Mitzvah). Also, members of the opposite sex are usually prevented from attending a *rite de passage.*[72] One might add that, in practice, for a very large proportion, perhaps for most, of Jewish boys who become Bar Mitzvah today, the experience does not result in the regular assumption of adult roles.

Conclusion

We have seen that adolescence is not everywhere or necessarily a period of storm and stress, but rather that the way of life of people may contribute to the presence, intensification, or relative absence of deep emotional conflict in adolescence.

We have seen, too, that the relative presence or absence of pressures upon adolescents may be related to a question of developmental emphasis in the culture. Among some peoples the heavier emphasis or stresses may be felt more so by others than adolescents. To some extent the developmental periods of greatest stress may be related to the extent to which cultural conditioning of children and youth for adult roles is relatively smooth and continuous or uneven and discontinuous,

---

[70]Whiting *et al., loc. cit.*
[71]Cohen, *op. cit.*, p. 103.
[72]*Loc. cit.*

and whether at various stages of development the individual has an opportunity to play or work at the roles which he is to assume in greater degree upon reaching adulthood.

The definition of adolescence, as a much broader concept than puberty, is dependent upon cultural factors—especially upon the unique areas of emphasis determined by the values and the way of life of a given society. Cultural factors, for example, largely determine the particular ways in which sexuality and other aspects of adolescence will be expressed in a society.

However, in most preliterate or primitive societies, the particular ways in which sexuality and other aspects of adolescence will be expressed, or the way in which people will change status from childhood to adolescence, or from adolescence to adulthood, are not left to chance. Definitions of statuses and roles tend to be fairly precise.

To assist children and youths to make the transitions to adolescence or to adulthood, puberty rites or *rites de passage* are utilized, although such ceremonials are not found in all societies. Such rites are less often found for males than for females.

In the United States and in other western societies, such *rites de passage*, especially to mark entry into puberty or adolescence, are rare. In preparation for adult status, they are again rare. The relative absence of such rites of passage would seem to contribute to the difficulty of transition of our youth from childhood into adolescence and from adolescence into adulthood.

Soviet Youth: Myth and Reality

George Sherman

Columbia University

Many observers of the international scene suggest that Russia, since Stalin, has been a culture in transition. Once a harshly regimented society, Russia now seems able to tolerate more diversity, more expression of individual and subgroup opinions and wishes. The author looks at youth within the context of a changing Russia. Soviet youth has been affected by change, and will influence future change. What this bodes for the people of Russia—and for the people of the world—makes for a tempting area of speculation.

"Let's suppose a man lives seventy-five years. For the first twenty-five he should study, for the second twenty-five he should travel the world, and for the last twenty-five he should rest, reflect and write—preparing for death."

Yuri, a twenty-nine-year-old Soviet geologist, was philosophizing. We were relaxing together on the fashionable hotel veranda at Sochi, the popular Black Sea resort, sipping Soviet champagne and savoring summer breezes from the dark water beyond.

Soviet propagandists would be aghast at Yuri's thoughts. In their mythology he is no ordinary geologist: He is one of the most dedicated of "the young builders of Communism." For the past four years Yuri has forsaken his native Moscow to drill for precious minerals beyond the Arctic Circle, near Vorkuta in European Siberia. For ten months of the year he lives on this North Soviet "New Frontier" in a small dormitory room of a hotel-hut. Vodka and hard work are daily sustenance on the frozen tundra. Soviet newspapers sing hymns to self-sacrificing young people like Yuri, who are supposed to be driven by love of country and devotion to Communist duty.

In Yuri's case, at least, the incentives are more prosaic. First, he is paid an inviting salary of 4000 roubles monthly. The average Soviet wage is 800. "Here in the South or near Moscow I could receive no more than 1500 a month," he said unashamedly. Second, Yuri receives two months' paid vacation every year. Normal vacations are three weeks to a month. Third, although Yuri has volunteered for his particular assignment, he pointed out that every Soviet graduate "pays" for his free education by working at least three years where the state employment office sends him. According to press reports, many of the educated young people hatch incredible schemes to evade work assignments outside the large metropolitan centers.[1] Finally, Yuri is not a Communist, nor does he desire to be one. "Membership in my professional union (*profsoyuz*) is enough for me," he said. Politics do not interest him, he made clear, and he became noticeably uncomfortable when they were mentioned. He dismissed a question about Stalin's forced-labor camp in Vorkuta with the simple explanation that all political prisoners had departed before he arrived. "Anyway, I have little contact with the local population," he said, and dropped the subject.

On the other hand, Yuri's curiosity about the outside world was insatiable. He had arranged to have his vacation in Moscow during the International Youth Festival in 1957. Rome was first on the list of foreign pilgrimages he planned. "Contacts, contacts and more contacts—that is the only way we Russians will learn to understand you foreigners," he exclaimed. Next year he would quit his job and return to Moscow to take a postgraduate degree. That would give him both knowledge and status (he already had money) to further ambitious travel plans. "The way things are going, I may visit North and South America in five or six years," Yuri prophesied. Who could contradict him? Such optimism is endemic in the Soviet era of "rising expectations."

[1]For example, an article in *Komsomolskaya Pravda*, June 23, 1956, p. 4, lashes out at physical education instructors who do anything to escape being sent out of Moscow to teach.

To meet young men and women like Yuri in the Soviet Union today is nothing unusual. To meet young people who are *not* like Yuri is also nothing unusual. One of the great changes in the post-Stalin period is the greater scope the enquiring outsider finds for probing the human variation behind the monolithic façade once presented to the world. The younger Soviet generation are the first complete products of Stalin's system. Anyone younger than his early thirties has had his whole life molded by a complicated combination of organized persuasion and police coercion. From the day a child can first understand the spoken word, he is gradually taught to subordinate his own desires to the demands of totalitarian society.

Against this background, the steady clamor in the press about "bourgeois hangovers" in the younger generation has a hollow ring. The West cannot be blamed for blemishes in the new socialist society. For over a decade after World War II the development of Soviet youth proceeded in almost complete isolation. Whereas their parents bore the brunt of forced industrialization and the forced collectivization of agriculture, this new generation has been nurtured on the havoc of war, schooled in the particular horrors of Stalin's reconstruction, and graduated into Khrushchev's "peaceful coexistence."

From this environment the new "Soviet man" is supposed to emerge. In literature, on wall posters, in newspapers, over the radio and television, he looms out larger than life. As an ardent member of the Young Communist League (the Komsomol),[2] he willingly devotes his leisure to "socially useful" work, he conforms morally and politically, he disciplines his innermost life to the will of Communist authority.

Mr. Khrushchev's drive toward "normalcy" has somewhat blurred that image. The model is still there, but is seems to have lost some vitality. Less arbitrary police controls, limited prosperity, and a general relaxation seem to have had their greatest effect on the young. They are less timid than their elders (who remember Stalin's purges) in exploring the bounds of freedom. In the process, many of the would-be robots are displaying the same virtues and weaknesses of youth the world over.

My purpose is not to analyze how far this virus of experimentation has spread among young Soviet citizens, or to estimate its ultimate impact on the society. Soviet society is still a very closed one, despite increased contacts with the outside world. The old myths are still religiously (although more gently) fostered from the top down. Numerous insights are now possible into underlying reality, but they are still only isolated fragments of unverified truth.

My purpose is rather to describe types of Soviet young people and their problems in the post-Stalin environment. Some have adjusted to that environment, some have not. My observations are based primarily on intermittent experiences with such people as Yuri over a five-year period (1955–1959). Wherever possible, they are supplemented by

---

[2]The emphasis here is on *ardent*, because mere membership of the Komsomol is little more than a formality today. By 1956 the Komsomol had 18,500,000 members aged fifteen to twenty-seven (A. N. Shelepin's "Report to the Twentieth Party Congress of the C.P.S.U.," *Pravda*, February 22, 1956, p. 8).

increasingly frank revelations on the part of the Soviet press and Mr. Khrushchev himself.[3] My main focus is on the large industrialized cities, whose better standard of living, cultural life, educational institutions, and factories attract congregations of young men and women. In these centers the persistent tussle between old myths and new realities is more readily observable.

The young people who have attracted most public attention at home and abroad are the *stilyagi*, the "style-chasers," the rough Soviet equivalent of the British "teddy boys" or the American "drugstore cowboys." In the beginning the *stilyagi* were not necessarily juvenile delinquents. They were boys and girls who appeared in public in "Tarzan" haircuts, bright American-style shirts and too narrow trousers or skirts — teen agers and beyond who called each other by American nicknames, illicitly recorded American jazz, and made primitive attempts at rock n' roll. In the end, however, the *stilyagi* have become a catch-all label in popular parlance for "anti-social" conduct — the "hooligans" who create drunken brawls, the black marketeers or "center boys" who trade counterfeit ikons for foreign tourists' clothes around the central hotels, the "gilded youth" who use their parents' influence to evade social duties and responsibilities.

A delving press has uncovered the spread of special slang among youth — labeled a "stilyaga-ism of speech." Young band musicians have begun to refer to their engagements as "playing at a funeral." One writer overheard the following conversation between students: "Well, let's fade. I still have to hit the hay; there's going to be a big shindig at a pal's shack."

The writer was even more dismayed at finding the "linguistic nihilism" spreading from students to workers. Instead of "Let's eat!" they are beginning to say, "Let's feed," or "Let's chop." Instead of buying something, the young workers now "grab" or "tear it off." The word "mug" is now used instead of "face," and the television set (*televizor*) has become the "telik."[4]

The line between innocent innovation and criminal delinquency is hard to draw in the Soviet Union. Any action not officially inspired and controlled is potentially dangerous to the regimented society. A kind of Victorian puritanism, inflexible and humorless, dominates the scene. Established authority makes full use of it to stamp hard on all overt signs of nonconformity. A vicious campaign in the press has sent the most extreme fads underground. Informal "comrades' courts" have been set up in factory and office to criticize and ostracize minor offenders — the girl who wears too much lipstick or the worker who arrives at work with vodka on his breath.

In Ivanovo, a textile town 300 miles northeast of Moscow, the sprawling Park of Culture features a row of life-sized posters ridiculing young culprits most recently apprehended by the People's Militia. These public caricatures change every two weeks. A girl worker, with

---

[3]For instance, Mr. Khrushchev has given the best exposé of the snobbishness of the elite system in Soviet higher education: "Memorandum on School Reorganization," *Pravda*, September 21, 1958, pp. 2–3.

[4]"On Slang and Fashionable Catchwords," *Neva*, Leningrad, September 1960, *9:* 200–203, as translated in *Current Digest of the Soviet Press*, 1960, *XII, 46:*15–16.

vodka bottle at her lips, lounges lazily on the sunny beach; Marina has spent two weeks in jail, the doggerel underneath explains, "because the sun made her insides too warm." Another caricature shows feline Alexandra, a "beautiful cat," preening herself before the mirror, "because she would rather have a man than work."[5]

The protection of standard culture for the masses has collided head-on with the drive for sophistication among educated and quite respectable young people. On the one hand, they are exposed to an increasing number of fashion shows, articles, and books on refined manners, and to more limited numbers of foreign cultural imports such as British and French film festivals, a Polish exhibition of modern art, a Czechoslovak glass exhibit, and several American exhibitions. On the other hand, the new fashions which spread from the capital to the provinces fall victim to organized Komsomol scorn.

Letters and articles in the Moscow press complain that roving bands of "Komsomol police" have hunted down and molested vacationing young men in bright shirts and young women in slacks on the streets of fashionable Sochi.[6] Stylish girls have had their hair chopped off with "sheer violence." Two young girls from the distant province of Amur in Siberia complain that they were treated "like *stilyagi*" in their village because they wore one-piece fitted dresses. Their Komsomol Committee told them: "Dress so that you will not be different from others!"[7] *Komsomolskaya Pravda*, the chief youth paper in the Soviet Union, has had to reassure Kiev residents that the "music patrols" set up by the Kiev Komsomol do not have the power to prohibit the playing of "good jazz."[8]

The effect of the excesses has been a slow swing of the social pendulum toward some kind of compromise over developing tastes. Official attacks on intolerance bring with them demands for an "ethic of mutual respect."[9] In practice, that seems to mean greater individual freedom in private or semiprivate, while paying lip-service in public to slowly changing social conventions. Public dance halls in Moscow, Stalingrad, and Sochi all still look much the same: Young people in open-necked shirts and shapeless dresses move around crowded floors to conventional waltzes, some folk-dance music, and nondescript foxtrots for the "masses." Komsomol police see that no one steps out of line. In the expensive restaurants and hotels, however, an air of relaxed sophistication is becoming more noticeable. In the National Hotel dining room in Moscow or the Gorka Restaurant in Sochi, popping champagne corks punctuate the occasional cha cha cha, rock n' roll, and other improvisations the dance bands have learned from the Voice of America. Toward the end of the evening several well-dressed couples may prove that the ban on "unorthodox dancing" is not uniformly enforced.

Changes are also going on just beneath the surface in the field of art.

---

[5] I saw these posters during a visit to Ivanovo at the end of July 1959.
[6] "Patrol in Knee Pants," *Komsomolskaya Pravada,* December 13, 1960, p. 2.
[7] *Ibid.*
[8] "Soviet Jazz Awaits Its Composers," *Komsomolskaya Pravda*, December 25, 1960, p. 4.
[9] "Patrol in Knee Pants," *loc. cit.*

Although "abstractionism," or "formalism," or "subjectless art" (in fact most experimentation) is officially condemned, some of the younger intelligentsia are tasting the forbidden fruit. A network of "private" Soviet art is spreading in the cities, aided by Mr. Khrushchev's drive for socialist legality. A friend in Leningrad who collects and disperses "modern art" for artist friends said he now had little fear that the police would invade his rooms simply to remove paintings from the wall. Officials of the Artists Union had threatened to inspect the studio of one of his clients, a well-known artist. They suspected he was dabbling in unorthodox art—as indeed he was. The artist (who is also well-known for his war record) bluntly replied he would throw out anyone who entered without permission or a search warrant. He would publicly display what pictures he chose. Any others were his own affair. The artist evidently carried the day, for the threat was dropped, and he is still painting.

The drive against the *stilyagi* has hampered but not destroyed the development of (Soviet-style) "beatniki" among the younger artistic and literary intelligentsia. Criticism has made them more discreet, less flamboyant. Neither by past training nor by present desire do they reject society. Not even the most radical would follow American beatniks in debunking the central tenet of Soviet life: the sacredness of work. As a young Soviet writer put it to me, anyone who does not at least pretend to work is soon investigated and chastised by his local "block committee."

The tendency of Soviet "beatniki" is to emulate what they consider the Left-Bank bohemianism of Paris. It is a faint whisper of a similar movement among young East European intellectuals, particularly in Poland, to make ultrasophistication their mark of separateness from "proletarian" society. In the semiprivacy of their artists and writers clubs, or in their homes, they may don the long cigaret holder, dark glasses, bright orange lipstick, or tight skirt. Perhaps the closest thing to public spontaneity comes in the groups of young people who gather on summer evenings in Moscow to read their poems before the statue of the Soviet poet-hero, Mayakovsky. The stereotyped imagery of socialist realism still predominates, but innovation is more evident. University newspapers and their literary supplements also begin to allow more scope for individual creativity. Take, for instance, the otherworldly quality and quietly religious resignation in the following lines.[10]

The Ikon

In a dusty, cobwebby attic
Turning its face from the world
An ikon with gilded crown hangs over a pile of torn boots.
For a time moonlight steals in through the cracked roof
Lighting evanescently
The red-haired one, unshaven with grey dust,
Yet still God's haughty image. . . .
Let the mice quietly gnaw each other to death

---

[10]From the literary supplement of the Moscow University newspaper, *Raduga*, 1958.

> While he, masked like a pill-box,
> Sees and hears nothing in the attic
> But waits. He awaits something nonetheless.

The controversy over modes of dress and social behavior is much more than the Soviet version of a universal problem with youth. It reflects a much deeper social conflict in the Soviet Union: the conflict between stifling paternalism and rebellious youth, characterized in less regimented societies as the "conflict between generations." According to Communist mythology, this conflict cannot exist in socialist society. All generations are supposed to be helpmates along the predetermined road to a new heaven on earth. In fact, however, Soviet society today is grappling with a central paradox. Old controls imposed in the name of that heaven are increasingly questioned by the young reapers of half-way prosperity.[11]

The problem can be sensed in the perplexed words of a middleaged engineer, speaking about his son: "Sometimes I do not understand him," he told me, "he wants everything in the world right away. He thinks too much about 'me,' and not enough about 'us.' " For this man and his generation, serving the "collective" was an imperative of survival. Stalin had been their idol; the suffering and sacrifices of the 1930's and 1940's, their religion.

For the young, this past lives only in stories or dim childhood memories. Their Soviet society is no longer revolutionary, it is established. Relaxation is as evident as is the increase in consumer goods that heralded it. For forty-odd years the Russians have been loudly beating their collective chest about the glories of building socialism. Now it is built. Many doting parents encourage their children to enjoy the youth they lost. People can afford to be less vocal and more confident. They begin to worry less about the socialist image and more about the substance of their own lives.

The virus of easy wealth is most deadly among the *lumpenproletariat.* Many of the real delinquents covered by "stilyaga-ism" are recruited from their ranks. They become the professional speculators who make their living on foreign goods, currency, and innumerable domestic rackets. Their inner bearings differentiate them from the *nouveaux-riches* and even more elite "gilded youth" who lavishly spend their own and their parents' money on scarce luxuries they consider stylish.

By comparison, the young speculators have been raised in working-class slums. They have seen their parents (many of whom were peasants new to city factories) work long years for a single room in a prerevolutionary apartment shared with four other families. One young worker I visited had obtained his privacy by a pasteboard partition around one corner of the room. The whole family had to cook over one gas jet on the communal stove in the communal kitchen of the apartment. Given such cramped quarters and full working hours for each adult—raising

---

[11]See *Komsomolskaya Pravda*, February 28, 1957, p. 1, for a decree of the Central Committee of the Komsomol which comes close to admitting this conflict of generations. The younger generation has not been through "the severe school of revolutionary struggle," it says, and therefore takes the "great achievements of the Soviet people" for granted or does not appreciate them at all.

children is more a responsibility of the "collective"—family life virtually disappears and the harsh life of the street takes over.[12]

The young speculator begins with a yearning to break out of these surroundings. He is impatient for a better lot, without the hard work which has brought parents and friends small reward. He dismisses the modest improvement of living standards since Stalin's death as inadequate. For him the glamor of Western "easy living" is irresistible. The means for making a quick—if illegal—fortune are close at hand. The advent of more foreign tourists, more Soviet trips abroad, and more private wealth combines with inferior consumer goods and a chaotic distribution system to provide a golden opportunity for black marketeers. Despite official strictures, these speculators make a good living while they fulfill a real economic function.

The price they pay is high. They are not only outside the law; they are totally outside the pale of respectability. And respectability counts for much in Soviet Victorian society. These young people dress well, eat and drink the best food and wines, but they are still *déclassés.* An amateur Soviet sociologist, himself quite respectable, described the type:

> They become empty human beings. They have nothing but their own fine appearance. They set out to push themselves to the top, but they end up belonging nowhere. No good family will have anything to do with these *stilyagi* except for "business."

Superficially, the wayward "gilded youth" have many of these same antisocial habits. They dabble freely in illicit foreign goods, from clothes to books. They are certainly as lawless and immoral. They take out their boredom in wild drinking bouts and parties in their parents' apartments or country *dachas.* They make free use of the family ZIM limousine, which technically belongs to the State ministry or enterprise. In private, however, these reprobates are regarded as the Soviet equivalent of Shakespeare's "Prince Hal." The parents' position in society constantly pulls them toward respectability, while the parents' influence prevents the "adolescent flings" from becoming public scandal. Time and age are supposed to bring the middle- and upper-class delinquents back to the confines of conventional society.

It must be emphasized at this point that the maladjusted young people described above do not mean that the whole rising generation in the Soviet Union are problem children. Quite the contrary. The bulk of Soviet young people emerge as conventionally minded as the Communist apparatus intends. This is particularly true of the young workers. My amateur sociologist friend described them as the "gold of the system." They are hardworking yet submissive. Paternal authority channels their thinking toward ever greater material rewards for increased production. Young "Stakhanovites" and "brigades of Communist labor" are praised at every turn for setting the pace on the production

[12]See George Z. F. Bereday, William W. Brickman, Gerald H. Read (eds), *The Changing Soviet School* (Cambridge: Riverside Press, 1960), p. 423, for the impressions of a group of American educators as to the effect of disorganized family life on delinquency in the Soviet Union.

line. Professional Komsomol "students" lead extracurricular political lectures and study groups in the factories after work hours. The factory collective, run by factory committee and trade union, makes sure they are integrated into social clubs and sports programs. Young workers are further encouraged to study in factory trade schools and technicums. The more intelligent and hard-working still have access (although more limited) to the prized professional institutes and even the university.

The result is a political passivity which seems assured so long as the over-all system remains stable. In the words of the sociologist cited above: "These young workers may grumble and protest when they receive 800 roubles bonus at the end of the month instead of the 1000 promised, but they soon tell themselves that 800 is better than the 600 they used to receive. So long as they have enough money and more things to buy, they are happy enough."

The same attitude is roughly true of most institute and university students, although they have scarcely any affinity with the working class. They judge the value of their education according to the status and money it will earn them, not on its intrinsic worth. In this, they are the logical heirs of Stalin's abandonment of egalitarianism in the early 'thirties for more prosaic reward incentives. All the powerful and influential occupations established during that period of the "building of socialism" can now be obtained only through the higher institutes and universities. Furthermore, the number of openings in each category are strictly tied to the needs of the plan. These limitations, plus the social values of a newly industrialized society, have dictated the upgrading of some professions and the downgrading of others. For instance, students specializing in engineering, chemistry, and physics have a higher prestige and will earn higher salaries than those in the humanities (a preparation for teaching), in law or in medicine—careers that are not in such great demand.[13]

The overwhelming emphasis on scientific disciplines is borne out in the educational statistics. In a thorough-going study, Nicholas DeWitt has found that in the sample year 1954, 60 per cent of Soviet classes graduating from higher institutes and universities were majors in engineering, physical, and other natural sciences. This figure excludes graduates of scientific pedagogical institutes which train secondary-school teachers. In the field of higher graduate and research degrees, the figure is even higher: 70 per cent of all advanced degrees in 1954 were in scientific fields.[14]

While the demands of the newly industrialized economy and the built-in bias of the economic plans undoubtedly promote this popularity of applied and theoretical science, powerful psychic and monetary incentives reinforce the appeal of the career for the young. My friend

---

[13]See George Z. F. Bereday and Jann Pennar, *The Politics of Soviet Education* (New York: Frederick A. Praeger, 1960), Ch. 4, "Class Tensions in Soviet Education," pp. 57–88, for a more comprehensive analysis of the conflict between egalitarianism and status in Soviet education.

[14]Nicholas DeWitt, *Soviet Professional Manpower* (Washington: National Science Foundation, 1955), pp. 167–169, 217. Mr. DeWitt also found that, while Soviet higher education graduated 40 per cent less than American colleges and universities, only 25 per cent of American bachelor degrees went to scientific and engineering students.

Yuri, vacationing in southern Sochi from the far North, is an example of the salaries and the opportunities open to young engineers. But any young man—or woman—chosen for research in one of the institutes at the top of the scientific hierarchy is also assured of working with the best equipment, of having every possible professional resource available, and of receiving good housing in the attractive (but crowded) urban centers. Success while young also holds out the promise of higher salaries, higher status, and the greater personal freedom given senior scientists.

Science offers the greatest possible retreat from politics in a system in which everything is political to a greater or lesser degree. As will be discussed shortly, young scientists, like other young people in institutes and offices, are subject to constant political supervision by Party or Komsomol "activists." If they overtly transgress the bounds of political orthodoxy outside their work, scientists suffer the same Party reprimands, loss of career opportunities, or even imprisonment, in extreme cases.

On the other hand, *inside* their work, research scientists (with notable exceptions such as biologists) do not have to spend their lives dodging Party doctrine. The intellect remains relatively unscarred by the demands of dogmatic truth. Unlike students or young professionals in such politically sensitive disciplines as history, art, and the humanities, scientists have an autonomy free of the day-to-day dictates of shifting ideological interpretation. Of course, this adds to the appeal of scientific studies and detracts from the appeal of the humanities. Any pitfalls which may lie ahead for the young scientist engaged in the most basic research—in the way of potential conflict with Marxist-Leninism—must seem a far-off danger, indeed, compared to immediate advantages.

One observer has characterized the resulting situation in the schools:[15]

> Arithmetic, algebra, trigonometry, geometry, the laws of classical physics, chemistry—these remain the same whether politically biased phraseology is used or not. . . . Thus the teaching of these subjects suffers less than those fields where an interpretive bias can be freely applied. These conditions are but the starting point in a race in which the sciences win and the humanities lose in the Soviet educational setting.

This "other-worldliness" of science—particularly research—in which scientists of all ages find intellectual satisfaction by losing themselves completely in their work, tends to give the profession a unity and to diminish that conflict of generations more evident in other fields. Older scientists and professors are genuinely revered for knowledge and talents easily divorced from the particular political and social setting. They are people to be emulated, not displaced. So, in the case of young scientists, the rationalization of their mentors' work under Stalin comes easily with the "proof" that their internationally recognized

---

[15]*Ibid.*, p. 41.

achievements were not directly tied to the revealed tyranny of the despot.

This is not to say, however, that the experimental faculty of scientific youth is uniformly walled off from Soviet life, or that the regime is content with the political attitudes of the scientific profession. Young scientists appear to be some of the most caustic critics of the over-all system, if not of the place their own profession has in it. During a visit to Harvard University earlier this year, the young Soviet poet Evtushenko (an aggressive "reform" leader since 1956) said that he preferred to read his poetry to young scientists and engineers because of their "fresh minds." He believed his work enjoys its greatest success among this group, who read it in their spare time. And back in the troubled fall of 1956, the questioning of Party truth seems to have been as widespread in the scientific faculties and institutes as in the liberal arts and humanities.

Mr. Khrushchev has thrown some light on this unrest among young scientists. In a recently published speech to "representatives of the Soviet intelligentsia," he singled out three anonymous young scientists to prove that no profession is too valuable to be above or beyond politics. He was discussing the disciplinary steps taken by the regime to still the storm of 1956. Mr Khrushchev said the three renegades had been thrown out of the Party organization in their institute for "anti-Party" activities. When a "famous academician" had telephoned to plead for the future of these "talented boys," Mr Khrushchev responded that their actions—unspecified—had not been children's play. He refused to relent, and went on to gloat over the calm such stern action had restored to the Soviet intelligentsia.[16]

Scientists, while perhaps more privileged than others of the intelligentsia, have much in common with certain young elite in other professions. The various frames of mind with which this young intelligentsia has emerged from the psychological upheaval of 1956 will be discussed in a section below.

The system of rewards through education has led to one of the greatest contradictions in Soviet society: Although common physical labor is loudly praised, children of the powerful professional groups consider themselves failures if reduced to it. Their world is increasingly separated from that of the working class. Professional military officers vie with one another to get their sons into the elite Suvorov and Nakhimov military academies. The budding civilian aristocracy asserts its exclusiveness through unpublicized special secondary schools, like the one near Sokolniki Park in Moscow, where instruction is carried on exclusively in English, French, or German.[17] The ballet schools in Moscow and Leningrad have become another important status symbol. Generally speaking, the well-equipped ten-year secondary schools in the cities are far surer stepping stones to success than their seven-year

[16]Although this speech was actually delivered July 17, 1960, it was not published until May 1961. N. S. Khrushchev, "Toward New Success of Literature and Art," *Kommunist*, May 1961, *7:* 6–7.

[17]*Ibid.*, p. 120. David Burg, a student in Moscow until 1956, writes that the children of Mr. Malenkov attended the English-language school near Sokolniki Park while he was premier. This confirms my personal observations during 1959 about the exclusiveness of this school.

counterparts still remaining in the countryside.

These educational gaps have conflicted sharply with the egalitarian features built into the over-all educational system from the revolutionary past. An upward mobility of workers and peasants has been encouraged in the name of that revolution. Everyone, regardless of social position or sex, has access to a free secondary-school education. Informal relationships between teacher and pupil, an overbearing emphasis in primary and secondary school on collectivism, and the enforcement of a common culture and language through centralized controls also have a leveling effect (although in the latter case poor instruction in Russian in the national republics hampers the advancement of these minorities in All-Union careers). This egalitarianism puts an unbearable strain on the higher educational establishments, which, by design of the economic plan, cannot absorb all secondary-school graduates.

With characteristic directness, Mr. Khrushchev has set out to undo Stalin's legacy through a wholesale shake-up of the educational system. "The chief and fundamental defect of our secondary and higher schools is the fact that they are detached from life," was his way of expressing it in September 1958.[18] He noted that in 1957 some 800,000 of 2,500,000 secondary-school graduates could not go on to higher education, but that they were prepared for nothing else. He discovered that only 30–40 per cent of students in Moscow higher schools came from worker and peasant families. He found that many families had a "haughty and contemptuous" attitude toward physical work and that their children considered factory and farm work "beneath their dignity."

Mr. Khrushchev's proposed solution: "polytechnical" education in secondary schools to "establish ties with life" (work); a requirement that all students entering professional institutes and universities have at least two years' work experience; and a much closer alignment of specialized studies with practical work. Although this radical proposal was somewhat watered down through negotiation with Soviet educators, essential changes were introduced at the opening of the academic year 1959-1960.

There is no space here to analyze all the changes and their myriad exceptions. It is also too soon to judge the final impact of the reforms, for they will not be completed until 1964. It must be stressed, however, that their aim is *not* to reduce the number of students in higher education or to throw a huge supply of unskilled child labor onto the market. That intention might have been read into Mr. Khrushchev's first pronouncements. In practice, however, the reform (at least in the big cities) has added one year onto the old ten-year middle schools and shifted the curriculum for the last three years toward more "knowledge of production." In the school I visited in Moscow, this means that, beginning with the ninth grade, students spend four days a week in the school, and two days in a "patron factory" learning industrial skills. The principal, Maria Skyartsova, said the extra year had also allowed them to broaden the teaching of literature, physics, chemistry, and

[18]Mr. Khrushchev's "Memorandum on School Reorganization."

mathematics, and to add a new course on world history since World War I.[19]

The aim is to change the orientation of students, not to reduce their numbers. Secondary-school graduates must be able to go into practical work; some may go on to full-time higher education in two years, others will have to be content with night school or vastly expanded correspondence courses.[20] The privileged ones who do become full-time day students are to be thoroughly reliable. According to new rules published early in 1959, they must have "good" recommendations from the Communist Party group, trade union, and Komsomol in the factory, as well as support from the factory director or collective farm board.[21]

Loopholes in the rules have already appeared. Given the power of the professional groups affected, those holes may be expected to become larger rather than smaller. First, at least 20 per cent of first-year students are still to be chosen directly from secondary middle schools, although the new admission rules are notably ambiguous about students of the humanities.[22] This general 20 per cent is a minimum figure; in fact, in 1959, 45 per cent came directly from secondary schools.[23] This leeway in avoiding the work requirements obviously intensifies, rather than relieves, that cutthroat competition among well-placed parents which Mr. Khrushchev attacked in 1958. They still pull every possible string to get their children into the higher schools. Second, it is doubtful that those children are going to acquire that "worker's mentality" Mr. Khrushchev so admires by serving time in a factory or on a collective farm, or that the manual labor is going to aid their future careers. Sons and daughters of ensconced officialdom are already claiming confidentially that they will find suitable apprenticeships in good laboratories or executive offices. Some I met felt the elite would have no difficulty in getting the necessary recommendations for university entrance well ahead of the end of the two-year period.

The immediate political imperative for these reforms grew out of the unrest in 1956-1957. The debunking of Stalin, a near revolt in Poland, a real revolution in Hungary, armed intervention, and their aftermath produced a crisis of confidence among the young intelligentsia which clearly frightened Mr. Khrushchev and his hierarchy. That latent conflict of attitudes between generations had never before come so close to the surface, nor had it ever borne such ominous political overtones. Here were privileged students—particularly in the elite institutes and universities of Leningrad and Moscow—who reacted to Khrushchev's revelations with a barrage of confused criticism, not with the embarrassed silence of their elders. They were young enough to question profoundly, old enough to know what to question. Although no one knows how many students displayed "unhealthy attitudes" in

---

[19]Middle School No. 49, which I visited on September 28, 1959.

[20]P. I. Polukhin, a spokesman for the All-Union Ministry of Higher Education, told me on December 4, 1959 that one-half of the two million students then enrolled in higher education were in night school or taking correspondence courses.

[21]*Pravda*, April 4, 1959, p. 4.

[22]*Ibid.*: This article seems to suggest that *all* students in these disciplines must have the preliminary work experience.

[23]According to P. I. Polukhin in the interview noted above.

1956–1957, enough existed at the very summit of Soviet education to warrant strong attacks in the press.[24] Soviet intervention in the Hungarian revolution and concomitant police coercion and social pressures at home finally silenced their protests but did not correct the condition underlying them. When Mr. Khrushchev later began demanding the resurrection of ties between the schools and "life," he really meant restoring firm ties between education and the Communist leadership.

Yet the reforms have come too late to affect the rebels of 1956-1957. Today they are no longer students, but they are not yet seasoned members of the "establishment." They are still grappling with the shock from the denunciation of Stalin, the thaw, the new freeze, and then the more careful relaxation since 1959. The result, I believe, is two recognizable strains in this part of the young intelligentsia: the "intellectuals" and the "men of action." Sometimes both strains coexist uneasily in the same person, sometimes not, but both types represent important ingredients in the present Soviet environment.

The "intellectuals" are the ones who have turned their backs on the establishment. They have not stopped questioning; they do not accept the materialistic red herrings Mr. Khrushchev has provided. They have a guilty conscience about the past. As one critic put it: "The intellectuals come straight out of Dostoevski, wailing and worrying about the future of society, about abstract ideas like 'justice,' but they can never make a decision, they can never do anything." In 1956, they were students who turned university seminars into serious political discussion groups and later expressed sympathy with the Hungarian rebels. Some were reprimanded, others were expelled, and still others, imprisoned. Now conditions have returned to "normal"; they are lonely, disillusioned and bitter.

"We have found out that when you beat your head against a stone wall, you break your head, not the wall," a dissident confided in Leningrad, more in sorrow than in anger. "The secret police have changed their tactics, they are more polite. Whether they call it arrest or education, however, their power amounts to the same thing. They are the stick, and the leadership of the Party wields it."

These young men and women in their middle and late twenties provide penetrating (and not always unsympathetic) insight into their more conformist fellows. "The bright young people see that this system has lasted over forty years and is growing steadily stronger," this ex-student said. "They believe the mistakes of the past are being corrected. So they conform. They fulfill all the outward norms, but in reality they are indifferent to politics. Do not think the lie they live is a conscious one. They honestly believe they are doing the right thing. Nagging doubts remain, but they are subconscious. That explains the loud enthusiasm for Khrushchev's great Seven Year Plan. If that suc-

---

[24]David Burg, "Observations on Soviet University Students," *Dædalus*, Summer 1960, pp. 520–540. This article gives a detailed report on student reactions to the events of 1956. See also S. V. and P. Utechin, "Patterns of Nonconformity," *Problems of Communism*, 1957, *3:* 15–23. *Komsomolskaya Pravda*, December 16, 1956 and December 28, 1956, tells of handwritten magazines in Leningrad bearing such names as *Fresh Voices* and *Heresy*. See also "Strength and Faith," *Izvestia*, September 6, 1959, p. 4, for an account of the Soviet handling of another student conspiracy.

ceeds, if the Soviet Union emerges with the highest standard of living in the world, these people feel their last troublesome doubts will die."

Some of the "intellectuals" are prone to analyze the effect of future prosperity. Some believe it will so mellow the "petty bourgeois" mentality of the ruling bureaucracy that nonconformists will be left more to their own devices. The progress of industrialization, the increased infiltration into Party ranks on the part of the rising technical intelligentsia, the slow expansion of "socialist legality" in day-to-day life—all these developments, they believe, may produce an "old-fashioned" dictatorship under which lip-service is still paid to totalitarian doctrine, but substantial areas of personal freedom exist. On the other hand, some of the more extreme believe the spiritual decay beneath the material prosperity will be the downfall of the whole Communist system.

"Have no illusions about the development of democracy here," were the bitter words of an anonymous man in his early thirties. We were sitting on high stools in the bar of the Sovietskaya Hotel, a meeting place in the capital of the "gilded youth." "The Russians are too submissive and disorderly. You speak of the power of education, but the men who rule us are educated. They are all philistines. Take the writers, for instance. No one compels them to write such trash now, but they are all afraid of losing their material well-being. I suppose when people live eight or ten to a room they have little time to think about anything besides finding some place of their own. But once they find that place and more besides, this system will just fall apart from moral decay." He paused to look around at the animated company on the dance floor from his perch on high, and added thoughtfully: "If Lenin returned, we would greet him in the way the Bible says Jesus was received: 'He came unto his own, but his own received him not.' We would say to him what Dostoevski's Grand Inquisitor told Christ: 'Go away and never come back!' "

Sometimes this lonely despair leads to a heart-rending outburst of patriotism. All else may fail them, but anguished love of Russia remains. "The troubles of today, yesterday, tomorrow—they are one small part of our history," suddenly exclaimed one troubled friend. "Mother Russia has survived before, it will survive again. Even if I were better off anywhere else in the world, I would still choose my Russia. I love it all—the crying, the laughing, drinking vodka, kissing one minute, cursing the next. You Westerners cannot understand that, can you?"

He did not wait for an answer. "Our temperament shocks you. We got it from the Mongols. Before the invasion, we were calm but disorganized. Today we are no longer calm, but we are still disorganized."

The "man of action" tends to dismiss these malcontents. For him, they are spiritual outcasts, powerless and meaningless. He compares them to Pasternak's Dr. Zhivago and himself to Lopatkin, the inventor-hero who triumphs over bureaucracy in Dudintsev's *Not By Bread Alone*. Zhivago is the man who claims to feel strongly about "right" and "wrong," but he irritates these young people because he can never choose sides. (Most have read only the selected excerpts of the book printed in the *Literaturnaya Gazeta* for October 25, 1958.) Lopatkin, on the other hand, is supposed to be "Soviet " to the core. He works and suffers through the system but comes out on the other side. One acquaintance compared Dudintsev's book to Chernyshevski's *What Is To Be Done?* of the last century. Both books had a "revolutionary" impact at different moments in history.

"Pasternak may write beautifully," he said, "but his ideas are outmoded. Dudintsev writes badly, but what he writes is social dynamite. I stayed up all night reading it."

The ideal young "man of action" claims he has reconciled himself to his system. He may be sensitive in his inner life, but he is utterly realistic about his social environment. Above all, he is diligent and ambitious. He respects power at home and abroad. By devious means he is working his way up in the ministries and industry to wield power. He joins the Communist Party to get ahead but thinks little of ideology. He reveres Lenin but admits that Marx could not foresee twentieth-century development. He (or she) aspires to dress like Americans, but neither envies nor fears the Americans. He wants to learn their technical—not their political—skills. He wants peace, for the success of his economic gamble depends on it.

The cynicism about world revolution is barely disguised. One evening in late 1959 in the Praga Restaurant in Moscow, I commented on the number of Africans on the dance floor: "They must be among the revolutionaries being trained here."

"Too well dressed," my companion took up the jest.

"Part of the Khrushchev era," I ventured.

"Then they are certainly not for world revolution," he countered.

The Chinese offend this attitude, no matter how prized or necessary an ally they remain. They offend because they remind. There they are, suddenly aping all the early Soviet antics with a vengeance. They blaze with a genuine revolutionary fervor that most thoughtful Russians long ago abandoned to the slogan writers. They sound a clarion call from the past which many would like to ignore but cannot. China has become the revolutionary conscience, irritating because it can neither be stilled nor forgotten. Even those young Soviet zealots who yearn to return to the revolutionary ideals of Lenin are put off by the seemingly inhuman discipline of the Chinese. Their own deeply ingrained chauvinism is offended by the rising national power of 650 million Chinese to the East.

By 1959 at least some Soviet students no longer tried to put the gloss of solidarity over this distaste for the Chinese mentality. "They volunteer for the hardest work during vacations and then refuse payment," one student almost shouted over the clanking of metal in the self-service canteen of Moscow University. "They seem to love political meetings. Nothing official like ours. Someone simply decides a subject, they all excitedly agree, and then spend days priming for it."

A student in Leningrad related what had happened when his dormitory Komsomol organized a "voluntary Sunday." These days used to be popular during the 'twenties and 'thirties, when people donated leisure time to social work and slum clearance. Times have changed, he said.

"This project was rubbish clearance. Twenty out of twenty-two

Chinese in the dormitory appeared. The other two were certified as ill. Do you know how many Russians turned up?" he asked rhetorically, and laughed. "Two out of three hundred—the organizer and the secretary of the Komsomol!"

The Komsomol or young Party workers are the basest offshoots of the "man of action" type. Superficially, they are sterling examples of the ideal "Soviet man." They are enrolled in the higher schools, receive diplomas in the various faculties, like all students, and at the same time lead all kinds of required "social work" on the side. They are the guardians of moral and political conformity in the Komsomol, to which more than 90 per cent of students belong. In fact, this minority of activists are unbelievably cynical. One observer has set their number at between ten and fifteen per cent of Soviet students.[25] Quite early in their student life, they sort out the mechanism of political power and fashion their careers accordingly. They learn the prescribed liturgy of Marxism-Leninism by heart and achieve progress through their ability to follow orders in enforcing it. Technically, they are elected to their Komsomol offices, but in fact, they are appointed by the bureaucratic apparatus. They are out of their depth when they have to engage in serious discussion outside the established framework, and they avoid it wherever possible. Mr. Khrushchev's sudden denunciation of Stalin and the moves to "democratize" Komsomol life in 1956 threw their ranks into complete disarray. The chain of command was temporarily broken, their confidence shattered, for no one from the top down knew any longer quite what line to enforce.

Now that the situation has been stabilized, these activists are firmly back in the saddle. They continue to exercise enormous power through the Komsomol role in the administration of the higher schools. The three-year work assignment a student receives on graduation depends as much on his Komsomol recommendation as on his grades. As noted above, the Komsomol also has new power in recommending which students are to be admitted to higher studies after working two years. The nature of these recommendations in turn depends on a student's willingness to serve in numerous "extracurricular" activities such as the voluntary Sundays or summer work on collective farms. This power over a student's future naturally leads to Komsomol meddling in the most intimate human relationships. Activists extract public confessions, enforce punishment, make certain that no one publicly transgresses the bounds of propriety. A rebellious student risks expulsion from the Komsomol, and this is tantamount to social ostracism and expulsion from the university.

Mr. Khrushchev's great problem is how to foster the "spirit of revolution" among the educated young while maintaining this essential Komsomol control. The contradiction between means and ends here sets the dimensions of potential tragedy in the Soviet leader's policy. On the one hand, he has fathered imaginative frontier plans for developing virgin lands in the Far East and South. Through these pro-

[25]David Burg, *op. cit.*, p. 525.

grams, more than half a million young people have moved out of Western Russia. He has also increased material incentives at all levels of society and has begun to fulfill some of the old promises about consumer prosperity. In the schools—beside polytechnical reforms for secondary day schools—he has instituted since 1956 a network of boarding schools (*internati*) which give increasing numbers of children from the age of seven on a proper "Communist upbringing" outside the family. By 1965 these *internati* are scheduled to have 2,500,000 out of the more than 30 million primary- and secondary-school pupils in the country. All these moves are attempts to maintain the momentum of Communist revolution without the excesses of Stalin.

On the other hand—working against those moves—Mr. Khrushchev's revelations about Stalin and the omnipresent hypocrisy of Soviet society today have destroyed much of the idealism necessary to maintain revolutionary momentum. Calculation rather than spontaneity is a young person's guide to success in the Soviet Union. Young people in both factory and university work out elaborate methods for escaping the snooping and the commands of the Komsomol without impairing their future. Among the students especially, service extorted in the name of socialist society is no longer an honor but a duty to be avoided wherever possible. Constant press attacks on the Komsomol's failure to enlist the "best" recruits for the virgin lands, coupled with reports of wild juvenile delinquency on the frontier, bear witness to the success of many evaders.[26] A growing emphasis on more persuasion and less coercion (with concomitant relaxation) only gives more scope for this evasion. The greater material rewards offered young people become incentives for more cynicism, not more idealism, because they can only be had by those who pay the price of enforced conformity.

Mr. Khrushchev's brand of Communism indisputably is opening up new vistas for Soviet youth. At the same time, the measure of those vistas must surely be the types of adults who emerge. The Soviet social scene is changing too rapidly to make any definite predictions. The answers lie well beyond Mr. Khrushchev, in what or who follows him. At this point, however, present signposts indicate, for better or for worse, that the on-coming adult generation little resembles the ideal Soviet Man of Communist mythology.

---

[26]See *Literatura i Zhizn*, Moscow, February 17, 1961, as reported in *The New York Times*, February 18, 1961, p. 1, for an account of gang warfare and murder among youths in Vladivostok.

Youth in France and the United States

Laurence Wylie

Harvard University

Compared with French adolescents, American youth are less restricted by tradition, more capable of exploring the unknown. Americans have greater freedom of choice but also experience more frustration in making and obeying decisions. In this article the author examines the importance of setting limits for adolescents. He finds that French and American societies differ widely on the concept of limits and that this difference accounts for much of the variance in French and American adolescent behavior. The reader might compare the two methods of child rearing to decide which is the more realistic preparation for living in the world as we know it.

Life is different for French and American adolescents. The differences, of course, are less obvious than those between widely separated, primitive cultures, and they are complicated by the social and geographical variations within modern, national cultures. In certain respects a New York boy in a college preparatory school may have more in common with a Parisian in a *lycée* than with a Negro boy in Harlem. The son of dairy farmer in Normandy may have a great deal in common with a boy on a farm in Wisconsin and very little with a boy in the coal country of northern France. Nevertheless, there is something about the adolescent experience of a French boy which makes it different from the normal adolescent experience of an American. The basic differences which exist between French and American adolescents transcend social class and are evidence of contrasts between the cultures themselves.

One way in which Americans and Frenchmen seem clearly to differ is in their conception of the rules that govern social behavior. The French generally believe that it is right for people to be forced to accept the sharply defined framework which man has projected onto the chaos into which he is born. Americans, on the other hand, generally feel that individuals should not be hampered in their free development but should discover for themselves the rules that govern the naturally ordered reality into which they are born. Taking these two attitudes as starting points, we can trace their effects on French and American adolescents as they face their common problems—the problem of learning to live with physically maturing bodies, the problem of trying to fulfil the image they have formed of themselves as adults, the problem of preparing to share in the responsibility of perpetuating their culture by having and educating children.

French children are taught very early the importance of man-made limits. A few years ago in an interview with a young French woman living in this country, I doubted that we could accomplish our business during the short time at our disposal when I realized that Madame's two-year-old son was obviously to be on hand for our discussion. My fears were unfounded, however. The child was put on the floor in a corner of the room with one toy. In front of him his mother put a cardboard box and said: "Pierre, there's a line running through the box. Your place is on that side of the line. Ours is on this side." To my amazement, the child respected the line which had been projected across the corner of the rug, and not until his mother and I had finished our business and she took away the box did he venture out from what had been for a few moments his own well-defined segment of existence.

From the time he is very small the French child learns that life is compartmentalized. The limits defining the compartments, furthermore, are established by forces beyond his control. Pierre was not consulted about whether he wanted to stay in one part of the room or another. He was not asked where he wanted the line drawn or indeed whether he wanted a line at all. Even the fact that the line was invisible was of no importance: this imaginary barrier was as forbidding as a wall of wood and plaster.

A French child grows up with an awareness of both kinds of barriers, one a material barrier defining our relationship with the physical world, the other a social barrier defining our relationship with people. He learns, furthermore, that each segment of existence calls for behavior appropriate to it. When he goes to school he continues to learn in the same compartmentalizing manner. He learns by rote, for example, the categories of history and geography and grammar that have been established by someone else—the authors of the textbooks or his teachers—and he then studies examples of these categories until he can recognize them by himself. Learning is essentially a matter of acquiring a clear awareness of the compartments of existence, of their distinctiveness, of their interrelationships.

In contrast to Pierre, most American children I know are being brought up in a quite different manner. The most extreme case I think of is that of a psychologist and his wife who as a matter of principle raised their child to be unaware of previously established limits. The child had no playpen. He could crawl about the house at will, which meant that an adult had to be with him every minute to make sure he did not hurt himself. He was never told that he must not do anything. He was offered alternatives, but he was not to hear the word "no." There was no special time or place for feeding, sleeping or toilet. In so far as it is possible, this child was supposed to establish his own limits as he explored the world.

This may be an extreme case of American permissiveness, but in tendency it is by no means uncommon. In fact, even the sort of training I had as a child fifty years ago, although far from permissive, was basically more like that of the psychologist's child than Pierre's. It seemed to me as I was growing up that I was surrounded by many rules and limits—"get to school on time"—"no skating or noisy play on Sunday"—"wash hands before meals"—"don't shock the women of the Ladies Aid Society." These were human rules. There were also the Ten Commandments, but they did not seem like rules because they were either too obvious to mention (like loving God and honoring my Mother and Father) or irrelevant in my life (like coveting my neighbor's wife or his ox or his ass).

In spite of this profusion of rules I realize now that fundamentally I was taught that rules as made or interpreted by men need not be respected at all costs. The basic lesson drilled into me was that I should try to behave as Jesus did or as He would have wanted me to behave. What He wanted was often not very clear, but at least two things were certain. One was that Jesus himself did not obey rules just because they were proclaimed by human authority, and the other was that He insisted God's kingdom should come "on earth as it is in heaven." I knew, therefore, I should not accept life as it is but should act so that I might help change things in preparation for God's earthly kingdom.

In school I was given the same feeling. History should not bind me. On the contrary, I was shown examples of great men who had swept aside man-made compartments and rules in order to bring about progress. My own ancestors offered good models: They had rejected the restraints of the old world and had come to the wilderness to build a better world. It took only courage to reject the accretion of the ages. In English class I learned by heart:

> Let the Past bury its dead!
> Act, act in the living present!
> Heart within, and God o'erhead!

So I grew up, as the psychologist's child will probably grow up, to reject the idea of a compartmentalized world into which I was born and which I must accept. Life was a continuum, and I was free to move within it to accomplish what I thought right. Between the extreme of the Methodist parsonage in 1910 and that of a psychologist's home in 1960 lies a basic attitude shared by most American families. Man should not be hampered by previously set boundaries.

The differences between the way a French child and an American child are brought up are greatly oversimplified here, but they point to significant generalizations about socialization in France and the United States. The French child learns that life has been compartmentalized by man and that the limits of each compartment must be recognized and respected. The American child learns that life is a boundless experience. The Frenchman recognizes that rules are a convenience, but that they are man-made and therefore artificial. The American believes he has discovered his rules for himself and that they reflect the essential structure of reality. For the Frenchman, reality is dual: There is the official reality of man-made rules, but it is only a façade concealing a deeper, more mysterious reality which may be felt by the individual in moments of introspection or revealed by art and religion. For the American, reality is a unity, and any apparent discrepancy between the ideal and the actuality is essentially immoral.

These two conceptions of reality and of the individual's proper relation to it inevitably help determine the reaction of French and American children to the problems of adolescence. Not only do the problems have a different significance to them, but the solutions they seek are different.

In France the vague but compelling stir of sexual development creates greater wonder and anxiety than it does in America. To a child who has been carefully trained to compartmentalize life rationally, the tempestuous quality of pubescence is threatening. It raises a doubt as to whether these feelings may not become so intense that they cannot be controlled within the framework provided by society. This anxiety is frequently expressed in French literature and films in a way the French find moving but Americans often find frankly ludicrous.

Recently I showed the French movie short, *Les Mistons*, to a group of college students which included both French and Americans. The movie portrays the panic of a gang of boys when they suddenly become conscious of the sexual development of a young girl. The girl and the young man she loves become the enemies of the gang, who react hysterically to the new desires they feel. The boys spy on the couple, torment them, mock them, even stone them. The characters in the movie do not speak, but a poetic commentary describes the situation as it develops. The European members of the audience found the movie a valid artistic expression of a situation that seemed true for them. The Americans found the whole thing ridiculous; the very conception of the movie seemed a joke.

In learning how to cope with his sexual urge, the French child, however, is helped by his training in recognizing proper limits of behavior. He may be more upset than the American child by the feelings that accompany puberty, but he is better equipped to handle those feelings. From early childhood he has been taught the necessity of controlling his impulses, of not expressing them freely. With puberty he is confronted with the most violent urge of all. The urge may frighten him, but he is at least used to exerting self-control.

The American child has had less preparation. Rather, he has been encouraged to express his feelings freely. Now suddenly the attitude of his elders is reversed. He is expected to exert self-discipline and not act out this new feeling at the very point in life when it is most difficult to do so. The injunction that he must restrain his sexual impulse is all the harder to accept, since at the same time the American adolescent learns another hard lesson—that there is a wide gap between the expressed standards of sexual behavior and actual practice. At church and school and home both boys and girls are told that it is wrong to express themselves sexually outside of wedlock. But walking home from school, in locker rooms, at the corner drugstore, from newspaper stories, from movies and magazines and TV, they learn that the ideal standards are false. The American adolescent must choose between observing the standards and feeling frustrated and cheated, or violating the standards, feeling guilt, and risking social sanction.

It is true that there is also a double standard in France. However, this double standard of morality comes as no surprise to a French child, since from the time he was very young he has been made aware of the duality of existence. Furthermore, the French tend on the whole to feel that man must accept the limitations of nature and not try vainly to deny them. Since sex is an integral force in nature it is better to accept and to pattern it rather than uselessly repudiating it or even dangerously distorting it.

A traditional means has evolved in France for the indoctrination of young people in the expression of their sexual feelings. The adolescent boy receives his experience and training from an older woman and then in turn initiates the girl—ideally, of course, his virgin wife—in the art he has learned. French literature and movies offer examples of this, but whether this literary expression mirrors actual behavior is a question which cannot be answered. Still, from what evidence we have, it does seem that the situation so frequently portrayed in the novels of Colette, for instance, bears some relation to actual practice.

To the American boy the very idea of sexual relations with a woman old enough to be his mother seems monstrous. He learns sexual techniques just as he is taught to learn all things—by venturing out, fumbling, experimenting, seeking advice from his peers or from any other source he can find. Eventually, for better or for worse, he evolves his own system. Today in the United States we seem to feel that sexual initiation should come naturally as the result of a burst of romantic passion. We have little information, but it appears that most American boys today receive their sexual initiation on the back seat of a car with girls roughly their own age, who have had their initiation in the same situation with an older adolescent. The romantic situation is enhanced by the beer in a "six-pack" the couple have drunk. This is not a very satisfactory experience for either one of the couple, and it has been suggested that the whole clumsy operation may help account for the feeling of inadequacy shared by many American adults.

The American reluctance to set limits creates another sexual problem for adolescents that is less troublesome for the French—that of determining a feeling of sexual identity. Even when they are very small, French children are rather strictly segregated by sex. Boys and girls are dressed differently, and are given different sorts of toys. They are treated differently and are expected to behave differently. From the age of five or six they are separated in school, even in the public schools. A strong feeling develops of belonging to *les garçons* or *les filles*, and each individual is left no doubt as to his affiliation.

For Americans, on the other hand, it seems wrong to deny a girl or a boy what is accorded to members of the other sex. Consequently, boys and girls are treated essentially in the same manner. As little children they are dressed alike, they may play with the same toys if they choose, and they are treated with studied impartiality. At school they are in class together and compete in exactly the same skills. At home they see the responsibilities of the parents divided by their mother and father on the basis of convenience and with little emphasis on which is properly a woman's role and which is properly a man's. Yet when boys and girls become adolescents, they are told that they are fundamentally different and should feel fundamentally different—or else they risk the dreadful fate of being labeled sexual deviants. With relatively little support, American youth is expected to achieve the proper feeling of sexual identity. The normal bisexuality of humans and the normal homosexual experimentation in our culture add to the confusion. The result is that adolescents feel an urgent need to prove to themselves and to others that psychologically they belong to the class with which they are anatomically grouped. As a result, girls go to extremes to make themselves appear feminine, and boys go to stupid and dangerous lengths to avoid being called "chicken." Homosexuality exists in France, but there is less confusion and resultant anxiety over sexual identity among normal French adolescents than among normal Americans.

By the time a child has reached adolescence he has formed a more or less precise image of what he and his culture expect of him as an adult. One of the principal problems for an adolescent then is to conduct his life so that he has the feeling he is achieving this ideal image of himself.

The average French child (and his parents even more than he) has a clear idea of the limits within which his ambition may be fulfilled. He knows to what social and professional class he belongs. There is no doubt about his family's traditional political, religious, and even aesthetic ideals, and he has been placed by both family and teachers in a well-defined intellectual category. Each of these classifications implies certain limitations and expectations so far as the child's future is concerned. For the normal French child, then, this clear definition of expectations makes the problem of fulfilling his ideal self-image relatively simple. He has only to accept and to live up to what is expected of him.

It is true that many more possibilities are open to French children, especially to gifted children of the farming and working class, than those of which they are aware. There is a tendency in France to assume that one's position in the social structure is fixed. Just as Americans assume there is more mobility in their society than there is, the French assume that there is less chance for change than there actually is. However, this misconception makes it easier for the French adolescent to accept the image he has of himself as an adult.

Of course, not all children can accept or live up to expected limits so readily. The most unhappy French adolescents are those for whom the limits are impossible. The less gifted child of an ambitious middle-class family who tries again and again to pass the *baccalauréat* examination, the independent child who refuses to be harnessed to fixed goals, the imaginative child who has elaborated an ideal quite different from that which society expects of him—such children have a hard time of it during adolescence. These exceptions are not numerous, however. They seem more common to us than they are in fact, because they offer the poignant cases from which novels and movies are made, and we form our idea of French life in a large part through such media. As a matter of fact, most French adolescents do accept the limitations laid down by society and do try to fulfil their ambitions within them.

Acceptance is made easier by a series of escape hatches which French society provides so that the individual does not feel himself annihilated by his acceptance of limitations. The French child has learned that if he accepts social constraints he will be left to himself. There is a tendency, therefore, for the French adolescent to escape into himself, to live in his private domain of thoughts, emotions, and fantasies. Even though one of the most common feelings may be hatred for *les autres*, the people around him who force him to conform superficially, so long as the adolescent's retaliation is confined to his feelings or even to verbal or artistic expression, society imposes no sanction.

Since children have seen that social regulations are in no way sacred but are only a practical means invented by man to permit human beings to live together, and since these regulations are so often frustrating, another traditional means of escape is for adolescents to form cliques and work outside the accepted social bounds to attain a common goal. The presence of this clandestine association, which Jesse Pitts has called the "delinquent peer group," is felt wherever children need to get things done in spite of rules. Americans visiting French schools are shocked by the hidden power exercised by an apparently well-disciplined class over their teacher. An effective *chahut* carried out by the conspirators may even ruin a teacher's professional career. A child who runs afoul of the conspiratorial system may be punished by the group in a way that seems shockingly cruel. The clique permits adolescents to accept social limitations and at the same time reject them. Furthermore, participation in a clique brings one of the cherished experiences of life—warmth of mutual association in a secret, illicit endeavor.

Among older adolescent boys this association is encouraged by society. In a sedate, conservative village in western France I have seen the *conscrits*, the group of nineteen-year-old boys who will go off next year for their military service, spend every Saturday night over a period of months getting drunk on wine furnished by their parents. One evening six of them were said to have drunk thirty bottles of wine while they waited for the rest of their comrades to arrive. This seems impossible and probably was, but at least it is an indication of the massive scale of these binges. They are not only tolerated but encouraged by adults as long as the adolescents do not jeopardize their future.

Generally speaking, then, society helps make the severe limitations it places on children more bearable. To fulfil his self-image, the French adolescent must learn to fit into the limits prescribed by society, and having accepted these boundaries, he utilizes the means available to express his individuality outside these limits.

The American adolescent is in a quite different predicament as he strives to achieve the ideal image he has formed of himself. His difficulty lies not in living up to expectations but in discovering what they really are. The only system of rules he has been taught is a Sunday-school sort of code, and as he grows up he learns little by little that it is not the code by which people actually live. The real code exists, but no one defines it openly.

Confronted by the fact that this double standard exists, American adults beat their breasts and admit their sins. Still they insist that the ideal code is the right one. Failure to live up to it is attributed only to the weakness of human beings who hopefully merit forgiveness when they confess their sins and show their good intentions. The adults' need to believe that everything will come out for the best in the long run is satisfied by placing the responsibility on the adolescents to make the ideal code function as it should. "Our generation has gotten the country into trouble, and we want you to get us out," Senator Barry Goldwater tells an audience of Young Republicans,[1] just as every adult speaker has told every adolescent audience in which I have been present since I was a child. Adolescents are not told how to do a better job, however. When they ask for advice, they are merely given further indoctrination in the ideal code. Middle-aged professional adolescents continue to insist at Sunday-evening meetings, summer conferences, in discussion groups and recreational organizations that the ideal is attainable. Dozens of books are written for teen-agers to be used in these meetings.

A typical book for adolescent instruction is Pat Boone's *Twixt Twelve and Twenty*,[2] in which the blurb says "Pat talks intimately to teen-agers about all the problems and joys of the exciting years." There are chapters on life such as "A Great Adventure," on "The Happy Home Corporation," "Habit Weaving," "God is Real," and "Dreams Do Come True." My informants tell me this book is rarely bought by adolescents themselves, but is purchased in large quantities by church organizations for use in young people's groups.

The reaction of most adolescents to the duplicity of adults is an outcry against sham and an increased emphasis on the value of sincerity. Newsstand dealers will tell you that there are four kinds of publications bought by adolescents themselves: comics, movie and confession magazines, technical magazines (cars, mechanics, sports, etc.), and above all *Mad* and its imitators. *Mad* is a specific antidote for Pat Boone. It shows that all the virtues which are extolled are in reality only a screen for vice. *Mad* delights adolescents by turning the official American value system upside-down.

In a recent number of *Mad*[3] from the collection accumulated by my children, the first article suggests a whole series of new textbooks to teach children life as it really is: "Today's children are developing into clods because old-fashioned textbooks still in use fail to hold their interest, fail to reflect life as it is lived now, and fail to prepare kids for what they face in the years ahead. To remedy this situation, we recommend that schools immediately junk their outdated texts and replace them with *Mad's* Modernized Elementary School Textbooks."

The proposed third-grade arithmetic is composed of problems like the following: "1 Elvis plus 12,000,000 Teenagers at 16 shrieks per

---

[1]*The Harvard Crimson*, May 3, 1961, p. 1.

[2]Pat Boone, *Twixt Twelve and Twenty* (Englewood Cliffs, N.J.: Prentice-Hall, Inc., 1958; and New York: Dell Publishing Company, 1960).

[3]*Mad*, No. 63, June 1961.

Teenager equals? Answer: $3,000,000 a year for Elvis!" The new geography manual would not have the traditional figure of Atlas on the cover but two Atlas musclemen, each supporting a half of the world. One is labeled "Good Guys" and the other, "Bad Guys." Children would be introduced to the *First Principles of American Civics* by a cover illustration showing a bum being paid to vote by a politician wearing a campaign button reading, "I like Me!" The following chart of real municipal government in the United States is shown on a sample page:

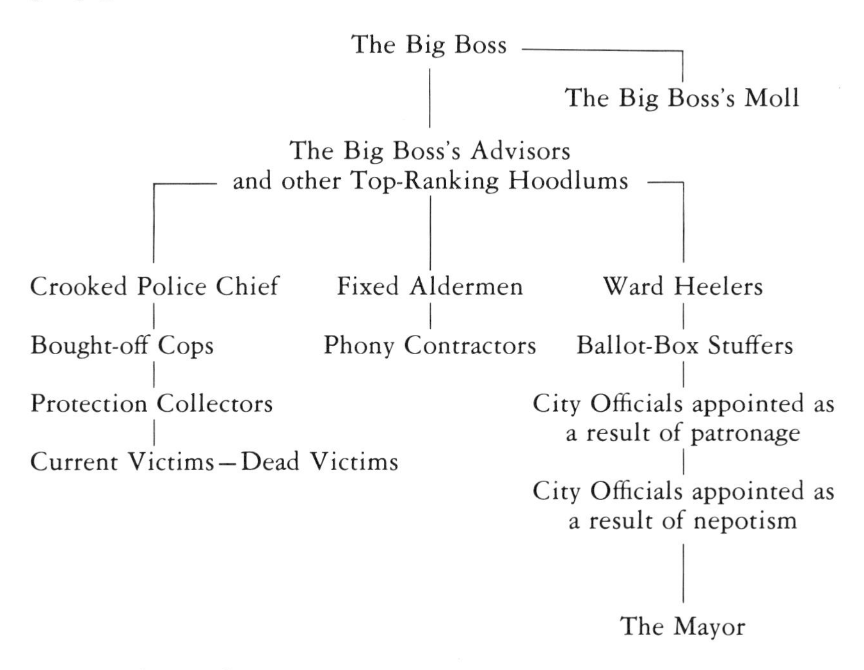

In *Mad* the adolescent finds a confirmation of his discovery that adults have furnished him a false blueprint of life. Government, school, family life, advertising, TV, movies, business—even *Mad* itself!—are exposed. *Mad's* symbol, the insipidly smiling Alfred E. Neuman, who maintains his ghoulishly cheerful expression while the most appalling things go on around him, stands for American culture itself as the adolescent experiences it. This idiotically smiling figure implies that all is for the best in the best of all possible worlds, in spite of overwhelming evidence to the contrary. Alfred E. Neuman is the American *Candide*, but with one difference: he never mentions God and religion. Even *Mad* could not get away with that.

The anguish an adolescent may feel when faced by a lack of a realistic moral code is portrayed in the James Dean movie, *Rebel Without a Cause*, a movie that draws a large audience of adolescents whenever it is shown. In the movie young Jimmy pleads again and again with his father and mother to tell him what he ought to do. He wants to know the rules. His parents shrink before his questions. His mother's only solution is to move the family to a different city every time Jimmy gets into trouble, in the hope that in a new atmosphere Jimmy will "behave." His father will reply only that "the important thing is to understand, just to understand." Jimmy is left to work out his problems for himself, in spite of his plea: "Tell me what to do! Please, Dad, just tell me what to do!"

It is painful for American fathers to witness this scene, for we as a group are committed to Jimmy's father's position. We believe that we need only give our children loving understanding, the Sunday-school rules, and a *Reader's Digest* philosophy, and that they will work it out for themselves. They usually do, but it is a hard assignment we give them, and one which the French adolescent is largely spared.

As French and American adolescents face the problems of realizing their self-image, the difficulty for the French is to live up to or contain themselves within the limits society had laid down for them. The difficulty for American adolescents is to discover behind the façade of the ideal system the real limits established by society.

The normal desire of young people in France and the United States to establish homes and families of their own poses another question. As we have seen, the contrasting attitudes toward limits have a direct bearing on the ways in which adolescents in the two countries face the problems of learning to live with their physically maturing bodies and to fulfil their image of themselves. This same influence is felt in the way the problem of "hiving off" is resolved in the two cultures.

The French adolescent is left in no doubt when questions arise concerning his role in the family. "So long as you live in this house, you'll do what we tell you to do!" says the French father in the normally regulated household. Although the mother may soften the harshness of this decree when she deals individually with the children, traditionally she backs up her husband. The child, the adolescent, and even the young adult child still living at home must accept what is at best the benevolent despotism of the father, although as we have seen, the father limits his authority to the realm of the action and usually does not try to control the ideas and feelings of his children. With his experience of clandestine action, an adolescent may be able with the connivance of a sibling, sometimes the mother (and sometimes even the father himself!) to carry out an action that may be formally forbidden. Nevertheless, there is no doubt where the seat of authority lies and what the limits are. When the chips are down, it is the father with the advice and consent of the mother who makes the decisions which regulate the activities of the ménage.

The dependence of the French adolescent on the family is increased by his lack of personal financial resources. The money a child earns is not his own but is given to the parents for the family treasury. This is true not only of young adolescents but often even of young, unmarried adults living at home. There are exceptions. A young middle-class boy or girl may work in the grape harvest in the country near the place where his family spends vacations and save the money to buy a scooter, but even in this case his keeping the money and buying the scooter must be approved by the parents.

Of course, a French father is obligated to give his child sufficient money for the leisure activities of his particular social group. A father who is too stingy is frowned on. Even worse, however, is the father who indulges his child too much. Recently, in the murder trial of Georges Rapin, "Monsieur Bill," who was eventually executed for killing a young woman in a singularly brutal manner, it was not the murderer himself who was most severely censured. The newspapers and the public vented their anger against the father. He had spoiled his son by giving him far too much spending money. He had even bought the young man a bar when he refused to take the respectable sort of job that might have been expected of an upper middle-class engineer's son. When the boy was being taken to the death cell after the trial, people followed the father out of the court and jeered him along the street. *Match* and other popular magazines carried photographs of the incident and pointed out in editorials that this was a good lesson for parents who do not teach their children to behave reasonably.

The older a French adolescent is, the more he tires of paternal authority and the ever repeated phrase: "So long as you live in this house. . . ." The effect is to strengthen his determination to become independent. As soon as he finishes his military service and professional training he tries to make a clean break and establish his own ménage. In France, as in the United States, the age for marrying has been pushed back toward adolescence, and like American parents French parents complain that children are marrying too young. The reasons for earlier marriage are different. In the United States, marriage is a romantic refuge from the bewilderment of life; in France it is a refuge from the severe restrictions of life.

In American culture a child is taught very young to fend for himself, to make his own decisions, to stand on his own feet. A good illustration of this is in the movie, *Four Families*, produced by the Canadian Film Board under the general supervision of Margaret Mead. Of the four babies shown in the film, the Anglo-Canadian baby was, of course, the most spoiled by modern conveniences. However, in some ways she had a harder time than the Indian, Japanese, and French babies because she was expected to care for herself in a way the other babies were not. During the ten-minute episode, the Canadian baby was constantly urged to venture out and take care of herself. She got a hard bump on the nose when she was encouraged by her father to take part in the rough play of her older brothers. When she cried, she was merely told, "There, there, it'll be all right." In the bath she was encouraged by her mother to fight for the possession of a washrag held by the mother herself. At the table she was expected to feed herself. In contrast to the other babies, who were fed again and lulled to sleep by their mothers at bedtime, she was put in her crib with a bottle and left alone to go to sleep.

As children in America grow older, we continue to encourage their independence. We encourage them to make money, to start their own bank account. They run errands, baby-sit, carry newspapers, sell lemonade—in fact, they often surprise their parents with the jobs they turn up on their own. They use their earnings as they want. "They are at a learning stage. I cannot think of any better way to teach them than to let them do it," says Gwen Bymers in support of this training in independence.[4] American children are also encouraged to make their own social ties outside the family. Instead of being limited, as French children are, to a group of friends known to the family circle, they venture out and make their own friends. American parents even utilize their children's friendships to make the acquaintance of the parents of their children's friends. At a very early age children here come to feel at home beyond the limits of the household. The fact that their household is open freely to outsiders further blurs any clear conception as to what home is exactly. There is not the wide, clearly defined gap between home and society that there is in France.

Within the American family there is seldom any insistence that the family has a way of doing things which a child must accept so long as he lives under the family roof. More often the child's argument, "But nobody else's family . . ." sets the standard of behavior. In deciding family affairs the child is given an equal vote with the parents, whose attitude is characteristically expressed by the phrase, "Let's work this out together." When a problem arises in which the adolescent's and the parents' judgments are in conflict, the outcome is ideally a compromise by which the child may get what he wants at the same time as the worries of the parents are allayed. There is no real tyranny in the American home unless it be that exercised by the adolescent who shames his parents for their unacceptable social behavior.

Far from being the autocrat who lays down the law in the family, the American father tries to become his children's friend so that they will want to turn to him for advice in solving problems that face them. Sometimes this friendship comes about naturally, sometimes it is forced. The accepted social code thoroughly approves this kind of comradeship. A caricature of the situation is described by Dobie Gillis, the "pint-sized Don Juan," adolescent hero of Max Shulman's *I was a Teen-Age Dwarf.*[5]

I'm a little embarrassed to tell you about our Palship Walks, but I guess I'd better. It's one of my mother's kooky ideas, which Pa and I fought against like a couple of madmen, but it wasn't any use at all because when Ma gets an idea in her head you can't knock it out with an elephant gun. . . . Ma got on Pa's back a few years ago about him not spending enough time with me. "Herbert," she screamed, "a man ought to be pals with his son. Why don't you take Dobie for walks on Saturday morning to talk to him about nature and engines and like that?" Well, Pa and I both started yelling like maniacs because we didn't want to go for a walk on Saturday mornings. What I like to do on Saturday morning is crack my knuckles. What Pa likes to do is stay in the sack. It is the one morning he doesn't have office hours. But Ma just ignored us and put on our jackets and pushed us out of the door.

So Pa and I stumbled around for a while, and it was pretty grim. At first he tried to talk to me about nature and engines, but that didn't work too well because I kept thinking about cracking my knuckles and he kept thinking about

---

[4]Gwen Bymers, in *The New York Times*, May 8, 1961, p. 47.
[5]Max Shulman, *I Was a Teen-Age Dwarf* (New York: Bantam Books, 1960), pp. 3–4.

> the sack. Finally we sat down against a big oak tree on a point of land overlooking the ocean and moped till it was lunch time and we could go home.
>
> After that we didn't make any attempts at conversation on our Palship Walks. We just high-tailed it out to the oak tree where Pa had stashed an air mattress in a hollow limb and I had stashed a copy of *Lolita*. Pa blew up the mattress and corked off a couple of hours while I read the book and then, both refreshed, we went home where Ma beamed at us and kissed us and gave us a special treat for lunch in honor of our palship.

And, of course, since "mothers know best," the father and son by sharing this exile did come to feel close enough for the boy to ask a question once, and the father gave him a straight answer. But the father had had to earn the right to help his son make a decision. The boy's business was the boy's business, after all, and the father had no right to interfere without being asked.

Ironically, although the American adolescent is encouraged to be independent, although he is free to make his own decisions, he is in no hurry to leave home. Life at home is comfortable. Even though he may marry young, he feels no need to make a clean break. Unless the young couple move so far away that they are of necessity separated from their parents' homes, they still linger about their old haunts and depend on their parents to help them as they always did. They drop in to have a wedge of Mom's cake or a drink of Dad's whiskey, or to get help in making draperies, or in giving a party. Eventually the parents become admirable baby-sitters. They cost nothing, they can be counted on to stay with the baby until all hours of the morning, and without doubt they know best what to do in case of an emergency. Eventually, it is the parents of the adolescents, not the adolescents themselves, who long for a clean break between the old home and the new home.

How different this is from the situation of the French couple who have had enough of the discipline of the parents' home and are eager to make the break themselves! In France it is the young couple which treasures its independence, maintains proper relations with the older generation but still insists on handling its affairs alone. The unhappy young French couple is the one that cannot find adequate housing and is obliged to live under the parental roof.

In the light of early training, how is this difference to be interpreted? Should the emphasis be on the confidence the young French have acquired from learning early and well what the limits are? Or should the emphasis be on the frustration these limits have created?

The same question must be raised concerning the American adolescent's reaction. Has his lack of feeling for what is and what is not made him unsure and tired? Does breaking away from his parents' home imply too great an effort, too much more searching? Or has his family experience made him so comfortable with his parents that he does not want to leave them?

Having begun this essay with broad generalizations concerning the difference between French and American culture and the impact of these differences on the lives of adolescents in the two cultures, we come now to the point where we no longer generalize so confidently but raise questions about what might be the truth. Who knows for sure the exact effect of child training? Doubts concerning our generalizations are strengthened by other considerations. Although we intended to speak of all adolescents, it is obvious that what has been said mainly concerns boys. Do these same generalizations apply to girls? Certainly not without some change.

Recent conversations with French parents raise another question. They complain now that their children have no respect for them, criticize them, insist on establishing their own rules. Is my picture of French family life outmoded? It would be so much simpler to speak of differences between American adolescence and adolescence in the Nuer tribes of the upper reaches of the Nile River. Then we could point to striking, definite contrasts about which there could be no doubt. Comparatively, the differences between French and Americans seem so slight. And yet they exist. No one who knows French and American culture will deny that there are substantial differences. How can we define them?

Recently a French colleague said that from his point of view French and American parents are today in the same predicament. He knows "how uncontrolled, how lacking in respect for tradition" American youth is. But times have changed in France. Children no longer accept the limits set by their parents. This French father says he could not get away with saying, "So long as you live in this house you will do as I say!" His children would only laugh and still do as they please.

On the other hand, there is more talk in the United States today about the importance of giving children a feeling for limits. In a recent article,[6] Ann Landers, human-relations counselor and newspaper columnist, suggests that American parents have allowed their children far too much freedom for their own good. Rules must be set and accepted by young people whether they seem to like it or not. This sounds like a step toward the French concept of discipline.

However, Miss Landers and my French friend are still far apart in their attitudes. The French adolescent children are not revolting against the very idea of limits. They are revolting against the particular set of rules which their father insists they accept. This sort of revolt is very much within the French tradition and in accordance with the idea that the young Frenchman insists on differentiating himself from his parents.

On the other hand, Miss Landers wants parents to assert rules as little as possible. She does not praise limits for their own sake:[7]

> All parents should allow their teen-agers to make a great many decisions for themselves. The vital question is where to draw the line. But wherever the line is drawn, remember that even a foolish decision can be a useful one if the teen-ager learns a lesson from the mistake. Just take care that you don't bail your youngster out of every embarrassing situation. . . . Your major job as a parent is to equip your child to lead an independent, productive, useful life. Live with your child, not for him. For the most part, let him take

[6]Ann Landers, "Straight Talk on Sex and Growing Up," *Life*, August 18, 1961.
[7]*Ibid.*, pp. 84, 88.

his own jumps but don't let him jump off a cliff to learn first-hand what's at the bottom. Be firm but be fair. Respect him and his rights and you won't have to worry about his respect for you.

When my French colleague is no longer shocked at his children's revolt, when he insists that they learn by making mistakes, when Miss Landers insists on the parents trying to pattern their children's lives, not merely preventing them from jumping over the cliff, then I shall agree that American and French culture have indeed become very much alike. Until then I shall continue to believe that this difference in attitude toward limits is a major factor in differentiating not only adolescent behavior but also many other aspects of French and American culture.

Youth and History: Individual Change in Postwar Japan

Robert Jay Lifton

Yale University

Anyone old enough to remember Japan before Pearl Harbor cannot help but be amazed by the dramatic change in Japanese life of the 1950's and 1960's. The author looks at the youth of Japan and sees causes and effects of change—both of which seem to contain good and evil. A drive for the individual freedom found in the West versus a security need for the traditions of the East constitutes a paradox the Japanese adolescent must cope with. Lifton elaborates on this and other themes in his analysis of the Japanese youth culture.

Youth confronts us with the simple truth, too often ignored by psychologists and historians alike, that every individual life is bound up with the whole of human history. Whether or not young people talk about their historical involvements—Americans usually do not, while Japanese tend to dwell upon them—these involvements are inevitably intense. For those in their late teens and early twenties find themselves entering, sometimes with the explosive enthusiasm of the new arrival, into the realm of historical ideas. And they bring to this realm their special urge toward development and change.

In Japan, the rather sudden emergence of outspoken "youth attitudes" has led to facile generalizations about the nature of young people's contemporary historical experience. There is first the claim (perhaps most popular in the West) that nothing is really changing, that although things may look different on the surface, deep down everything (and everyone) in the "unchanging East" is, and will continue to be, just as it (and they) always has been. And there is the opposite assertion (a favorite of Japanese mass media) that young people have changed absolutely, and beyond recognition, so that they no longer have any relationship to their country's past. To avoid these polarities, I have found it useful to think in terms of the interplay between inertia and flux in cultures and individual people as well as in inorganic matter. For in Japan one discovers that inertia (maintained by traditional psychological patterns) and flux (stimulated by pressures toward change) can both be extremely strong—that individual change is at the same time perpetual and perpetually resisted.

In my work with Japanese students[1]—done mostly through intensive interviews—I have tried to focus on ways in which they experience and express the wider historical change taking place within their society. I have looked for consistent psychological patterns among them and have then tried to understand these patterns as both old and new, both specific and universal. That is, each is related to the psychological and social currents of Japanese cultural tradition; to psychobiological tendencies common to all mankind; and to forces of historical change, particularly modern and contemporary, in Japan and throughout the world. (I shall refer in this article mainly to young men, since they are most directly involved in the historical issues under consideration. The discussion applies to young women too, but the special features of their changing situation require their own full treatment.)

It is impossible, of course, to make an exact determination of just how much the cultural, universal, or historical factor is at play. But I have found it necessary to take all three into account in order to gain perspective on any immediate observation. This form of perspective seems particularly relevant for Japanese youth, but it is perhaps no less relevant for any other age or cultural group. I have also stressed the *direction of change,* on the assumption that the psychological experiments of outstanding young people can to some extent anticipate future directions in which their culture at large will move.

Historical Dislocation

The most fundamental of these patterns is the absence in contemporary Japanese youth of vital and nourishing ties to their own heritage —*a break in their sense of connection.* It is not that Japanese youth have

[1]This study of Japanese youth, supported by the Foundations' Fund for Research in Psychiatry, is still in progress. The research subjects I have interviewed are largely an elite group, attending leading universities and women's colleges in Tokyo and Kyoto, and in many cases possessing outstanding abilities as students and student leaders. I am grateful to Dr. Takeo Doi, with whom I have consulted regularly during the work; and to Mr. Hiroshi Makino and Miss Kyoko Komatsu for their general research assistance, including interpreting and translation.

been unaffected by the cultural elements which had formerly served to integrate (at least ideally) Japanese existence—by the Japanese style of harmony and obligation within the group life of family, locality, and nation; and by the special Japanese stress upon aesthetics and the liberating effect of beauty. Indeed, such elements are all too present in the mental life of young Japanese. But they are now felt to be irrelevant, inadequate to the perceived demands of the modern world. Rather than being a source of pride or strength, they often lead to embarrassment and even debilitation.

This lack of a sense of connection extends to their view of the contemporary society which they are preparing to enter. The word "feudalistic" (*hōkenteki*) comes readily to their lips, not only in reference to rural Japan but to "Japanese" forms of human relationship in general; and "monopoly capitalism" (*dokusen shihonshugi*) is the derogatory phrase for the modern—one might almost say postmodern—society that dominates the large cities. Underneath this semi-automatic Marxist terminology is the profound conviction of the young that they can connect nowhere, at least not in a manner they can be inwardly proud of. "Society" is thus envisaged as a gigantic, closed sorting apparatus, within which one must be pressed mechanically into a slot, painfully constrained by old patterns, suffocated by new ones.[2]

Yet the matter is not quite so simple. What is so readily condemned cannot be so summarily dismissed. By turning to two individual examples, we can begin to recognize the inner paradox and ambivalence of this historical dislocation.

A student leader (whom we shall call Sato) in his early twenties described to me the following dream: "A student [political] demonstration is taking place. A long line of students moves rapidly along . . . then at the end of the line there seems to be a festival float (*dashi*) which other students are pulling." Sato laughed uncomfortably as he told his dream, because he could begin to perceive (as he explained later) that it seemed to suggest a relationship between student political demonstrations and traditional shrine festivals. This embarrassed him because such political demonstrations and the student movement which sponsored them (the *Zengakuren*, or All Japan Federation of Student Self-Governing Societies) had been for the past few years the central and most sacred part of his life, in fact the only part that held meaning for him; while a shrine festival, symbolized by the large float, seemed to him something quite frivolous, or worse. He was particularly struck, and dismayed, by the fact that it was *students* who were pulling the float.

In his associations to the dream, he recalled the shrine festivals he had witnessed in the provincial city where he had attended high school; these he remembered as dreary, unanimated, motivated only by commercial considerations, and ultimately degenerate, stimulating in him feelings like those he sometimes experiences when face to face with very old people—a combination of revulsion, sympathy, and a sense of contamination. But he contrasted these negative impressions of relatively recent shrine festivals with the romantic and beautiful atmosphere of great shrine festivals in the distant

---

[2]This in many ways resembles the "apparently closed room" which Paul Goodman describes as confronting American youth (*Growing Up Absurd*, New York: Random House, 1960). But rather than the "rat race" which American youth encounter, Japanese youth are more concerned with their society's stress upon one's place or slot, which, once assigned, is (at least, occupationally) difficult to change.

past, as described in many court novels he had read. And he also thought of smaller festivals held at harvest time in the rural area of central Japan where he was born and had spent his early childhood. He spoke vividly of the sense of total relaxation that came over the entire village, of the bright decorations and gay atmosphere around the shrine, of the exciting horse races made up of local entrants, of big feasts with relatives, of masked dances (*kagura*) giving their renditions of the most ancient of recorded Japanese tales (from the *Kojiki*), of fascinating plays performed sometimes by traveling troupes (*ichiza*) and at times by young people from the village. Sato emphasized that in his dream he was a bystander, standing apart from both the political demonstration and the festival-like activities. This he associated with his recent displacement from a position of leadership within the student movement (because of a factional struggle) and with his feeling that he had failed to live up to his obligations to colleagues and followers in the movement. One meaning he gave to the dream was his belief that the student movement, now in the hands of leaders whom he did not fully respect, might become weak and ineffectual, nothing more than a "festival."

But the dream suggested that Sato was a "bystander" in a more fundamental sense, that he was alienated from those very elements of his personal and cultural past which were at the core of his character structure. These same elements—still the formative essence of his developing self, or self-process—had not only lost their vitality but had become symbols of decay. The dream was partly a longing for childhood innocence and happiness, but it was also an effort at integration. Thus in his nostalgic associations Sato commented that if he really did ever see students pulling a *dashi* in that manner at the end of one of their demonstrations, "I would feel that the world was stabilized," by which he meant in a personal sense that if he could harmoniously blend the old things he carried within himself with the new things to which he aspired, *he* would be stabilized. Like so many young people in Japan, Sato outwardly condemns many of the symbols of his own cultural heritage, yet inwardly he seeks to recover and restore those symbols so that they might once more be "beautiful" and psychologically functional.

Another frequent individual pattern demonstrating the break in the sense of connection is one of exaggerated experimentation, of exposing oneself or being exposed to an extraordinary variety of cultural and ideological influences, each of which engages the young person sufficiently to affect his developing self-process, but never with enough profundity to afford him a consistent source of personal meaning or creative expression. Consider the confusing array of identity fragments (as numbered below) experienced by one rather sophisticated Tokyo-born young man whom we shall call Kondo—all before the age of twenty-five.

As the youngest son in a professional family, he was brought up to be (1) a proper middle-class Japanese boy. But when he was evacuated to the country from the age of eight to eleven during and after the war, his contacts with farmers' and fishermen's sons created in him (2) a lasting attraction to the life and the tastes of the "common man." He was at that time (3) a fiery young patriot who was convinced of the sacredness of Japan's cause, revered her fighting men (especially his oldest brother, a naval pilot saved from a *kamikaze* death only by the war's end), accepted without question the historical myth of the Emperor's divine descent, and "hated the Americans." Japan's surrender came as a great shock and left him (4) temporarily confused in his beliefs, but toward the first American soldier he met he felt curiosity rather than hostility. He soon became (5) an eager young exponent of democracy, caught up in the "democracy boom" which then swept Japan (especially its classrooms) and which seemed to most youngsters to promise "freedom" and moral certainty. At the same time, Kondo also became (6) a devotee of traditional Japanese arts—skillful at singing and reciting old Chinese poems (*shigin*), passionately fond of old novels, and knowledgeable about *kabuki* drama and flower arrangement (*ikebana*).

During junior high school and high school years he was (7) an allround leader, excelling in his studies, prominent in student self-government and in social and athletic activities. Yet he also became (8) an outspoken critic of society at large (on the basis of Marxist ideas current in Japanese intellectual circles) and of fellow students for their narrow focus on preparation for entrance examinations in order to get into the best universities, then get the best jobs, and then lead stultifying, conventional lives. He was (9) an English-speaking student, having concentrated since childhood on learning English, stimulated by his growing interest in America and by the size, wealth, and seemingly relaxed manner of individual Americans he had met and observed. Therefore, when he found himself unaccountably (10) developing what he called a "kind of neurosis" in which he completely lost interest in everything he was doing, he decided to seek a change in mood (*kibun tenkan*) by applying for admission to a program of one year of study at an American high school.

He then became (11) a convert to many aspects of American life, enthusiastic about the warmth and freedom in human relationships, and so moved by the direction and example of his American "father" (a Protestant minister and courageous defender of civil rights during McCarthyite controversies) that he made a sudden, emotional decision to be baptized as a Christian. Having almost "forgotten" about his real family, he returned to Japan reluctantly, and there found himself looked upon as (12) something of an oddity —one friend told he "smelled like butter" (the conventional Japanese olfactory impression of Westerners), and others criticized him for having become fat and somewhat crude and insensitive to others' feelings. Eager to regain acceptance, he became (13) more aware than ever of his "Japaneseness"—of the pleasures of drinking tea and eating rice crackers (*senbei*) while sitting on floor mats (*tatami*) and sharing with friends a quiet and somewhat melancholic mood (*shoboi*), particularly in regular meetings of a reading group to which he belonged.

Yet he did not reintegrate himself to Japanese student life quickly enough to organize himself for the desperate all-out struggle to pass the entrance examination for Tokyo University, failing in his first attempt and thereby becoming a (14) *rōnin* (in feudal days, a *samurai* without a master, now a student without a university) for one year, before passing the examination on his second attempt.[3] Once admitted to the university, he found little to interest him and rarely attended classes until—through the influence of a Marxist professer and bright fellow-students in an economics seminar—he became (15) an enthusiastic *Zengakuren* activist. His embrace of the *Zengakuren* ideal of "pure communism," to be achieved through world-wide workers' revolu-

[3]Nowadays, more than half the students admitted to Tokyo and Kyoto Universities have spent at least one year as a *rōnin*. Because of the prestige and better job opportunities accorded graduates of these leading universities, students prefer to spend an extra year (or sometimes two or three years) working to gain admission, rather than attend a different university.

tions, and his participation in student demonstrations and planning sessions gave him a sense of comradeship and fulfillment beyond any he had previously known. But when offered a position of leadership during his third year at the university Kondo decided that his character was not suited for "the life of a revolutionary" and that the best path for him was a conventional life of economic and social success within the existing society.

He left the *Zengakuren* and drifted into (16) a life of dissipation, devoting his major energies to heavy drinking, marathon *mahjong* games, and affairs with bar girls. But when the time came, he had no difficulty (because of his Tokyo University background and connections, as well as his ability) in gaining employment with one of Japan's mammoth business organizations. His feelings about embarking upon (17) the life of the *sarariman* (salaried man) were complex. He was relieved to give up his dissipation and find a central focus once more, and in fact expressed an extraordinary identification with the firm. He stressed the benefits it bestowed upon the Japanese economy and the Japanese people, and sought in every way to give himself entirely to the group life demanded of him—to wear the proper clothes, behave appropriately toward superiors and colleagues, and effectively flatter customers (allowing them to seem most popular with bar girls and to win at *mahjong*). At the same time, he retained a significant amount of inner despair and self-contempt, the feeling that capitalism was "evil," and that he himself had become a "machine for capitalism." He had fantasies of total escape from the restraints of his new life, including one of murdering a Japanese or American capitalist, stealing a great deal of money, and then spending the rest of his life wandering about Europe and America amusing himself; and he would also, in unguarded moments, go into tirades against the constricted life-pattern of the "typical salaried man" (*sarariman konjo*).

He attempted to resolve these contradictory feelings by making plans to introduce reforms into his firm that would ultimately encourage greater individual initiative, promote efficiency, and allow for more genuine personal relationships; toward this end he began a study of American writings on human relations in industry. At the same time he was constantly preoccupied with promoting his rise within the firm, with becoming in time a section head, a department head, a member of the board of directors, and if possible not only the president of the firm but also one who would be long remembered in its annals and who would come to exert a profound influence upon all Japanese economic life.

To be sure, neither Sato nor Kondo can be said to be "typical" of Japanese intellectual youth; rather, they express in exaggerated form the experimental possibilities to which all Japanese youth are exposed. (Relatively few become *Zengakuren* activists, but all are confronted with the *Zengakuren* moral and ideological claims which dominate the campuses; even fewer get to America, but none is unaffected by postwar American influences). Even in the majority of youth, who seem to plod unquestioningly through university and occupational careers, there is something of Sato's quest for the past as he works for a revolutionary future, something of Kondo's diffusion, sudden shifts in ideological and group loyalties, and final ambivalent compromise.

What about the family relationships of Japanese youth? Is there a break in connection here as well? I have found that virtually all my research subjects—whether brilliant students, playboys, plodders, or

Zengakuren leaders—tend to remain very much in the bosom of their families, nourished by the readiness of Japanese parents to cater to their children's wants and encourage dependency—even when such children have reached manhood or womanhood. This continuity in family life seems to be the balancing force that permits Japanese youth to weather their confusing psychological environment as well as they do. But the continuity is only partial. On matters of ideology and general social outlook, most Japanese students feel completely apart from their parents. A typical constellation (actually experienced for a time by Kondo) is the following: the "radical" son remains on intimate (in fact, mutually idealized) terms with his mother; she is sympathetic to his point of view, confident of the "purity" of her son and his fellow students, although understanding little of the intellectual issues involved; his father, with no firm ideological convictions of his own, disapproves, silently, ineffectually, and from a distance, so that father and son are rarely in open combat. The son's emotional state is less one of "rebellion" than of continuous inner search.

What, then, are some of the wider historical factors associated with this break in the sense of connection? We must first look back beyond World War II and the postwar period to the latter half of the nineteenth century, and particularly to the Meiji Restoration of 1868. Before then, Japanese culture, although by no means as even and consistent as sometimes painted, had maintained an effective stress upon lineage, continuity, and on long-standing Japanese and Chinese moral principles—cemented by the extraordinary experience of more than two hundred years of nearly total isolation from the outside world. At the time of the Meiji restoration, however, the Japanese faced a very real danger, not only of being militarily overwhelmed by the West but also of being ideologically, institutionally, and culturally overwhelmed as well. The early slogans—"Revere the Emperor, Repel the Barbarian" (*Sonnō-jōi*); and "Eastern ethics and Western science" (*Tōyō no dōtoku, Seiyō no gakugei*)[4]—and the ensuing pattern of an uncritical embrace of things Western, alternating with recoil from them in fundamentalist horror, revealed *the continuing effort to reassert Japanese cultural identity within a modern idiom.*

Thus, ever since the time just before the Meiji Restoration, Japanese, and especially educated Japanese, have looked to the West with a uniquely intense ambivalence. They have felt impelled to immerse themselves in Western ideas and styles of life in order to be able to feel themselves the equal of Westerners, and at the same time they have waged a constant struggle against being psychologically inundated by these same Western influences. In the process they have experimented with a greater variety of ideas, of belief-systems, of political, religious, social, and scientific ways of thinking and feeling than perhaps any other people in the world. And they have as individuals learned to move quickly and relatively easily from one of these patterns to another, to compartmentalize their beliefs and identifications

[4]Ryusaku Tsunoda, William Theodore de Bary, and Donald Keene, *Sources of Japanese Tradition* (New York: Columbia University Press, 1958), pp. 592 and 606.

and thereby maintain effective psychological function.[5] (We would expect an American youngster who actively experienced as wide and conflicting an array of personal influences as Kondo to be incapacitated by his identity diffusion.) Japanese youth are still engaged in the psychological-historical struggle carried over from the time of the Meiji Restoration.

The defeat in World War II, therefore, did not create the conflicts I have been describing but rather intensified them. Yet the intensification has been of a very special kind, adding important new dimensions to the postwar situation. Most important here was the humiliation of the defeat itself, because in that defeat Japan experienced not only its first great modern "failure" (after a series of extraordinary successes) but also had its mystical-ideological concept of *kokutai* undermined. *Kokutai*[6] is usually translated as "national polity" or "national essence," but it also conveys the sense of "body" or "substance," and its nature is impossible to define precisely. Included in *kokutai* are the concepts of "national structure," particularly the emperor system; "national basis," the myth of the divine origin of Japan and of its imperial dynasty; and "national character," those special Japanese moral virtues, stemming from both native and Confucian influences, that are considered indispensable for individual behavior and social cohesion (embodied in *Bushidō*, or the Way of the Warrior). Although *kokutai* is a relatively modern concept—manipulated for political purposes during the Meiji era and again in association with pre-World War II militarism—it had profound roots in Japanese cultural experience and embraced something in the cultural identity of all Japanese.

Most young people (with the exception of "rightists") no longer take *kokutai* seriously; they dismiss it as the propaganda of militarists, and even find it laughable. Nevertheless, the dishonoring of *kokutai* has created in many Japanese youth a sense of their own past as dishonored, or even of Japaneseness itself as dishonored. The sudden collapse of *kokutai* revealed its tenuousness as an ideological system. But it also created an ideological void and thus encouraged the polarizing tendencies that still haunt Japanese thought—the urge to recover *kokutai* and make things just as they were, and the opposite urge to break away entirely from every remnant of *kokutai* and make all things new.

Nor can intellectual youth feel comforted by Japan's extraordinary postwar industrial development. As the first generation of Asians to grow up in a country which, at least in its urban aspects, resembles the modern industrial West, they are also the first to experience the dehumanizing effects of mass society (though they sometimes attribute these to capitalism alone). Moreover, they link this industrial develop-

[5] I do not mean to suggest that this modern historical experience is the only cause of the Japanese tendency to compartmentalize their beliefs and identifications. Moreover, there is a good deal of evidence that the same tendency existed during the seventh, eighth and ninth centuries In relation to Chinese cultural influences. See Ruth Benedict's discussions, "Clearing One's Name" and "The Dilemma of Virtue," in *The Chrysanthemum and the Sword* (Boston: Houghton Mifflin Company, 1946).

[6] For discussions of *kokutai*, see Maruyama Masao, "Chōkokka-shugi no Ronri to Shinri" (Theory and Psychology of Ultranationalism), in *Gendai Seiji no Shisō to Kōdō* (Thought and Action in Current Politics), Tokyo, 1956; Tsunoda, de Bary and Keene, *op. cit.*, 597–598; Richard Storry, *The Double Patriots* (Boston: Houghton Mifflin Company, 1957), p. 5; and Ivan Morris, *Nationalism and the Right Wing in Japan* (London: Oxford University Press, 1960). I am also indebted to Professor Maruyama for personal discussions of *kokutai* and *shutaisei*.

ment to the "old guard" among their politicians and businessmen, from whom they feel themselves (or wish to feel themselves) completely removed. They find insufficient satisfaction in the democratic freedoms they enjoy—they often do not *feel* free—and they condemn themselves for being attracted to the rewards of their own society.

The collapse of *kokutai* also ushered in a new era of increased receptivity to outside ideological currents. But when young intellectuals now look to the West, they find the Western world itself in a state of profound uncertainty and disillusionment in relation to much of its own great tradition of humanism, individualism, Judeo-Christian religion, and private economic enterprise. They see in Communism a powerful, expanding force, with profound intellectual, emotional, and moral attractions (especially in the case of Chinese Communism), but they have been sufficiently sensitive to the organizational cruelties of Communism for much disillusionment to have set in here as well. Still inspiring and untarnished in their eyes is the social revolution occurring throughout most of Africa and Asia (and in other relatively underdeveloped areas, such as Latin America), whose dynamism has great appeal. But the youth are inwardly torn between their "Asian" identification with this movement and their "Western" separation from it—that is, by the experience of Western-inspired "modernization," which (superimposed on their previous geographical and cultural isolation) has set the Japanese apart from the rest of Asia and has enabled them to accomplish many of the things other Asian countries are just now setting out to achieve.

Surely, it is not only in postwar Japan that such a break in the sense of connection has occurred. To what extent can we say that universal factors are at play? Here we must first consider the everpresent ideological gap of the generations, found in varying degrees in all cultures and at all periods of history. Thus, Ortega y Gasset claims that "the concept of the generation is the most important one in the whole of history."[7] He points out that the twenty-year-old, the forty-year-old, and the sixty-year-old create three different styles of life which are blended into one historical period, so that "lodged together in a single external and chronological fragment of time are three different and vital times." Ortega y Gasset calls this "history's essential anachronism," an "internal lack of equilibrium," thanks to which "history moves, changes, wheels and flows." In other words, this generational gap is the psychobiological substrate of the historical process, imperfectly blended with it but necessary to it. Moreover, the occurrence of "youth problems" and "youth rebellions" throughout the world suggests that the gap is universally enlarging. The rapid technological and social change affecting all mankind has created a universally shared sense that the past experience of older generations is an increasingly unreliable guide for young people in their efforts to imagine the future. And individual identity diffusion becomes for many young people everywhere a virtual necessity, a form of sensitive (though often

[7]José Ortega y Gasset, *What is Philosophy?* (New York: W. W. Norton & Company, 1960), pp. 32–39.

costly) experimentation with historical possibilities. In Japanese youth, cultural and historical influences have brought about diffusion and dislocation of unusual magnitude.

Selfhood

One of the ways in which young people attempt to deal with this predicament is by stressing a developing awareness of their own being, by delineating the self. They do this in many different ways. They speak much of individual freedom in relation to family and society, and strongly criticize the negation of the individual person in traditional (and contemporary) Japanese practice. They respond strongly to those elements of Marxist thought which refer to self-realization. And they frequently combine their Marxism with existentialism, for they are drawn to the ideal of personal freedom they find expressed in the writings of Jean-Paul Sartre and in his life as well. They criticize great nations like Russia and America for what they perceive to be a tendency toward mass conformity and a denial of self. And many criticize their own student political movement on the same basis, despite strong sympathy for it otherwise. Still others conduct their self-exploration through an attitude of negation, through the mood of nihilism and passive disintegration that has frequently appeared in Japanese literature and social behavior; students have this kind of attitude in mind in their use of a coined word meaning "feigned evil" (*giaku*).

Also related to this urge to liberate the self is the extremely widespread fascination, even among intellectual youth, with American Western films. Both Sato and Kondo attend them regularly, and have revealed a variety of reasons for their appeal: the exhilarating spectacle of young men and women engaged in purposeful adventure, free from conventional pressures of social obligation (*giri*), and creating a new way of life solely by their own efforts; the sense of geographical openness and of unlimited possibility; the admirable figure of the hero—his simple courage, direct (unambivalent) action, and tight-lipped masculinity; and the excitement and precision of the gunplay. All this, of course, is contrasted with their own situation in present-day Japan. They perceive in "Westerns" a world of ultimate freedom, in which the self is clearly defined, unrestrained, and noble even in its violence.

But underneath this ideal of selfhood, however strongly maintained, one can frequently detect an even more profound craving for renewed group life, for solidarity, even for the chance to "melt" completely into a small group, a professional organization, or a mass movement, and even at the cost of nearly all self-assertion. Those most concerned with selfhood have often told me (as Kondo did) that their moments of greatest happiness come when they feel themselves, in a spiritual sense, completely merged with groups of young comrades. And I have repeatedly observed their despair and depression when separated from groups with which they have been profoundly involved, or when unable to establish meaningful group relationships. For Japanese of all ages, in virtually any situation, have a powerful urge toward group formation: when they wish to do something startling (intellectual, artistic, social, or political), they are likely to go about it by forming, joining, or activating a group. The extraordinary array of student circles, of cultural, professional, political, and neighborhood groups—the "horizontal" groups so prominent at all levels of society—makes Japan one of the most group-conscious nations in the world.

One feels this tension between the ideal of individualism and the need for the group in the concern of young people with that much-discussed, elusive, sometimes near-mystical, but always highly desirable entity known as *shutaisei. Shutaisei* literally means "subjecthood," and is a modern Japanese word derived from German philosophy, coined by Japanese philosophers to introduce into Japanese thought the German philosophical ideal of man as subject rather than object. But the word has had its vicissitudes: some philosophers who were sympathetic to the prewar Japanese ideology sought to combine *shutaisei* with *kokutai* (thereby almost reversing its original meaning); while in the postwar period it has been a central concept in intra-Marxist debates about man's nature and responsibility in relation to the historical process. Continuing in this postwar trend, young people use *shutaisei* to mean two things: first, holding and living by personal convictions—here *shutaisei* comes close to meaning selfhood; and second, having the capacity to act in a way that is effective in furthering historical goals, and (at least by implication) joining forces with like-minded people in order to do so—here the word means something like social commitment. The young Japanese themselves tend to be confused by the conflicts which seem to arise from these two aspects of *shutaisei.* Their greatest difficulty is in realizing to their own satisfaction its first element, that of selfhood; and the sense of "smallness" or the "inferiority complex" which they talk so much about seems to reflect the great difficulty the Japanese have in perceiving and believing in a relatively independent self.

Yet the very groups to which youth are drawn may themselves become arenas for the struggle for selfhood. In this group life there is always a delicate balance between competition (often fierce, though usually suppressed), mutual support and encouragement, and (perhaps most important) constant comparison with other members as a means of self-definition. Moreover, their struggle for selfhood in combination with their historical dislocation has resulted in a burst of literary and artistic creativity among them; such creative accomplishments rarely resolve their dilemmas, but they are energetic efforts to come to grips with them.

Traditional Japanese patterns of group and individual behavior throw a good deal of light upon the present situation. For, in Japan, the stress upon the group as the "cellular unit"[8] of society and the negation of consciousness of self has been carried to an unparalleled extreme. The relatively closed ("vertical") groups constituting traditional society (family, locality, clan, and nation) became the source of all authority in Japanese life. (An outspoken critic of *Tokugawa* society character-

[8]Kawashima Takeyoshi, "Giri," *Shisō* (Thought), September 1951, as quoted in Nobutaka Ike, *Japanese Politics* (New York: Alfred A. Knopf, 1957), p. 29.

ized its group hierarchy as "tens of millions of people enclosed in tens of millions of boxes separated by millions of walls."[9]) More than this, these groups have often become something close to objects of worship, resulting in a characteristic Japanese pattern which we may term *deification of the human matrix.*[10] In a culture with a notable absence of universal principles, men have found their sacred cause in defending the integrity of their particular human matrix.

This pattern finds its central symbolization in the idea of the divinity of the Imperial family, the Imperial family having been considered since ancient times the "living totality of the nation." It found later expression in the *samurai's* absolute submission and loyalty to his feudal overlord, which in turn supplied a psychological model for the modern practice of national Emperor worship. Therefore, it was not simply the experience of *Tokugawa* isolation which brought about the cliquish intensity of Japanese group life, as is often asserted; rather it was the earlier tendency to regard the Japanese human matrix as sacred which created (and then was reinforced by) *Tokugawa* isolation. The Japanese have long had an unconscious tendency to equate separation from the human matrix (or exile) with death—expressed linguistically in the common Chinese character used in the Japanese words *bōmei suru* (to be exiled, literally, to lose life), and *nakunaru* (to die).

All this has resulted in a language and a thought pattern in which "there is . . . no full awareness of the individual, or of an independent performer of actions . . . no inclination to attribute actions to a specific performer."[11] It is the combination of historical inability to delineate boundaries of the self with the modern urge to do so that creates the inner conflicts I have described.

This historical tendency has its counterparts—indeed, they are partly its results—in child-rearing practices and in resulting individual psychological patterns. Japanese children in relation to their parents (and especially to their mothers) are expected to show the desire to *amaeru. Amaeru* has no single English equivalent. It means to depend upon, expect, presume upon, even solicit, another's love. According to Dr. Takeo Doi, this pattern of *amaeru*—or *amae*, the noun form (both words are derived from *amai*, meaning sweet)—is basic to individual Japanese psychology and is carried over into adult life and into all human relationships. Doi argues further that the unsatisfied urge to *amaeru* is the underlying dynamic of neurosis in Japan.[12] We can also say that the *amaeru* pattern is the child's introduction to Japanese group life; brought up to depend totally on his mother (and to a lesser extent his father and older brothers and sisters within the family group), he unconsciously seeks similar opportunities later on in rela-

---

[9]Fukuzawa Yukichi, as quoted by Maruyama Masso, "Kaikoku" (The Opening of the Country) in *Kōza Gendai Rinri* (Modern Ethics), Tokyo, Chikuma Shobō, 1959.

[10]Much of the following discussion is based upon Nakamura Hajime, *The Ways of Thinking of Eastern Peoples* (Tokyo: Japanese National Commission for UNESCO, 1960), pp. 304-433.

[11]*Ibid.*, p. 307.

[12]Doi Takeo, "Jibun to Amaeru no Sesishin Byōri" (The Psychopathology of the Self and Amaeru), *Seishin Shinkei Gaku Zasshi* (Journal of Neuropsychiatry), 1960, *61*:149-162; and "*Amae*—A Key Concept for Understanding Japanese Personality Structure," (unpublished manuscript). Dr. Doi emphasizes correctly, I believe, that the emotions surrounding *amaeru* are by no means unique to the Japanese but are particularly intense in them.

tion to others who are important to his welfare. The lesson he learns is: you must depend on others, and they must take care of you. It is difficult for him to feel independent, or even to separate his own sense of self from those who care for him or have cared for him in the past. The spirit of *amaeru* still dominates child-rearing practices; and the desire expressed by many young Japanese (especially women) to bring up their own children "differently," more "as individuals," is a form of recognizing that this spirit conflicts with aspirations to selfhood.

The question arises whether there is in the Japanese historical and cultural tradition a tendency opposite to those we have mentioned, one stressing greater independence, more self-expression, and less submission to group authority. Many Japanese feel that such a native tendency did exist before it was submerged by the repressive atmosphere of Confucian orthodoxy, and they point to such early Japanese writings as the *Manyoshu* (a collection of verse recorded during the seventh and eighth centuries) as depicting considerable spontaneity of emotion and independence of spirit. This is a question I will not attempt to take up; but I believe one can say that, despite this early ethos of spontaneity, there remains a rather weak tradition for the ideal of individuation which young people now embrace.

For the concepts of selfhood and of commitment (which implies selfhood), of *shutaisei*, stem almost entirely from Western tradition: from classical Greece of the fourth century B.C., from Judeo-Christian monotheism, from the Renaissance and the Reformation, and from the later philosophical schools which grew out of these traditions. Vital to these Western traditions has been a spirit of universalism—concepts of the universal God, the universal Idea, and the universal State— with which the individual self could come into nourishing symbolic contact and thereby free itself from the influence of more immediate and particularistic human groups. This kind of stress upon individuation has been limited primarily to a very small part of the world, mostly Western Europe and those areas populated by Western Europeans. Non-Western cultures have been profoundly stirred by it, to adopt a form of *self-expression via the group*. The alternative is a retreat from selfhood into a modern form of collectivism that makes emotional contact with earlier group traditions.

It is perhaps unnecessary to add that the process of individuation has hardly run smoothly and is far from "complete" in those Western cultures where it evolved. Moreover, the exciting appeal of selfhood has created, first in the West and then in those countries influenced by the West, what we might term a myth of absolute individualism, the fantasy of the self existing in total independence from all groups. This, of course, ignores the psychological interdependence between individuation and community.

The dual aspects of *shutaisei* reflect an awareness in young Japanese of the need for both. But they cannot achieve either aspect of *shutaisei* without modifying their overwhelming need for immediate group acceptance, since this can stifle not only selfhood but true social commitment as well. Their inner question is not so much, "Who am I?" (the problem of identity) as, "Can I perceive my own person as existing with a measure of independence from others?" (the problem of self-hood).[13]

Logic and Beauty

Young Japanese repeatedly assert their desire to be logical, objective, scientific, to be in every way tough-minded. They stress their urge to *warikiru*—a verb which means "to divide" but which now conveys the sense of cutting through a problem, giving a clear-cut and logical explanation. They are quick to criticize one another's attitudes as *amai* ("sweet"), meaning wishful, rather than realistic (*genjitsuteki*) in one's expectations; or as *kannenteki*, meaning prone to philosophical idealism, overtheoretical, and also unrealistic. A still stronger condemnation is *nansensu* (nonsense) which has been used particularly widely within the student movement to dismiss dissenting opinions and convey the sense that such opinions are a logical impossibility.

These "undesirable" (and "illogical") tendencies are in turn related to one's background and probable future: those judged guilty of them are likely also to be called *botchan*, meaning "little man" or "sonny," and suggesting the softness and self-indulgence created by favored middle-class circumstances; *puchi-buru*, the Japanization of petty bourgeois, which conveys utter contempt in its very sound; or *sarariman* (salaried man), the *bête noire* of Japanese youth in the wider social sense, signifying the selfless, mindless, amoral, modern Japanese automaton, whose thought and life are utterly devoid of "logic" (and which, it must be added, most young Japanese expect to become).

Yet accompanying this strongly held ideal of logic is an inherent predilection for nonrational, aesthetic responses, and this predilection becomes increasingly evident the better one gets to know a young person. Dedicated political activists have told me that they were inspired to join the revolutionary movement through the examples of the heroes of novels by Gorky, Rolland, and Malraux. One *Zengakuren* leader, a central figure in the mass political demonstrations of 1960, told me he had been "profoundly moved" (*sugoku kangeki shita*) by the "absolute sincerity" (*shinjō o tsukusu*) of the revolutionaries in Gorky's novel *The Mother*, by their capacity to hate their exploiters and at the same time to love one another, and that he later found his fellow *Zengakuren* activists to be in the same way inwardly "beautiful" (*utsukushii*). Such sentiments were also prominent in Sato and Kondo.

This emphasis upon the sincere (*seijitsu*) and the pure (*junsui*) applies to not only politics but to all experience. And among the majority of students (those who are politically moderate or apolitical) there is often a guilty sense of their being unable to match the "purity" and "sincerity" of *Zengakuren* leaders, despite their feeling otherwise critical of their behavior. Many speak of their desire to live seriously and

---

[13]This idea of "self" is closely related to that of Susanne Langer, who states, "The conception of 'self' . . . may possibly depend on this process of symbolically epitomizing our feeling," *Philosophy in a New Key* (New York: Mentor Books, 1948), p. 111; and also that of Robert E. Nixon: "Self is the person's symbol for his own organism" in "An Approach to the Dynamics of Growth in Adolescence," *Psychiatry*, 1961, *24*:18-31.

honestly; the word they use is *shinken*, whose literal meaning is "true sword," and which suggests the kind of inner intensity one might find in art or religion or in any dedicated life.

When talking freely, they make extensive use of the rich Japanese vocabulary of aesthetic and emotional experience—*kimochi* (feel), *kibun* (mood), *kanji* (feeling), *kankaku* (sense), *kanjo* (emotion or passion), *kan* (intuitive sense), *funiki* (atmosphere) etc.; and *akarui* (bright) or *kurai* (dark), to convey their impression of almost any event or person. They have an unusually strong aesthetic response to the totality of a situation, and both their immediate and enduring judgments depend greatly on the extent to which purity and beauty are perceived. I believe that one of the reasons for the attraction of Marxism as an over-all doctrinal system is its capacity to evoke this sense of aesthetic totality, of the universal "fit" and feeling of truth. At the same time, Marxism readily lends itself to the equally necessary stress upon "scientific logic" and tough-minded analysis.

The reliance upon aesthetic emotions extends into personal relations, too, in which one finds that these students combine a considerable amount of distrust and criticism (especially toward their elders) with a profound romanticism, a strong tendency to idealize human emotions. Their "wet" (in the slang of postwar youth) quality is especially evident when falling in love: the young man, perhaps after speaking a few words to a young woman in a casual, more or less public situation, or perhaps after simply catching a glimpse of her, sends an impassioned letter declaring his love and accepting the responsibility (meaning his readiness to consider marriage) for having done so; and in the relationship which follows, the letters exchanged (almost entirely devoted to descriptions of feeling and mood) often seem to be of greater importance than the rare meetings for talks in coffee houses. To be sure, there are more "modern" ("dry") relationships also, but it is surprising how frequently one still encounters this older "Japanese" form of love affair among students.[14]

The efforts to resolve this tension between aesthetic emotion and logic sometimes result in rather problematical attitudes toward ideas in general. At one extreme is the desperate urge to cast off the alien "logic"—the distrust of all ideas, theory, or even talk, and the stress on the pure and spontaneous (aesthetically perfect) act. This pattern is most intense in political rightists, who are rare among intellectual youth, and in certain postwar literary movements whose leaders have emerged as university students, expressing disdain for the intellect in favor of a cult of the senses.

The opposite tendency, and the more frequent one, is to elevate logical and scientific ideas to the status of absolute, concrete entities, which then take on aesthetically satisfying properties and become incontestable—a form of scientism. But one must add that many show great sensitivity in groping toward a balance between their logical and aesthetic inclinations, allowing themselves an increasing capacity for

---

[14]In looking toward marriage, most students express a strong preference for "love marriages" rather than the more traditional "arranged marriages." But despite this general trend, a considerable number, when the time comes, resort to the older pattern of family arrangements.

precision and logic while neither disdaining the nonrational nor worshipping a pseudo-scientific form of rationalism.

These conflicts become more understandable when we consider that Japanese youth are heirs to a tradition utterly unique among high cultures in its extraordinary emphasis upon aesthetic experience and the neglect of logical principles. The aesthetic emphasis includes not only a remarkable body of art and literature but also a consistent concern with sensitivity to all varieties of beauty and every nuance of human emotion. Such aesthetic sensibility can even become the criterion for human goodness, as suggested by Motoori Norinaga, a leading figure in the eighteenth-century Shinto revival, when commenting (approvingly) upon the morality of *The Tale of Genji* (the court novel of the early eleventh century):[15]

> Generally speaking, those who know the meaning of the sorrow of human existence, i.e., those who are in sympathy and in harmony with human sentiments, are regarded as good: and those who are not aware of the poignancy of human existence, i.e., those who are not in sympathy and not in harmony with human sentiments, are regarded as bad.

There is a corresponding stress, found in almost every Japanese form of spiritual-physical discipline (Zen *jūdō, kendō karate*), on achieving emotional harmony, purity, and simplicity: a form of aesthetic perfection in which conflict (ambivalence) is eliminated. But among the "impurities" and "complexities" got rid of are ideas and rational principles. Again, Motoori Norinaga:[16]

> In ancient times in our land, even the "Way" was not talked about at all and we had only ways directly leading to things themselves, while in foreign countries it is the custom to entertain and to talk about many different doctrines, about principles of things, this "Way" or that "Way." The Emperor's land in ancient times had not such theories or doctrines whatever, but we enjoyed peace and order then, and the descendants of the Sun Goddess have consecutively succeeded to the throne.

Averse to detailed general principles, the Japanese have tended to turn to their opposite, to brief, concrete, emotionally evocative symbols, as in the short verse forms of *Tanka* and *Haiku*. In the political-ideological sphere, however, this propensity for evocative word-symbols, for what one Japanese philosopher has called the "amuletic" use of words,[17] has had more serious consequences. Words like *kokutai, nipponteki* (Japanese) and *Kōdō* (Imperial Way) seem to have given their users a magical sense of perfection; and this same tendency has made Japanese particularly susceptible to slogans associated with military expansionism. These amuletic words and slogans, within the framework of *kokutai*, offer a sense of aesthetic totality, of both moral righteousness and group invulnerability. And the Japanese language itself reflects the tendencies we have mentioned in its unusual capacity for

---

[15] Tsunoda, de Bary, and Keene, *op. cit.*, p. 533.
[16] Nakamura, *op. cit.*, p. 471.
[17] Tsurumi Shunsuke, as quoted and summarized in Morris, *op. cit.*, Appendix I, pp. 427–428.

describing beauty and capturing emotional nuance and in its contrasting limitations in dealing with precise ideas—such that it "has a structure unfit for expressing logical conceptions."[18]

When Japanese students condemn the "irrationalism" of their tradition, they are repeating the attitudes of generations before them, going back to the middle of the nineteenth century; and even today intellectuals of all ages feel themselves to be (rightly or wrongly) an island of logic amid a sea of emotionalism. Their stress on logic represents a cultural countertrend, a rebound reaction against a tradition which has not only neglected scientific and rational thought but also has often condemned it. Such a cultural sequence can readily lead to a form of worship for the thing that has been historically denied, and this makes it difficult for many young Japanese to retain full access to the aesthetic sensitivities still at the core of their self-process.

Turning to the universal aspect of the question, we find that the Japanese have been unique only in the *degree* of their stress upon aesthetics and neglect of logic. Their style of symbol-formation (following the terminology of Susanne Langer)[19] has stressed "nondiscursive" elements which rely upon a "total," or essentially emotional and aesthetic, form of reference, in contrast to the relatively great stress in the West on "discursive" (or logical) symbolic forms. But advanced logical skills are a relatively late accomplishment, in a historical as well as an individual psychological sense, and are always superimposed upon an earlier, nonrational, mental structure. Moreover, the high development of logical thought has created in modern Western man an artificial separation of mind into logical and nonlogical categories. The glorification of the former and the derogation of the latter has left men dissatisfied with the myths and symbols they used to find enriching, although it hardly seems to have eliminated their irrationality. It can be said that this separation of mind has been the price Western man has had to pay for his modern achievements, including that of selfhood.

Japanese intellectuals, expecially young ones, are now seeking similar achievements and paying a similar price. Yet Western man has had some second thoughts about the matter, not only in spiritual quests but also in the realization that original discoveries in such logical disciplines as mathematics and the physical sciences depend importantly on aesthetic and other nonrational experience. In the same light, one suspects that the recent emergence of gifted Japanese mathematicians and scientists reflects not only the rapid development of logical thought in post-Meiji Japan but also the capacity of outstanding Japanese to bring to bear upon their intellectual work elements of their exceptionally rich aesthetic tradition.

Directions and Principles

It is clear by now that the psychological directions in which young people in Japan are moving (and in which Japan itself is perhaps mov-

[18]Nakamura, *op. cit.*, p. 465.

[19]Langer, *op, cit.*, pp. 75-94. I would stress that this is a *relative* difference in emphasis between Japanese and Western patterns of symbolization.

ing) are spasmodic, conflicting, and paradoxical. Yet we can discern reasonably definite patterns and crucial pitfalls.

There is first the conscious ideal, the symbolic direction which a large portion of young people chart out for their own character structure. They wish to be, and are to some extent becoming: "new," progressive, innovative, and antitraditional; active, individually independent and socially committed (possessors of *shutaisei*); logical, realistic, tough-minded, and scientific. Summing up the spirit of this ideal path, we may call it "active-Western-masculine."

In opposition to this direction is their negative image,[20] the things they wish to avoid becoming, but which deep in their mental life (because of their individual and cultural experience) in many important ways, they *are*. They do not want to be: "old," unprogressive, acquiescent, traditionalistic; passive, wholly dependent upon others and socially uncommitted (lacking *shutaisei*); irrational, unrealistic, wishful and unscientific. This path we may term (according to the way they perceive it) "passive-Japanese-feminine."

The inner struggle between these two sets of elements is continuous. The actual psychological task—and one which Japanese have been performing since the seventh century[21]—is that of making use of "old" tendencies when creating new patterns, always careful that the new patterns do not do violence to what is emotionally most important in the old tendencies. Thus young Japanese are seeking to recover their own past even as they move away from it; to maintain their sense of group intimacy, even as they achieve greater individuation; to live by their aesthetic sensitivities, even as they attain greater logical precision. In outstanding youth, much of this process is conscious and self-evaluative, while in the majority it is largely unconscious. In all, the distinction between what is "ideal" and what is "negative" becomes less absolute as it is found necessary to make use of both sets of elements. And even the most mentally adventurous can at most achieve only a slight modification of the psychological patterns which form the core of their developing self-process. But that is achieving a great deal.

The two great problems young people face are, on the one hand, totalism (or psychological extremism),[22] and on the other, a complete surrender of ideals, or what might be called "moral backsliding." They themselves articulate the second problem clearly, the first more vaguely.

Totalism may take (and has taken) two forms. There is the *totalism of the new*, in which young people carry the elements of the "active-Western-masculine" ideal to the point of creating a closed ideological system (usually derived from Marxism) in which there are combined

---

[20]This "negative image" is closely related to Erik H. Erikson's concept of "negative identity," except that it is not, as in the case of the latter, something that youth have been warned not to become, but rather a part of their culture within themselves which they condemn. The general point of view in this article is influenced by Erikson's psychological approach to historical events, especially *Young Man Luther* (New York: W. W. Norton & Co., 1958). See also Zevedei Barbu, *Problems of Historical Psychology*, (London: Routledge & Kegan Paul, 1960).

[21]Nakamura, *op. cit.;* and Yoshikawa Kōjiro, "The Introduction of Chinese Culture," *Japan Quarterly*, 1961, *8:* 160-169.

[22]I have discussed this tendency at greater length in my book, *Thought Reform and the Psychology of Totalism* (New York: W. W. Norton & Company, 1961).

elements of extreme idealism, scientism, a moral imperative for bold (sometimes violent) action, and a degree of martyrdom. Such totalism has been prominent in the student movement, although actively espoused by only a small minority; and even among this minority, many later struggle against their totalism by questioning the "openness" of the ideology and the nature of their own involvement in it.

The *totalism of the old* disdains the symbols of logic, science, and *shutaisei*, in favor of a traditionalistic reversion to *kokutai;* violent homicidal assaults are made by young rightist fanatics in order to "protect" and "restore" the sacred Japanese identity. Among university students, one encounters, rather than the overt expression of this form of totalism, a certain amount of covert identification with it on the basis of the rightists' youthfulness, sincerity of feeling, and purity of motive.

We have already mentioned some of the elements in Japanese culture which lend themselves to totalism—patterns of abolute self-negation and exaggerated dependency in relation to a deified human matrix. But there are also important cultural elements which resist totalism: a long-standing tolerance toward diverse influences from the outside; a distrust for things which are immoderate or forced (*muri*); a general acceptance of bodily functions and an attraction to the sensual pleasures of this "floating world" (*ukiyo*); and the more recent disillusionment with chauvinistic nationalism and an attraction toward (if only partial comprehension of) moderate democratic patterns. Moreover, what G. B. Sansom refers to as the great sensitivity of the Japanese to the surfaces of existence tends to give a hysterical rather than a profound or totalistic quality to Japanese expressions of extremism.

The second great problem, that of "moral backsliding," involves giving up one's ideals in order to make one's peace with organized society (as we saw in the case of Kondo), and reflects a long-standing Japanese tendency known as *tenkō. Tenkō* means conversion, a form of about-face, and usually suggests surrendering one's integrity in order to merge with a greater power. In this sense, every youth is expected to have, and every youth expects to have, an experience of *tenkō* on graduating from his university and "entering society," and this is sometimes compared with the *tenkō* of intellectuals who gave up Marxist and democratic ideals during the 1930's to embrace some version of *kokutai.* Thus *tenkō* is basic to Japanese psychology: it reflects patterns of aesthetic romanticism, obscurantism, and often shallow experimentation with ideals prior to *tenkō* itself; and it also reflects the ultimate need felt by most Japanese to submit and become part of existing authority, to gain a safe place in a human matrix, rather than risk standing alone. Young Japanese go back on their ideals because their society virtually forces them to; but their own emotional inclinations contribute to this "self-betrayal."

Yet much of what I have described may be understood as youth's efforts to resist *tenkō* and to acquire a new form of integrity. Without and within, their struggle is no easy one. But they bring to it a special intensity that has long characterized their culture.

It is their intensity which helps one, when working with Japanese youth, to think more vividly about general principles. And from this study I believe it is possible to attempt a few general formulations on the relationship between youth and history.

Historical change is not in its most elemental sense brought about by "technology" or "science"; it is human in origin, a product of creative and destructive expressions of the human organism. We have said that the gap between the generations supplies a basic psychological substrate for historical change. But there would be no generational gap—that is, every son would think, feel and do as his father did—were it not for another psychological tendency: the inherent urge toward exploration and change, which is part of the growth process and exists side by side with the more conservative human tendency to hold on to old emotional patterns and adapt to things as they are. The urge toward change becomes closely linked with man's efforts to master his physical environment; it is the source of the ideas, discoveries, and technologies, which in themselves exert so great an effect in reshaping man's experimental world that their own human origins are obscured and often forgotten. The more rapid the over-all process, the greater the generational gap—or, one might say, the shorter the time required for a "new generation" (a youth group with new attitudes) to appear.

Young people in their late teens and early twenties are central to this process, not because they make great historical decisions or discover great truths, but because they feel most intensely the generational gap and the inner urge toward change. At an age when self must be created or defined and identity discovered, their strong response to ideals and ideologies produces pressures toward change—sometimes constant, sometimes explosive—in all societies. (I suspect that even in "primitive" or in "static" societies, careful historical study would reveal evidence of the generational gap and the inherent urge toward change, however these may have been suppressed by techniques of "initiation" into existing patterns of adult life.) In our present era social change has been so rapid and the effects of the "second scientific revolution" so momentous that we are in the midst of universal historical dislocation. Consequently, youth experiences traditional symbols painfully; and the family representative of traditional authority, the father, tends to "disappear." Youth bands together, partly in an effort to set its own standards, partly to experience collectively ideologies that promise to bring about further change felt to be imperative, and partly in the (less conscious) effort to recover something from its own past that might lead to greater stability.

Historical change in all cultures, except those which are the vanguard of such change (now those of America and Russia), depends very greatly on outside influences, particularly on influences coming from the vanguard cultures. Gifted young people are extremely sensitive to these outside influences but are also ambivalent to them. They are attracted to their liberating elements and at the same time are fearful of having their own cultural identity overwhelmed; and their ambivalence can lead to sudden shifts from near-total embrace to near-phobic avoidance. Moreover, outward acceptance can be a means of maintaining a deeper resistance. Yet even when this is the case, these outside influences do bring about gradual changes in individual psychology. Such changes become significant when core elements of self-process within a particular culture are permitted expression in the new combination taking place.

Finally, youth's intensity in relation to the historical process gives it a particularly strong potential for totalism. This potential is most likely to be realized when young people feel hopelessly dislocated in the face of rapid and undigested historical change, and when they are convinced that their society will afford them no recognition without moral backsliding. But the capacity of young people for self-examination within a social and historical framework—sometimes exasperating in its seeming narcissism—can be an effective source of resistance to such totalism. It can also open up new possibilities in the desperate universal task of coming to grips with the ever accelerating, ever more threatening movement of history.

Teen-Age Culture in Contemporary Britain and Europe

John Barron Mays

Liverpool University

As recently as two decades ago, one would have been hard pressed to find evidence of a teen-age culture in either Britain or Europe. Today such evidence is abundant. Dr. Mays describes the contemporary youth culture and finds the determinants of its character in the structure of adult values. He suggests that where adults are uncertain about the social role that young people should have, one will find adolescenthood to be a time of ambivalence and frustration.

ABSTRACT: Youth culture of Western Europe shows marked similarities with the United States and is almost certainly a product of similar social and economic influences. In the postwar years, new problems have arisen partly as a result of the comparative affluence and security now enjoyed by greater numbers than heretofore and partly because of the pace at which these changes have occurred. Uncertainty of role and status results sometimes in an acute alienation between the generations. Repudiation of traditional values has produced rebellious behavior of an unprecedented kind, and there has been a sharp increase in violence and hooliganism among certain sections of the community. At

From *The Annals*, Vol. 338 (November 1961), pp. 22–32. Reprinted by permission of the author and The American Academy of Political and Social Science.

the same time, a tendency toward political apathy, distrust of officialdom, and the pursuit of short-term hedonistic goals are further indication of youth's fundamental dissatisfaction. In all countries, commercial interests have exploited this situation by providing a specialized teen-age market, and this has further emphasized the differing attitudes of young and elders. The literary field has witnessed a corresponding protest against "the Establishment," whereby many of the frustrations and, also, the stifled idealisms of youth have been given expression. The mingled hostility and confusion of young people presents educational agencies with a vital challenge and opportunity for constructive work.

It is generally agreed that, in those Western European societies which have attained a predominantly industrialized and urban culture there is a problem of adolescence, variously designated the teen-ager or, merely, the youth problem. It is essentially a matter of adjustment between the age groups and the generations and concerns ways in which social status and economic independence, as well as psychological security and individual autonomy, are attained by the rising generation, who, while no longer defined as children, are yet barred from the full responsibilities of adult citizenship. The behavior of some young people is considered by the older members of the society to be hostile, aggressive, and socially disruptive to a degree that was unknown before the Second World War. The consequences of this state of affairs are anxiety on the part of adults and uncertainty in the minds of youth as the two age and status groups confront each other across a deep divide of mutual alienation. Earlier physical maturation, for which there is some recent medical evidence, may also have contributed to the precocity of many young people's behavior and so further alienated the youthful from the middle-aged.

The Two Generations

Most of the people who now occupy positions of power and authority in comtemporary society grew up and were educated in the 1920's and 1930's. As they entered upon the responsibilities of adult life, they were confronted by trade recession, economic depression, and rising tension between the dichotomous ideologies of fascism and communism. Many of them, before they had cast their first vote, found themselves involved in the atrocities of total war, the very future of their culture threatened by abominable forces. When the military conflict with Nazi Germany ended, they tried to make for themselves and their young families a society free from the kinds of fears that had dominated their own youth. Peace, economic security, social welfare, and equality of opportunity were the objectives they set themselves to attain.

But the present day teen-agers who grew up in the 1940's and 1950's have no knowledge of their fathers' world. To them, mass unemployment, endemic poverty, an underprivileged majority, the obscene threat of fascism are little more than legends of the Napoleonic struggle were to our Victorian forebears. Those who have not lived through bitter years of unemployment and the agony of the Munich crisis can never know what such things mean to the older generation. We have to remember that today there are many adolescents who know next to nothing of Adolf Hitler and the Nazi mass extermination camps, or of the anguish of the Spanish Civil War, or the painful frustrations of Abyssinia. For this generation, many of our memories are like fairy tales and our excoriating experiences sound like myths. We have to face the fact that, from the 1930's to the 1950's and 1960's, there has been a social revolution and that our culture has undergone profound changes.

With slight variations, the phenomenon of conspicuous youth is to be found in every European capital. In each country there is an individual quirk of behavior or sartorial differentiation, but essentially the picture is the same. Different names—Teddy-boy, *Halbstarke, Lederjacken, Stilyagi*—epitomize similar outward manifestations of peculiarly reactive juvenile mental attitudes. The often delirious addiction to rock-and-roll has taken by storm such dissimilar capitals as London, Paris, and Moscow. Indeed, the content of contemporary youth culture knows no material boundaries.

Since the Second World War, young people have everywhere impinged forcibly on the adult consciousness. Their immense vitality and economic strength on the one hand and their inertia, uncertainty, and lack of moral purpose on the other are everywhere commented on, usually adversely, as though youth existed in a social vacuum untouched and uninfluenced by movements in the adult world. The brash ebullience and undisciplined energies of proletarian youth in contemporary Britain are perfectly reflected in the personality of Arthur Seaton, the central character in Alan Sillitoe's widely read novel of working-class life in the Midlands, *Saturday Night and Sunday Morning.* His self-assurance and assertiveness, his sexual promiscuity and easy-going amorality typify a reaction which is common among certain sections of young people in all the great European cities today. At the same time, it is fatally easy to write off youth as utterly Philistine and barbaric. In Britain, the rank and file of the Aldermaston marchers who annually demonstrate for the cause of nuclear disarmament is made up of the teen-age group. Moreover, it is general experience that girls present many less problems than boys, largely, no doubt, on account of their earlier age of marriage and the readiness with which the vast majority of them accept responsibilities for homemaking and child care in their early teens.

Every generation of parents has to face the problem of understanding its own children. Such understanding often demands a full and painful self-appraisal from which the majority of adults shrink. There is, in fact, no such thing as a "youth problem" as such. There is only the network of problems in which both young and old are simultaneously involved. That this is so can be seen by a realization that the vast majority of social work is concerned with the care of children and with the maintenance of stable family life. The two activities are inextricably interwoven and equally vital for the future welfare of our society. Neither can be understood *in vacuo* or treated in isolation.

Stresses of City Life

Children and young people are especially exposed to the stresses and strains of an urban culture and many of their problems of adjustment, including much delinquency and hooliganism, are attributable to this source. Anxiety-disposing forces operating in the general social structure include the multiplicity of choices presented to young people in all phases of their development, increasing geographical mobility of families, greater social mobility between the various income groups, the high speed of social and technical change, a confusion of ethical values, and a general climate of public opinion disposed to questioning the validity of traditional beliefs and standards. Against this kind of background, the increase in purchasing power and comparative economic security in adolescence have, in many sections of society, resulted in further instability. Young people have now obtained the freedom of action and the strength to rebel against frustrating factors in the social structure. They can no longer be ignored or brushed aside as minors and inferiors or kept in their subordinate place by threats or firm discipline. It is important to realize, too, that similar problems and stresses afflict young people of all classes and income groups alike, though possibly at differing periods of development.

It is impossible to say how far the youth cultures of contemporary Europe have been derived from American models or to what extent they are the product of indigenous influences. Certainly, in every Western country, there are similar conditioning forces at work, and it is these things which young people in Germany, France, Britain, and the United States of America have in common which are important, not their superficial local trappings.

Similarities in attitude and basic behavior clearly spring from a common state of mind which may be described as self-consciously hostile and defensive. Modern urban youth, at least a substantial section of them, want to look different from the rest of the community. They want to talk, to behave in a distinctively teen-age way. Only thus can they assert both their solidarity, one with another, and their critical disapproval of the adult world.

This is, of course, not an entirely novel situation. Young people must inevitably feel themselves, to some extent, in conflict with their parents' values and ways of living. Some kind of rebellion against authority is necessary in the process of growing up at all. Before the vessel can move under its own steam, it must cut its moorings. What is significant in European countries today, however, is the degree to which this reaction has been carried. What is remarkable is the vehemence of the gesture with which youth nowadays has repudiated the middle-aged. There are possibly pathological symptoms in the exaggerated way in which a minority of young people flaunt their difference. To mock and to shock seems to be an end in itself rather than the necessary clearing away of cant and humbug before a new resurgence of the creative spirit.

The reaction in Britain has followed somewhat less exaggerated lines than in some parts of the United States. There are not many traces in Britain of typically "beat" influences. A few young "weirds" do, from time to time, congregate in urban cellars or, astonishingly enough, at fashionable seaside resorts or in ancient country houses. But they are almost always no more than pseudo-beats, engaged in self-dramatization, rather than total rejectors of the social structure who find nothing left to live for beyond the acceptance of their own hysteria and ultimate inanity.

In Britain, it is the "Angry Young Man" rather than the "Rebel Without a Cause" who epitomizes the more serious youth's reaction to the mess and injustice which he has inherited from his elders. It is the playwright Arnold Wesker or the poet Christopher Logue, rather than James Dean, who reflects youth's sharp rebellion here, and theirs is an intellectual and esthetic revolt as much as anything else. Logue, indeed, is closer to Shelley than to Lipton. Logue's period in prison, his gun-running career and subsequent cashiering from the Army, and his spell on National Assistance are the melodramatic episodes in an essentially poetic, hence creative, career.

The Angries in England have engaged in a war against the sham façade that masks reality, while the beatniks seem to be more concerned with rejecting a way of life which appears to them to be totally sham and corrupt. The Angries are social reformers rather than world-rejectors. This description hardly seems to fit the genuine hysteria of Venice West. But, undoubtedly, the "angry" movement in Britain has been an intellectual and artistic resurgence as much as a desire to throw the whole of our society overboard. Indeed, writers like John Osborne who protested and derided their way to the top of the tree have adjusted very easily to their early affluence and prestige. Theirs is the old story of the literary *coup d'état* which usually paves the way for a new and different kind of intellectual establishment.

Social Work with Youth

In Britain, the Youth Service has been developed as a part of the informal education of young people between the ages of fourteen and twenty to enable them to make the best use of their adolescent years.[1] By and large, both the statutory and voluntary youth work has been born of middle-class unease over the apparent aimlessness and potential aggression of working-class and lower income group youngsters. It has aimed at providing them with creative outlooks for energies which might otherwise be channeled into antisocial activities and is essentially a bureaucratic response intended to palliate the social strains generated by class differences. It is generally conceived as something which the community as a whole does for its young people.

In recent years, there has been an interesting reaction on the part of a small section of young people against this somewhat patronizing attitude. Spontaneous groups of teen-agers have combined to run their own organizations, meeting their specific teen-age needs in ways that

[1] *The Youth Service in England and Wales*, H.M.S.O. 1960, Cmnd. 929.

are satisfying to them rather than to educationalists who have hitherto monopolized youth work. The promoters of these clubs which are run by teen-agers strictly for teen-agers claim to epitomize adolescent culture. They talk of restoring the genitive case to youth work, of making it truly the service of youth by providing the kind of physical setting and freedom of activity more akin to the students' union of a university than to the orthodox club.[2] Here, in a relaxed atmosphere, they can jive and rock, enjoy coffee and cuddles, or merely sit broodily staring at blank walls or at avant-garde murals.

Antisocial Behavior

In Britain, as elsewhere, much attention has been focused upon the unattached adolescent. It is estimated that not more than one third of all boys and girls between the ages of fourteen and twenty are members of acknowledged organizations. The unattached who patronize the coffee bars, who occasionally take to drugs, and who are sometimes involved in outbursts of inexplicable violence keep on hitting the headlines. A further source of anxiety is the juvenile suicide rate, which includes all social classes and which has more than doubled for the seventeen to twenty age group in recent years. Sexual experience in the fullest sense in the premarriage period is also on the increase, as is demonstrated by the Registrar General's 1958 statistics, which showed that the number of mothers between the ages of twelve and sixteen (before the legal age of consent, that is to say) has doubled over the past twenty years. It remains, however, a comparatively negligible, proportion of live births. Nevertheless, the trend is upward and in the wrong direction.

Hooliganism, insofar as such a term can be defined, also seems to be more common than it used to be. Vandalism on railways has been a feature in certain parts of the country. Stones and debris have been thrown at locomotives, injuring the drivers, and blocks and obstacles capable of causing derailment have been deliberately placed on the tracks. Even undergraduate rag days have, in some university towns, attained a degree of rowdiness and violence hitherto unknown and have led, in some cases, to court proceedings.

There is a general belief that the present generation of young people in all European countries is more antisocial than its predecessors. Juvenile delinquency is almost everywhere thought to be on the increase, new forms of criminal behavior having developed in response to new opportunities, of which the increase in motoring offenses is a notable example. Juvenile crime in Britain—that is to say, reported crimes known to have been committed by those over eight years but under eighteen—has more than doubled since 1938. This is, in fact, a typical situation throughout Western Europe.

Drug addiction among teen-agers is more common, although, compared with the United States, the problem in Britain is minimal and is

[2]Ray Gosling, *Lady Albemarle's Boys*, a Young Fabian publication (London: Fabian Society, 1961).

confined to a few of the more decadent areas of the big cities, especially London. Drunkenness is also more extensive among the seventeen to twenty-one age group than ever before, and the increase in crimes of violence among the same section of the juvenile population—who, significantly, were born during the war years—is notable.

Ganging is associated with the rowdier elements of urban youth, although there is no reason to believe that this phenomenon is more extensive or more serious than it used to be. English juvenile gangs, on the whole, are not highly organized, nor is there a striking uniformity of character or motive in those youths who consort together for comparatively short periods during the time of their adolescent difficulties. Such gangs as exist usually frequent regular meeting places in coffee bars, pubs, cafés, or, occasionally, in vacant buildings and ruins. More organized groups are to be found in specific districts in London called "manors." Affrays between gangs occur, especially at dance halls, and it is clear on such occasions that outlets for violent behavior are sought for their own sake.

It is not uncommon for groups of twenty and more city boys, sometimes with girls in tow, to arm themselves with knives, bicycle chains, studded belts, and even cut-throat razors and to sally forth by bus, taxi, private car, and motor bike to dance halls fifty miles away with the express purpose of seeking out the local youth gangs and provoking a fight. On a less dramatic scale, groups of boys on foot come together and wander about the cities looking for mischief and fun or, in their words, "kicks," wherever such opportunities are to be found.

It is natural for the adult members of the community to be alarmed by such manifestations of lawlessness and apparent social alienation. But the problem can be exaggerated, and it is important to remember that it is phasic in character, that the vast majority of young people do not find it necessary to express themselves in such melodramatic and negativistic ways, and that, even of those who do, only a fraction are so psychologically disturbed that their bad behavior lasts beyond the teen-age period.

The majority of those who rebel in this period would, given adequate support and firm but sympathetic leadership, adjust to their growing-up problems in socially acceptable ways. But the failure of older members of the community, especially of parents and educators, to give them adequate support, makes them temporarily easy victims for the illegal promptings of a handful of seriously maladjusted and emotionally disturbed instigators.

Although such pathological symptoms are confined to only a small proportion of young people, many observers find them indices of the fundamental malaise of modern industrial society. Richard Hoggart[3] speaks of "a sort of spiritual dry rot amid the odour of boiled milk" afflicting contemporary youth, and, to Dr. Kurt Hahn,[4] they are symptomatic of the five great decays of modern life: decay of physical fitness, of self-discipline, of enterprise, of skill, and of human compas-

[3] *The Uses of Literacy* (London: Penguin Books, 1958), p. 204.
[4] *The Observer*, London, November 13th, 1960.

sion. Indications of mass hysteria are to be found in the wild, unrestrained adulation of pop singers and the mushroom growths of fan clubs. The new pin-up is not a seminude dancer but an attractive proletarian male with a mournful face, wearing open-neck shirt and leather jacket, or even a plump young rock-and-roller in his pajama bottoms.

The Teen-Age Market

There undeniably is much adult stimulation behind the teen-age cult. That this is sometimes of a nature to encourage an undesirable precocity of behavior can be seen in the advertisements for brassieres for ten-year-old girls which are to be found in some periodicals and shops and in a general willingness to stimulate the sexual appetite by stressing glamor and man-appeal to promote the sales of certain kinds of articles. Commercial entertainment promoters plug adolescent tastes and thereby help to fixate them. The fantasy of the new status group of youth, idealization of both revolt and despair, the encouragement of promiscuous sexual activity on an experimental basis—known to teen-agers as "having sex"—are recurring themes in the media young people seem to enjoy.

For the first time in British history, the adolescent age group has enough purchasing power to make them a worth-while market for commercial exploitation. Mark Abrams has recently shown that the age group fifteen to twenty-five, which in 1959 contained approximately five million unmarried youths, after putting aside £70 millions as savings, spent some £830 millions a year.[5] While this does not comprise a very substantial proportion of the nation's consumer expenditure, it nevertheless is a new phenomenon.

In prewar days, the youth market was negligible and not worth exploiting, but, since the war, teen-age incomes have, in fact, risen faster than adults'. Moreover, there are some fields of spending in which young people's custom is vital for sustained prosperity. The clothing, cosmetics, and soft drinks markets, together with the cinema industry and gramophone record trade, depend to a considerable extent upon adolescent affluence. Mark Abrams has calculated that the average unmarried male in the age group has about 71/6d. a week free spending money left over after his basic commitments have been met, while a female has rather less, about 54/-. Generalizing, Abrams says that "the quite large amount of money at the disposal of Britain's average teen-ager is spent mainly on dress and on goods which form the nexus of teen-age gregariousness outside the home. In other words, this is distinctive teen-age spending for distinctive teen-age ends in a distinctive teen-age world."[6]

Until recently, the British teen-age market was almost entirely working class. Because in prewar days the teen-age market virtually did not exist, commercial promoters had no experience of the appropriate

---

[5]Mark Abrams, *The Teen-age Consumer* (London: London Press Exchange Ltd., 1959).
[6]Mark Abrams, *op. cit.*, p. 10.

ways for milking adolescent affluence and had to turn to the United States for their models. And it is still valid in 1960 to characterize the teen-age culture and market as predominantly proletarian in style. But there are indications that children of higher income group families are coming under the same influences and that, for the first time, middle-class culture finds itself under strong pressure to change from what is a predominantly working-class way of life. Even boys in grammar schools sometimes favor Edwardian and Italian clothes styles, frequent soft drink bars, adore pop music, and spend their evenings drifting around with peer group members in loosely knit gangs. Similar influences, at least in regard to dress, speech, and behavior are also discernible in some British universities, especially in the provinces.

Teen-age male spending is considerably greater than female spending, but there is very little difference between working-class and middle-class boys, the former having slightly more pocket money. A substantial gap, however, exists between working-class and middle-class girls. The latter have, on the average, a third more than their proletarian counterparts. As far as the pattern of spending goes, young people of all classes and both sexes show a marked similarity: Clothing and footwear take the major slice, followed by food, transportation, drinks (soft and hard), cigarettes, and entertainment.[7] It is certainly not a picture of either complete recklessness or utter depravity; it is merely one of personal indulgence, which seems to follow closely the general attitude of the time which counsels us to enjoy ourselves to the limit of our means while we can—the attitude, indeed, appropriate to an age nurtured in comparative affluence and shielded against utter calamity by welfare services.

At the same time, there is a monotony in the endless round of juvenile social life and teen-age culture. Music and dancing, the semitribalistic, drugging, modern jives and jitters, dressing up, experimenting sexually are all no doubt activities which meet genuine adolescent needs, but there is a lack, in the lower social groups in particular, of what, for want of a better term, we may call intellectual stimulation. In small towns and suburbs much time is spent in milk-bars and cafés listening to the jukebox in mild and mindless dissipation. Theirs is a life of sensations rather than of thoughts. The world of art, literature, and social thinking pass most of these young people by or, as they would say, leave them cold. Again we may point to Arthur Seaton in *Saturday Night and Sunday Morning* as the type of youthful Philistine amoralist who never reads a serious book, enjoys a high material standard of living, but is a complete sensualist.

Education

The shorter working week, longer holidays, and greater security have not produced an upsurge of interest in education. Very many working-class children leave grammar schools at the earliest possible

[7]Mark Abrams, *op. cit.*, pp. 10–11.

age without following the full four-year course leading to the General Certificate Examination.[8] What we may call the pursuit of banality characterizes many working-class youngsters' lives. While bourgeois children may apply themselves more seriously to study, it is often solely with a view to gaining the necessary credentials to admit them to the more lucrative and higher status jobs. The cult of enjoyment and security, at one stage removed, lies behind much British educational endeavor. Education is a means to greater luxury rather than a preparation for "the good life." It has suffered severely from "bourgeoisification" in recent years.

In contemporary Britain, the treatment and training of adolescents varies strikingly between the classes. Parents who can afford to do so tend to send their children to private schools where they stay until seventeen, eighteen, or even nineteen.

The so-called "public" boarding schools, which are, in fact, exclusive and private, are still in great demand and have actually extended their influence since the end of the last war. In these schools, the children of the upper classes live segregated and highly specialized lives. Boys are not encouraged to consort with girls and vice versa. In some British public schools, talking to members of the opposite sex is still regarded as a breach of discipline dealt with by corporal punishment. The prefect, and its allied fagging system, is still widely enforced, permitting bullying of juniors by seniors. The older pupils attain higher status and prestige through this system and, in this way, are encouraged to remain conformists. Petty regulations are made for the express purpose of enforcing control by discipline and tradition. Games are compulsory. Much time is spent in chapel and in preparing for confirmation in the Church of England. The concept of manliness is emphasized, and there is much concern about team spirit and the qualities of leadership.

Public school education solves the problem of protracted dependency and extended adolescence by creating an artificial youth culture in which the young person is segregated from the opposite sex and the lower social classes until he is on the brink of manhood. He is then transferred to a university, preferably Oxford or Cambridge, where most well-known schools have foundation scholarships and where, once again, he is made a member, albeit this time with greater privileges and much more freedom, of a specialized, highly favored, and altogether artificial community until such time as he is ready to take an appointment in the civil service or train for management in his uncle's factory.

This picture is admittedly an extreme one. There are some private schools, even of the boarding variety, which have reacted against the typically Spartan system of the traditional English public school and where young people are enabled to develop their personalities and their talents in a free and more realistic atmosphere.

Many middle-class and most lower-middle-class children are educated at free Local Authority or at the older locally endowed grammar schools and are, thus, in a position to live at home and to mix in a

[8] *Early Leaving*, a report of the Central Advisory Council for Education (England), H.M.S.O., 1954, pp. 18–19.

more heterogeneous community. Those who are able to pass the General Certificate Examination at advanced level often pass on to universities, usually the newer red-brick provincial variety, and train for professional and similar high status careers.

But the children of the wage-earners, although they have in increasing numbers since 1944 entered the local authority grammar schools, are still, in the main, educated at secondary modern schools only until the age of fifteen. These schools, which cater to some 70 per cent of the nation's children, are usually nonvocational in character and tend not to take any external examinations, with the result that former students are neatly barred from entering the more influential and better paid fields of employment. They usually take the skilled, semiskilled, and unskilled manual jobs. The educational system, therefore, tends to reinforce and perpetuate class divisions and to reproduce two main social groups with different cultures and life chances who confront one another in mutual incomprehension and distaste.

Middle- and upper-class children are, therefore, protected during their adolescence from many of the stresses of modern life. As members of a social and educational elite, they are groomed for a future which is both attractive and realizable, whereas the children of less fortunate homes are faced very often with conflict, anxiety, and uncertainty resulting from the rapidly changing pattern of social and economic organization.[9] They leave school at fifteen to take jobs in industry or the retail trades where, all too often, no adult has time or responsibility to supervise their adjustment to the strains of the new life of the adult world. Frequently, the actual work is dull, repetitive, lacking prospects, although the pay may be adequate enough. As a result, the young worker tends to live for his off-duty hours when he can revel in the compensations of those uncreative banal amusements so conveniently provided for his delectation by people whose only concern is to profit from his predicament.

The working-class boy is, thus, especially subjected to stresses and temptation during his adolescent working years. Girls, by comparison, see a different road ahead of them, a way leading, after a brief wage-earning and money-saving period, to marriage, homemaking, and maternity. But, for the boy, the whole future depends on what happens to him in the years immediately following the end of formal education.

The Youth Employment Bureaus, usually attached to Local Education Authorities in Britain, endeavor to give some vocational guidance and also to operate a rudimentary after-care service for those who have recently left school. All too often, however, the youth employment officers find it a difficult task to do more than place children in jobs offering reasonable remuneration, whether or not they are really suitable for the type of work involved. It is not uncommon to find that even their minimal services are declined by children and parents alike and that their advice is ignored.

---

[9]For a fuller exposition of this theme in the context of contemporary British society, see *Education and the Urban Child*, ed. Professor T. S. Simey (Social Research Series; Liverpool: Liverpool University Press, 1961).

Conclusion

From the foregoing, it should be clear that youth as a period of social and psychological development presents serious problems in all Western European societies and that these are, in origin though probably not in degree, similar to those encountered in American society. They arise primarily from the uncertainty of adults regarding the role that young people should be given in the life of the community. As a result of this uncertainty, which communicates itself like electricity to youth itself, young people are often confused and ambivalent about their own status. They are forced into experimentation, which is often disastrous and usually offensive to the older members of the community. The pace at which changes have occurred in recent years has caught young and old off balance; parents are particularly vulnerable to the doubts, indecisions, and anxieties to which changed economic conditions and the dissemination of psychological notions have exposed them. At the same time that some of the attributes of maturity have been granted to young people, there is also a contrary tendency to extend the period of dependency in other directions to a later age. The adolescent period of the teen-age covers roughly a decade, and, to many minds, this is unduly prolonged. And, behind the greater economic security and increased welfare that, as a result of the general leveling process, all sections of society enjoy, there is also the shadow of the bomb and total war, which, while it may not figure very largely in the minds of young people themselves, foments a general psychological climate of anxiety and despair. In a time when moral values are everywhere challenged, discussed, and denied, childhood and youth inevitably become times of deep perplexity and instability. Only in the English public schools is an effort made to hold the environment fixed and certain, in tune more with an age which has forever gone, and, because of its very unreality, it is questionable whether such an educational setting can train men capable of coping successfully with the even more rapidly changing conditions that face civilization in the second half of the twentieth century.[10]

Elsewhere, there are significant indications of the doubt, cynicism, and despair, a distrust of politics, and an acceptance of purely materialistic and hedonistic goals, especially among young people in prosperous Western Germany, which have made this present age one of supreme educational challenge. Rebellion and disaffection in youth is at once a hopeful and a disturbing condition. It is the task of education in the widest sense of that term to promote and regulate social change, and to do this successfully means, among other things, assisting young people to rebel against certain unworthy aspects of the social structure without, however, encouraging moral deviation. At the same time, it must ensure their allegiance to the fundamental philosophy which is the foundation of our civilization and which should, in theory at least, inspire every permanent social institution.

---

[10]See A. D. C. Peterson, *Educating Our Rulers* (London: Duckworth, 1951), especially pp. 51–63.

Communist Chinese and the American Adolescent Subcultures

Lucy Jen Huang Hickrod
and G. Alan Hickrod

What has the Communist Chinese adolescent in common with the American adolescent? How do they differ? The authors compare Chinese with American adolescence, each within the context of its culture. Thus this article examines aspects of Communist Chinese society and American society. The former is a subject of which most Americans are totally ignorant; the latter subject is one about which most Americans are confused. This article provides an incisive, though not necessarily comforting, analysis of how societies shape their youth.

Sociological research on Communist China is severely limited by the fact that western-trained sociologists, at least those traveling on an American passport, are not permitted to enter, let alone practice on, the mainland of China. Consequently, the standard techniques of the journeyman sociologist, the case method, questionaires, interviews, nonparticipant observation, etc., cannot be used at present. In such a situation social scientists have had to fall back upon the translation and analysis of documents issued on the mainland and intended by their authors for internal, rather than external, consumption. Whenever possible this technique is supplemented by the results of interviews conducted with emigrés from the mainland. The senior author has used this technique elsewhere to describe changes occurring in the structure and function of the Chinese family under Communism.[1] It should be admitted that such an approach is open to the charge that the primary data are biased: that is, that the research runs the risk of confusing behavioral reality with the image that the régime wishes to convey in its internal publications. There are two answers to this. First, the internal publications include a good deal of "self-criticism" which is likely to contain other than propaganda elements, and secondly, direct empirical observations are neither feasible nor possible under present conditions. The use of emigré data is probably more suspect, since those who flee the regime are likely to be biased in their interpretations of regime policies and actions. Any type of social science research which attempts to deal

From *The China Quarterly*, No. 22 (1965). Reprinted by permission of the publisher.

[1]Lucy Jen Huang, *The Impact of the Commune on the Chinese Family*, a monograph published by General Electric Co., Santa Barbara, California, December 1962; "Some Changing Patterns in the Communist Chinese Family," *Marriage and Family Living*, May 1961; "The Communist Chinese Attitude Towards Inter-Class Marriage," *The China Quarterly*, October-December 1962; "A Re-Evaluation of the Primary Role of the Communist Chinese Woman: The Home-maker or the Worker," *Marriage and Family Living*, May 1963; "The Problem Child and Delinquent Youth in the Communist Chinese Family," *Marriage and Family Living*, November 1963.

with a totalitarian society, be it sociological, economic or political, is open to similar criticisms. The purpose of this article is to present information concerning adolescent and student behavior under Communist rule, subject to the aforesaid limitations, contrasting it with certain aspects of American adolescent and student behavior.

Role Models In Education

Wilber Brookover, W. W. Charters, Jr., and Neal Gross have urged that research be undertaken in the United States to describe the process by which teachers in the American public schools are perceived as "models" by their students. It is thought likely that several aspects of student behavior may be explainable on the basis of the perceived image of these "significant others."[2] Gross has pointed out that there may be a plurality of models depending on the reference group orientation, self-concept and actual group memberships of each teacher.[3] This "plural model" situation is noticeably lacking in Communist China. There, the model is a carefully constructed bundle of values, goals and norms, believed by the dominant social organization, the Communist Party, to be useful in furthering the aims of its ideological movement. The solution of all social problems is thought to lie in the successful emulation of certain virtures possessed by the Communist cadres and activists, including teachers at all levels of formal education. The veneration of the scholar in pre-Communist China has made the education system a particularly potent asset for the Communist Party.

Techniques used to control delinquency and to maintain discipline in the classrooms in China are particularly revealing. To cope with these problems, ingenious teachers of grade school pupils often report using the approach of role identification. Famous heroes and heroines of the past and present are cited as shining examples for emulation. One teacher, when faced with forty-eight sixth graders with various emotional and behavioral problems, decided to use the hero-worship approach. She took them to visit the tombs of famous Communist martyrs and told stories about them. They brought flowers and pledged before their heroes' graves that they would strive to become deserving members of the Young Pioneers as well as better students. Many were said to be "in tears."[4] Another teacher, after finding out that five of her pupils stole and picked people's pockets, prescribed a book entitled *My Whole Family* which consisted of the heroic deeds of a patriotic woman in Communist China.[5] Yet another teacher was successful in changing the delinquent ways of her incorrigible pupil "Tiger Meng" by giving him texts to read such as "Not a Moment's Rest from Work,"

---

[2]See Wilber Brookover, "Teachers and the Stratification of American Society," *Harvard Educational Review*, Fall 1953; Neal Gross, "A Critique of Social Class Structure and American Education," *Harvard Educational Review*, Fall 1953; W. W. Charters, Jr., "The Social Background of Teaching," N. L. Gage, *Handbook of Research on Teaching* (New York: Rand-McNally, 1963).

[3]Gross, *op. cit.*

[4]Ting Chih-siu, "Plant Red Seeds During Childhood," *Women of China*, No. 12, December 1961.

[5]*Women of China*, No. 18, September 1958.

passages lauding the tireless worker who would not waste a moment's time because he was "building the motherland."[6] Sentiments such as those expressed in the article, "Foster the Next Revolutionary Generation in Co-ordination with School Education" run through most of the major editorials of newspapers and magazines in China.[7] There can be little doubt in the minds of Communist Chinese youth which role model to emulate in this process of growing up. The effort exerted by the Communist Party in all areas of life provides a consistent and clear-cut role model for all citizens, especially the youths.

By contrast, American youth appear to be caught in a rather complicated role-conflict situation. Robert Herriott has described this in terms of a "parent-school-peer" influence triangle.[8] Furthermore, the dominant force in this triangle appears to change from one decision-making situation to the next. Wilson and Rogoff have described the effect of differing community influences upon educational aspirations of youth.[9] Different role models are presumably being held up for emulation in different American communities. The findings of Ellis and Lane suggest that the emulation of role models varies among different socioeconomic classes of students and among different levels of academic ability.[10] Contrary to the more pessimistic position of some students of sociology of education,[11] it would appear that some teachers may be rather effective in shaping the aspirational levels of at least the more academically able portions of lower socioeconomic youth. However, the effect of this may be to increase the conflict between either the home-role, the peer-role, or both, and the school-role of the students involved. Studies bearing on this matter appear often in the journals and the details of the general process will doubtless be clearer in the future. The over-all impression, however, is one of a relatively high level of role-conflict for a sizeable number of students. The "mixed-up-kid" may prove to be more than simply an American slang term.

Continuity Versus Discontinuity Between Adolescent and Adult Roles

In societies characterized by a high degree of technological development it would appear that discontinuities between adolescent and adult roles are more likely to occur than in societies at less advanced stages of production. Longer and longer periods of formal education are needed to equip youth to take their positions in the labor force of the more complicated societies. Technological change in these socie-

[6]Chang Dien-er, "Little Tiger Meng Has Changed," *Women of China*, No. 16, August 1959, page 7.

[7]*Jen-min Jih-pao (People's Daily)*, January 2, 1962.

[8]Robert Herriott, "Some Social Determinants of Educational Aspiration," *Harvard Educational Review*, Spring 1963.

[9]Alan B. Wilson, "Residential Segregation of Social Classes and Aspirations of High School Boys," *American Sociological Review*, December 1959, and Natalie Rogoff, "Local Social Structure and Educational Selection," in Floud and Anderson Halsey, *Education, Economy, and Society* (Glencoe: Free Press, 1961).

[10]Robert Ellis and W. Clayton Lane, "Structural Supports for Upward Mobility," *American Sociological Review*, October 1963.

[11]Robert A. Bell, "Social Class Values and the Teacher," in R. A. Bell (ed.) *The Sociology of Education: A Sourcebook* (Homewood, Illinois: Dorsey Press, 1962).

ties also dictates that youth will more often than not take work roles unlike those of their fathers and mothers. Furthermore, the need for a flexible labor force presumably necessitates broad layers of general knowledge upon which additional layers of specialized knowledge are superimposed. One aspect of this latter problem is the discontinuity between the classroom task of the student and the work role task of the adult. Coleman has made some suggestions for reducing this "role gap" through the introduction of what amounts to "game theory" in teaching methodology.[12] Discontinuity between adolescent and adult roles springs also from sociological and psychological sources as well as the particular stage of economic development of a country. There is a considerable literature on this point with notable contributions by Benedict, Parsons, Davis and others.[13] The transition of American youth from adolescent to adult is therefore apt to be abrupt and disturbing for a number of socioeconomic reasons. Bloch and Niederhoffer believe this to be one of the major elements in juvenile delinquency.[14]

By contrast, the Communist Chinese youth has an easier transition, since the ideals of a good citizen apply to youth as well as to older citizens. In prescribing ideal characteristics of a citizen under the Communist regime, the leaders have proclaimed a five-fold model called the "Wu Hao"[15] citizen. Every Communist citizen is encouraged to cultivate the "five good" roles: Good worker or producer, good neighbor, good scholar or student, advocate of good health and advocate of good life. These ideal roles are not only for adults to perform but also for the young to emulate, for men as well as for women. In the role of a good producer, the adult may serve as an office worker, farmer, laborer, tradesman or militiaman while the adolescent and the child may function in a supporting role, such as weed picker or manure collector in the rural area or a helper in the family sideline occupations, such as planting trees or raising pigs. Young students are expected to study as hard as advanced scholars, and adults are encouraged to perform well in their night classes and spare-time schools as well. In the role of an advocate for good health, hygiene and sanitation, the young Chinese are encouraged to help in such efforts at home as well as in school. As a part of sanitation movements, organizations from all walks of life launch clean up campaigns simultaneously. *Women of China* often publishes cartoons showing kindergarten pupils on their way to school with a satchel on the shoulder, each of them carrying a fly swatter in one hand and a sling shot in the other, helping the nation to get rid of flies and grain-eating sparrows. This journal once printed a story concerning a tired father, arriving home from a long day at the office. He asked his young son to kill 200 flies for him to take to the office the next day as his assignment. His son informed him that in his grade

---

[12]James S. Coleman, *The Adolescent Society* (Glencoe: Free Press, 1961).

[13]Ruth Benedict, "Continuities and Discontinuities in Cultural Conditioning," *Psychiatry*, No. 1, 1938; Talcott Parsons. "Age and Sex in the Social Structure of the United States," *American Sociological Review*. No. 7, 1942; and Kingsley Davis, "Adolescence and the Social Structure," and "Causes of Parent-Youth Conflict" in Kingsley Davis, Harry C. Predmeier, and Marion J. Levy, Jr., (eds.) *Modern American Society* (New York: Holt, Rinehart, and Winston, 1947).

[14]Herbert A. Bloch and A. Niederhoffer, *The Gang, A Study in Adolescent Behavior* (Philosophical Library, 1958).

[15]*Women of China*, January 1956, p. 17.

school he had the same assignment, and that he could not complete the assignment for both. The regime's movement to combine study with labor for all age groups allows a smooth transition of roles from adolescence to adulthood. Qualities of a good neighbor and that of an advocate for good life can be cultivated in all ages, at all times: Attributes such as thrift and simplicity, helpfulness and unselfishness, can also be cultivated among all groups at all times. Deviation from such ideal "virtues" is often described in enemy image terms such as "capitalistic" or "reactionary," which are proclaimed to be the cause of all personal and social problems. From juvenile delinquency[16] to extreme individualism, from spousal estrangement[17] to interclass marital adjustments,[18] cultivation of the "Wu Hao" model is presumed to "cure" everything. The prescribed socialist morality and Communist ideology represent the major values and attitudes for all "good" citizens, preferred roles for all, adolescents or adults. The similarity between the "Wu Hao" model and the major role model presented in the literature of the Calvinistic theocracy of early New England is striking and obvious. Communist Chinese and Puritan parallels can be found in thrift, hard work, simple attire, deligent scholarship and a number of other social characteristics.

The technological aspects of this situation are worth emphasizing. In the advanced society fertilizer, D.D.T. and construction equipment all reduce the amount of labor that little unskilled hands can do. The automobile removes the delivery boy on his bicycle from the local scene. Mechanized farm equipment replaces the after-school "chores" of the farmer's son. The high school lad finds that his summer jobs have begun to disappear. Finally, the high school graduate finds that post-high school education is needed simply to gain a full-time position with more than a modest wage attached to it. To be sure, this development provides certain social benefits. The economy can forgo larger and larger amounts of labor by teen-agers. If this time is well invested then there should be considerable social gains. Observers of the American educational process, however, pointing to a presumed "fun orientation" in American high schools have at least implied that this "released time" an advanced economy has available is perhaps not being well invested.

The Student Subculture: Fun Oriented Versus Service Oriented

Discontinuity between adult and adolescent roles is believed to be so great in the United States that student "subcultures" are said to exist: groups, that is, which exhibit values and norms sufficiently different from the larger society as to exert an independent force on the behav-

---

[16]Lucy Jen Huang, "The Problem Child and Delinquent Youth in the Communist Chinese Family," *Marriage and Family Living*, November 1963.

[17]Lucy Jen Huang, "Some Changing Patterns in the Communist Chinese Family," *ibid.* May 1961.

[18]Lucy Jen Huang, "The Communist Chinese Attitude Towards Inter-class Marriage," *The China Quarterly*, October-December 1962.

ior of their members. Burton Clark, building on the work of Martin Trow, has presented a typology for both college and high school student groups.[19] Four types of college subcultures are identified: a "nonconformist" group which is deviant, bohemian and intellectually oriented but somewhat undisciplined; an "academic" group, which balances social activities with intellectual pursuits; a "vocational" group which is interested in acquiring job skills as quickly and painlessly as possible; and the "collegiate" group, which emphasizes football, husband-hunting, beer busts, panty raids and other such extracurricular activities of the American undergraduate. David Gottlieb has demonstrated the predictive power of a typology of this kind with respect to college achievement and has made some interesting comments about differences in life styles, reference groups and other factors, among these subcultures.[20] The high school subcultures are reduced to an "academically oriented" subculture made up of conscientious and responsible students; a "fun subculture," interested in hot-rodding, disc-jockey parties, school athletics, most popular girl contest and cheerleadership; and a "delinquent subculture," the switchblade, black jacket, junk-pushing group. As Clark notes, it is not at present possible to state which of these groups dominates American secondary education, except that the delinquent group probably does not, save under central city slum conditions. Different schools are likely to be dominated by different subcultures. With reference to this Havighurst has suggested a socioeconomic index to measure the socioeconomic status of a particular school district.[21] The degree to which student subcultures can be predicted or described by "objective" social class measurements and the degree to which they must be approached via attitudinal research would, however, appear to be moot at this point.

Even before the Communist regime, Chinese children were brought up quite differently from Americans. Other than being younger than adults and older than babies, the pre-Communist Chinese adolescents did not stand out as possessing values and norms different from the adult years. The young, children and adolescents, were given household chores to perform according to their physical capacity to assist adults in the family. The traditional Chinese respect and deference for elders required the younger generation to assume a role of relative obedience and submission to the will of parents and teachers. Adulthood to the average Chinese children of pre-Communist days represented freer and more independent years, if not happier. Most Chinese children probably wished silently to grow up quickly.

One may say that the average pre-Communist Chinese childhood and adolescence was a miniature adult existence, only less privileged and more suppressed. The transition from pre-Communist to Communist values in child rearing and education has been characterized by several stages. During the initial period of readjustment to the Social-

[19]Burton Clark, *Educating the Expert Society* (San Francisco: Chandler, 1963).

[20]David Gottlieb and Benjamin Hodgkins, "College Student Subcultures: Their Structures and Characteristics in Relation to Student Attitude Change," *School Review*, Autumn 1963.

[21]Robert J. Havighurst and Bernice L. Newgarten, *Society and Education,* 2nd ed. (Chicago: Allyn and Bacon, 1962), Chapter XIII.

ist indoctrination and the anti-rightist and anti-landlord movements, many young men and women were encouraged to persuade their parents to confess their past guilt and reform. "During the Five-Anti movement in 1952 in Shanghai over 600 members of the New Democratic Youth League in Futan University were pressured into going home to persuade family members to confess their crimes."[22] Thousands of other young men and women students followed their example and attempted to persuade their parents to confess, exposing them to the government should they refuse. Cases[23] of the younger generation denouncing their parents were to be found often in books, press and periodicals during the first few years of the Communist regime, showing at times a nightmarish picture of parent-youth relationships. During the mid-1950s leaders of the regime began to show concern over the momentum which the Five-Anti movement had started. Articles[24] appeared warning the younger generation, especially the adolescents, from being too unfilial and harsh with their "backward" or "capitalistic" parents. There has since been a revival or re-emphasis of Confucian ethics governing the new Communist family relationships. The younger generation has been under the constant guidance and supervision of adults under Communist Party indoctrination, a task in which parents, teachers, organization leaders and commune directors of the city and countryside all participate. Thus during this early period it might be said that a revolutionary student subculture existed and that it was necessary for the regime to take a hand in curtailing its excesses.

Press and magazine articles of the 1960s have revealed a strong Party policy aimed at making Communist Chinese adolescents and children "useful" members of the nation. Articles entitled "Educate Your Children to be Heirs of Communism,"[25] "Inculate in Children the Yenan Work Style of Arduous Struggle,"[26] "Over 600 Students of Department of Physics, Chungshan University, Participate in Labor and Actual Struggle in the Countryside and Receive Class Education,"[27] "Chinese College Students Take Up Productive Labor,"[28] "Ardently Love the New Society, Resolutely Obey the Job Assignments of the Motherland,"[29] and "Step Up Education of Middle and Primary School Students to Foster Ardent Love for Labor,"[30] flood the front pages and key editorial columns. They report such items with the following sentiments:

> Students of this year's senior and junior middle graduation classes of Liangyang Middle School, Uangchiang hsien, were recently organized to take

---

[22] C. K. Yang, *The Chinese Family in The Communist Revolution* (Cambridge, Mass.: Technology Press, 1959), p. 179.

[23] Robert J. Lifton, *Thought Reform and the Psychology of Totalism* (New York: W. W. Norton, 1961), pp. 344–345.

[24] "Maltreatment and Abandonment of Parents Shall Not be Permitted," Editorial, *China Youth*, No. 23, December 1, 1956. See also: Yao Yuan-Fang, "From Filial Piety to the Treatment of Parents," *China Youth*, No. 21, November 1, 1956.

[25] *China Youth*, Nos. 9–10, May 7, 1962 pp. 13–15, 22.

[26] *Chung-kuo Ching-nien Pao (Chinese Youth)*, November 23, 1960.

[27] *Kuang-ming Jih-pao,* August 21, 1963.

[28] *Chinese Youth*, August 24, 1963.

[29] *Kuang-ming Jih-pao*, July 24, 1963.

[30] *Ibid.*, June 27, 1963.

part in agricultural labor and the rural campaign of education in socialism in the nearby Pingkang commune, thereby coming in contact with the practical current class struggle in rural areas and receiving very good training and impressive class education.[31]

Editorial comments of *Women of China* reported on International Children's Day (June 1) that Chinese parents "cultivate in the children the fine characteristics of living amid hardships and frugality, studying hard, having love for labor and for the collective, and abiding by law, etc., . . ."[32] Students from such large cities as Peking and Shanghai all participate in farm labor.[33]

The above citations from press and mainland magazines would seem to indicate that adolescents in Communist China have little time or opportunity to form a distinct subculture, even if they wished to. Youth are under constant supervision of the Party apparatus, school authorities and parents, in both their work and study. There is some slight evidence that rebellious groups of youth have existed in certain educational institutions. An emigré[34] from Communist China, who arrived in the United States in 1961, reported that at his Preparatory School for Overseas Students he had once led a group of students in a protest against the long hours of manual labor (four hours per day) that were required in addition to attending regular classes and study time. The administration of the school conceded and even revised the work schedule to two hours per day. However, the administration also announced publicly that this student had "volunteered" to go to a work camp in a rural area of China as an example of his devotion to the needs of the peasantry. The informnant reported that he could not remember so "volunteering," despite repeated attempts to get him to do so while working eighteen hours a day in this camp for six months. If this was a sample of an adolescent subculture, it was immediately nipped in the bud due to its interference with the general aims of the regime. Groups of problem children or delinquent youth with tendencies toward a more hedonistic life have little opportunity to develop, due to the close supervision of Party personnel. Due to the Party emphasis on scholarship and education many problem children who were found to have stolen money often bought books, pens and stationery with this money, while others simply stole pens, books and other educational articles from stores or libraries.[35] Judging from the above, any student subcultures in Communist China would be likely to be service- and study-oriented and therefore not distinguishable from the larger society.

Coleman finds that American student subcultures at the high school level have a nonscholastic ethos about them. Specifically, more of his sample would prefer to be remembered as "star athletes" than "bril-

---

[31]*Nan-fang Jih-pao (Southern Daily)*, June 21, 1963.

[32]*Women of China*, No. 6, June 1, 1963.

[33]"More Than 60,000 Middle School Students in Peking Participate in 'Three Autumn' Productive Activities in the Countryside," *Peoples Daily*, October 21, 1963; and "Over 60,000 Univ. and Middle School Students in Shanghai Go To Take Part in Autumn Harvesting and Sowing in Suburban Areas," *Peoples Daily*, October 21, 1963.

[34]Emigré interview, Case No. 2, September 1962.

[35]Huang, "The Problem Child and Delinquent Youth in the Communist Chinese Family," *op. cit.*

liant students." The situation of the female student appears particularly acute. The role model that is being held up for emulation for her, according to Coleman, is that of a "chorus girl, model, movie and television actress and call girl."[36] Although the extent and strength of this nonscholastic ethos is currently under debate, its very presence provides a striking contrast with student orientations in Communist China.

Contrasts between the "fun" aspects of the American student social worlds and the "service"-oriented aspects of the Communist Chinese student world doubtless have their roots in the value systems of the larger society. The ethic of individualism carries with it the privilege to waste time and energy as well as to invest it. At any rate, given the orientation of many American educators toward the values of a pluralistic and individualistic society,[37] a certain inefficiency in the educational subsystem will likely be tolerated as it is, indeed, in other subsystems of the society. The brief contrast we have been able to make between what adolescent group life appears to be like in Communist China and what it is thought to be like in the United States may serve to highlight the "costs" of various student subcultures relative to the well-being of the larger society. Few, if any, American educators, or sociologists for that matter, would desire to harness the educational system to the economic and political goals of the State so completely as appears to have occurred under the Communist régime. On the other hand, even a free and affluent culture should be aware of the social, psychological, and economic price it pays for maintaining a "fun" subculture within its framework.

---

[36]Coleman, *op. cit.*, p. 51.

[37]See the general position of Harold L. Hodgkinson, *Education in Social and Cultural Perspectives* (Englewood Cliffs, New Jersey: Prentice-Hall, 1962).

Discussion Questions for Chapter 4

1. How do you describe "adolescenthood" in America as compared with adolescence in the nations discussed in this chapter? Is it more or less wholesome with respect to growth and development?
2. Why do modern societies seem less able to provide for a "smooth" adolescence than primitive societies seemed able to do?
3. How might American society profit from the anthropologist's cross-cultural studies of adolescence?
4. Is the stress and turbulence associated with adolescence inevitable as societies become more complex?
5. How might one predict the future quality of relationships among nations by looking at the nature of "adolescenthood" in each of them?

Chapter 5
Promoting Healthy Adolescence in American Society

It is no doubt helpful to adolescent development when those who teach, counsel, and in other ways interact with the adolescent recognize characteristics and problems of special significance during this phase of maturing. It is insufficient, however, merely to describe the adolescent and to compare him with the nonadolescent and adolescents in other cultures. The teacher, the counselor, the parent need to examine behavioral alternatives for nurturing the wholesome development of their charges. They need to know how to assist the adolescent to accomplish the developmental tasks of greater importance during adolescence.

The readings in this chapter were chosen because they say something about how adults can assist the adolescent to become what he is capable of becoming. The orientation of the chapter is, essentially, that adolescents can and do respond to counseling; that personality can be creative—if adults permit it; and that while there are esoteric needs during adolescence, the adolescent is a human being first and foremost, thus he has the same basic needs as everybody else.

Counseling Adolescents

Glen T. Nygreen

Lehman College

A most difficult challenge to many adolescents is how to maintain a healthy balance between liberty and order. More than a few need the help of a counselor in this effort. The author suggests that the counselor occupies a position of "high trust" and recommends qualifications for counselors. He recognizes, too, that even the most qualified counselors are subject to the anxieties concomitant with counseling. His formula for successful counseling considers the "humanness" of both counselee and counselor. Judged by your experience with counseling, how much in focus is Nygreen's point of view?

"A counseling situation is one involving two anxious people. The one who is the more anxious is the one who is helped."

This definition may have been offered factiously by the counselor who framed it but it is descriptive of the life situations which confront adolescents. People tend to hold stereotyped views of adolescents. In ordinary conversation young adults are lumped together with implied condescension in such terms as "teen-agers," "college students," "high schoolers," or "hot rodders." Such labels, of course, are substitutes for more careful thought and speech but their ubiquitous use testifies to their effectiveness in communicating a commonly held impression. They imply a common anxiety about the manners and behavior of the younger generation. An adolescent caught up in a one-to-one situation with an older adult is very likely to encounter such stereotypical thinking and be sensitive to the very real anxiety which underlies it. The older adult may, indeed, be a very anxious and insecure person where the young are concerned.

The adolescent, too, is anxious in such encounters. Relatively inexperienced, the adolescent tries various modes of behavior to see what happens. From his own reactions and the reactions of others he adopts as habits preferred forms of behavior. The constellation of his behavior patterns we call personality. His unsureness as he experiments is what we mean by anxiety. An adolescent and an older adult caught up in a common situation thus face the interaction of two anxiety patterns.

The role definitions of parents and teachers create further dimensions of anxiety. Such persons may not feel free to adopt varying ideological positions. The parent may be anxious about how other adults will judge his competence in parenthood if he fails to produce a socially adjusted young adult. The teacher knows he cannot meet the expectations of all parents and supervisors so he may look for the most common expectations. These are usually perceived to be the production of young adults with predictable behavior patterns within the accepted limits of social manners. These role concepts of parents and teachers conflict directly with those of adolescents. For the adolescent, testing the limits of socially acceptable behavior is a learning technique. Furthermore, the adolescent knows he must function not only in a dominant adult world but also in dynamic interaction with a distinctive adolescent subculture. In the counseling situation, these older adult and adolescent anxiety patterns interact to produce an atmosphere within which change can take place.

The purpose of the counseling situation is to produce a change in the understanding and anxiety level of one of the participants. If the object is to produce such a change in the adolescent as counselee, then the counselor must be a person of larger understandings and lesser anxieties. At the same time the counselor must perceive that he cannot be all-knowing and free from his own anxieties. He must be free to learn from the adolescent through their interaction. He should also be able to communicate with openness to create the possibility that he might reduce his own anxieties.

The dictionary defines freedom as self-determination. The adolescent is reaching toward freedom in many ways. He is testing the limits of his family world, discovering that there are definitions and experiences outside his family with which he must come to terms as he has earlier with his family. Sometimes this stretching toward a larger world is threatening to the self-concepts of parents and they react with attempts to restrict and to channel or control this reaching out process. Such a family situation may be filled with mutual love and concern and yet be one in which communication between parents and adolescent have broken down completely. Much of the anxiety of adolescence can be traced to these misunderstandings, the adolescent not perceiving that family attitudes may be motivated by affection and caring, the parent not recognizing that the acceptance and open affection of parents is the polar point in their lives against which all other experiences are being judged.

The society which men build is a bulwark against the chaos of the universe. The order established necessarily involves some restriction on absolute individual freedom in order that social order may prevail. The process of learning the requirements of this social order we call socialization. Individuals learn this first in the family, later in the school and in informal interactions. Some family and neighborhood environments are more effective than others in socializing individuals. Some individuals learn these requirements more quickly and more completely than others. Church, school, family, and the other institutions of society legitimate these rules in various ways. Obviously, some individuals will have difficulty in adolescence if their earlier experiences have been less effective in teaching these rules or if they have been less apt pupils of the world of experience.

When individuals fail to learn these rules of social order or are denied opportunities for effective learning, society resorts to social control. The agents of social control are such groups as police, courts, and those holding offices in the social structure. An administrator of a school or social agency, for example, is always subject to the expectations of others that he will act in such a role when the social order is challenged by the actions of individuals who either have not learned the rules of order or who deny their applicability to them.

The adult who finds himself in a counseling role with an adolescent must be sensitive to these conflicting role expectations. The counselor is viewed by many as being an agent of the social order. Currently we use the term "establishment;" we hear those who challenge the current rules of order refer to counselors as "part of the establishment." Thus both the agents of the status quo and those who challenge them expect the counselor to act in considerable part as supporter of the way things are. On the other hand, the counselee in coming to the adult is uttering a cry for help. His coming represents in some way an awareness that he is unable to reconcile the requirements of liberty and order. He wants to exercise his individuality, to realize himself as a person, to develop an identity meaningful first to him and then to others. He perceives the social order as denying this to him, as forcing him to accept an imposed order, of requiring conformity as the price of existence. What the counselee may expect to find in the counselor and what he wants to find may be in sharp contrast.

In such a situation the concept of individual self-determination becomes a powerful weapon in the hands of the counselor. If the counselee does not find the counselor attempting overtly to represent or to defend the way things are in society, he may then be able to share his feelings with confidence that they will be accepted as social facts to be dealt with objectively rather than normatively. This is implied in the school of thought in counseling psychology which is called Rogerian or nondirective. This does not mean that the counselor will not find it appropriate at some time to speak about his own structure of the world about him but rather that he will deal directly with the experiences and feelings of the adolescent to help him bring his own world into order.

I recall a woman who found herself alone in the world with the full responsibility for rearing two small children. She was eminently successful. They both became campus leaders in college, honor students, and today they are both professional persons in their own right. Both are married and have stable families. When I was about to marry I asked her if she had any advice for me about the rearing of children. She replied, "I know only one thing about children. You have to hold them with an open hand."

My thesis is that freedom and self-determination is the basis of all effective counseling. Who are the counselors? Parents may be counselors. Teachers, too. The salesman who carries on a conversation, the attendant in the gasoline station, the conductor on the train, the clerk in the office, and everyone who interacts with others can be a counselor. The determining point is the attitude with which the interaction is approached. If the actor perceives others as possessing worth and dignity and accords to them the right to self-determination he will be performing in a counseling manner.

To some persons we accord the title counselor because they possess special skills in helping others to resolve the persistent problem of the balance between liberty and order. Such persons have had long training and supervised experience before they are entitled to be called counselors. Their educatioal backgrounds include many courses in various aspects of developmental psychology. They have studied sociology to gain an understanding of the environmental and societal factors which bear upon social and personality development. They have made themselves experts on the institutions of society—family and school and church. To be appointed as a counselor in a professional setting is a place of high trust, so much so that legislatures are turning increasingly to a licensing procedure in order to assure that those who represent themselves as professional counselors are in fact properly qualified to carry such a trust.

Armed with these qualifications, a counselor is equipped to begin the process of working with adolescents. He knows that individuals need freedom to explore and test the limits of their worlds. He knows that the environment which surrounds the adolescent is constantly changing, must in fact change continually in relation to a particular individual if he is to grow in competence and confidence. He understands the ways in which the technology of our time has changed the experience patterns of growing up. He recognizes not only that adolescents are subject to more and varied stimuli than were earlier generations but that they do not have the freedom to avoid these stimuli. The environment is more insistent, from the demanding ringing of the telephone to the crowdedness of the common urban condition. The individual does not need to imagine how others live; he sees their life styles portrayed in papers and magazines, on television, and demonstrated about him in towns and cities.

The counselor is aware that the need to hold back from tasting some experiences while having the freedom to try others faces both adolescents and their parents. It is the balancing of these needs in terms of the insistent peer group pressure which helps create problems. This suggests that adolescents today have to make more decisions than ever before. In a simpler day, young adults were not faced with the necessity of making as many decisions as early in life as is true today. Today's decisions are more complicated. Our society is more interdependent, and the available leisure and freedom from physical toil adds new dimensions to the life planning through which adolescents must progress.

We often hear the charge that young people yearn for freedom but ignore the dimension of responsibility which must accompany any meaningful freedom. "Freedom with responsibility" has become a common challenge from older adults to adolescents. Younger people sometimes retort that the only time they hear this from older adults is when the adults are trying to restrict or control the activities of the younger. Counselors must be careful not to use the dimension of responsibility as a mechanism of control. Responsibility is meaningful only when it is freely assumed. Only when the adolescent has come to terms with the requirements of the social order and the insistent needs of his individuality can he assume what older adults call full responsibility.

After all, the requirements of the social order were created by man in order to serve his needs. The isolated individual on the shores of a remote woodland lake may be free from restrictions of communal society but he would be so preoccupied with satisfying his elemental needs for food and shelter and clothing that there would be no time left to enjoy the so-called freedom which he sought to obtain. Leisure, or the freedom to devote one's time to whatever pursuits one chooses, is a result of the complex interdependence and advanced technology which our society has achieved.

Nonetheless, the requirements of the communal life have been viewed by many scholars as "unnatural." This was the view of Sigmund Freud who held that the communal life prescribed by culture was based upon coercion and the renunciation of instincts and thus was in opposition to the animal and instinctive nature of man. From these and other views we have come to view the anxieties of modern man as attributable in some part to this basic problem of reconciling liberty and order.

If a counseling situation is one involving two anxious persons, then it is incumbent upon the counselor to have come to terms himself with this basic developmental problem. Until he has done so, he cannot accord to the other in the counseling situation the right to self-determination which the resolution of the counselee's questions demands. The problem is a continuing one for all men. It is never finally settled. It may very well be, then, that in some counseling situations it is the counselor who is helped.

One more consideration. Studies of adolescence in various cultures demonstrate that what we glibly call "adolescent rebellion" is not a necessary concomitant of the maturing process. The adolescent who does not display rebellious manners is not necessarily repressing his feelings. The adolescent who does display rebellious manners is not necessarily going through a natural process. It is not the manners employed but the objects toward which rebellion is directed that are important. To display rebellious manners without a meaningful objective is usually self-defeating behavior.

We look to maturing adolescents to focus our attention upon the dimensions of possible change which need our attention. For youth to rebel against the injustices of society, to challenge the evasions and hypocricies of our ways of life, to demand the right to freer and more open expressions of opinion and attitudes and interests are all admirable and valuable expressions if society is to change and continue viable. The goal of counseling is to enable persons to cope more effectively with the world about them and to enable them to leave the world a better place for individuals as a result of their efforts. Change is necessary in every society. Only those who know how to exert their efforts effectively so as to work with and through others can accomplish significant change.

The essential wisdom is still to "know thyself." This is the goal of counseling.

Crises in Normal Personality Development

Gordon W. Allport

At best, a teacher or counselor must remain uncertain about his effect on the personality development of adolescents. The author's studies suggest that only rarely does a teacher have a profound influence on the growing character of his students—and then it is more incidental than planned. He also points up crisis areas where adolescents need help and recommends to counselors and teachers a theoretical approach based on normal personality development.

There is one trick every teacher knows: When trapped in a state of ignorance throw the question back to the class. Without suspecting the teacher's predicament, bright students will often rescue him.

This is the strategy I employed to learn something about crises in normal personality development. I passed along the assignment to my class of one hundred captive undergraduates, and they obligingly provided me, through their own autobiographical writing, with the insights that I articulate now. Parenthetically, let me say that in my opinion no teacher or counselor has the right to require intimate autobiographical documents from students. Yet when given a completely free choice, the large majority will choose to write in the autobiographical vein. For the few who would find the experience too threatening, it should not be prescribed.

Influence of Teachers

First I shall report a minor investigation related to our main topic. I asked the hundred students, mostly sophomores and juniors, four questions with the results reported here. My first question was "Approximately how many different teachers at school and college have you had up to the present stage of your education?" The hundred respondents mentioned a total of 4,632 teachers. The three remaining queries were concerned with varying degrees of influence exercised by the teachers on the development of these students. With the percentages indicated as having played formative roles in student lives, the questions and their answers were as follows:

> How many teachers had a very strong or powerful influence on your intellectual or personal development? (8.5 per cent)

From *The Person in Psychology* by Gordon W. Allport. Reprinted by permission of the author's estate and the Beacon Press.

> How many others would you say had a reasonably strong, well-remembered influence? (14.8 per cent)
>
> How many do you remember only vaguely, or who seem to have had no substantial influence on your development? (76.7 per cent)

We are immediately struck by the fact that more than three-quarters of the teachers are remembered only vaguely and are credited with no appreciable influence, whether intellectual or personal. As teachers, we all know the shock of discovering how little impact we have had. A former student of mine brightened my day by remarking, "Years ago I took a course with you, but all I can remember about it is that the textbook had a blue cover." He grinned pleasantly while I shuddered inwardly.

Only about eight per cent of teachers are reported as having a very strong influence, and about 15 per cent are credited with a less strong but well-remembered influence. Another way of stating this finding is to say that the average teacher (assuming all teachers are equally effective) "gets through" to less than a quarter of the class, and exerts a really strong influence on not more than one student in ten.

Varieties of Influence

Asked to tell when and in what way they were influenced the students give us three facts of special interest. First, about half of all their examples deal with experiences of intellectual awakening. For example,

> She encouraged me to read poetry and drama beyond the class assignment.
>
> In chemistry the instructor asked us why bubbles appeared overnight in a water glass. When we said we had never wondered about that, he told us that everyone must question even the most common and seemingly trivial things.

And about half of the examples deal with personal development:

> She made me see that others did not judge me as harshly as I was judging myself.
>
> He had so much warmth and humanity that I wanted to be like him.
>
> She seemed tough and disagreeable, but was so kind and helpful to me that I realized I must think twice before passing judgment on anyone.

A second insight, based on the large array of illustrative incidents, reveals the remarkably *casual* nature of the influence. In hardly any case could the teacher or counselor have known that what he was saying at a given moment would make a lasting impression upon the growing mind and character of the student. Elsewhere (*1*) I have argued that in teaching values and attitudes it is not the deliberately adopted curriculum that is effective; it is rather the *obiter dicta*, the parenthetical remark, the "little true things," and above all the example of the teacher that count. And what holds for teachers no doubt holds for the counselor, too.

Finally, and most relevant to my topic, is the finding that in elementary school there are few remembered influences of special strength. Apparently development is gradual at this time, and the teacher does not often bring a sudden and traumatic experience of "dawn" to the pupil. Only 12 per cent report any strong or even appreciable teacher influence in elementary school. Fully 88 per cent of the reports date the occurrences in high school (58 per cent) or in college (30 per cent, with the college years still incomplete).

So it is in middle and late adolescence where the role of the teacher is most vivid to the student. It is in this period, according to Erikson *(4)*, that the identity crisis is in the ascendance. The young person seems to be moving from past childhood into present adulthood in a jerky manner. Development is not continuous like a hill; rather, it is episodic like a flight of stairs. It is this episodic or crisis character of development that brings both challenge and opportunity to the guidance officer.

Nature of Crisis

What precisely is a "crisis"? It is a situation of emotional and mental stress requiring significant alterations of outlook within a short period of time. These alterations of outlook frequently involve changes in the structure of personality. The resulting changes may be progressive in the life or they may be regressive. By definition, a person in crisis cannot stand still; that is to say, he cannot redact his present traumatic experience into familiar and routine categories or employ simple habitual modes of adjustment. He must either separate himself further from childhood and move toward adulthood, or else move backward to earlier levels of adjustment which may mean becoming disorganized, dropping out of school, escaping from the field, developing hostilities and defenses, and in general becoming a thorn in the flesh of the teacher, the parent, the counselor, the dean, and occasionally of the police. Sometimes, following a crisis, the adolescent will become stabilized anew after four or five weeks of severe disorganization; but in many cases the trauma retards development for a year or more, and may even leave a lifelong scar.

Turning now to my data, drawn from college undergraduates, we ask first about the phenomenology of crisis. What does it "feel" like to the student? Common is a sense of numbness and apathy. Upon entering college, the youth finds fewer strict role-prescriptions than at home. He is no longer tied to his domestic filial role, to the highly structured routine of high school, to his siblings, to his church connections, to his teen-age subcultures. He has left his possessions behind—his stamp collection, his television, his girl friends, his boy friends. All his familiar roles are in suspension. As one student writes,

> The complete freedom of college is itself a crisis. For the first time I live in close contact with people who are not members of my family. They don't even resemble people I have known before. They have different opinions, different origins, and different emotions. I feel numbed by it all.

Interestingly enough, this sense of hollowness does not necessarily have its maximum effect during the freshman year. The excitement of new scenes and especially frequent correspondence with and visits back to the home town keep the silver cord intact. The student feels that he should prove to his parents, teachers, friends, that he can master the college environment and thus please them and win their approval as he has done in the past. The impending crisis has not yet overwhelmed him (or her—for what I am saying is as true for college girls as for boys).

It is the sophomore year that seems (from my data) to be the year of crisis *par excellence.* Suddenly it becomes no longer tolerable to live one's life for the edification of people "back home." The time has come for the child of the past to be separated once and for all from the adult of the present. Here are typical phenomenological statements of this stage of the crisis:

> I feel I have been dragged into something against my will.
>
> I feel like a rat in a maze.
>
> I want to be a law unto myself, but cannot.
>
> It seems suddenly that the decisions I make must be valid for the rest of my life.
>
> To shake off parental norms and values seems to me the most important thing I must do.

The life of the past and the life of the future seem suddenly to be at cross purposes. There is often an intolerable feeling of suspended animation. Recrystallization is not yet possible. The youth is waiting still to make a choice of careers, a suitable marriage, and to find an integrative philosophy of life which his diverse college courses are too discordant to supply.

Apathy and Anxiety

It is small wonder that apathy and a paralysis of will often occur. But apathy is only a mask for anxiety. The whole framework of life is disturbed. Whereas the majority of students contrive gradually to build a new framework in spite of, or perhaps because of, the goals of anxiety, yet a large minority cannot cope with the situation unaided.

From my data, I would estimate that three-quarters are able to take the progressive road in creating their new frame of existence. About one-quarter cannot immediately do so. Proof of this point is that the dropout rate during undergraduate years is surprisingly high—over 20 per cent at Harvard, about three-quarters of the cases representing voluntary withdrawals (*3*). The dropouts present a special problem of guidance. Blaine and McArthur (*3*) write,

> The drop-outs as a group ultimately do quite well if properly handled. We attempt to establish a relationship, however brief or tenuous, with these students, not so much to prevent their leaving school, but rather in the hope of giving them some insight into the determinants of their difficulties so that their dropping out can be ultimately converted into a meaningful constructive experience instead of mere failure."

After a year or two of constructive work elsewhere, the majority of voluntary dropouts return to college and graduate. But they could not have met their crisis by remaining in the environment that was the context of their conflict.

The regressive road is surprisingly common. Among eventual dropouts, but also among other students, we find such self-destroying behavior as quitting classes, a compulsion to do trivial things, playing bridge until four A.M., drinking bouts, feelings of unreality, fugues, and general debauchery. The candid documents received startle me a bit by the extent of plain juvenile delinquency among my innocent-appearing students:

> One student finding himself unable to handle his conflicts over choice of career and over friction with his roommate, indulged in plagiarism on a term paper in such a way that he would be caught and forcibly separated from college. In this case a wise instructor, catching him in the transgression, turned the occasion into constructive counseling, forgave the deed, and put the lad onto the progressive rather than regressive road.

Here I venture a theoretical digression. The problem, as I see it, is one of interiorizing motivation. To put it in a student's words: "I am fed up with having everybody else cheer me on. I want to work to please myself rather than others, but I don't know how to do it." This plaintive statement points to a serious dilemma in our educational process. In school, the child is rewarded and punished by good grades and bad grades. Even in college, As and Bs are pats on the back, Ds and Fs are punishments. To gain love, the student must read books and toe the academic line. Finally, he obtains his degree (which is a symbol of academic love) and is freed from this external form of motivation. What then happens?

We know that a shockingly high percentage of college graduates rarely or never read another book after receiving their bachelor's degree. Why should they? Their love now comes from their employer, their wife, their children, not from the approval of parents and teachers. For them, intellectual curiosity never became a motive in its own right. External rewards are appropriate props in early childhood. But we educators, being limited by current inadequate theories of learning, do not know how to help the student free himself from the props of reward and develop a functionally autonomous zeal for learning. With our slavish dependence on reinforcement theory, I think it surprising that we arouse as much internal motivation as we do. In any event, we cannot be proud of the many educational cripples who after graduation, lacking the routine incentive of college, sink into intellectual apathy.

Crisis Areas

The counselor or teacher, of course, cannot wait for better theories of learning. He is confronted here and now with crises in the concrete. Four areas of conflict, judging from my data, are especially common.

Intellectual crises. First, there are students whose problem is one of intellectual malplacement. Among my cases, a large number report that in primary and secondary school they were too bright for their class. The penalty is one of boredom lasting down into college work, which they still do not find challenging enough for their abilities. At the same time, double promotions in elementary and high school are not a solution. To be placed with older children often creates social difficulties far more serious than boredom. In fact, the evil consequences reported from double promotion are so numerous that we should challenge this particular solution of the bright child's dilemma.

The opposite type of intellectual crisis is also common. It is the deep disturbance that often results in college from intensified competition. It is statistically impossible for most students to maintain the same relative superiority in college that they enjoyed in high school. While this fact does not trouble the majority, it is a critical experience for those who depend on scholarship aid or who frame their self-image almost entirely in terms of scholarly pre-eminence. They are suffering a severe narcissistic wound.

Specific inferiorities. A second area of crisis is the old, familiar "inferiority complex." Besides the sense of intellectual inferiority just described, we encounter deep disturbance due to physical handicaps or to plain physical appearance, with resulting shyness, loneliness, and misery. To be poor at athletics creates a crisis for males, probably more acute in high school than in college. To be a member of a minority group likewise creates an inevitable crisis somewhere along the line. Here again I suspect the major adjustments and defenses are prepared before the college age. Occasionally, the inferiority concerns guilt due to moral lapses. One student is still haunted by her dishonesty which enabled her to pass a certain course three years ago. She has felt miserable ever since about this critical experience and badly needs a means of expiation.

In this connection we may speak of religious crises. While they are uncommon in my sample, Havens (6) estimates that at any given time 12 per cent of college students have a critical concern, and sometimes acute crises, due to their religious conflicts. I suspect the concern is even more widespread, but since it pertains to one's whole ground of being, it is seldom configurated as a specific crisis at a given moment of time.

Another area, seldom mentioned but surely important, is the ideological crisis of modern society as a whole. Youth is inevitably worried, as are adults, by our uncertain future. Elsewhere I have discussed the withdrawal of American youth from their social and political context (5). Both the earlier and present data show an almost exclusive concern among American youth with their own lives. Compared with autobiographic writings of youth in other cultures, the American documents are far more self-centered, more privatistic. They are too baffled to articulate their distress, and so take refuge in their private concerns.

Sex and Family

Sex conflicts. Needless to say, our candid discussions of crises frequently, in fact usually, report acute sex conflicts. Extremely common are breakups in boy-girl relationships which are usually taken as a disaster only slightly less fatal than the end of the world. Such breakups are so recently experienced that college students do not realize that they will, in spite of their present feelings, eventually make a good recovery.

We should face the fact that at least in the early years of college life crises in the sexual sphere are for the most part frankly genital in their reference. The biological drive is so powerful that the youth is concerned with it almost by itself. Its integration into mature love, into marriage, into career plans, into an embracing philosophy of life, exceeds his present capacity. He is likely to think that genitality by itself is maturity. Sexual gratification is frankly the aim, often with devastating consequences. At this stage of development, the students have much to say about sex and little to say about mature love.

Family conflicts. I have left until last the most pervasive area of conflict and crisis. I am referring, of course, to the situation that exists between every adolescent and his parents. It is not enough to say that adolescent rebellion against the parents is the rule. Of course it is; but my documents show that the whole history of the relationships from the time of earliest memories is important. Almost any irregularity in normal family life is felt bitterly and may trouble a student even into adulthood. A mother who is neglectful or self-centered, or perhaps overpossessive and neurotic, leaves traumatic traces in the child's life. A father who is ineffectual and weak, or cruel, or absent (if only for wartime service) leaves the child with a lasting feeling of protest.

One document of unusual maturity notes that many college students seem to need their parents as scapegoats. They find it comfortable to blame parents for their own shortcomings. Perceiving that their parents are not all-powerful, all-wise, and all-perfect, they can say, "Well, no wonder I am having a hard time growing up; they didn't raise me right." Thus, an adolescent, having no genuine ground for complaint, may yet soak himself in self-pity, not being mature enough to relate his restricted image of his parents to the totality of human nature—not yet ready to appreciate the fact that his parents, considering human limitations, may have done a good job. Even if the job was not especially good, the adolescent seems not yet able to appreciate his parents' good intentions as an important value in their own right. From talking with many parents, I hazard the hypothesis that normally it is not until the age of 23 that a child encounters his parents on a mature, adult-to-adult basis.

This brief account of crises emanating from the parent-child relationship leads me to a final point. My students were required to discuss their crises from the point of view of personality theory. They were free to employ any of the theories they were studying in my course. Most of them took Freud. (I may add that the reason was not because Freud was their instructor's favorite author.)

The Conditions of Theory

Now my observation is this: Their Freudian interpretations seemed to fit well if and when the family situation in early life was disturbed. When the father was absent or ineffectual, when the mother was notably aggressive, when there was deliberate sex stimulation within the family—in such cases, it seems that the Oedipal formula provides a good fit, together with all its theoretical accoutrements of identification, superego conflict, defense mechanisms, castration threats, and all the rest.

When, on the other hand, the family life is reasonably normal and secure, a Freudian conceptualization seems forced and artificial. If we say, by way of rough estimate, that 60 per cent of the students try a Freudian conceptualization of their own cases, about 10 per cent turn out to be wholly convincing and theoretically appropriate. The remaining 50 per cent appear to be somehow contrived and badly strained.

I am wondering whether the same ratio might be applicable to cases that come to counselors. If a counselor or a therapist approaches every client or patient with the preconceived belief that his life must fit a Freudian frame of conceptualization, he may win in a minority of the cases, but lose in the majority.

Even where a Freudian approach is clearly justified, exclusive adherence to it may distract the counselor from many significant developments within the life—for example, from the present functional significance of religious and aesthetic values, from the competence and interests that extend beyond the neurotic core, from the client's conscious plans for the future, and from his "will to meaning" and existential concern with life as a whole.

Every person concerned with guidance, or for that matter with teaching, needs as background some general theory of the nature of human personality *(2)*. Our tendency, I fear, is to draw our theories from the realm of illness and deviance. It is somehow tempting to apply psychiatric rubrics to all personalities, for psychiatric rubrics are vivid, incisive, dramatic, and easy. Our conceptual banners bear such sloganized concepts as Oedipal complex, character disorder, identity diffusion, schizoid, acting out, and maybe an array of dimensions drawn from the Minnesota Multiphasic Personality Inventory. All such concepts, of course, have their proper place. But personality theory for guidance and teaching needs also to be woven of less lurid fabrics.

Youth, whatever neurotic threads may lie in his nature, is busy with his realistic perceptions, with his gradual learning and quiet coping, with the slow extension of selfhood, with noncritical failures and successes, with developing a generic conscience and a personal style of life. Even in the throes of crisis, he seeks in undramatic ways to consolidate his gains and continue on the path of becoming. A theory of personality adequate to undergird the art of guidance will keep such non-dramatic facts in mind. Crises in normal personality development are important, but so too is the slow growth of each youth's unique style of life.

References

1. Allport, G. W. "Values and Our Youth," *Teach. Coll. Rec.,* 1961, *63,* 211–219.
2. Allport, G. W. "Psychological Models for Guidance." *Harvard Educ. Rev.,* 1962, *32,* 373–381.
3. Blaine, G. B., & C. C. McArthur. *Emotional Problems of the Student.* New York: Appleton-Century-Crofts, 1961.
4. Erikson, E. *Childhood and Society.* New York: Norton, 1950.
5. Gillespie, J. M., & G. W. Allport, *Youth's Outlook on the Future.* New York: Doubleday, 1955.
6. Havens, J. A. Study of Religious Confiict in College Students. *J. Sci. Stud. Relig.,* 1963, *3,* 52–69.

The Climate of Learning: Historical Perspectives and Implications for the Learner

Valda Robinson

Fordham University

Learning in a classroom, on an athletic field, or in the privacy of one's study is a very complicated process. The factors affecting what and how well one learns are multiple, complex, and interrelated. In this paper, the author looks at a very large concept, "climate," as a variable in learning. She discusses the topic with the view that climate is real, tangible, and controllable and that it both reflects and shapes the value structure of adolescents.

Reprinted by permission of the author.

Anyone who has ever been a student has felt intuitively something called a "climate of learning." A student can describe certain classrooms, high schools, and colleges as ones that make him want to "work hard and learn more." Conversely, in others the atmosphere seems conducive to a student's "just getting by," regardless of his initial motivation or ability. What is this concept referred to as "climate"? Is it as real as the London fog or the New York smog? Is there such a thing as an "atmosphere" that permeates the psychological state of the student and promotes, hinders, or channels his learning?

This idea has been of interest to educators and to psychologists for a long period of time. At the beginning of the twentieth century, it was referred to as an intuitive concept that everyone felt was true. However, within the past fifty years, it has been studied scientifically. Evidence now indicates that the idea is more than intuition; it can be described and submitted to scrutiny.

The first person to write on the subject was the educator, Dewey. He believed that a particular environment, an atmosphere where the teacher was encouraging and understanding, was the optimum place for learning to occur. As early as 1916 he indicated how important atmosphere was when he wrote, "We never educate directly, but indirectly by means of environment."[1] The student learns as much by the climate in which the lesson is presented as by the excellence of the presentation itself.

Not until two decades later was this concept again discussed, this time by a psychologist, Murray. The environment was described by Murray as having an actual force acting on the individual. To understand an individual's behavior one had to understand the nature of this force. "The potency of an environment may be called *press*," and ". . .the conduct of an individual cannot be formulated without a characterization of each confronting situation, physical and social."[2] A student in a classroom is *pressed upon* by the climate that is prevalent, and his learning is changed, channeled, or influenced according to this press.

This idea of climate aroused the interest of Lippitt, and, in 1939, he conducted research that is considered to be a classic psychological study. He focused on the reactions of four groups of preadolescent boys when they were confronted with three kinds of adult leadership: democratic, authoritarian and laissez-faire. He kept a running account of social interactions, as well as other types of data. The data showed that each particular social climate definitely affected how the individuals reacted to tasks and to each other. The adult leader's role was a strong determiner of the interaction, with the autocratic and laissez-faire leaders both inhibiting "psychological freedom."[3] Thus, Lippitt, in his study of the effect of a particular climate on behavior, provided the first experimental investigation into the theories of Dewey and Murray as related to the classroom. He was able to show scientifically

---

[1]John Dewey, *Democracy and Education* (New York: MacMillan Company, 1916), p. 22.

[2]Henry A. Murray, *Explorations in Personality* (New York: Oxford University Press, 1938) , p.40.

[3]Ronald Lippitt and Ralph K. White, "An Experimental Study of Leadership and Group Life," *Readings in Social Psychology of Education*, ed. by W. W. Charters (Boston: Allyn and Bacon, 1963), p. 152.

that an adult leader (in a classroom, the teacher) could determine whether or not the students would feel psychologically free to learn and whether or not they would react positively to tasks and to each other. If students have ever been exposed to a teacher regarded either as "a dictator" or as "a weakling" (authoritarian or laissez-faire), they have probably experienced a classroom climate in which there was student hostility toward the teacher, toward the subject matter, and sometimes (because of frustration) even toward each other.

If a classroom has a climate, it would seem to follow that an entire school also has a climate. Newcomb, at about this same time, decided to conduct a study at Bennington College, a study to show that the college had a particular climate, a press that would influence students' behavior and thinking. From 1935–1939 he studied the Bennington faculty and students by means of questionnaires, written reports, and interviews. His specific purpose was to measure the attitudes of students, faculty members, and parents on a scale of political liberalism, and to follow the students' attitudes over a period of time. He discovered that the students tended to move toward the more liberal attitudes of the faculty and to move away from the attitudes of the parents. Thus, this college did seem to have a climate, and Newcomb felt that the longer the students were exposed to it, the more its influence was felt.[4]

From these two studies, the small-group study by Lippitt and the Bennington College study by Newcomb, two parallel developments tended to evolve. Evidently this phenomenon of climate not only existed within single classroom settings, but it also was pervasive and could permeate an entire school or college. Thus, one group of researchers focused on the classroom alone, while another group studied the school as a community.

Lippitt's study of climate evoked interest in measuring "social-emotional climate" in a classroom setting. Whereas Lippitt was chiefly interested in the overall effect of an adult's leadership in establishing a climate, Withall wanted to measure the effects of specific teacher behaviors in a classroom. He offered the first clear definition of climate. "Climate is considered . . . to represent the emotional tone which is a concomitant of inter-personal reaction."[5] He categorized teachers' verbal behaviors in a classroom with a Climate Index, reducing responses to one of seven categories: reassuring, feeling of understanding, proferring information, neutral, directive, reproving, self-supporting. By noting exactly what a teacher *said* in a classroom, the researcher could "take the temperature." Was the teacher understanding, creating a comfortable place for learning, or was he directive and reproving, causing the Climate Index to "fall"? The researcher could detect if the teacher was understanding, creating a comfortable place for learning, or if he was directive and reproving, causing the Climate Index to "fall."

Both Lippitt's and Withall's studies had focused on high school students. Robbins, interested in discovering if the older student could

---

[4]Theodore M. Newcomb, *Personality and Social Change* (New York: Dryden Press, 1943), p. 168.

[5]John Withall, "The Development of a Technique for the Measurement of Social-Emotional Climate in the classroom," *Journal of Experimental Education*, XVII (September 1948), p. 349.

become insulated against the climate of a classroom, studied college classrooms. Using Lippitt's categorizations of autocratic, laissez-faire, and democratic, she found a healthy growth in the democratic group, no accomplishment in the laissez-faire group, and an atmosphere of competetiveness, conflict, tension, hostility, or quietness in the autocratic group.[6] Even the more mature college student is not insured immunity against the atmospheric pressures found in the classroom.

Mitzel and Rabinowitz extended the study of climate downward, conducting intensive studies in elementary school classrooms. Using Withall's technique of a Climate Index, they found that teachers differed very much from each other in their classroom verbal behaviors.[7] Cunningham and Henry had earlier directed attention to this idea of consistency of classroom climate. They believed there was much frustration for the student who had to move from one climate to another. The principal and the faculty should decide, in fairness to the pupils, what kind of climate they wanted to establish.[8] One would expect little productive behavior of a person who had flown from the Florida sun to the Vermont snow and back to the Florida sun within the same day. Likewise, little productive learning could be expected of a student who, in moving from a classroom climate to one completely different, had to devote his energy and attention to acclimating himself to the new and different atmosphere.

Writers continue to elaborate on Dewey's 1916 idea of classroom climate. All extend Dewey's descriptions, but they retain his basic concepts. Johnson, in 1957, urged a classroom climate to be one "to grow in." His theory was that a student—to learn—must be ready physically, intellectually, and emotionally, and that it was the teacher's task to provide a climate for emotional well-being, a "therapeutic climate." To provide this therapeutic climate, the teacher must accept children, be secure with administrators, peers, parents, and pupils, provide stimulating classroom work, set limits on behavior, encourage group feelings of belongness, and have comfortable physical surroundings.[9] Hoffman, in 1962, also emphasized the importance of the teacher. He must not only create an accepting atmosphere, but he must also be aware of *when*, *how*, and *where* to challenge pupils.[10]

Arsenian studied the attitudes of the classes of 1938, 1939, and 1940 at Springfield College, Springfield, Massachusetts. He used an instrument, the Allport-Vernon Scale of Values, to measure the attitudes the students had on arrival, and if these attitudes changed. This study was somewhat similar to Newcomb's earlier study of what happened to the Bennington College students over a period of four years. Arsenian found that the philosophical orientation of a college acted as a selec-

---

[6]Florence Robbins, "The Impact of Social Climates Upon a College Class," *School Review*, LX (May 1952), p. 284.

[7]Harold E. Mitzel and William Rabinowitz, "Assessing Social-Emotional Climate in the Classroom by Withall's Technique," *Psychological Monographs*, LXVII (1953), pp. 1–19.

[8]Ruth Cunningham and George Henry, "Classroom Climate," *Education Digest*, XV (March 1950), p. 47.

[9]O. B. Johnson, "The Teacher's Role in Providing a Climate to Grow In," *NEA Journal*, XLVI (April 1957), p. 236.

[10]Earl Hoffman, "Good Classroom Climate, the Teacher's Function," *National Association of Secondary School Principals Bulletin*, XLVI (December 1962), p. 6.

tive criterion in both admission and retention. As Springfield emphasized "human engineering" in its academic program, it tended to admit, in general, those students who had high concern for people, in areas designated as "political, religious, and social." The students who were admitted whose values differed greatly from these tended to drop out before graduation, and those who did stay to graduate had a significant change of values, becoming even more concerned with people than when they had entered as freshmen.[11] Thus, it appears that a student who is admitted to a college either adapts to its climate of learning or leaves!

In 1957 a study sponsored by the Hazen Foundation was published, a study to illuminate the consequences of basic courses in the social sciences and to ascertain what factors contribute to the development of constructive social values. The study became much broader, however, and the final report covered an overall profile of values of American college students, the value outcomes or college education, the influence of curriculum, the impact of instructors, the effects of teaching method, and the relationship between student personalities and teaching methods. The study concluded that colleges do have very different climates, that ". . . the intellectual, cultural or moral climate of some institutions stands out from the crowd . . . with a distinctive quality of this kind, an institution acquires a 'personality' in the eyes of its students, alumni, staff."[12]

Knapp and Greenbaum, interested in exploring further the concept of intellectual climates, studied the collegiate origins of persons who had earned (or who were pursuing) with scholarship aid a Ph.D. at 25 selected institutions. They found that a *few* institutions were far superior in producing promising scholars. The distribution of the collegiate origins was highly skewed, indicating that the intellectual climate of some schools was far superior to that of others.[13] Some colleges, then, definitely exert an intellectual press on the students. An able student exposed during college to a rigorous intellectual climate will be highly influenced to obtain a scholarship and continue study toward an advanced degree.

Perhaps the persons who have studied "campus climate" most intensively have been Pace and Stern. Pace has stated climate ". . . is a little like the weather. It is talked about and it is felt, but it is difficult to explain."[14] Withall had measured classroom climate by means of a Climate Index. Pace devised a College Characteristics Index to measure the environmental press or expectations of a college. From this Index, he has been able to make climate profiles of colleges, profiles made up of the following clusters: humanistic intellectual, scientific intellectual, practical, group welfare, rebellion. If students are aware of a college's climate, the climate tends to exert a direct influence on

---

[11]Seth Arsenian, "Changes in Evaluative Attitudes During Four Years of College," *Journal of Applied Psychology*, XXVII (1943), p. 347.

[12]Philip Jacob, *Changing Values in College* (New Haven: Hazen Foundation, 1957), p. 10.

[13]Robert Knapp and Joseph Greenbaum, *The Younger American Scholar: His Collegiate Origins* (Chicago: U. of Chicago, 1953), p. 93.

[14]C. Robert Pace, "Evaluating the Total Climate or Profile of a Campus," *Current Issues in Higher Education, 1961*, ed. by G. Kerry Smith (Washington: Association for Higher Education, 1961), p. 171.

their behavior.[15] If the students know they are in a school considered to be "rebellious," this very awareness tends to press or encourage each individual student toward rebellious behavior. This college climate is very complex, however. It is more than just the student characteristics, or just the manner of teaching, or just the curriculum—but is composed of the integrated whole of these.[16]

Stern has collaborated with Pace on studies using the College Characteristics Index, but coupled with an Activities Index, a measure of the students' needs. Not only does the college have expectations of the students, but also the students have expectations of the college. By comparing the student needs to the college press, one can explore many factors, such as: Does the college change the students or do the students change the college? Is it better for the college press to have greater demands for excellence than the students want? For example, what happens when a student who is not highly motivated academically attends a college with an intellectual climate? Will the climate increase his desire to study or will the climate merely create anxiety in the student? If there are many students like him, will the intellectual climate itself gradually change? Sanford has summarized this interrelatedness as "complicated higher order processes" that must be carefully observed before anyone can make sweeping generalizations concerning the general "climate" of a college.[17] For example, if a student selected a certain college on the basis of Pace's description of its college climate, he still could not know what he would be after four years in the institution. To ascertain the student's final characteristics, one would have to know the following: What was he when he arrived? What were his expectations of the college? What was the college climate of learning? What experiences did he have while in the college? These factors are all interrelated; each sets upon and is acted upon by others. While he may become more intellectual because of an intellectual college climate, the climate itself may become somewhat less intellectual because of him!

High schools, as well as colleges, have climates of learning. However, less study seems to have been focused on high schools. Perhaps this is because the high school climate is not as distinctive as the college climate, the high school student population is more heterogeneous (while colleges select and are selected by students), and the high school students are still influenced by the climate of the home (while college students are usually living away from the parents.)

Stern modified the College Characteristics Index into a High School Characteristics Index. He utilized this on a study of a freshman class of 2000 entrants at a major Eastern university to find the characteristics of the high schools from which the students had graduated. It was discovered that there was a wide variety of high schools described. The private schools were described as offering greater intellectual stimulation, the parochial schools were noteworthy for their fostering of dependency

---

[15]Pace, *op. cit.*, p. 173.
[16]Pace, *op. cit.*, p. 174.
[17]Nevitt Sanford, "Higher Education as a Field of Study," *The American College*, ed. by Nevitt Sanford (New York: Wiley and Sons, 1962), p. 69.

and conformity, while the public schools encouraged a lack of dependency relationships between teacher and pupil.[18] Therefore, even in a high school, an overall climate of learning appears to be pervasive, affecting the learning processes of all the students.

As students' values and needs contribute to the college climate of learning, they also influence the high school climate. These needs are often referred to as "social" and strongly influence the academic motivation of adolescents. Perhaps the most well-known study of "social climate" is the one performed by Coleman. He investigated the qualities most admired by high school students and found what one would have guessed. The role of the intellectual, the scholar, was *not* the one most highly valued by either boys or girls. The boys would most like to be athletes; the girls would most like to be popular.[19] If the adolescent peer culture exerts this kind of press, the "learning climate" is considerably diluted by the overpowering atmosphere of social striving.

Thus, for the psychologist and the educator, interest continues concerning "climate of learning." The hunches of Dewey have been shown to be truths. Each classroom has a distinctive "climate of learning." Each college and each high school also has a distinctive "climate of learning." Thus, a student is influenced by more than the ability he has and by more than the motivations that have evolved from his earlier experiences in and out of school. What he learns and if he learns may be largely determined by this pervasive climate. What is the press exerted by the *teacher* towards learning? Does he value it highly? Does he conduct a classroom that is emotionally warm and healthy? What is the press exerted by the *students as a group*? Do they think it is more important to be popular than to learn geometry? What is the press exerted by the *entire school*? Are the chief activities sponsored by the school athletic events and dances? If the teacher expects and fosters an excitement toward learning, if all the other students want this, and if the entire school values this, the student has much less chance of *not* learning. Given these conditions, even the least inspired student tends to be caught up in an overall air of expectation and intellectual excitement. In such an atmosphere, sometimes even in spite of himself, the student will say about studying, "I seem to be evading it less and enjoying it more."

Attitudes toward learning *do* "depend on the weather."

---

[18]George Stern, "Continuity and Contrast in the Transition," *Orientation to College Learning*, ed. by N. C. Brown (Washington: American Council of Education, 1961), p. 58.

[19]James S. Coleman, *Social Climates in the High Schools* (Washington, D.C.: U.S. Government Printing Office, 1961), p. 7.

Can the Adolescent Be Creative?

Eugene M. Nuss

University of Bridgeport

Creativity is a much discussed and written-about subject among today's behavioral scientists. In this article the author describes the creative process in its generic dimension and identifies certain personal and social variables that affect creative behavior. He suggests that there are strong forces operating in the lives of many adolescents that serve to inhibit their creativity. His tentative answer to the question, "Can the Adolescent Be Creative?" offers direction to those who would assist the adolescent in manifesting his natural creative potential.

Americans are told by rhyme and verse that a no-man's land exists somewhere between childhood and adulthood. It is known as adolescenthood. Those who trespass there are labeled adolescents, or teen-agers; sometimes they are euphemistically referred to as "youth." Their stage of development is often described as suspended animation, during which they take uncertain steps toward the reality of adulthood and retreat more than occassionally toward the fantasy of childhood.

Adolescence is real enough, however, for this is the stuff of which adults are made. What the adolescent can or cannot be is what he will or will not become as an adult. An honest teen-ager becomes a reliable grownup; a loyal adolescent, a responsible citizen (Ask any teacher or politician.)

Can the adolescent be creative? (An exercise in rhetoric? Not necessarily.) In another chapter of society's favorite book we learn that there is a dearth of creative persons and that more are needed to solve problems old and new, which man has seen fit to invent. If the adolescent cannot be creative, then it is unlikely he can become that most desired, creative adult. Moreover, some of the sages relate that American society exhibits an almost irresistable urge to regiment the thought and action of its every member (including adolescents), much to the detriment of creativity and, of course, progress.

Traditionally as mysterious as even adolescence, creativity is now the object of a ubiquitous movement to explore and explain its nature and nurture. It is believed that an understanding of the creative process is essential to developing a healthy, productive society. Thus it seems necessary to describe creativeness before attempting to answer the question, "Can the adolescent be creative?"

Creativity Revisited

The current interest in creativity may well be in its apogee, but concern for this phenomenon is not new. Recorded history refers to man's fascination (and suspicion) for creativeness as early as the Ancient Greeks. What is fresh and encouraging about the recent study of creativity is that it is reasonably scientific and increasingly empirical. Complementing philosophical and aethestic notions about creativity, the findings of empirical research have helped shape a new image of this most complex of human traits. The new view of creativeness differs sharply from traditional thinking and suggests rather convincingly that man can indeed cause himself to behave more creatively.

The traditional concept of creativity held that creative potential existed only in the geniuses—the anomalies of the species. By equating creativeness with giftedness and special talents, only Archimedes, Galileo, Mozart, Einstein, i.e., "The Illustrious Ones," could be considered creative. This assessment suggests a dichotomous distribution of creative potential—the haves and have nots. It also makes unlikely the empirical study of factors associated with creative behavior. For example, there are never enough recognized geniuses alive at any one time to make feasible a cross-sectional comparison of the genius with the nongenius. Further, any logitudinal study of the genius must proceed in retrospect and, consequently, reflect the distortions of time and the social nostalgia in vogue at the moment. Finally, when the product of the genius, or gifted, is used as the sole criterion of creativeness, the processes preceeding and concomitant with creative production tend to be viewed as incidental to the finished product—thus largely ignored.

The "new view" describes creative potential as a universal characteristic of human nature; it focuses on the processes inherent within the creative act; it gives much attention to the generic dimension of creativity; it is concerned more with the how and why of creative behavior—less with an evaluation of the products of such behavior.

This more recent perspective on creativity reflects the thinking and research of behavioral scientists who emphasize uniqueness as a basic universal of human nature. Their assumption of human individual uniqueness is supported by the geneticist's observation that the odds two individuals will inherit identical genetic patterns is about 8* X 10^{29} to 1; by the physiologist's findings indicating that the internal functioning of each human body has a style all its own. Given these assumptions, it follows that sensory data will be received and evaluated by physical equipment that is unique to the individual. Thus reality will be experienced by each person in a manner naturally different from how anyone else experiences it. It is further reasoned that one's responses to reality are also naturally unique (some would say idiomatic) and that herein lies the genesis of creativity.

---

*(or 8 billion raised to the 23rd power).

Creativity Defined

As one might anticipate, definitions of creativity are many and varied. There is to be found, however, a common theme among most definitions advanced as part of the recent inquiry into the creative act. Simply stated, the essence of creativity is the capacity for spontaneous expression of individual uniqueness. Empirical researchers tend to view the creative process as the manifestation of the ability to integrate sensory data into new forms, thus creating the capacity to respond to new and routine situations in novel and original ways. A less research-oriented definition holds that to be creative is to experience life naturally, i.e., in one's own way; to utilize one's own resources in solving problems; to maintain one's integrity in all relationships with the environment. These descriptions are relevant to the generic aspects of creativity—to the basic behavioral processes central to being creative. They suggest that creative behavior can be nurtured (or inhibited) by controllable forces operating upon and from within the individual, and that in order to promote creative behavior it is necessary to identify and evaluate those forces.

Creativity Researched

Researchers in creativity have isolated personal and social variables which seem to relate to creative behavior. Their studies give much attention to the developmental phases of childhood and adolescence where, it is felt, the behavioral antecedents of adult creativity can best be recognized and influenced. It should be noted that a preponderance of the creativity research is descriptive (correlational), rather than experimental; thus one must speak tentatively about the ways and means to creative production. However, descriptive research has provided many promising leads to the experimenter and action researcher. Most important of these leads is the testable hypothesis, without which fruitful experimentation is impossible. In a most general sense, the findings of descriptive research suggest that before one attempts to nurture individual creative behavior he must recognize the personality dynamics of the individual, the environment in which he functions, and the interaction of the individual with his environment.

When one examines the adolescent and his creative behavior it is imperative to keep the individual in focus and at the same time recognize that adolescenthood implies certain modal characteristics peculiar to the adolescent group. Generalities about adolescenthood are useful in understanding the behavior of an individual only if they are interpreted within the specific context of his (unique) personality. Thus it seems promising to approach the question, "Can the adolescent be creative?" by examining social and personal dynamics of special significance during adolescence which also seem closely related to creative behavior. An awareness of how these factors operate normatively can provide the conceptual framework within which the assessment of individual creative potential is possible.

Creativity and Self-Acceptance

Perhaps the most universal trait that distinguishes high-creative persons from low-creative is high level self-acceptance. Feeling good about one's self seems necessary to being one's self, i.e., perceiving and responding to life as an individual. One who lacks self-confidence learns low self-esteem and can hardly be expected to display spontaneity and independence in his approach to problem solving. The low-esteem person is more likely to imitate, to conform, to yield his integrity when his views differ from others, especially from the expectations of his peers. The stereotype of the American adolescent is more nearly that of the low-esteem person than the high-acceptance individual. Indeed, adolescenthood in American society is characterized by conditions which seem designed to create a confused self-image.

In the physical dimension, the adolescent must contend with a body that is changing rapidly and dramatically. For example, physical size is a common source of anxiety to the adolescent. "Will I become too tall?" (Girls) "Will I become tall enough?" (Boys) The smoothly functioning body of the child becomes less efficient; it requires more food, and, in spite of increased attention, is inclined toward unsightly skin blemishes. More energy is required for growth, thus a changing energy pattern must be coped with. Sexual maturity is accompanied by a host of developments, the nature of which can only be vaguely anticipated—never fully understood. In brief, normal physical developments during adolescenthood require an adjustment in self-evaluation. Each adolescent is forced to take a new look at himself. The look is, in and of itself, unnerving. If what he sees fails to measure up to his (actually society's) expectations, self-esteem will suffer a sharp blow.

Sociologically, the adolescent in America is at best a marginal person. He contributes little to the economic viability of his society; he does not enter into the decision-making processes which shape his culture. He is expected to assume certain responsibilities labeled adult, yet is denied most of the rights and privileges of adulthood. The adolescent is too big to re-enter the world of children, though not mature enough (so say his elders) to be considered a bona fide adult. His response to this state of limbo is to create a society of peers which spends large amounts of energy imitating and antagonizing adults. It is within this peer society that the adolescent seeks, without notable success, to learn his true identity.

What many do learn is that they very badly need the peer group as an only refuge from adult rejection. However, even the value of the peer group is open to question, for adults are still needed, and soon this age-mate sanctuary must be abandoned for a try at the respectability of adulthood. Denied a meaningful role in his greater society, the adolescent might well be expected to entertain doubts about his self-worth. If he should also fail to win acceptance in his peer society, his doubts could become self-deprecating certainities.

There are also psychological forces which, especially during adolescence, have a significant impact on self-evaluation. The press to achieve independence ". . . to be something other than my father's son . . ." is strong in most adolescents. However, independence is not an unmixed blessing; indeed it tends to produce an attraction-avoidance conflict. To sever ties with the people who have taken care of most of his past needs is not altogether painless for the adolescent. One might expect that some degree of guilt will be experienced by all adolescents who contemplate the move toward emancipation. Moreover, independence has an inherent dark side. What about needed financial support? or, emotional backup, if one doesn't quite make it on his own? If desires to leave the nest produce sufficient guilt, intense anxiety can seriously affect self-esteem. Conversely, an overpowering fear of the world beyond the nest can have the same effect. How the adolescent views his move toward independence; how he goes about achieving it; and how successful he is in this effort, will greatly affect his assessment of self-worth.

There seems to be, then, characteristics of adolescenthood which militate against high self-esteem: an unpredictable physical body; an indeterminant social role; a conflict-producing drive for independence. If these variables function to fashion an adolescent dissatisfied with self, distrustful of self-responses, then the capacity of that adolescent to be original, to be divergent, to be creative is seriously limited.

Creativity and Conformity

The position of the adolescent on a conformity-autonomy continuum serves as another focal point for the study of creativity during adolescence. Empirical studies indicate that conformity is the antithesis of creativity, and pressures to conform are often described as being overwhelming during adolescence. Location near the conformity end of the continuum implies that one will seek to avoid controversy, be reluctant to examine experience for meaning, or value, and exhibit a generalized fear of standing up or out. The conforming person is motivated to meet standards set by others, to follow, to imitate—in short, to avoid situations which require the expression of his unique self.

To what extent the adolescent becomes a conforming person is largely a function of the strength of the conformity pressures he experiences, and how he is able to cope with them. The strongest forces, in this regard, emanate from the school, the peer group, and the home.

Conformity in the School

A large amount of adolescenthood is spent in school. It is difficult to imagine that any of society's institutions requires more conformity of its clientele than does the public school. Physically, economically, and intellectually the school is group- rather than individual-oriented. Typically, the teacher-pupil ratio precludes individualization of instruction; convergent thinking is emphasized, while divergent thought and imagination are frequently sacrificed in the interest of the standardized test. Pupil evaluation is primarily concerned with comparing students with each other, and in so doing fails to indicate individual achievement in terms of individual ability and goals. The school communicates to its pupils expectations, standards, and models which are prerequisite to academic success. And adolescents are taught early that academic success bodes well for future social and economic well-being. Thus the school in America offers passageway to the affluent life for those who can and will conform to its modus operandis. Conformity may appear to be a small price to pay for the credentials required of the respectable citizen. It is of some importance to note that many of the most creative students fail to conform sufficiently well to become also the most academically successful. A close inquiry into the subject reveals that academic success, as measured by achievement tests, correlates poorly with high creativity as measured by tests of creativity.

Conformity in the Peer Group

Every adolescent is a member of the peer society simply by virtue of his being an adolescent. Not every adolescent is an accepted member of a peer group, however. Entrance into the face-to-face arrangement known as the peer group is easy for some, difficult for others, but exceedingly important to adolescents generally. For it is in the peer group that the adolescent learns much about what is most important to him, including how to function as an independent sexual being in a society that is reluctant to extend him status as such.

To what extent peer group membership requires the surrender of individuality no doubt varies among groups and certainly among individuals. However all group membership requires some degree of conformity and standardization. When the need for group acceptance is of paramount importance to the adolescent, and when he finds it difficult to win such acceptance, he may readily succumb to group dictates. In fact, he may eagerly seek anonymity within the pack as the sine qua non of his belongingness. Alienation and isolation from the child and adult worlds tend to motivate the adolescent to seek status as an individual within a group of his peers. Once there, he is susceptible to the potent influence of the group. When this influence promotes conformity, he will most likely conform.

Conformity in the Family

If the family unit fails to take into consideration the uniqueness of its members, it, too, will function as an agency of excessive conformity. When child-rearing practices, child-parent relationships, and rewards and punishments communicate to the adolescent that his position in the family rests entirely upon his becoming what others wish him to be, self-confidence and creative potential are poorly served. If threatened withdrawal of love is used as a weapon to effect submission, the expression of uniqueness will be supressed.

Adolescent behavior in America must assuredly produce anxiety for most parents. Basically, this is because the adolescent is breaking away from the family constellation. As he breaks away, he adopts new identifications and behavioral modes which, to his parents, represent the loss of control over and support for their young. To parents with little understanding of adolescenthood, this anxiety may become intense and result in frantic attempts to retain dominion over their rebellious offspring.

Finally, parents are judged by others and by themselves pretty much on the basis of how well the behavior of their children conforms to the expectations of society. Thus a parent's ego needs are affected considerably by the behavior of his adolescent son or daughter. The insecure parent, to protect himself, may demand of his child a pattern of behavior that in no way takes into account the child's unique characteristics or needs. When this occurs, the adolescent is pressured to conform to expectations and standards even though these prescriptions are at best myopic, at worst psychotic.

Conclusion

Creative potential in its generic dimension may be understood as a universal characteristic of the human species. However, its manifestation through behavior, though natural, is not inexorable. There is no guarantee that the inquisitive child will become an imaginative adolescent. Americans have made adolescenthood a time of trial, a period of uncertainity and confusion. There are strong environmental forces which tend to enervate creative potential during adolescenthood by lowering self-esteem and denying self-uniqueness. The school, the peer group, and the home must share the major portion of the responsibility for conformity pressures on adolescents. In a general perspective, it appears that these three core agencies of society collaborate, albeit unwittingly, in producing a level of conformity in excess of the limit most desirable for individual growth and development. When the question is asked, "Can the adolescent be creative?" it seems appropriate to reply, "Perhaps, but for most it isn't easy."

The Feminine Identity: 1970

Esther M. Westervelt

Teachers College, Columbia University

In order to understand how an adolescent girl psychologically becomes a female adult one needs to conceptualize a feminine identity. The author believes that the American feminine identity is changing—and that this change is all to the good. She holds that the new view of femininity allows for the possibility that being a woman has its own satisfactions. This is quite a departure from the concept of the traditional American woman wherein she must find her satisfactions through serving her husband and children.

This morning, as you can probably guess from the title, I am going to permit myself a luxury. Instead of talking to you about what is, reviewing the research, and that sort of thing, and discussing how we got where we are, as I often do, I am instead going to talk about what *may* be in the relatively near future. Perhaps a social scientist would say, "I am going to dream." Well, that is so, and it is all right, I think, because we dream too little—especially I think those of us who are concerned with the education and the guidance of girls. It sometimes seems to me that we try to prepare girls to walk into the future by imposing on them the perspective we get from walking backwards or from looking at just where we are now. We look at our own lives and our own problems and we project them upon the future of the girls.

It seems to me—and I am going to say this right at the outset—that today's girls, especially today's college girls, are quietly and most unselfconsciously setting about becoming the kind of woman that up until now has mostly been only imagined. The women that I think these girls are going to become will be feminine in the fullest sense of the word. They will know how to use their feminity to the fullest. They will use it not as a weapon which protects them as a disadvantaged group from those who have imposed the disadvantages—that is to say, men—but as a vehicle through which they will enhance and enrich the lives of all around them and their own. No matter what these girls do, they will think and act and feel like women and be proud of doing so. They will admire the qualities of men, but they will not wish to emulate them. They will not, however, set themselves apart from the world of men and carve out, as it were, a small and secluded sphere of society which will be a woman's domain. Their lives will be wholly interwoven

Reprinted from a report on *A Faculty-Student Dialogue on Group Guidance for Undergraduate Women* by permission of the author and Betty Jane Lloyd (Editor), Carnegie-Mellon University, Pittsburgh, Penn., 1965.

into the social fabric of their times in work, in play, in politics, in civic leadership, and in the home.

Well, those are the rough outlines of my dream and I believe it is coming true. I am going to discuss the evidence with you or a little of it, anyway, this morning. But before I go any further, I think that something should be said about what we mean by the word identity since I use it in the title and since the title implies that it can be used in a way that in fact it cannot be used. Identity is an individual's sense of individuality, his perception of both his own uniqueness and the ways in which his uniqueness is important to other people—that is, of the ways in which he belongs to his world and his time. Since identity is a highly singular thing, it should not properly be used as a collective noun. But I excuse myself for doing this this morning because one of the most important factors which affect anyone's sense of identity is sex. What I am really talking about, then, is not identity in all of its singularity for every individual, but about how the fact of being a woman will influence the sense of identity of women in general in the years ahead—their sense of uniqueness and belongingness.

Now, it is most important to remember that identity is as much a matter of feeling of belonging to the world outside oneself as it is a feeling of being unlike all others in that world. Although it may seem odd, these two dualities of identity are fully interdependent; that is, the less one feels that one belongs and is recognized as belonging to a significant society, the more difficult it is to perceive oneself as a unique and significant and worthy individual.

Of late years, as you know, we have heard much about the diffused identity crisis in girls, especially girls of college age. Bettelheim, Erikson, and others have suggested that this arises from pressures on girls in our society and in similar societies to adopt a role that conflicts with the pursuit of their individuality and with their full participation in the larger society. In other words, the natural desire of girls for marriage and motherhood seems to require the adoption of a role that demands less than a woman has to bring of herself as an individual to life, and that sets women apart from the concerns and activities of the world beyond the home. Many who discuss this subject ask, "Is this true even of brighter, better-educated girls?"

Well, there was, in fact, considerable empirical evidence from studies of college girls in the 1950's to support this claim; but it seems to me that if this was indeed the case in the 1950's, we need not be surprised. In the first place, we had by then acquired some decades of history of increased separation of the home from society—of, in other words, the life of the home from the work of the world. Each year less and less of the world's work was done in the home, and we ended up with the split-level trap and all that. Furthermore, the 1950's were heirs of strong social pressures that arose from World War II and its disruption of domestic life. Having been in the War myself—I know many of you here have been too—I can well remember how highly prized a dream, how much of a paradise beyond all possible paradises seemed just a little white cottage with a picket fence around it and all the world shut out—perfect peace! It was a much glorified goal for those of us who were young and looking forward to the end of the war at that time. It seems inevitable that the turmoil of the 1940's should have left the 1950's a legacy of strong pressures for stability in the society and for the individual security represented by home and intimate companionship, the peace of escape from the pressures of the outside world. But it is not very difficult to see that new forces are at work in the 1960's, that more and more peoples are participating in more and more ways in attempts to solve the problems of our society. And those people are girls as well as boys, women as well as men.

There was another force at work in the 1950's, and in earlier decades of the 20th century, which we might touch upon. It is a fact that the more sophisticated we became about psychology, the more apparent it has become that there is marked lack of agreement about what the psychology of women really is. (Not, of course, that we've reached any consensus on a psychology of men!) Yet people who wrote about women and prescribed for women, some psychologists among them, often did not make explicit their psychological assumptions; this resulted in certain very strong conflicting pressures on women the source of which was not apparent. The nature of the underlying confusion may become more clear if I briefly digress to roughly outline the three major sets of assumptions about feminine psychology which have been operant since about 1900, and which have underlain many of the conflicting prescriptions for women's lives.

Let me first say that these three major schools of thought disagree about the genesis of sex differences and about whether the differences between the sexes are basically quantitative or qualitative. That is to say, they disagree about whether one sex is merely more of everything than the other, or is, instead, different in ways that do not lend themselves to simple ordinal measures alone.

The Freudian view is the best known. It clearly reflects our Judean, Christian, and Graeco-Roman heritage and regards sex differences as basically quantitative rather than qualitative. "Anatomy is destiny," as Freud said, and for women, disaster. Since you can best appreciate the quality of Freud's thinking from his own words, I will quote a collection of his remarks on the psychology of women which reflect more than thirty years of his study on the subject.

> The anatomical distinction between the sexes must leave its mark on mental life. After the sight of the genital organs of the other sex, the girl feels herself at a great disadvantage, falls victim to penis envy, and this leaves ineradicable traces on her development and character formation. As a result of the discovery of the absence of the penis, women are as much depreciated in the eyes of the girl as in the eyes of the boy and later perhaps of the man.

I would like to pause here to tell those of you who don't know it that, in writing this passage, Freud is referring to a five-year-old girl and a five-year-old boy. Then he goes on to say:

> The feminine situation is only established, that is to say, the woman only becomes secure, when the wish for the penis is replaced by the wish for

> the child. More violence is done to the libido when it is forced into the service of the female function than to those of masculinity. This may be based on the fact that the achievement of the biological aim is entrusted to the aggressiveness of the male and is to some extent independent of the cooperation of the female. Women have but little sense of justice, and this is no doubt connected with the preponderance of envy in their mental life. We may also say of women that their social interests are weaker than those of men. A man of 30 seems a youthful and in a sense an incompletely developed individual of whom we expect that he will be able to make good use of the possibilities of development. But a woman of about the same age frequently staggers us by her psychological rigidity and unchangeability. There are no paths open to her for further development.

Of course, it is very obvious that Freud took the point of view of a man in developing a psychology of women. You see, all he did was to assume that because men liked being men, women would certainly like to be men too; and, therefore, they must feel deprived because they weren't. This is just really the simple basis of his psychology for women; and obviously such a view rejects the possibility that feminity has its own satisfactions as a way of being—an identity. It suggests that for all but a few women satisfaction must be found in husband and children and, according to Freud, mostly in sons. This of course is very obviously a result of the Hebrew tradition; because, as you know, in the Hebrew tradition sons are highly valued, especially by the mother.

A second position, which has been held at one time or another by various cultural anthropologists, including Margaret Mead in her earlier works, is that sex differences are a cultural artifact. At first, this seems the extreme antithesis of the Freudian position. But, in fact, it is not because it also assumes that there are no qualitative differences between the sexes, only quantitative ones. But it differs in that it attributes these quantitative differences to culture rather than to anatomy. Alfred Adler was an exponent of this point of view, and these are some statements from Adler written at about the same time Freud wrote some of the remarks quoted.

> The lesser capability of women is a palpable fable. A girl is daily subjected to the argument that girls are less capable than boys and are suitable only for unessential activities. A girl comes into the world with a prejudice sounding in her ears, which is designed only to rob her of her belief in her own value, to shatter her self-confidence, and destroy her hope of ever doing anything worthwhile. One of the bitter consequences of the prejudice concerning the inferiority of women is the sharpest division and pigeon-holing of concepts according to a scheme. Thus, masculine signifies worthwhile, powerful, victorious, capable, whereas, feminine becomes identical with obedient, servile, subordinate. Character traits which would seem to prove this fallacious contention of the inferiority of woman prove themselves at a closer observation nothing more than the manifestation of an inhibited psychic development. We do not maintain that we can make what is called a talented individual out of every child, but we can always make an untalented adult out of him. That such a fate overtakes girls more frequently than boys in our day and age is easily understood.

As you can see, Adler is saying that we limit girls' opportunities for full development of all their capacities simply by not expecting women to assume certain roles in the society, and that this is so no matter how much education we offer them because it isn't the education, it is the expectations that count. Given equal expectations, women would truly have equal opportunities and would, in effect, be as "masculine" as men. They would be comrades and co-workers at every level. But there is nothing in this point of view to suggest that women, because they are women, have anything to contribute to the world that men cannot contribute.

A third position, which historically speaking owes much more to Oriental culture than to those of Europe emphasizes the qualitative differences between the sexes. It assumes that anatomy is destiny, psychologically speaking; but it also assumes that social health as well as biological functions depend on psychological sex differences. While Adler and Freud were publishing the views I have mentioned, Carl Jung expressed this third idea.

> How is man to write about woman, his exact opposite, for woman stands just where man's shadow falls so that he is only too liable to confuse her with his own shadow. The elementary fact that a man always pre-supposes another's psychology as being identical with his own, aggravates the difficulty and hinders a correct understanding of the feminine psyche. Women psychology is founded on the principle of Eros, the binder and deliverer, while age old wisdom has ascribed Logos to man as his ruling principle. Whereas, logic and objective reality commonly prevail in the outer attitude of man, or at least are regarded as an ideal, in the case of woman, it is feeling; but in the soul the relations are reversed. Inwardly, it is the man who feels, the woman who reflects. Hence, man's greater liability to total despair, while a woman can always find comfort and hope.
>
> We deceive ourselves greatly if we suppose that many married women are neurotic only because they are unsatisfied sexually or because they have not found the right man or because they still have a fixation on their infantile sexuality. The real ground of the neurosis is, in many cases, the inability to recognize the work that is waiting for them of helping to build up a new civilization. We are all far too much at the standpoint of the nothing—but psychology. We persist in thinking we can squeeze the new future, which is pressing in at the door, into the framework of the old and the known.

Most of these words were written in either around 1915 or 1916 and in the 1920's. But just last spring, Eric Erikson (I am sure many of you read this), discussing penis envy in women, said:

> The existence of a productive inner bodily space has a reality superior to that of the missing organ. This inner space gives woman a commitment to nurture, an openness to other people, the ability to wait and/or endure, a preference for conservation rather than manipulation. But women are tempted quickly to go back to their place whenever they feel out of place.

And I would like to say parenthetically here that the more the outside world is organized *by* men, then the more it is organized *for* men, and the more women feel out of place in it.

> Leading women are all too often inclined to lead in too volatile, moralistic, or sharp a manner as if they agreed to the proposition that only exceptional and hard women can think. The influence of women will not be fully actualized until it reflects without apology the facts of the inner space and the potentialities and the needs of the feminine psyche. It is as yet unpredictable what the tasks and roles, and opportunities and job specifications will be once women are not merely adapted to male jobs, but when they have learned jobs to themselves. Mankind now obviously depends on new kinds of social inventions and on institutions which guard and cultivate that which nurses and nourishes, cares and tolerates, includes and preserves.

Well, these three points of view have been with us for quite a long while, although, as I said, they are very often not made explicit. For instance, in the Spring 1964 issue of *Dædalus* in which Erikson's words appeared, there was an article by Alice Rossi, which many of you may have read. The basic assumption of the article by Alice Rossi was an Adlerian one: that you just set the same expectations for both sexes and then sex differences will disappear; and that this will be a very good thing, since they are just a handicap to the female sex. This, in a sense, is almost the same—or so it seems to me—as saying that a woman really doesn't have a right to be a woman but rather must mold herself to fit the shape of whatever world she finds herself occupying. If this world happens to be masculine—that is, a world dominated by men and male values—then it will be necessary for her to just get over the troublesome but essentially insignificant fact of being a woman, if she wants to participate in it.

Erikson's view, which I am sure you can perceive is also my own, is that the sexes are complementary and that this state of affairs is socially essential. Therefore, the health of a society depends on a feminine style of participation by women as well as on a masculine style of participation by men.

It seems to me that, despite a continuing flurry of debate, muddied waters are beginning to clear. Women are beginning to find their place in the world of today, after a long period of dislocation created by social, economic, and political revolutions which in the past two centuries dislodged women from their traditional security as essential economic and social contributors to the total society, and which also produced the popularizers of social science whose attempts to rationalize this situation have kept us all feeling guilty about what we were or were not doing as women. It seems to me that women are about ready to rejoin society as fully feminine and fully participant individuals.

Now some of my thinking is based on hunches and on my own quite unscientific observations of today's adolescent girls, especially college girls; but there is also some empirical evidence for this belief from quite recent studies. Two examples are Zissis' report on the life planning of 550 freshmen women at Purdue University (Cecilia Zissis, "A Study of the Life Planning of 550 Freshman Women at Purdue University," *Journal of the National Association of Women Deans and Counselors*, Summer 1964) and the Ross study of the top 1 per cent of women at Michigan State University, which followed some of its subjects through the college years and into the year following graduation (Dorothy

Robinson Ross, *The Story of the Top 1% of the Women at Michigan State University,* Counseling Center, Michigan State University, September 1963, mimeographed).

I would like, however, to discuss just one such study with you. This study has two interesting aspects—its data, and the author's interpretation of the data. Like the rest of us, social scientists have to place their own interpretations on what they see, and sometimes this results in a report of data which suggests something quite different to some readers than the author's interpretations indicate that these data suggested to him. Such was the case with my reading of Mervin Freedman's report of some of his research in the last issue of the *College Personnel Journal.*

This was a study of 50 girls in a highly selective college for girls, continued over the four years they were in college. These girls have graduated since 1960. Both interviews and objective tests were used to obtain the findings. The report does not describe the instruments in detail but from what I could gather, it seemed to me that this study was unusually well-designed to elicit findings which were not a distortion of the data sought. So many of the studies of girls in the 1950's were inadvertently designed to produce reports of perceived role conflict, because they were sprinkled with questions about, "Do you plan to be married or have a career? Do you think there will be a conflict if you get married and have children and go to work?" and so on and so forth—questions which were very direct and very loaded. This study seemed to have none of these weaknesses. The subjects were induced in various ways to report their ideas about their futures; loaded questions were not used.

In reporting his findings, Freedman classifies them under several different headings, the first of which is "What Constitutes Women's Role." His data indicate that girls in his study do not take the conventional attitude of expectancy of housewifery, motherhood and conventional feminine behavior as the be-all and end-all of women's existence. In other words, Freedman says they do not fit the description of a typical American woman suggested by Betty Friedan in *The Feminine Mystique.* In fact, the majority of the girls he studied were disposed to disapprove the idea of marriage as the only goal in being a woman, dependence on superficial social life, pettiness and gossip for personal outlets, not having interests outside the home and family, being too tied to the children, etc. The majority were clearly not inclined to value conventional feminine characteristics and behavior.

There was some indication even and their attitudes were quite opposite in that they seemed to feel that masculine activities and traits are superior to the feminine, although not necessarily desirable for themselves as women. Of course, these results are very reminiscent of those found by Shenk and McKee in 1957 when they found that both college men and college women rate women lower than men on the possession of desirable traits, which, of course, is not the same thing as saying that girls, therefore, want to be like boys.

Despite the feeling of these girls that marriage should not be the only goal in life, the great majority, of course, aspired to marriage and motherhood. But, in addition, the large majority indicated that they also expected some kind of career or vocation outside the home.

The second heading under which Freedman discusses his findings is that of "Career and Marriage." Most of the students who plan to have careers and marry, which was about 70 per cent of the total, did not forsee conflict between their marriage and motherhood plans and their career aspirations. But this was not because they felt their career patterns could be identical to those of a man. Rather, these young women seemed to see clearly that they would have to plan for flexibility in career activities—either for brief interruptions for motherhood or a cutting down on time spent on career when the children were young. Most of the young women anticipated that complete interruption of their careers would be very painful for them personally but might be necessary for the sake of the children when they were very small. The majority reported that should such an interruption be absolutely necessary, they intended to retain intellectual activities and interests outside the home during such times. On the other hand, most of the girls anticipated much happiness from their lives in the home and family. They didn't feel, in other words, that all of their reward was going to come from outside activity. This study bore out other studies in its finding that women who were most career-minded were also more intellectual, unconventional, independent, and flexible in their thinking and outlook; and those who could not see the possibility of combining marriage and career at all (these were in the very small minority in this study) tended to be high on scales of authoritarianism, etc.

The third heading under which the author classified his data is "The Ideal Position of Women in American Society." The great majority of his subjects believed that American society offers them, as educated women generally, ample opportunity for fulfillment. I thought this was interesting and exciting. They recognized the existence of certain kinds of professional discrimination against women and attempts to restrain women intellectually; but their prevailing attitude was that no barriers to women's development are insurmountable; that is, any woman can manage to do whatever she wishes provided she possesses the appropriate capabilities, which, of course, includes the desire to do so. The majority of the students felt that the ideal position of woman in our society is one in which women have equality and freedom in that she is not prevented from doing what she wants and is accepted as an equal human being. The majority of the students also forsaw greater independence and equality for women in the future. They felt that there will be a greater emphasis on being a person rather than being a woman.

The final category under which the author classifies his findings is "Attitudes toward Feminism." Now this is closely related to what has just been said. Here Freedman comments that perhaps what stands out most in the interview is the relaxed quality of the students as they confront the issues of women's roles, marriage and career; and this kind of attitude is what I had in mind when, in the introduction, I said that I think today's girls are quietly and unselfconsciously going about shaping new kinds of lives.

Many of the women students were quite explicit in stating their disapproval of emotionality and fervor regarding issues related to the woman's role. They obviously hold the popular stereotype of the feminist of the 19th century; that is, the notion that she was typically a single woman, most aggressive and probably not very attractive. Of course, as you know, the contrary is the case—most of those feminists who struggled so hard were married and mothers and many of their husbands were outstanding men. If the girls in Freedman's study ever learned this, they have forgotten it, and possibly also forgotten that in the 19th century women were still, legally speaking, an oppressed minority who had little control over their own lives or property. Since then all this has changed, thanks in large measure to the feminists and their many masculine supporters. Girls today are not concerned with such issues; there is no reason they should be. Freedman seemed to feel that his subjects differed from the feminists in that these girls believed that women will always want marriage and a family first. It is my own view that not only most women but also most men see marriage and a family as a primary goal in life. It is important to note in this connection, that the girls did *not* say, "If I had to choose I would take marriage rather than something else," because they weren't asked that kind of question.

As already observed, almost all of the students believed that they will be able to do what they want, that they can decide their own fate, and that marriage is not a fate in itself, but that it will take planfulness to achieve all their goals. To me these findings are very interesting, and you can see why. But even more interesting were some of Freedman's comments in his discussion of his interpretation of the data. He says that he sees in these findings the revival of the primacy of home and family. In fact, one of the sub-paragraphs is headed "Revival of the Primacy of Home and Family." He sees these girls retreating from competition with men. Now the data, at least as reported by Freedman in this article, do not seem to me to lend themselves to such an interpretation. To me they suggest that today's young women are able to see the home and family as an essential part of their lives and a central part, but not the only part, of their total responsibilities, and that so far as competing with men is concerned, they are more interested in being vital women than in being pale carbon copies of men. They are not, of course, yet ready to say the latter in quite those terms because our society has so long overvalued male attributes of aggressiveness and dominance and all the related traits that it is just not easy for a girl to say, "I value my particular feminine qualities as highly for me as I do masculine qualities for a man." Nonetheless, I think such a feeling is coming very close to the surface in their lives.

One thing I didn't mention in Freedman's findings is that a number of the girls expressed their understanding of the fact that it would not be a wise thing to overtly compete with men, especially their husbands, since the male ego is a rather tender plant. And it is! I was impressed that girls this young understood so well that they could achieve their goals without having to adopt a masculine pattern of aggression and competition. To me this was not only a mature perception but also a very marked expression of feminity, but Freedman didn't see it quite this way. He feels that "these young women may be implicitly or unconsciously preparing for a future in which conventional work and careers assume less importance than they do now and in which leisure, recreation, play, and relationships among people, rather than things, assume increasing importance." In other words, Freedman is suggesting that only masculine values are functional in the world of work and that "conventional work and careers" are, by definition, masculine and must be pursued in a masculine fashion. It is very interesting that, although everything which he reported his subjects as verbalizing has to do with *work* and *responsible activities* outside the home, yet he suspects that unconsciously and implicitly they are thinking about *recreation, leisure,* and *relationships with people.* His interpretation may be an expression of the male ego and of masculine values. I apologize to Dr. Freedman and to the males here for suggesting that there is another—a feminine—perspective on these data, which might be different, but it is a possibility.

For instance, I have often wondered if the reason psychologists called this feminine trait that they isolated on so many tests "passivity" is because, being males, they couldn't think what else to name it. It seemed to be the opposite of aggressiveness and dominance which males understand so well; perhaps for this reason it seemed to them to have no characteristics of its own. It may be that the same limitations of the masculine perspective have influenced Freedman's interpretations.

In any case, Freedman's extremely careful and important study does seem to indicate a marked change from the 1950's, in that its subjects are not looking upon their lives as a series of compartmentalized and conflicting activities and roles. Instead they are seeing their lives as an integration of many activities, roles, and responsibilities, with such integration made possible by both flexibility and continuity. I doubt very much that girls like these are going to spend much time worrying about the long discussed "role conflicts" of women. (I think that, thank heavens, we are about to hear the end of that discourse.) They seem to see their lives as comprised of many activities which are related and which can fit together and which it is their privilege to enter upon. They are not desirous of being competitors against men, but they are eager to be partners with them. They understand that a woman's role in such a partnership may be more comfortable, both for her and for the male, if it is the less competitive and she less aggressive and the less overtly dominant, but this is not to say that they therefore think that they have nothing to contribute themselves. They are, I suspect, discussing the ways in which a woman contributes, as contrasted with the ways in which a man contributes to society. They look forward to the delights of home and motherhood but they look forward also the activities outside of the home and they are fully aware of the difficulties that combining these two may impose at certain times in their lives. They don't intend to shirk the difficulties nor any of the duties but they also feel that they need not be over-emphasized at the price of leaving some of the activities out of their lives.

Now to one of my generation who has known college girls of other kinds and other years this represents quite a change, and it's a change in the direction of greater maturity, greater breadth of vision, and more recognizion of what it means to be a woman—whether or not these girls can verbalize this. There was a time (this was in my day) when college girls expected that they would just have both marriage and a career, or some other satisfying external activity, but they really gave no thought as to how these goals would be achieved. Somehow, everything would happen—somehow the world was their oyster and it would all work out. And in fact for many, it didn't, and then in later years they had to undergo a second adolescence, some of them—and this was most painful, but they were more fortunate than those who never did enter upon the second adolescence.

Of course then there was a later generation, affected by World War II, the girls of the 1950's, (which was similar, I think, to the girls in the late forties) who tended to cast their lot entirely with domesticity. But now these women are re-entering the world outside home—these women who graduated from college in the forties and early fifties—I counsel with a number of them, as you know, and supervise students who counsel with many more—and I'm troubled greatly by the fact that even coming back too many of these women carry with them a load of guilt, and along with the guilt, of course, ambivalence about participation in the public sector of society. They're troubled with such questions as "Is it wrong for my husband's ego for me to do this?"—whatever this may be and usually not anything too terrific. Even though their children are now all adolescent, they wonder whether they shouldn't be home whenever the children happen to be home. They can't be comfortable in the knowledge that there is a place for them as women in the larger world and that they're actually needed there. It seems to me that the girls in Freedman's study are not going to suffer this way; that they're going to be comfortable with the knowledge that they belong to the outside world as well as home. They won't have to suffer this confusion and guilt.

Well, these, briefly, are some of the reasons that I think the young women of the nineteen-seventies will have an entirely different sense of feminine identity than their immediate forebearers, and I would like to mention just briefly some of the ways in which I think that identity will express itself in their lives.

First, I think these girls will be planful—as they are now planful—but not too planful. You know I've been speculating a great deal lately about whether, in trying to make girls plan as if they were boys—plan for this at this time and then that later on, and so on and so forth—we aren't beating our heads against a stone wall. I have been speculating about whether some of Erikson's notions, some of the things the trait psychologists didn't find out, some of the things that may be the components of this thing called "passivity" don't have to do with women having a stronger orientation to present time than men do, with women being, in other words, less oriented towards the future, less able to see or be terribly concerned about themselves at thirty, forty, fifty.

You know that we're always complaining that girls just won't try to imagine what it would be like to be that incredible age of thirty-two, and so on, but it may be that this is just not possible for them. That is, perhaps this is not the way women in general think about their lives or themselves. It may be that women have to be caught up in the here and now, immersed in the quality of their present experience, and in their associations with the individuals and activities which comprise it. When they think about the future, they think about it in much broader, more general, and less personal terms, unlike boys and men who think, "I will go to graduate school and then I will make this kind of an advance, and then that,"—and who can be quite disturbed if they are not able to see the future this clearly, or if it doesn't work out the way they planned. In general, women, as you know, accept more easily than men the unanticipated losses and obstacles encountered in the course of life; their suicide rate is lower; they seem better able than men to tolerate and recover from the stresses of war and social disruption, to maintain some semblance of order in the face of the dislocation or destruction of home, family, and security.

These are some of the reasons I think the girls of today will be planful, but not compulsively so; and that their planning will relate to the big things they want out of life, rather than be tied to narrow specifications of exactly how they will advance toward long-range goals—especially, perhaps, long-range vocational goals.

Secondly, these girls will adapt themselves to circumstances without allowing circumstances to dictate the pattern of their lives. In selecting a vocation, they will tend to choose a field that appeals to them but also one that seems doable in the setting of the kind of life they want to live. If, for example, they expect that their husband's work will keep them moving from place to place for some time, they may enter a profession which they can practice wherever they go, rather than a kind of work which necessitates employment by an institution, business firm, or industry. They may tend to evaluate a job more in terms of the satisfaction they get from doing it than in terms of the opportunities it offers for promotion. So far as their activities outside the home are concerned, they will be willing to live with uncertainty, and not be ready to throw in the sponge just because they can't see very far ahead at a given moment. I suspect that being able to see ahead in the lives of their husbands and children will be far more important to them than charting broad highways to achievement of their own. In all their activities, they will be flexible but not lacking in unity of direction.

Third, these girls will not be ashamed of having a sense of commitment to something outside the family or the home; nor will they be prey to the terrible discomforts of externally induced guilt. They will be comfortable in the knowledge that a society that carries on most of its work outside the home needs its women outside the home as well as in it.

Just last evening I was unexpectedly detained in my office by an emergency call from a student, a beautiful young woman who has three very young children and who is going through the painful struggle of trying to do graduate work part time while depending on baby-sitters for the children. Those of you who have done this know what a nightmare it can be. But this is not the problem that is getting her down.

What is getting her down is her terrible sense of guilt. This guilt is induced by the attitudes of her mother and the neighbors, who despite her husband's willingness for her to do what she is doing, constantly urge her to stop her studies and stay home with the children. She is not carrying an unduly heavy load of course work and is in fact away from home only for a few hours twice a week. But because she belongs to a generation a little older than today's girls, one whose indoctrination about the feminine role came chiefly from the women's magazines and the popularized distortion of certain theories of child development, her psyche is fertile ground for the growth of such guilt. She will need to have more intensive counseling than I have the time to give, but I think that she will be able to use such counseling to resolve her difficulties and continue with her graduate work.

If her kind of problem is not to recur again and again in the lives of girls who come after her, both those of us who educate girls and the girls themselves have the responsibility to face squarely the unrealism and the dangers of continuing to dichotomize the values associated with women's work within the home and that outside it, as if the first were truly feminine and essential and the other not. It is particularly important that college girls achieve this realization, not only because they are well prepared to contribute to society in many ways, but because less privileged girls and women will follow the lead they set, and this is very important in a society like ours in which the high dependence of most families on cash income from wages makes it economically essential for many women to work outside the home. As educators of girls, we should make our goal to help our students to become what they are ready to become—individuals possessed of a sense of direction and of a feeling of commitment to the world in which we live, and neither apologetic nor ashamed that they have to be more than just keepers of the hearth.

If all that I have so far suggested about these girls turns out to be true, then their lives will be characterized in yet another way. They will participate ably, readily, and joyously in each period of their lives as these arrive. We will not, I hope, see as many of certain kinds of faces on middle-aged women as we do today. I don't know how many of you have sat and sadly watched such faces—the kind you can see on Madison Avenue in New York, for example. Sometimes I wait in the car for my husband while he does an errand there and because he's terribly pokey I have lots of time to watch the human scenery going by. It is really appalling to me to see so many women with beautiful mink covering drooping shoulders, and above the mink, bitter, unhappy, empty, expensively made-up faces. These women are not more than middle-aged—at an age when life brings its richest gifts—but their eyes seemed to be turned inward on despair. They are trying terribly hard to look twenty years younger, which is of course an absolutely hopeless effort. The time may come when women will be able to do this, but this would not give new life to the spirits of women like these. One cannot *be* twenty years younger. Twenty years of early adulthood bring life experiences, joys and sorrows, losses and gains, ecstatic moments, and ways of living that cannot come again. One's children grow up and one's parents grow older or die. Middle-age brings its own joys and satisfactions, which are not those of youth and which do not depend upon a veneer of youthful looks. It seems to me possible that girls who are planful, flexible, inspired by a sense of direction and a feeling of commitment will be able to enjoy and welcome each period of life as it comes and not be at one point looking frantically forward and at another point desperately backward.

Finally, if the data from Freedman's study mean anything (and I think they do), the girls of today will grow into women who are neither competitors nor handmaidens of men (nor handmaidens of their children). They will be partners of men and nurturers of children. As partners, they will be able to carry their share of economic and social responsibility as wives, mothers and citizens in a complex, mobile and affluent society, with no need to be either shrill or coy. As nurturers, they will give themselves willingly to the task of helping their children, which means helping the children to grow away from them, free from the need to smother, to hold their children, or to compete with them later on.

Women of the kind I have been talking about have long existed, but they have not been typical. And I think it is important to remember that the most thoughtful and fascinating men of many periods in history have written about such women, or dreamed of them, or created them in fiction—and in real life have admired or loved or married them whenever they found them. Of the many we might name, I will mention only John Stuart Mill, Bernard Shaw, Franklin Roosevelt.

I would like to close with a quotation from another most interesting man, Laurens van der Post, an Englishman who grew up in South Africa, and who, as many of you know, writes beautifully and sensitively about Africa and other things. The words I am about to read were written about his mother when she was seventy-five years old and managing, single-handed, a farm in a remote section of Africa. Although van der Post approved of her activities, her other children did not, and were constantly urging her to leave the farm and take up a quieter life. In support of his own stand in the matter, van der Post wrote:

> It has often occurred to me that the heavy burden of bearing and rearing children—my mother reared thirteen—has, in a sense, been irrelevant to the deepest and most vital purpose of her life. I have never been able to believe that a woman's task in life is limited to her children. I can quite well conceive that in my mother, as with more and more women of our own day, there is an urge to creativeness which lies underneath and deeper, above and beyond the begetting of children. These women have a contract with life itself, which is not discharged by the mere procreation of their species. Men recognize and try to honor this contract in themselves as a matter of course. Their contribution to life vibrates with their passionate rebellion against the narrowly conceived idea that would restrict their role to that of protectors and feeders of women and children. They do not acknowledge and respect the same thing so readily in women. Perhaps until they do the world will not see the full creative relationship that life intended there should be between men and women.
>
> —LAURENS VAN DER POST,
> *Venture to the Interior*

I would like to add that it seems to me that as women themselves become more fully women, more able to release and express their feminine creativity, more free to live more of the life available to them at any one time, so too will men become more fully men, more imbued with masculine creativity, and also more close to the women with whom they live. It is my belief that the girls whom we are educating are aware of the broad and challenging terms of their "contract with life." As educators, I believe that we have a contract with them and with their world of tomorrow to recognize and nurture this awareness, to free these girls to be more fully women than women in our time have been able to be.

Needs of Negro Youth

E. Theodore Jones

Martin Luther King, Jr., School of Social Change,
Crozer Seminary

Are the needs of Negro youth any different from the needs of non-Negro youth, or are they merely more intense? Dr. Jones examines the question and suggests that American society has failed to provide adequately for need fulfillment among Negro youth. His discussion of cultural factors which frustrate the Negro is frank and undoubtedly disconcerting to the white establishment.

This chapter might be more appropriate in the section dealing with "Adolescence in Cross-Cultural Perspective" since of all major ethnic adolescent groups in America the Negro adolescent is both most isolated and insulated racially speaking. The historic roles of cities and the social processes in assimilating and establishing a base for upward migration for all European minorities and to a limited extent Oriental and Far East immigrants simply failed to function in the case of Negro Americans. As a result, as an ethnic group they stand outside the main stream of American normal middle class society in the sharing of its patterns of political and business management, in involvement in its economic and cultural institutions, in attending its exceptional private and suburban schools, and in the executive councils of its national church bodies. *Newsweek*'s special article of November 20, 1967, titled,

Reprinted by permission of the author.

"The Negro in America What Must be Done," subtitled the opening section as follows: "The cold fact is that the Negro in America is not really in America."

The needs of Negro youth are manifold and cannot be isolated from fundamental economic, cultural, and psychological needs of the race as a whole. The adolescent enters the threshold of personhood seeking an image he does not know in a world he rarely understands, with a body that he is just discovering. He has a mixed desire to be an individual who wants to assert himself while at the same time fearing to lose the little security and reassurance that only family can offer. This difficult period of ambiguities, a sort of half-way house between childhood and manhood, in some sense reflects the psychological struggle of the race in its ardent desire to throw off the stigma of second-class citizenship while at the same time adapting to the majority system.

From one point of view the riots may be seen as a logical result of the historic stunting or distorting of the Negro's self-image. He has been allowed openly to think of himself only as an adolescent, half-grown man. He has been locked in the role of one who would grow into manhood and self-sufficiency but has been firmly held in check. We know what difficulties inevitably arise when growth out of adolescence is ever thwarted. In terms of the results of a simple and long-continued thwarting of growth into maturity and manhood, the irrationality of the recent riots could be more than sufficiently explained. The wonder is, so Dr. Kenneth Clark has suggested, that there have been so few riots![1]

Psychological Needs

The Negro adolescent is seeking today for an image, a self identity that fulfills a need, a need of personal significance and acceptance. Political and civil rights legislation of the past three to four years have awakened in him a search for personal dignity and freedom. The negative connotation of the term Black in the White-Black syndrome is not only being reexamined, the term Black is being reinterpreted, reinforced, and elevated to a positive symbolic badge of ethnic identity. The Negro adolescent needs the reassurance of personal acceptance and racial dignity. He watches the TV screen, reads daily papers, books, and magazines, and observes the school process or system and finds little affirmation of Black worth or constructive roles and contributions of Black men and women to the on-going American scenario.

Judging by the faces he sees, the commercial jingles, the soap operas, the dance ensembles, the regular serial programs, and news broadcasting, the tragedy of the Black man is that he is practically a nonentity. And one is left to wonder where have all the 22 million of them gone, since the daily public media involve so few of them. It is this daily pace of life that establishes the psychological wall of separation.

---

[1]Nathan Wright, Jr., *Black Power and Urban Unrest* (New York, N. Y.: Hawthorn Books, Inc., 1967), p. 167.

And suddenly the question of identity has become compellingly important . . . . Even the term "Black" has become a badge of honor instead of the fighting word it always was in a society whose every day vocabulary includes "black mail," "black list" and "black day" . . . . The search for identity is growing up," says Bayard Rustin.[2]

Educational Needs

Two important facets of an adolescent's world are his primary group relations such as family and neighborhood friends on the one hand and, on the other, his school life, where social role and personal aspirations are motivated. For the middle-class child both these agencies play supportive roles. The opposite is quite often the case for the urban adolescent in the ghetto community. Family stability is often threatened by economic deprivation and insufficient employment opportunities. Welfare payments often make up for father's absence or nonsupport. The adolescent boy or girl grows up in an environment where economic insecurity and social rejection or unimportance is the order of the day. His school world is populated with other deprived poor. The pressure toward mediocrity is inescapable.

Crowded ghetto schools suffer the handicap of a sterile middle class—a professionally oriented curriculum that fails to or cannot adapt its offerings to the needs of the child. As a result the system itself aids and abets a situation of hopeless irrelevance. The writer sat with a group of girls in Harlem for one semester in the Spring of 1966. All were employed at Haryou. They were high school pushouts ranging in age from 16 to 19. All had become pregnant before being expelled. The group counseling project was directed by the Guidance Laboratory at Teachers College, Columbia University. Among the expressions of reaction to their past experiences, one stands out.

This girl had had her baby and had begun night school for a high school equivalency certificate. Kuder Interest Tests and others clearly revealed an inclination to a people-centered or social service career. As clearly as can be recalled the following is her assessment of events leading to her giving up on school and the system.

> I was making good grades in P. S.—but I knew they were not really challenging me. They didn't make me feel proud because I didn't have to do anything for them. Several times when we took our math and English tests, the classroom teachers would stand outside the door and talk with another teacher. This would last for the entire period of the test. We all had nothing to do but make good grades. It was a joke! I got tired of just fooling myself. So I dropped out to breathe some clean fresh air in the parks.

Some seventy per cent of Negro families live in the urban inner city. Since 1955 an increasing proportion are in the inner core and the ghetto areas. Racial segregation has left the ghetto schools overcrowded, understaffed, and with a high turnover of teachers. The irrelevancy of the school system and its curriculum to the slum world and ghetto cul-

[2] "The Negro in America," *Newsweek* (November 20, 1967), p. 10.

ture of the urban poor speeds up corrosive frustration and deep despair. As a result attrition rates are high, but must not be interpreted so much as failure on the part of the student as failure of the system to realistically involve its students in the educational process. In this form of cultural morass all suffer. Good teachers leave, inexperienced teachers are unable to cope with the situation. Incompetent teachers merely try to discipline and hold the class together. The more astute students transfer out and in time there remain people of low aspiration and low performance level.

> "Racial segregation, like all other forms of cruelty and tyranny, debases all human beings—those who are its victims, those who victimize, and in quite subtle ways those who are merely accessories."[3]

Life in the crowded inner core city deprives the Negro adolescent of the opportunity for adequate exposure to other groups and life styles to gain any objective concept of himself. Soon the separate isolation produces a sort of psychological insulation, whereby the adolescent turns upon himself in a negative sort of way. In time he despises himself and those around him as symbols of despair and failure. Gang warfare is an extreme form of diversion of psychological hostilities.

> Since every human being depends upon his cumulative experiences with others for clues as to how he should view and value himself, children who are consistently rejected understandably begin to question and doubt whether they, their family, and their group really deserve no more respect from the larger society than they receive . . . . To the Negro child the most serious injury seems to be in the concept of self-worth related directly to skin color itself.[4]

A recent statistic for a large Northern urban center revealed that 45 per cent of its white high school graduates were going on to college while only 15 per cent of its Negro graduates were college bound. In fairness one could not say that the school was totally at fault. Certainly the home, neighborhood environment, peer group influence, family structure, and economic security all are factors that play into the equation. But somehow the school, as the social institution of educational leadership designed to pull together all the talent and potential latent in the adolescent, is the last bright hope in the community.

The failure of ghetto schools to achieve some socially desirable goals reflects many needs, unmet in the system. School boards and systems are often hindered by bureaucracy and traditionalism. Institutions are generally suspicious of change. Schools are usually resistant toward innovations in patterns of management, designing of curriculum content, inviting home and community involvement and student expression in the basic decision-making processes. The resultant is an adolescent world in which the structures of social power, and this includes schools, all seem allied in a conspirary against the best interest of the

---

[3]Kenneth B. Clark, *Dark Ghetto* (New York, N. Y.: Harper & Row, 1965), p. 63.
[4]*Ibid.*, pp. 64–65.

Negro adolescent in the urban inner core. These students are not insensitive to this highly incompatible situation.

> Discrimination is even in the school I attend right now. I know my teacher is very prejudiced because I have certain questions that have to be answered for my knowledge, but he will never answer. He would always call on a little white boy to give the answer. I told him one night, to his face, that if he didn't want to answer my questions just tell me and I would leave. There are always other teachers. He didn't say anything. He just looked at me and figured I was going to—so he said, "Well, maybe next time." There is no next time, this is the time and I'm not taking a second best from any white man.[5]
>
> *Boy, Age 17*

Is There Hope for a Solution?

The critical issue at the heart of the urban school crisis now is the shortage of time left. While "hope may spring eternal in the human breast," the time factor plays a big part in determining whether the hope of saving the ghetto children from social and economic annihilation can be fulfilled. The crescendo of dissatisfied parents, frustrated school boards, overworked and disillusioned teachers and despairing Negro adolescents indicates the growing need for a complete overhaul of the public education system and a reformation of curriculum content and sources of policy decision.

Some innovative steps have been initiated through federal legislation. Three of the most dramatic of these were:

1. Title I, the diversified and wide-ranging section of the 1965 Elementary and Secondary Education Act that authorized more than $1 billion in educational services specifically for disadvantaged, low-income school children.
2. The Teacher Corps, the one imaginative program that really shook the educational establishment, perhaps for the first time in decades. It implemented the functional idea of sending enthusiastic teams of specially trained and sensitized teachers into slum schools.
3. Head Start, the culturally enriching preschool program for ghetto children.

Many other varieties of programs have been attempted, some by private foundations, some through university research, and many through school and community joint approach for relevance in education. However when one considers the vast and crowded population of adolescents in the metropolitan ghettos it is obvious that the surface has not yet been scratched. Nothing less than a revolution in our schools is needed if the degenerative effects of functional illiterates in urban slum schools is to be removed. Negro adolescents stand in desperate

---

[5] *Ibid.*, p. 3.

need of such a revolution amidst corrosive effects of an irrelevant school system.

> It is borne out by the familiar statistics of Negro educational inferiority: a 60 per cent greater dropout rate than whites, an average reading level three years behind whites by grade twelve, a miniscule handful of college applicants. But the demolition of the guiding concept of equal educational opportunity is most forcibly underscored in preferential treatment that educators themselves have regularly given white middle-class schools. In Washington, D.C., for example, the school board actually spent $100 more per pupil in white schools than in Negro schools—until it was restrained by a court order last summer.[6]

Conclusion

The pervasive crisis in personal identity, educational development, and social acceptance felt and expressed by the Negro community is perhaps a frightening experience for the adolescent. So universal are the symptoms that, whether South or North, Negro youth are becoming increasingly impatient with status quo conditions that debilitate. Whether it is long summers of unemployment, or crowded tenement ghettos that increase in density as urban renewal dislocates more and more low income families to build high rises for the establishment, or de facto segregation maintained in the schools by the power-backed neighborhood school association, time is running out. No human can contain deep despair forever. Steam will find a vent and frustration long stored will out. But the culprits in our explosive crisis are not these forgotten rejects, but the WAS (White Anglo-Saxon) establishment that maintains, profits from, and perpetuates slums, restricted residential areas, subaverage inner core schools, and a totally irrelevant curriculum. The recent report of the President's Riot Commission states it graphically.

> School facilities should be available during and after normal school hours for a variety of community service functions, delivery of social services by local agencies (including health and welfare), adult and community meetings, recreational and cultural activities. Decentralization and the establishment of Parents Advisory Councils will afford the community a means through which to communicate needs for such services and to play an active role in shaping activities. In addition to making better use of the major capital investment in school plants, this approach will encourage ghetto residents to regard their schools not as alien institutions but as vital community centers.[7]

In an effort to literally listen to a thoughtful and articulate youthful student who migrated to the North from Alabama four years ago, the writer invited her opinion on the needs of Negro adolescents as she sees and feels about them. This student lives in a family of six chil-

[6] *Newsweek.*, p. 17.
[7] Report of the National Advisory Commission on Civil Disorders (New York, N. Y.: E. P. Dutton & Co., 1968), p. 451.

dren. Their widowed young mother is a private nurse. The student is a freshman at Drexel Institute and on the dean's list. Her response to the writer appears in full text without editing.

> I think that one of the foremost needs of Negro adolescents is to have a strong motivating force behind them in the form of parents or older siblings. We all need someone we can look up to and respect and admire, someone who we would want to pattern our lives after and someone to give us encouragement in the fulfillment of our life goals and dreams.
>
> I feel that if all youth had this strong motivating force behind them there would be fewer dropouts and juvenile delinquents.
>
> We also have a strong need to attain self-confidence. There are too many of us who still feel inferior to our white counterparts. This feeling of inferiority is one of the reasons why students with great potential will overlook a top-rated college or university because they feel that there are too many whites with whom they could not possibly compete effectively and go to a second rate college when they actually could have performed well in the top rate school but let this feeling of inferiority keep them back.
>
> We as young Negroes must learn to work together. We must come to realize that the only way we will attain our desired goals is through teamwork. We must overcome jealousy of those who have in some way attained some of their goals and those that have attained these goals must not look down upon those who seem to do nothing to help themselves. We must learn to work for the betterment of the entire race while we strive to work for the betterment of ourselves.

Other needs of Negro adolescents are stable and wholesome home environments, enriching cultural contacts, supervised recreation and social diversions, and the influence of positive religious direction or leadership. Obviously economics lies at the bottom of many of these needs. Employment opportunity, sufficient tax revenues, enlightened local government, and concerned chambers of commerce are all relevant factors.

One way to remake the image of the ghetto youth is to reform the community in which he lives. This means that sound education must be made a viable part of public schools in the ghetto, that the provision of adequate resources and stable faculty is a better corrective than bussing kids for 20 miles only to return them to the despair of the ghetto. It means that police personnel need to be reeducated to become protectors of the poor rather than symbolize the alien strong arm of a brutal system.

The over-arching need for the Negro adolescent is for hope and for a feeling that he has a future and that destiny is concerned with that future. That future is however tied into the future of the white youth who is tied to the future of his country.

The task of education at this point is inescapable. The student minority cries out for recognition before it is too late. The following terse analysis of our predicament is cogent.

> The irony of the situation is enough to make strong men weep. Here, unmistakably, we have students concerned to ask the crucial questions—identity, meaning, right and wrong, the good life—and they get in response not

bread but a stone. Here we have a generation blessedly capable of moral outrage, and it is the bitterest of anomalies that the humanities should be dying among students capable of moral outrage in a morally outrageous world. Almost without exception the response of the universities to this profound hunger for education, for compelling examples of human courage and compassionate intelligence, has been mean, parochial, uncomprehending, or cold. Above all, cold.[8]

[8]William Arrowsmith, "The Future of Teaching," address delivered to the American Council on Education, St. Louis, October, 1966.

Discussion Questions for Chapter 5

1. When one counsels adolescents, are there "special" considerations that recognize the nature of young adulthood that should be observed?
2. What should be the role of the teacher or counselor during crisis periods of normal personality development? Do you believe the teacher should be a strong factor in value development among adolescents?
3. How might the culture be rearranged in order better to nurture creativity among adolescents?
4. Does it appear to you that the needs of America's Negro adolescents can be fulfilled? What changes in society must occur if these needs are to be met? What implications are there for Negro youth and America if these needs are not met?

Glossary of Statistical Terms

Gerald D. Winter

St. John's University

Abscissa Horizontal reference line of a graph, the *X* axis.

Analysis of covariance An extension of analysis of variance to include more than two related variables.

Analysis of variance A method used to determine if the difference found between a dependant variable and one or more experimental variables is more than would be expected by chance.

Arithmetic mean An average of a series of numbers or scores. It is determined by adding all of the scores and dividing by the number of scores.

Array A series of numbers in order of magnitude.

Attenuation The lowering of correlation because the measures involved were low in reliability.

Average The score obtained by adding all of the scores together and dividing by the number of scores; arithmetic mean. It is used as a measure of central tendency.

Average deviation The spread between the mean of the differences and the mean of the distribution.

Bar diagram A horizontal or vertical graphic representation of a series of quantities.

Bimodal Having two modes.

Bionomial distribution The distribution of frequencies or probabilities of discrete scores that do not change in gradual transitions.

Bionomial expansion A mathematical method for deriving the probabilities of scores.

Biserial correlation The measure of the relationship between variables that are continuously measurable but are reduced to two catagories.

Centile A distribution of scores that are divided in hundredths. A centile may be any score on that distribution.

Central tendency Term used to represent the characteristics of a group as a whole. An approximation to the "true score." Measures of central tendency include: mean, median, mode.

Chi square The measure used to determine if the frequences observed in a sample population differ significantly from expected population frequencies.

Class interval The range of scores between the upper and lower boundaries of a class.

Confidence level The risk that the value of a statistic is affected by chance. The risks are usually stated in per cents. i.e. 1% or 5% levels of confidence.

Constant A value that remains unchanged under all conditions.

Contingency table Tables showing the frequency of an occurrence.
Control group A group that is matched with the experimental group and undergoes all of the variables that the other group is exposed to with the exception of the experimental variable.
Correlation The degree of relationship that one variable has with another. A perfect relationship is expressed as +1, and −1 is used to express a relationship that is totally negative.
Correlation coefficient The number that is used to express the degree of relationship.
Covariance The tendency for two variables to change together.
Critical ratio The measure of stability, the ratio of the statistic to its standard error.
Curvilinear relationship The graphic representation of two quantities when the graph is other than a straight line (curved).
Decile One of the points in a ten-point distribution where each point represents one tenth of the distribution.
Degrees of Freedom The number of units that can vary without changing the mathematical involvement.
Dependent variable A variable whose changes are considered caused by changes in one or more other variables.
Deviation A departure from the average or expected.
Distribution A systematic compilation of data according to a certain characteristic of value of that data.
Equated groups Groups that are identical or as close to identical as possible according to certain predetermined characteristics.
Experiment A test or trial of something in accordance with a scientific method that has been established.
Experimental design The method by which an experiment will be conducted.
Experimental group The group that is being examined and exposed to the conditions set forth in the experimental design.
Exponent The number written to the right and above another number that shows the power to which the number is being raised.
***F* test** An estimate of the probability of a difference between two samples which involves the differences of the means of the samples and the differences between the standard deviations of the samples.
Factor analysis A method used to examine scores and correlations of scores from tests for consistency due to a specific characteristic of the tests.
Frequency distribution The number of times a given event occurs and the number of values of the variables that are found.
Geometric mean An average taken by multiplying the scores and taking the root of that number of scores; i. e. two scores take the square root, three scores take the cube root.
Grouping Process of placing scores in catagories or ranking them.
Homogeniety Characteristics of a group of items that make them alike, or similar, in quality.
Hypothesis A reflection or estimate on the part of a researcher as to the outcome of experimentation.

Independent variable The variable whose changes are not considered to be due to the changes of another variable.

Learning curve A graphic representation of results of practice in learning over a period of time.

Level of confidence The degree to which you have confidence in a result; the risk level of a statistic.

Level of significance The value at which a difference becomes important or meaningful in a relationship.

Line of best fit A line that most typifies the scores of a scattergram.

Linearity The ability to be represented by a straight line.

Matched groups Groups that are the same or as close to the same as possible according to known criteria.

Mean The average—a measure of central tendency.

Median The middle score in a distribution. The value or score that divides a distribution in half.

Mode The score that most frequently appears in a distribution.

Multiple correlation The relationship that exists when there are two or more related variables used for prediction.

Multimodal When there are two or more modes.

N The number of cases used in an observation.

Nonparametric The method of analyzing data where there is no assumption of a normal distribution.

Normal curve A frequency distribution curve that assumes a normal distribution. The values for this curve are obtained when the number of cases is infinite and the variation follows the law of probability.

Normal distribution The distribution that occurs when the number of cases is infinite and the variables are subject to the law of probability.

Null hypothesis A statement that there are no significant differences between the variables under study. If the findings indicate that there is a significant difference, then the null hypothesis is rejected.

One-tailed test A test of statistical stability where one variable can be only more or only less than the other variable.

Ordinate The vertical reference line of a graph, the *y*-axis.

Parameter A characteristic of a hypothetical, infinite population.

Parametric Adjective of parameter.

Partial correlation The degree of relationship between two variables when one or more other variables in their relationship have been omitted.

Percentile A score that divides a group into parts with each part representing one hundreth of the total.

Phi coefficient A measure of a relationship when two variables are divided into two discrete groups.

Point biserial correlation The degree of relationship between two variables when one is continuous in nature and the other is a dichotomy.

Population The defined aggregate of subjects.

Power The number of times a value or a number is multiplied by itself.

Probability The number of times an event is likely to occur and the number of ways the event may occur with different combinations of variables.

Quartile A score that divides a group into four parts with each part representing one fourth of the total.

Random sample A method of sampling that insures that all subjects have an equal opportunity of being picked.

Rank order correlation A method of determining the degree of relationship between two variables when these variables have been ranked according to increase of values.

Ratio A relation in degree between two numbers.

Regression coefficient The value that represents the slope of a regression line.

Regression line A line of best fit between variables on a scattergram where the representation is graphic.

Reliability The degree to which a device will yield the same results on sequence of administrations.

Rho coefficient A form of correlation for squared rank differences; also called rank difference correlation.

Sample A part of the population that is taken as representative of the population as a whole.

Sampling techniques The method by which samples are drawn.

Random sampling A method that insures that every individual has an equal opportunity to be chosen.

Biased sampling A method in which there is a systematic error; one group has more of a chance of being chosen than another.

Stratified sampling A method to help prevent bias and assure more of a representative sample; subgroups of populations are considered when the sample is drawn.

Purposive sampling A sample that is arbitrarily selected because there are indications that the cases chosen are representative of the population as a whole.

Incidental sampling A sample that is taken because it is readily available; sometimes called accidental sampling.

Spearman-Brown formula A formula used to estimate the reliability of a test when the test is altered by adding or subtracting items of a similar nature.

Standard deviation A measure of the variability of a whole distribution. It is a measure of how much the scores in a set or group differ from the mean, on the average. It is generally considered to be the most stable measure of variability and is the most frequently used. It is abbreviated as either SD or σ.

Standard error The measure or estimate of error of sampling that affects the statistical device being used.

Standard score A derived score that uses the standard deviation as its basis. Standard scores are comparable whereas raw scores are not. Converting to standard scores gives opportunity for comparison.

Stanine A score that divides a group into nine parts with each part representing one ninth of the total.

Statistical inference The process by which generalizations may be made from statistical data.

Statistics The science or art of gathering scores and treating them mathematically so that relationships can be expressed and chance and significance be established.

***t* test** The ratio of a statistic to its standard error. The significance of the t is dependent upon its size and the number of degrees of freedom.

Tetrachoric correlation The relationship between two variables both of which are continuous and normally distributed but where each falls into only two classes.

Two-tailed test A test of statistical stability where one variable can be either less or more than another; used to see if differences obtained are more or less than chance.

Type I error When the null hypothesis is true but is rejected statistically.

Type II error When the null hypothesis is false but is not rejected statistically.

Universe The total of all existing things in a system that is definable.

Validity The degree to which a device measures what it purports to measure.

Concurrent validity Measures the test results with performance in a particular skill.

Construct validity Measures the degree to which a test item is a sample of behavior being defined and the degree to which the items collectively measure the same thing.

Content validity The measure of degree to which a device measures what it is supposed to by studying the content of the device.

Empirical validity The measure of the degree to which a process works in practice with a sample population.

Face validity A casual idea of determining how a test measures what it is supposed to by looking at the title of it.

Validity coefficient An estimate of the degree to which a test measures what it is supposed to by studying the content of the device.

Empirical validity The measure of the degree to which a process

Variable A quantity that is subject to change.

Variance A measure of the extent that one score differs from another.

***X* axis** The horizontal reference line on a graph.

***Y* axis** The vertical reference line on a graph.

***z* score** A standard score.